D0897729

ALL OVER THE MAP

Books by Michael Sorkin

The Architecture of Hardy, Holzman, and Pfeiffer (1981)
Exquisite Corpse (1991)
Variations on a Theme Park (editor) (1992)
Local Code (1993)
Wiggle (1998)
Giving Ground (editor, with Joan Copjec) (1999)
Other Plans (2001)
Some Assembly Required (2001)
The Next Jerusalem (editor) (2002)
After the World Trade Center (editor, with Sharon Zukin) (2002)
Starting from Zero (2003)
Analyzing Ambasz (editor) (2004)
Against the Wall (editor) (2005)
Indefensible Space (editor) (2008)
Twenty Minutes in Manhattan (2009)

ALL OVER THE MAP

Writing on Buildings and Cities

MICHAEL SORKIN

V

VERSO

London • New York

First published by Verso 2011
© Michael Sorkin 2011

1 3 5 7 9 10 8 6 4 2

Verso
UK: 6 Meard Street, London W1F 0EG
US: 20 Jay Street, Suite 1010, Brooklyn, NY 11201
www.versobooks.com

Verso is the imprint of New Left Books

ISBN-13: 978-1-84467-323-0

British Library Cataloguing in Publication Data
A catalogue record for this book is available from the British Library

Library of Congress Cataloging-in-Publication Data
A catalog record for this book is available from the Library of Congress

Typeset in Fournier by Hewer Text UK Ltd, Edinburgh
Printed in the US by Maple Vail

To my students

Contents

Preface

The majority of the pieces in this collection were first published in *Architectural Record* magazine and I'd like to thank Robert Ivy and Clifford Pearson for offering me a place to say pretty much what I chose for so many years. A couple of the longer essays appeared in the *Harvard Design Magazine* and I'm indebted to William Saunders for his staunch support and encouragement. Many of the 9/11-related pieces in this volume were collected in *Starting from Zero* and I'd like to give a shout out to the great Dave McBride, formerly of Routledge, who saw that volume through. (I did debate leaving these pieces out but the volume seemed wrong without them, and so I've included a substantial selection, some trimmed, others merged to eliminate repetition and breathless deadline lapses. Forbearance please for remaining auto-cannibalization, self-plagarism and the overworking of many words and phrases, including "Manichean," "difference," "effects," "public-private partnerships," and "zillions.") Thanks too to Tom Penn for his comradely midwifery and to Verso for a third vote of confidence in this fellow traveler. Special thanks to Trudy Giordano, Maia Peck, and Zoë Blackler for their help in organizing the manuscript and tracking down many a misplaced file.

The period covered in this volume coincides with my directorship of the Graduate Program in Urban Design at the City College of New York, and I express my gratitude to my dear friend Dean George Ranalli for giving me an open space in which to work (not to mention tenure and health insurance) and for helping to gather a congenial and dedicated group of colleagues to further the mission of this extraordinary institution. While the Trots and the Stalinoids may no longer throw spitballs from their separate tables at the cafeteria, CCNY continues its grand tradition of progressive tolerance and its goal of making higher education available to all. I do love the thrill each year of welcoming students from across the planet to share the adventure of imagining happy, just, and sustainable futures for our cities. I dedicate this volume to them.

Introduction

About twenty years ago—at the height of the historicist belch of architectural PoMo—I taught a studio at the University of Pennsylvania. One day, as I strolled into the building fresh from the train, I came upon an exhibition of drawings of student projects all done in the then fashionably phony-baloney classical style (just following the orders), rendered in dispiriting watercolor washes and brown ink. Rounding a corner, I came upon the great Aldo van Eyck—a hero from my own student days—who was also teaching at the school that semester. He was in the process of ripping the drawings from the wall in a fury. People rushed from nearby offices, horrified. Indeed, I was somewhat horrified myself, having seen the work of my own students at Columbia vandalized by someone who disagreed with my purportedly wild approach—an outrage. Confronted by the dean, Van Eyck ceased his trashing and, when asked how he could do such a thing, delivered the memorable line: "Democracy means no freedom for fascism."

Baldly stated, but telling. Van Eyck was testing the line between free expression and what he saw as architectural hate speech, one of the primary negotiations of a democratic polity. Architecture can never be a purely private event, and unpacking the elasticity of public space and its ability to stimulate, accommodate, or suppress diverse (and unpredicted) forms of individual and collective expression has underlain much of my work, both written and drawn. Make no mistake: there is a crisis in the public realm and its grossest manifestations range from car bombs in Kabul to CCTV cameras in London, from defensive "street furniture" in Manhattan to the rampant privatization of everything. No matter how you slice it, a shopping mall will never be a public square, nor men with guns the mark of the open city. The focus of my project—whether via critique or proposal—has been on the ways in which such issues find their meaning in form . . . and forms of redress.

The essays in this book are, in large part, shaped by a series of American disasters, each of which has caused a special crisis for spatial liberation. This anthology takes up where my last one left off, late in 2000. In November of that year, George W. Bush was elected to the US presidency. Less than a year after that, the 9/11 attacks took place. Then the wars in Iraq and Afghanistan. In 2005, Hurricane Katrina struck the Gulf Coast, laying bare the egregious divisions of race and class that had only deepened under the rule of Bush and his corporatist wantons, and throwing into relief the real ramifications of the swelling debate over climate change. That in the midst of these nightmares the formal side of architecture continued to enjoy a remarkable efflorescence is not exactly paradoxical—periods of great accumulation from the Pharaohs to the Medici to the sheiks of the Emirates to the Masters of the Universe on Wall Street will beget monuments—but it begged the question that has perplexed me from the start of my career: how to simultaneously value artistic expression largely directed to the privileged and to rail against a world going to hell in a hand-basket because of a crisis in equity.

There is no simple formulation for this, and I apologize if my practices can seem a skosh schizophrenic: I've denounced the perquisites of big money in print while simultaneously designing a fancy hotel in the office. In exculpation, I can only beat my breast and suggest that there's a certain Peter/Paul strategy of compensatory practice. Even my studio is now physically divided in two with its for-profit (I wish!) and its non-profit sides. My own room straddles the demising wall designed for the IRS and, as the for-profit side pays for it all, the arrangement is the spatial signifier of donated time. Looking over the writing in this and previous volumes, though, I can see that the texts—unlike the 50/50 implication of the virtual division of my office—are strongly weighted to the social side. For that matter, so is the designing, particularly in a long specialization in urbanism, work at a scale that can genuinely be judged for its public arrangements and effects.

In fact, scale and organizational complexity are crucial to a distinction between architecture as an effect and as a producer of effects, whether social, political, environmental or aesthetic. The sumptuary architectures of the Republican decades—from McMansions to museums—can surely be read as effects of a commercialized culture, of seductive (and deceptive) interest rates, of an increased inurement to inequality and planetary peril. This must be decried. The problem, though, in dealing with an art form that is defined by the fact of its necessarily extra-artistic content and behavior is always in testing the implications of the differing—and sometimes competing—claims on it. No work of architecture can presently be judged without considering its impact on the "natural" environment. Nor should any work be exempted from consideration of its styles of collaboration in securing the common space of exchange among people and publics. But we must never criminalize the pursuit of the beautiful, nor depend on the simple vulgarity of arguments that the artistic superstructure is the deterministic outcome of some economic or political base. The work in this volume is informed by the fact, however nuanced or indirect, of a connection.

If there's an area of conflict in writing about architectural projects that represent enormous expenditure on luxury objects, the necessity of doing so springs from a few motives. One is that a beautiful and pleasurable architectural experience always inspires, provided its use isn't an overwhelming affront. Another is to hold the feet of my brother and sister architects to the fire for the insensitivity of their egregious money-grubbing and for the vapid, end-of-history (or hermetically arcane) explanations that seek to naturalize such practices as the only alternative. Still another has been to insist that the discourse of architectural and urban effects must be understood in terms of its invariable relevance to our planetary environmental meltdown. Building is responsible for nearly half of the carbon emissions that are wreaking such planetary havoc, and the differential rates of consumption—of materials, of energy, of space, clean air, labor, capital—embodied in construction make the crisis clear. A much rehearsed but telling example is the simple fact that were everyone in the world to consume at the American rate, the surface area of two additional planets would be required to supply all the stuff. We are up against real limits, and architecture can be decisive. Finally, I have never hesitated to call architects on doing work that's truly inimical to justice, whether that work is the instrument of the displacement of living communities, window dressing for repressive regimes or toxic ideologies, the medium of imprisonment and surveillance, or the distributor of ill-gotten gains. And, by extension, I've been intolerant of the criticism and theorizing that abets all of this.

The period from which these pieces come also saw the deaths of two individuals of special importance to me, a pair who represent the antinomies of contemporary architecture in stark relief. The first of these was Philip Johnson, against whom I have directed a bushel of diatribes—including a few in this volume. Johnson was clarifyingly emblematic of everything revolting about architectural culture, from his long love of the Nazis and his unspeakable anti-Semitism, to his club-house conduct of architectural patronage, to his rich boy's casualness with privilege, to his promiscuously banal sense of style, his fey irony, his upper-crust superficiality and the pack of sycophants who really should have known better but continued to allow themselves to be bought on the cheap. Basta! Good riddance! Shut the door!

The truly deep loss was Jane Jacobs. Jacobs redirected the tone of the urban question in America away from both blithe suburbanism and the savage "renewal" by demolition of urban neighborhoods and centers. She was the compleat urbanist, operating as a thinker, a polemicist and an activist. That I have long lived in the same neighborhood where Jacobs formulated her most trenchant and specific analyses of urbanity and won her most enduring victories "on the ground" is no coincidence. We all construct our quotidian utopias, and Greenwich Village—and New York City—have been a big part of mine from a tender age. Jane Jacobs was a poet of effects, a brilliant and engaged observer of the intercourse of space and the scope of human action and prospect. She was an economist in the hoariest sense, a student of the relational systems and structures that beget exchange. The seamlessness of the connection between her economism and her urbanism is a model of analysis and engagement, one that generated her profoundly ecological view of cities.

Jacobs inspires for the directness of her style, the restlessness of her curiosity, her rejection of disciplinary compartments, and for keeping up the fight to the very end. She is also an avatar of the sixties, a formative decade for me (I am often bashed nowadays as an unreconstructed fossil of the era), and a reminder that the delirium of those days stood on the shoulders of revelatory critique—the key texts were produced not by us whelps but by our elders during a special half-decade of wonders. *The Death and Life of Great American Cities* (1961) was published in a heroic context in America, one that includes Lewis Mumford's *The City in History* (1961), Rachel Carson's *Silent Spring* (1962), Betty Friedan's *Feminine Mystique* (1963), Martin Luther King's *Letter from a Birmingham Jail* (1963), Herbert Marcuse's *One-Dimensional Man* (1964), and Ralph Nader's *Unsafe at Any Speed* (1965) among many others. This constellation of work greeted me when I got to college and continues to define the core of my critical concerns. To these works of constructive intellectual insubordination were shortly added the more bodily vectors of sex, drugs, and rock and roll. The rest is not yet history.

When I collected my first volume of essays in 1991, my introduction bid a stirring farewell to critical writing, promising that I'd devote myself exclusively to architectural practice henceforth. So much for promises. A dozen books later, here is another one. It probably won't be the last. Of course, writing is an architectural practice—*ohne Theorie, keine Revolution* and all that. However, as I have been obliged to rediscover repeatedly since the pieces in that first volume were drafted in the fearless flush of resistance to the onerous world of commissions and compromises, I had written myself into something of a corner. I've bitten quite a few hands, many of which, it turned out, might otherwise have been feeding me. Nevertheless, architectural flesh always proved tasty to me, and the urge to chomp has continued. In retrospect, it's clear that my sunny animus was costly and I haven't found much architectural work in this town. And much of my design work has itself been adversarial, a long march of counter-proposals for vexed situations that have won me a certain amount of cred but haven't exactly opened the door to the plump commissions that a person of feeling such as *moi* thinks his due. Ironically, my studio now has a number of projects in China, a place where I am known almost entirely through images.

Still, I've persisted, and a great deal of work has been drawn, if not built. My studio has become a specialist in what we call "unsolicited master planning." This work has also informed my writing, which has tried to balance the claims of social justice with the unassailable specificities of taste. At a time when the homogenizing impacts of global capital are one of the greatest threats to our subjective differences, artistic invention is an ever more crucial hedge against the depredations of planetary sameness. So, the parallel inventions of writing and designing have shared aims: the struggle for a progressive environmental politics and a simultaneous broadening of architecture's artistic horizons. In both my own work and that for which I have been an advocate, I've tried to help secure an expressive space that is at once free and focused. Much of my affirmative writing has thus been in support of comrades on the disciplinary margins: the starchitects don't lack for flacks.

Although my own formal proclivities grow unabashedly from a number of sources—including the alternative modernities represented by architects like Michael de Klerk, Bruce Goff, Oscar Niemeyer, Konstantin Melnikov, Hermann Herzberger, Alvar Aalto, Antonio Gaudi, Erich Mendelssohn, Bucky Fuller, and, of course, Frank Lloyd Wright. I also have a special affinity for the Camillo Sitte branch of urbanism, one that finds particular inspiration in the crazy-quilts of Prague, Fez, the Hutongs of Beijing, or the juxtaposition of twisty streets and rotated skyscrapers in lower Manhattan. I especially love the spontaneous weirdness and exaggeration of hippie communes, the caves of Cappadocia, the towers of Yemen, or the stoned-out-of-his-gourd chops of Guarino Guarini. What I don't like is uniformity, especially rolled out as The Only Way, whether in the form of the modernist *existenzminimum*, the suburbs, or the *Prisoner*-esque New Urbanist package: there will always be some limits to tolerance. Interrogating such limits is the task of criticism. This is what Aldo Van Eyck was up to.

Do forgive the piety of all of the foregoing. It's motivated by my inner Pangloss, by a deep desire to live and work in a world that's decent, delightful, and beautiful. A world where everyone has the right to architecture.

1

The Second-Greatest Generation

Never Trust Anyone Over . . . ?

For the past twenty years I have been over thirty, the actual milestone having occurred slightly before the lapsing of the 1970s (which was when much of the 1960s actually occurred). And I'm not the only one. As the boomer bulge in the bell curve grinds toward oblivion, we are driven to ask: what has the aging of youth culture meant for architecture?

Youth, of course, *is* strictly a cultural matter. My generation is by self-definition—the only definition that ever counted for us—young. Architecture, the "old man's profession," has never been congenial to us (among others). We certainly returned the favor: bridling at the "man," many of us rebelled, abandoning architecture, heading for the woods, building by hand, advocating for communities, drawing, making trouble, laying the groundwork for the cultural revolution.

This didn't really work out as we planned. The world seems not to have changed along the lines of the image we had for it. Somehow the "liberating" mantra of sex, drugs, and rock and roll changed into the nightmare of AIDS, Prozac, and MTV. How much of a hand did we have in this cultural devolution?

The Clinton Library

Limiting politics to resistance or selling out has not served us entirely well. Our own first president illustrates the sheer porousness, the corruptibility, of these categories. Clinton is not exactly *one of us*, in the same way that any member of student government during the late 1960s was not exactly one of us, but rather something between a quisling and a geek (depending on whether one focuses on politics or style). Now we are witnessing the spectacle of two co-generationalists running for the presidency. These— the eternal frat boy and the sell-out student government type—give the lie to certain fantasies about the triumph of the counterculture. Sixty percent of George W. Bush's class at Yale—the class of 1968, no less—voted for either Richard Nixon or George Wallace. Al Gore elected to go to Vietnam. Patrician universities, with their solid ruling-class values and their various schools of social architecture, have a way of countering countercultural agendas, it seems.

And they have a way of promoting the middle of the road. When the time came for Clinton to choose an architect to design his shrine in Little Rock, did he turn to an architect his own age? Did he seek to radicalize the repository via form or effect? Not at all. He made his choice from the slightly older generation, choosing an architect not quite old enough to be his (absent) father but certainly old enough to Wally his Beaver. The first boomer administration runs from its roots, affecting the same brain-dead Hollywood style that answers the question "Rock and Roll Museum?" with "I.M. Pei" (designer of the first "modern" presidential library). And we haven't heard much lately from the presidential sax, not since Clinton was trying to persuade us that he shared our values (we'll keep our pain to ourselves, thanks).

Blah Blah Blah

The political rebellion of the 1960s announced itself in the characteristic speech of the late twentieth century: first person. But the self-promoting, self-conscious "I" of my generation has been hobbled by our awareness of the unconscious, which has hovered over us like a specter. This unconscious has not only promised the possibility of a "liberation of desire" from social constraint, it has also rallied skepticism of our best intentions. The unconscious, after all, *always* trumps the conscious as a cause of action and thus of political striving. Beneath the desire to do good lurks a neglected child. Behind the orderliness of minimalism lies crap in the pants. Politics itself has been reduced to just another symptom; it dares not promise a cure for fear of being labeled the dupe of its own neuroses.

Whether this is a proper reading of Freud is really not the issue; it is the reading that undermined our sense of the world's reliability and our own political will, producing a special generational uncertainty principle. We all have our styles of superego, and this combination of license and guilt has distinguished us, on the one hand, from the "greatest generation" of our parents who—dammit—had something unequivocal to fight for, and, on the other hand, from the Gen X-ers and Y-ers, the Reagan*jugend*, whose traumas seem so *fifties*, inflicted by the pressures of consumption, rather than rebellion. Thus questions of influence acquire for us a special anxiety. The unflagging hegemony of the sixty-something and seventy-something cadre that rules, that formulated the parameters of the depoliticized, desocialized post-modernity that swept architecture in the seventies and eighties, needs a violent shaking from the left.

2

No More Second-Hand Dad

What to do when the parents in your own family romance are the stalwarts of the avant-garde? That we received our lessons in artistic rebellion at twice-second-hand somewhat diminished our sense of their originality. Avant-gardism is about rupture, overthrow, the father-murderous rage of art. Classic early-twentieth-century avant-gardism wanted a radical reworking of the visual aspect of architecture *and* a reinvention of the process of production.

The postmodern "avant-garde"—compromised by a sense of having inherited both its credentials and its topics—is a somewhat different creature. Its intellectual agenda has remained caught in the avant-garde dream of its ancestors. It thus re-covered much of the ground explored half a century ago, redoubling the received critical discourse with its own metacritical commentary, interpolating another layer of interpretation between the "primary" investigation and its own. The magazine *October*, for example, the bible of post-modernity (and exemplar for our own theorizing), continues to be held hostage by its obsession with surrealism, as with some lost idyll. And architecture carries on with fresh formalisms of the broken (or the perfect) square.

Try as we might, we haven't been able to get Oedipus out of our edifices; inherited property still defines us. A false patriarchy continues to structure the discipline and practice of architecture, in which a fraternal order of equals is presided over by a simultaneously dead and obscenely alive father, father Philip, in this instance.

Life in the Past Lane

This stalled fascination with former revolutions is the result of a failure of nerve and of invention. It is also evidence of the ideological and psychological trauma that has beset our attempts to formulate an avant-garde in rebellion against an avant-garde to which we desperately desire to remain faithful. The result has been a kind of fission. One by-product is the hyperconservatism of our melancholy historicists. Another is the would-be radicalism that has produced visually novel buildings and rudimentary bridges to the world of the virtual, but which still clings to dusty desires for legitimacy.

The lesson we have been unable to learn is that it takes a lot more rebellion than we have been able to muster to remain faithful to the heritage of the avant-garde.

Market Share

I am not sure the *New York Times Magazine* did us any favors with its gossipy, prurient cover story on Rem Koolhaas, our momentary laureate. Depicting him as a kind of edgy Martha Stewart who refuses to judge any endeavor "a good thing," whose mission is the "mission of no mission," the *Times* tried to inscribe his fundamental cynicism into the format of the hero-architect, *Fountainhead*-style. Of course, the paper went for the Hollywood version. Gary Cooper may have behaved like Frank Lloyd Wright, but the models in the background were strictly Gordon Bunshaft.

Sound familiar? The challenge of collapsing the tastemaker and the ideologue is sure to test one side or the other dramatically. Is it possible to be Paul Auster, Sam Walton, and Kim Il Sung at the same time? Will Rem succeed in branding the generic?

Africa Shops at Prada

Jetting into Harvard to administer his shopping seminar, Rem snags a job designing Prada stores. The press praises his strategy of branding: no design "identity," instead *a space where things happen*, "an exciting urban environment that creates a unique Prada experience." A TV camera in the dressing room will permit you (TV's *Big Brother* is another Dutch import) to view yourself from all sides at once. Will thousand-dollar shoes move faster when surveilled from all angles? Will there be an algorithm to airbrush away our worst features? Must we buy this privatization of culture? Does the postmodern critique of the museum, the call for tearing down its walls, do anything but free art for the shopping mall? I'll take Bilbao, thanks.

The trouble with an age of scholasticism is that you talk yourself into the idea that *anything* is politics. By the time it's devolved from direct action to propaganda to critical theory, to the appropriation of theory, to the branding of theory, to the rejection of theory, something is lost. Critique stokes its own fantasy of participation. On the one hand, this produces boutique design as social practice, and, on the other, it segues into the more rarefied reaches of recombination. My Russian colleague, Andrei, has been smoking cheap cigarettes that someone brought him from back home. The bright red pack is emblazoned with a picture of Lenin in high sixties graphic style. The make is "Prima," the brand "Nostalgia," the smell appalling. What's next? Lenin Lites and Trotsky 100s? Must we succumb to the speed of this? Can't we slow the whole thing down?

Nostalgie de la Boue

This new nostalgia (the nostalgia for packaged nostalgia) is everywhere. Now that my generation rules the media, part of us keep busy looting our experience for the rudest forms of exploitation. If you've turned on your TV lately, you might have seen *That Seventies Show*, a slick package of affects, the decade as a set of tics and styles. The expropriation continues to the limits of corporate memory. Advertising nowadays is lush with 1960s themes as fiftyish account executives preside over the wholesale trashing of the culture that nourished them. "I Feel Good"—a laxative. "Forever Young"—invidious irony—incontinence diapers. On *Survivor*, flaming torches turn the game-show paradise island into Trader Vic's.

Nostalgic for 1950s and 1960s styles, yet too hip not to be troubled by the accumulated political baggage of the project, this cadre of media masters offers a stance of almost pure cynicism. "I am saying this, but I don't actually believe it; In fact, I don't actually believe anything, because it is no longer possible to do so." With Niemayer or Lapidus or Harrison as the soundtrack (and the Stones, perhaps, playing on the answering machine), they seem to want to suspend indefinitely the moment when they would be obliged to take a position.

A micro-generational conflict now exists among those for whom the 1960s represents a source of anxiety, those for whom the decade still represents possibility, and those for whom it is simply ancient history. Most invested in the middle alternative, I grapple with this legacy, but the particulars grow vague (the feeling stays evergreen).

That Vision Thing

Our fantasies did have vision—the product, mainly, of the working out of certain congruent themes of prior modernisms. Those domes and inflatables and garbage housing were not just technologically and environmentally prescient; they also figured—whether in civil rights or Woodstock variants—in political ideas about the extension, openness, and spontaneity of spaces of assembly. And the canny melding of technological control with an "anti"-technological ideology gave birth to appropriate technology.

The alternative visuality of the 1960s, however, has had only the most marginal impact on architecture. (Many breathe a sigh of relief.) The psychedelic style that included Fillmore posters, the Merry Pranksters bus, and Sgt Pepperesque couture required a certain lag before becoming appropriatable by architecture. We liberated the 1970s supreme Soviet—Venturi, Stern, Moore, Graves, et al.—from the kitsch closet and made it permissible for them to love Vegas and the roadside. But they always had to rationalize their love, to capture it for their outmoded agendas and fantasies of control. We responded with disengagement and irony, as usual.

The "appropriated" art of so many artists of my generation was a typically limp response, immediately gobbled up by the art machine. Having bought into a critical history that denigrated intentions, we then bought into our own ironical reappropriation of intentionality via obsessive proceduralisms and poetic trances. Too late. Narcissism is not the same as self-confidence. Even Seinfeld has been cancelled.

Vive la Différence!

The Whole Earth Catalogue and *Our Bodies, Ourselves* are our holy books, good news for a political body and a contested environment both. These really were milestones: we're all a little more gay now, a little closer to the earth, a little more skeptical about the system's "choices." The politicization of the personal (as the formula *should* have been) demands idiosyncrasy beyond the tonsorial and sartorial. Pity about our architecture. So many interesting sites wasted.

It Isn't Easy Being Green

We always hear that green architecture "looks bad," and most of it does. At the end of the day, though, separating your trash is probably a greater contribution to world architecture than Bilbao. Well, maybe not Bilbao.

2000

2

Herb's Content

Does the *New York Times* architecture critic Herbert Muschamp keep writing about the same things?

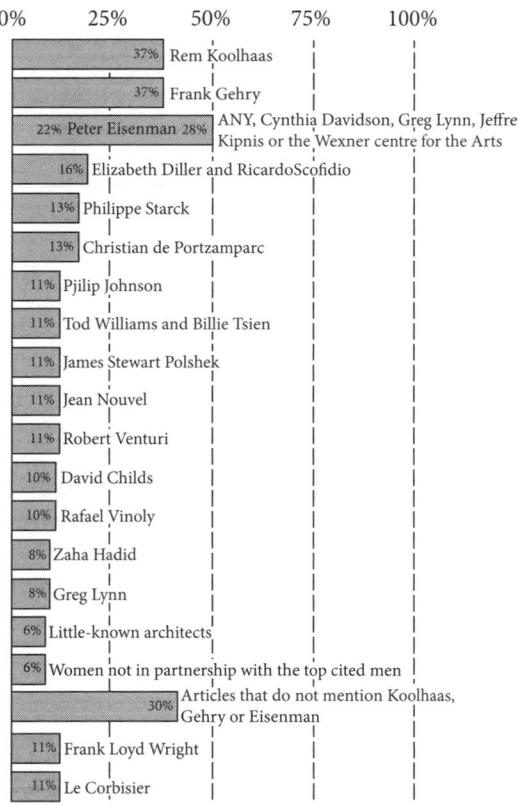

0%	25%	50%	75%	100%

37% Rem Koolhaas
37% Frank Gehry
22% Peter Eisenman 28% ANY, Cynthia Davidson, Greg Lynn, Jeffrey Kipnis or the Wexner centre for the Arts
16% Elizabeth Diller and RicardoScofidio
13% Philippe Starck
13% Christian de Portzamparc
11% Pjilip Johnson
11% Tod Williams and Billie Tsien
11% James Stewart Polshek
11% Jean Nouvel
11% Robert Venturi
10% David Childs
10% Rafael Vinoly
8% Zaha Hadid
8% Greg Lynn
6% Little-known architects
6% Women not in partnership with the top cited men
30% Articles that do not mention Koolhaas, Gehry or Eisenman
11% Frank Loyd Wright
11% Le Corbisier

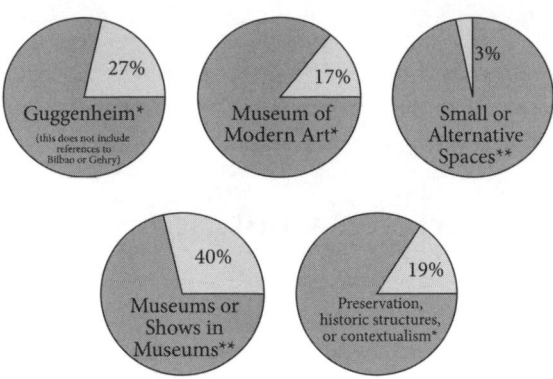

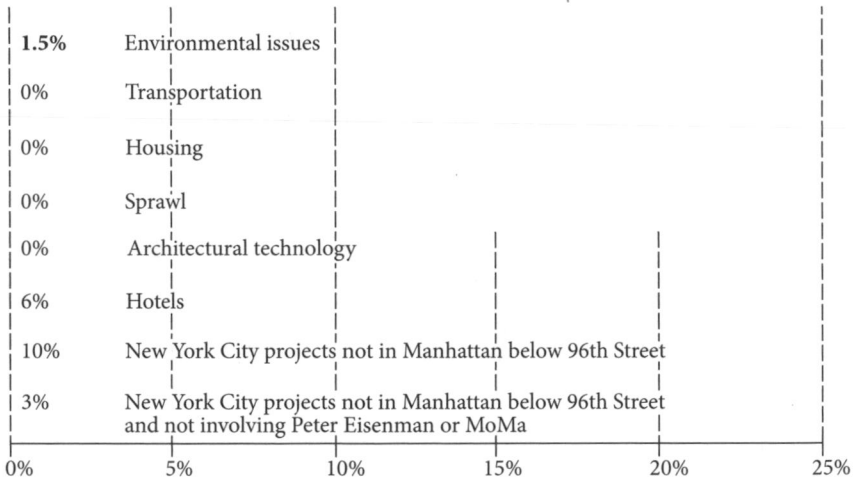

* Percentages of articles that mention subject at least once   ** Percentage of articles about subject
Data calculated from articles written by Herbert Muschamp for the New York Times from January 2, 2000 to April 11, 2001,
totaling 63 (including news items obituaries)

1.5%   Environmental issues

0%   Transportation

0%   Housing

0%   Sprawl

0%   Architectural technology

6%   Hotels

10%   New York City projects not in Manhattan below 96th Street

3%   New York City projects not in Manhattan below 96th Street
and not involving Peter Eisenman or MoMa

0%   5%   10%   15%   20%   25%

Longest consecutive run of a single name: Rem Koolhaas, nine out of eleven articles

Most mentions of a single name in an article about a subject other than the person mentioned: six, Rem Koolhaas

Most Hollywood references in a single article: twelve (Chateau Marmont, Pedro Almodóvar, King Pleasure, Alfred Hitchcock, *That Touch of Mink*, *The Best of Everything*, *Rear Window*, *West Side Story*, Grace Kelly, Jimmy Stewart, film sprockets, and film noir; in a story about a hotel by Jean Nouvel)

Number of paragraphs required to deploy the above references: five
Favorite non-American architectural nationality: French

Second-favorite non-American architectural nationality: Dutch

2001

3

Notes on a Tennessee Town

In my suburban Washington, DC childhood, I had a remarkable next-door neighbor, a grandfatherly figure called Bob Coe. Bob was a landscape architect—trained at Harvard—whose early career had been spent with the Olmsted brothers. A man of sincere liberalism, he signed on with the Tennessee Valley Authority (TVA) in the 1930s and was responsible for landscape design at a number of sites throughout the project.

The one that he spoke of most, though, was Norris—a planned community built in 1933–34 to house TVA workers who were building a giant dam nearby. Bob had lived in Norris, and it was there that he met and married his wife, Kay, a preternaturally kind Tennessee native who taught first grade for over fifty years. The two of them spent hours each week working in their beautiful garden which was, for me, a paradise—the most lovingly cultivated half-acre I have seen before or since. I assumed Norris was a variation on this garden.

A couple of months ago, I finally had the opportunity to visit Norris and take a dam tour down the Clinch and Tennessee. Norris is lovely: the garden city layout of the town is carefully informal and sensitive to the hilly topography, and it contains a number of astute spatial deployments, including a repeated grouping of three houses around a common lawn that struck me as beautifully scaled and latently convivial. Throughout the town, I thought I could recognize Bob's rich, serpentine and layered sensibility in landscaping grown lush.

The original houses that have survived are very small and inexpensively built, but have a compact elegance. One mustn't overstate the consequences of 350 houses: the current atmosphere leans toward the funky, and Norris remains a very small place with a few modest shops and services, two schools, and several TVA labs and workshops. The vibe is tender, though—even moving. Kids are wandering the pathways at dusk. Neighbors are chatting in the commons.

Here, I thought to myself, was a genuine town, built out in the optimistic idiom of interwar modernity. At Norris, and nearby Oak Ridge, there's a lingering aura of purpose that exceeds the site planning. The plan conveys a way of seeing spaces as continuities, flowing in scale from the town to the river to its watershed to regional topography to the organization of the nation and beyond. The spectacular dam down the hill and the beautifully managed river are there to testify to what a town can do. A place with a grounding beyond economy, this is not a company town but its flipside. Its rationalism is gentle and its layout sinuous. Those curves—understood as the contour-following outgrowth of a compact with nature—reflect a strong feeling for the welfare of the environment: an ecological vision, an idea of sympathy, not of discipline.

A recent visit to Taliesin revealed another classic intersection between form, ideology, and organization. Taliesin continues to draw both the shape and the reasons for its routine from the religio-architectural principles laid down by "Mr. Wright." To the degree that these principles are complicit and shared, the place works wonderfully in both its hierarchy and its collectivity. Like Norris, the architectural frame still functions adaptably despite the inevitable ebbing of the force of the cultural project of Wrightian architecture. And the specificity is superb; a complex that continuously reads its own site.

Not long after my trips to Norris and Taliesin I spoke at one of the periodic conclaves of the Congress for the New Urbanism (CNU), this one in Ann Arbor. I have had a modest career in the past few years playing Tim Leary to Andres Duany's Gordon Liddy at these events, offering hyperbolic dissent to his neo-traditional, generic planning strategies. The argument has some merit: it's no accident that Seaside and Celebration have become icons for creepy social control, symbols of fraud and camouflage, private interest masquerading as public, the opposite of Norris.

Not living in a very civic time, we do get a huge overproduction of surrogates and appropriations of civil life—the Disney effect. How to resist? I don't suggest that we must be Shakers or rural electrifiers to find reasons for shaping townscapes. But real town life is not simply a matter of consumption, of mass customization, or even of market-driven "choice." Not an original insight but one shared, I'm happy to think, by many in the CNU. Indeed, I became skeptical of my own interlocutory position at that conference in Ann Arbor. I felt a bond with the range of projects presented by a softer, more formally disinterested wing, including Peter Calthorpe, Bill Morrish, and Anne Vernez-Moudon, among others.

Norris is something I think all of us might agree on: we're all trying to keep alive the idea of a town, of the next Norris. Norris is no Disneyland— it's malleable, and the intentionality is soft. It was founded in a real fantasy of the *demos*. The New Deal really was a big deal for a lot of people— Bob and Kay among them. The cluster of ideologies and strategies behind it readily attached to (and were shaped by) both the pastoral planning of the garden city movement and the organizational vision in the exponential thinking of Patrick Geddes, Benton MacKaye and other godfathers of the experiment. Refitted now for other ways of living, Norris succeeds in its revalidation of the founding plan by contemporary events and in its retention of strong atmosphere and community.

There are two big issues confronting town building today, and they are the same ones that produced and were addressed by Norris: environment and equity. Towns both organize and steward the environment, anchoring the natural economy. They are themselves produced from the countryside and, at the same time, they are its annihilation. Environmentally informed planning is the medium for declaring a truce. The recent flash of Bush terror—a scorched-earth policy from hell—showed how close to the surface the paranoia about recolonizing hard-won boundaries for sprawl is. This is a true civil emergency, and planning is the only answer.

Planning always engages questions of equity. In America, equity resides in property, and a town plan represents its division. But a real town creates a proprietorship that exceeds property: town plans are the medium of negotiation between public and private rights, and freedom and power are as legible as can be. The plan is the mechanism for quantifying parity or scarcity—of space, of environmental quality, of architecture.

The beauty of Norris lies in its smooth enclosure of these desires. Its light lie on the land, its distributive dream, its modesty, and its aspirations for a culture and region larger than itself make it a model.

2001

4

After the Fall

Buildings have caused the death of 6,000 people. What can architects do? Surely, this horror should force us to examine fundamental assumptions— about the integrity of structure, about the logic of such concentrations of people, about height. What else?

We are, to be sure, embarrassed by our ambulance-chasing brethren who urge that we rebuild exactly as before. Or higher still. Or prettier. Or more robust. Or all four. The owner has pledged to reconstruct immediately and has laid on a distinguished high corporate architect, ready to get back to business.

But something has shifted and we embarrass ourselves by rushing out to spend again, by fantasizing about 150-story towers that will take an additional hour to evacuate when the next disaster strikes, by thinking about the next thing, by having no second thoughts about anything we might have done.

Visiting the site of the disaster in its immediate aftermath, I struggled to take in the somber beauty of twisted steel, the pulverized rubble that seemed too small to contain all of what was there before. I worried that something in me also had to die, some capacity for enjoyment, if only the shopworn sublime of aestheticized horror. At the grocery store an hour later, I cringed at choosing between a peach and a plum, at picking pleasures in a time of grief.

And the culture slogs on.

In a letter to the editor, Philipe de Monetebello calls the twisted remains a masterpiece.

Karlheinz Stockhuasuen declares the attack to be "the greatest work of art imaginable for the whole cosmos." Broadway reopens with self-congratulatory bravado and unconscious irony. After the first post-disaster performance of *The Producers* the cast takes the stage—dressed in their Nazi uniforms—to lead the audience in singing "God Bless America."

Dan Rather weeps on Letterman.

In Kabul, our reporter visits a barbershop with a hidden camera. He has come to photograph an adolescent boy getting a "Titanic" haircut, like Leonardo DiCaprio's. Later, interviewing a turbaned member of the Taliban, the correspondent replays this scene, rubbing the boy's act of resistance in his bearded face. "Such things are not possible in Afghanistan," the mullah replies.

And what about for us? Clearly some familiar way of facing the world must die now. The *Times* has already suggested postmodernity as a likely casualty. This is not a moment for slippery relativism and ethical agnosticism, for the aestheticization of everything, for any obtrusive visuality. But how can we absorb the images presented to us day and night without simple recourse to old routines and strategies? How must we judge ourselves, judging?

The official demonization of the terrorists paints them as implacably other, pure evil—agents of nothing we could have helped produce. But the terrorists fascinate us, in part because they are the dark side of something we have not simply predicted, but advanced. This extends beyond the initial arming of and collaboration with bin Laden during the Soviet Afghan war to deeper, more conceptual connections. Al Qaeda—"the global network"—is just one tick away from our own global business as usual.

Osama bin Laden is one of us, the Patty Hearst of radical Islam, a trust fund revolutionary ready to go the extra mile. Heir to a construction dynasty, with a client list to make the most jaded architect jealous, bin Laden studied civil engineering and frequented the bars of Beirut, betraying an early penchant for structure and modernity.

Radicalized out of his gilded youth by the war in Afghanistan, Osama bin Laden became the extreme instance of globalization. His network of autonomous franchises, regulated by infrequent signals from headquarters, delivers its product with just-in-time precision, deploying the full spectrum of media—from cell phones to satellite links to complex and illicit private banking arrangements and high-tech forgeries—with incredible discipline and facility. The operatives who destroyed the World Trade Center were well educated and able to quickly grasp the most sophisticated technology. These are not hopped up savages, dreaming of black-eyed virgins: these are our children.

Mohammed Atta, the apparent operational ringleader of the plot, received a master's degree in city planning from a university in Hamburg, which also housed the nucleus of a radical Islamic cell. His thesis advisor was quoted yesterday speaking admiringly about Atta's diploma research on the historic planning of Aleppo, Syria. The professor had not suspected that Atta would be implicated in the most violent act of urbanism America has ever seen.

One of the most widely retailed images of the downfall of modernism was the implosion of the Pruitt Igoe towers in St. Louis, designed, like the Trade Center, by Minoru Yamasaki. This image has been absorbed into both architectural discourse and popular culture as a totem of corrective violence. September 11 was the biggest implosion ever, staged in the most media-saturated environment on the planet and captured from every angle, stamping out every other image. The unbelieveable crash. The unbelievable collapse. The unbelievable aftermath. Concluding that it's too good not to broadcast, the media moguls have cleaned it up nicely for mass consumption, given it a PG rating by expunging shots of bodies falling, washing out the sight of blood, branding the event for easy, uncritical, consumption, to play over and over like Challenger or the Hindenberg or Kamikazes striking carrier decks.

The global network that destroyed the towers was neural, enabled by the infrastructure of empire. Without the internet, no terror: these monsters are the dark side of the creature we have ourselves designed, operating in its unregulated space and driving its assumptions to their furthest conclusions. The killers visited a mad act of urban renewal on behalf of their own idea of one world. Down went not simply the leading architectural icon of global capital but the most concentrated symbol of human density, of the coming together that has, in one form or another, guided urbanism from its beginnings.

The most in-your-face image here downtown is on Canal Street, a billboard for the latest Schwarzenegger film with a huge Arnold in the foreground, the usual mayhem behind him. The name of the film—the release of which has been delicately delayed by its producers—is "Collateral Damage."

Perhaps it is time for architects to cease their celebration of branding and "pure" communication to try to be of some real service to the planet.

Architectural theory has been talking for some years of building as the pure space of events.

Here is an event.

What shall we build now?

And who will decide?

The only answer to terror is an excess of democracy.

2001

5

What Remains

Traffic returned to the streets of my neighborhood today after the cordon was moved south to Canal Street. It was the day of Bush's tardy visit and the sky was filled with the futile darting of fighter jets, commanding anxious looks upward with every pass. I made my way through the police lines to my studio—only a few blocks from the World Trade Center—and sat around numbly for most of the day. Outgoing communication was down and I couldn't respond to the dozens of email and phone messages wondering if we were all alive.

In the evening, I returned home and switched on the television to learn the latest and to watch the riveting pornography of planes smashing over and over into buildings, the eruptions of flame, the horrific collapse, ashamed at my own fascination. Like the restored traffic in the streets, the traffic of commerce had also returned to the airwaves and the dour talk was again interrupted by commercials, happy faces commanding us to buy SUVs and stock up on useless commodities.

Solidarity and civility had bloomed in the days following the attack as barriers of diffidence fell and comfort and information flowed freely between strangers. Acts of kindness and friendship multiplied and the public's demeanor became somber and respectful. We comforted each other with small exchanges of information and feeling, and by the powerful egalitarianism of disaster. The city's official response was magnificent, astonishing. The streets below 14th Street were closed to traffic and nobody but local residents was allowed in. The result was an eerie calm as people, quiet and restrained, took possession of the empty streets as after heavy snowfall. The weather was mockingly beautiful and the city was, in this way, at its very best: quiet, free of cars, crisp, cooperative. Only when the wind shifted and the dreadful smell of incineration permeated the air was there a sensory reminder of the hell nearby, belying the cool. And everywhere, the ash fell.

Before Tuesday, I'd been thinking about what to write for this column. I had been asked to conform to the theme of preservation and planned to focus on Frank Gehry's new boutique for Issey Miyake down the street.

I was going to discuss the narrow focus among architects and critics in which "preservation" has been reduced to a battle of styles; the endless debate over the virtues of modern building versus historicism—the official default when building in old neighborhoods like mine. I was going to argue that we've lost sight of the ecology of place and that it's not enough only to preserve the visually familiar in beloved environments—we must also be sensitive to established ways of living, to daily habits, to the need for home.

Gehry's boutique would have been exhibit A in all of this because it would surely have been beautiful, the work of our most artistically accomplished architect. I would probably have mentioned too my annoyance at the trendy boutique having replaced something actually useful: an organic food store that had been there for years.

But now, confronted by the agonizing absence of the Twin Towers from our field of vision, I am thrown back into thinking of architecture as an element of citizenship. Must it now be subsumed in the rhetoric of defiance and victory? Will we continue to look at architecture as the answer?

There has been a brave and understandable clamor for rebuilding. After all, this was the city's preeminent icon, and we must not hand a symbolic victory to terror by allowing it to disfigure our legendary skyline. Those terrorists—who obviously understood the World Trade Center's structure and construction—used architecture as a means of mass murder. Architecture became an accessory to the crime. The economic and narcissistic logic behind the form of the Twin Towers put people at risk.

Risk assessment—like "threat" assessment for the military—is always a component of architecture. Among the risks the designers of the World Trade Center deemed acceptable was a one-hour climb downstairs for people attempting to flee the upper stories of the building, a climb impossible for the disabled. One of the tradeoffs they made against this risk was the elimination of asbestos fireproofing around the structural steel. There has been much discussion about whether the building—which sits along a primary approach route to La Guardia airport—was designed to survive the strike of a plane. The answer circulated in the media was that yes, indeed it had been, but only from the smaller type of aircraft in use when the structure was built. The question remains, though, about which harm's ways a building should be in.

For now, I'm uncertain about what should be done to heal the site. Perhaps this is the moment for a decisive break from the machismo of scale that foregrounds values of size and cost above all other signifiers of success and power. Perhaps this is an opportunity to reimagine architecture, not from a position of either power or paranoia but from one of compassion. Maybe this site shouldn't even be rebuilt. I shudder at the trivial objects of memorial that will ultimately be offered, the ornamented island of calm amidst the gigantic new construction.

Perhaps this is a scar that should simply be left. Perhaps the billions should be spent improving transportation and building in neglected parts of the city, neglected parts of the world.

As the endless loop of planes crashing into buildings plays over and over in our heads, it has joined our image bank of disasters, morphed into special effect. It's depressing how many of those interviewed have referred to Bruce Willis, *Independence Day*, *The Towering Inferno*, the earthquake ride at Universal Studios.

But already the tragedy has invented its own memorial. On every lamppost and mailbox, fence and facade, thousands of images have been posted—photographs of the missing, advertising the ineradicable despair of their loved ones. All over the city people stop to stare at these pictures, taken when things were normal, formal portraits and tourist snaps, family photos, graduation shots. We all look to see if we recognize these faces— and though we breathe with quiet relief whenever we don't, every picture still feels familiar, every photograph could have been our own or that of someone we love. I am not chronically paranoid but I'm good and worried. Not so much about the next attack (though I am still afraid to fly) but about the reconstruction of our city and of our culture. The victory for terror lies in our own frightened willingness to give up on the values that are under attack, values that lie at the core of what makes good architecture and urbanism: facilitating the face-to-face creation of places of privacy and personal sanctuary, setting the pleasures of community, foregrounding the beautiful.

Asked for an ID every morning by a guardsman in combat dress, listening to the president blustering about "smokin' them out of their holes, getting them running, and whipping them"—with the "them" as yet unknown—I fear for us all, for where we'll have to live from now on.

2001

6

First Response

As the recovery operation progressed and clearing Ground Zero became the focus of energy, we were approached by a local builder to suggest a form of temporary enclosure for the site. This was to physically protect the public from the perilous process underway, to cordon the workplace from intrusion, and to accommodate the large numbers of people pressing to visit. Our initial proposal was for a large earthen berm surrounding the site. Since we felt it was important both to secure and to mark the place, this enclosure took the form of a circular crater. It had an obvious symbolism while still being substantial enough to remain in place for as long as it took to agree on a future for the site. Concerned about acting in haste, we wanted to mark a place of reverence and deliberation, not solve the "problem" of Ground Zero. With that in mind, we contemplated more durable materials for the project, including stone and brick. We wanted to create views from the rim of the crater down into the void that would be left. We

felt a discussion of what should be done to recover the place had to exceed the limits of the site and extend, not just to the rest of downtown, but to the city as a whole. We also imagined that the temporary enclosure could have effects beyond Ground Zero. The initial notion was for it to become a point of origin for greening and pedestrianization, for the healing ministrations of nature, and for a network of human connections, leading both to and from the place of tragedy.

2001

7

The Center Cannot Hold

In his farewell to office, Rudy Giuliani—standing in St. Paul's Chapel, adjacent to the World Trade Center site—declared: "I really believe we shouldn't think about this site out there, right behind us, right here, as a site for economic development. We should think about a soaring, monumental, beautiful memorial that draws millions of people here who just want to see it. We have to be able to create something here that enshrines this forever and that allows people to build on it and grow from it. And it's not going to happen if we just think about it in a very narrow way."

Giuliani's speech reminded me of Eisenhower's leave-taking from the presidency, in which he warned the nation against the growing anti-democratic power of the "military-industrial complex." In both cases, the cautionary appeals resonated because of their sources, one a military man and architect of the Cold War, the other a mayor whose leadership favored planning by the "market." Giuliani's heartfelt call for restraint ran counter to the back-to-business approach that has dominated official thinking since the tragedy. This has included obscene job-grubbing on the part of the architectural community and robust talk about responding to the terror by rapid rebuilding, bigger than ever. The Lower Manhattan Development Corporation (LMDC), empowered to decide the future of the site, is headed up by a patriarchal ex-director of Goldman Sachs whose credibility seems untainted by the spectacle of his own firm abandoning Manhattan for New Jersey. With the exception of a single community representative, the board is composed of the usual business crowd. Their initial consensus seems to favor the construction of a vast amount of office space on the cleared site of the fallen towers with the memorial simply a modest component. Meanwhile rumors grind on about the working drawings, apparently already on the computers at Skidmore, Owings & Merrill.

Fortunately, the competition for authority over the site is both structural and complex. The Port Authority, Larry Silverstein (the ninety-nine-year leaseholder), the LMDC, the federal, state, and city governments, survivor groups, the local community, the business improvement district, the Battery Park City Authority, the Transit Authority, and myriad other civic and private interests are jostling to be heard and influential. If nothing else, this fog buys time for contention and for the serious consideration of alternatives.

What is clear is that, despite the currently soft market, some of the 15 million square feet of lost space needs to be replaced sooner rather than later, and downtown's dysfunctions repaired to allow the city's economy to re-establish jobs and networks lost in the attack. The eventual need is not simply for replacement space: The "Group of 35"—a business-heavy organization chaired by Charles Schumer and Robert Rubin—predicts that an additional 60 million square feet of office space will be required by 2020.

The question is where to put it, and some will clearly go to lower Manhattan. Railroading the restoration of the status quo by looking at the site as no more than its footprint, however, guarantees that we learn nothing from the tragedy and let the opportunity for better thinking slip away.

My studio is not far from the Western Union building at 60 Hudson Street, known to architects as the home of the New York City Building Department. Since September 11, this building has been the subject of unusual security, surrounded by concrete barriers and half a dozen police cars. It appears to be the only site outside the confines of Ground Zero to enjoy this level of fresh protection, and the reason seems to be the building's longstanding role as the nexus both for telecommunications cables coming into New York City and trunk lines to the nation and the world, a logical next target for terror according to some scenarios. Ironically, a system at the core of urban disaggregation depends on joining huge dispersed networks on a single site.

Today, our dominant urban pattern—enabled by the instantaneous, artificial proximity created by phones, faxes, emails, and other global electronic networks—is the rapid growth of the suburban "edge city," a sprawling realm, that has become the antithesis of a traditional sense of place. But this "non-place urban realm," the location to which security-conscious firms are now retreating, is the result of more than just new communications technology. The suburbs were fertilized by massive government intervention in highway construction, by radical tax policy, by changes in the national culture of desire, by racism, by cheap, unencumbered land, and by an earlier fear of terror. The prospect of nuclear annihilation that made urban concentrations particularly vulnerable was on the minds of many planners during the Cold War, both in the USA and abroad. The massive de-urbanization in Maoist China was also the direct result of nuclear anxiety. This dispersal, from center to suburb, facilitated by the Interstates—our erstwhile "National Defense Highway"—was likewise more than simply good for General Motors: both the auto-maker and the USA were playing the same stratego-urban games.

The effects of this pattern of urbanization were in many ways antithetical to the presumptions behind the space of lower Manhattan. Here, concentration has long been considered crucially advantageous. The possibility of conducting economic affairs face to face, the collective housing of related bureaucracies and businesses (the famous FIRE: finance, insurance, real estate) that makes up the majority of business downtown), the dense life of the streets, the convenience of having everything at hand, are the foundation for the viability of the main financial district for the planet. Its characteristic form—the superimpostion of skyscrapers on the medieval street pattern left by the Dutch—has given downtown its indelible shape.

Any changes reconstruction brings must deepen this formal singularity, expand the possibilities of exchange, and broaden the mix of uses supported. While it's a bromide to apologize before suggesting that the tragedy can be turned to advantage, the enormous disruption in the life of the city has already had a number of constructive effects. Here in Tribeca—ten blocks from Ground Zero—traffic is dramatically reduced on local streets, the polluted sewer of Canal Street is suddenly tractable, and deep civility abides many months later. The emergency car-pooling and limited access instituted as the result of the disaster are equally positive.

The radical act of the terrorists opens a space for us to think radically as well, to examine alternatives for the future of all of New York City. It is no coincidence that we have constructed a skyline in the image of a bar graph. This is not simply an abstraction but an extrusion, an utterly simple means of multiplying wealth. Where land is scarce, make more. Lots more. There is a fantasy of Manhattan as driven simply by a pure and perpetual increase in density. But while our dynamism is surely a product of critical mass, all arguments for concentration are not the same. Viewed from the perspective of the city as a whole, the hyper-concentration of the Trade Center was not optimal by any standard other than profit, and even that proved elusive.

Density has a downside in over-crowding and strained services, but this is not necessarily the result of the hyper-scale of any particular building. More critical than specific effects on the ground are the consequences for densities elsewhere. While anxiety over corporate and population flight to the suburbs comes from a general fear of both economic and social losses, the all-eggs-in-one-basket approach slights other areas of the city themselves in need of jobs, construction, and greater concentration. Manhattan's gain has been the boroughs' loss: the rise of the island's office towers historically marks the decline of industrial employment throughout the city, and has obliged the respiratory pattern of one-directional commuting. A new means of producing wealth with new spatial requirements has—over the century—completely supplanted its predecessor.

With thousands of jobs already relocated out of the city, a solution to the "practical" problems of reconstruction can and must engage possibilities well beyond the confines of the downtown site. While the billions that will be available for new building—from insurance, from federal aid, from city coffers, from developers—are certainly needed to restore health to the enterprises formerly in or servicing the Trade Center, it seems reasonable to question—given the probable level of this investment—whether such massive expenditure should be focused exclusively here rather than throughout the city at additional sites of need and opportunity, places development could transform.

The majority of New York City's population and geography does not lie in Manhattan: the island comprises only 8 percent of the city's land area and 19 percent of its inhabitants. Moreover, according to the 2000 census, the residential growth of the island since 1990—slightly over 3 percent—lags far behind the explosive growth of Staten Island (17 percent) and Queens (nearly 15 percent) and the dramatic increases in the Bronx (10.7 percent) and Brooklyn (7.2 percent). Manhattan, however, remains the city's economic engine, producing 67 percent of its jobs and 46 percent of its retail sales.

These imbalances have fundamentally reshaped the city. The great infusions of capital and the artificial fortunes of the last decade have propelled the price of real estate in much of Manhattan to the stratosphere, accelerating the flight of the middle class and the poor and making Manhattan increasingly monochrome. We continue to revere our island as a place of thick, urbane interaction, and cling to the fantasy of the great mixing engine of difference, of a city with many quarters housing many kinds of people. Increasingly, however, the differences in Manhattan's neighborhoods are merely physical. This uneven development and accelerated metamorphosis has had dramatic effects, distorting the character of our urbanity decisively.

Here in Tribeca, we are at the end of a familiar cycle in which a neighborhood moves from a mix of warehouses, manufacturing, offices, and housing, to an "artistic" neighborhood, and now to the climax form of gentrification, an extreme high-end residential *quartier*. The corollary is that the jobs and people formerly employed here have either been eliminated or moved elsewhere: to the Hunt's Point Market in the Bronx, to low-wage environments offshore, to the suburbs, or to the new bohemias of Williamsburg or Long Island City. We have scrupulously preserved the architectural character of Tribeca, but at the expense of its human one.

With the exception of Chinatown, Manhattan south of 110th Street has become a faded mosaic of former ethnic enclaves and cultural variety. Increasingly, the city's ethnic and cultural quarters are being solidified outside the borough, in Flushing, Greenpoint, Dumbo, or Atlantic Avenue. Although the city remains a beacon for immigrants—both from home and abroad—the sites of intake and expression are not what they were, having been preserved to death. Manhattan is ceasing to be a place to get a start and becoming inhospitable to striving, less and less like New York.

But big changes can also suggest big opportunities for burgeoning neighborhoods struggling to find form, or merely to keep up. Not all disaggregation leads to sprawl; better, perhaps, to call it reaggregation. But it is also a notion that can be useful in cultivating character and encouraging development within more traditional, compact cities like New York, itself the central place for an enormous region. The point is not to make New York more like Phoenix or Los Angeles, but to make the city as a whole more like New York.

Because of its dynamic population and superb movement infrastructure, New York City can become a model of a new kind of polycentric metropolis, with Manhattan remaining its *centro di tutti centri*, its concentrated vitality unsapped. In fact, Manhattan is itself already polycentric: the disaggregation represented by, for example, the easy movement of financial and legal services firms from downtown to midtown in recent years suggests that there is a certain fluidity to the idea of proximity within the city, that convenient movement and strong local character can substitute for immediate adjacency within an overall context of density.

Reinforcing New York's special polycentricity would return the city to something of its pre-twentieth-century character by restoring a network of autonomous, comprehensible places. Such a "village" stucture—the origin of the great city of variegated neighborhoods—is again made possible by the technology behind the ephemeral and flexible nets and flows of the twenty-first century. Because it is aspatial, this malleability need not simply lead to generic sprawl but can fit within—and reinforce—any pre-existing infrastructure of neighborhood differences.

Cultivating this "natural" polycentricity would multiply opportunities for more self-sufficient neighborhoods where people walk to work, to school, to recreation and to culture. Such places would satisfy many of the needs that impel people to seek the densities and economies of the suburbs and edge cities. By regenerating local character, the energy of intra-city reaggregation could reinforce the expressive singularity of each of the neighborhoods to which its energies were applied—the Asian flavor of Flushing, the Latin American atmosphere of the Bronx Hub, the African cultures of Harlem.

This would be an advance on the wing-and-a-prayer style of current planning, in which good intentions are simultaneously frustrated by imprecise plans and the absence of economic drivers to set them in motion before changing times render them irrelevant. By joining physical planning to direct investment and to zoning and economic incentives, we can redistribute uses to a set of centers outside Manhattan where land and transit connections are available and economical—places like Flushing, Jamaica, Queens Plaza, Sunnyside, the Bronx Hub, St. George, and Downtown Brooklyn, among others. These sites—also identified in the report of the Group of 35—are not mysterious either in their needs or their suitability.

Planning comprehensively could help assure the mixed-use character of these places by including residential construction matched to the numbers of new workplaces, a pattern that has already begun downtown, where substantial office space has actually been eliminated by conversion to residential use. Indeed, in the last ten years forty office buildings have been converted to residential use downtown, part of an 18 percent population growth in the area below Canal Street. The sense of locality that grows from a well-finessed mix would be further reinforced by the decentralization of cultural growth (the City Opera, the Guggenheim, the Whitney, the Met, and the Jets are all seeking space) and by encouraging the development of new cultural, healthcare, educational, and commercial institutions to enhance the variety and life of these neighborhood centers.

YANKEE STADIUM
BRONX HUB

125TH ST.

FLUSHING

QUEENS PLAZA
SUNNYSIDE

DOWNTOWN
BROOKLYN

JAMAICA

ST. GEORGE

© Michael Sorkin Studio

It is critical, however, that these centers be envisioned and planned as semi-autonomous and not simply as ancillary. Downtown Brooklyn is already one of the largest "central places" in America but continues to be thought of as a back-office for Manhattan. The key is zoning for sustainability and difference, not simply for a series of mini-Manhattans. Although the skyscraper is a preeminent symbol of twentieth-century technology and of the culture of the corporation, other paradigms must now emerge as values change. The economic driver that has impelled these heights will be usefully moderated in smaller centers which foreground strong environmental values and in which land prices are restrainedly moderate.

Downtown Manhattan is the commercial district with the highest public transportation usage in the country. Eighty percent of those who come to work here—350,000 people a day—arrive on mass transit. A comprehensive re-examination and reinforcement of this pattern is crucial to sustaining the city, but must be approached non-centrifugally to facilitate movement not simply in and out of Manhattan but between the developing centers of lived life, reinforcing the repatterning. Our waterways, in particular, offer a tremendous opportunity for creating such links with great economy. In addition, the city's large areas of public greenspace and municipally owned property can be used to begin to create a third transport net—for pedestrians, bikers, and nonaggressive zero-emissions vehicles—to supplement the street grid and the subway.

Business-as-usual in New York City is more than the compulsion to repeat patterns of the past: our talent is creating the new. In the case of downtown Manhattan, however, it is also important to recognize that this is an area of the city that is near completion, its project of build-out and of formal invention is almost done. The construction of the World Trade Center, the isolation of Battery Park City by an over-wide highway, the nasty scale of many newer high-rises, the abandonment of the piers, the elimination of manufacturing and small-scale commercial activity, and the elevation of the East Side Highway are all assaults on a satisfying paradigm of great scale contrasts, rich architectural textures, and pedestrian primacy that lies at the core of what's best about downtown. Restoring this is the task at hand, and it cannot be accomplished in Lower Manhattan alone.

2001

8

Six Months

Last week—the six-month anniversary of the World Trade Center attack—I walked down to see the towers of light on a foggy evening. The clouds lay low and the effect was startling and dramatic, occluding and revealing the powerful skyward beams shrouding downtown in an other-worldly glow. It was completely beautiful and a little frightening, a genu-ine sublimity that could be taken for what it was, inspiring a feeling quite different from the embarrassed awe that shamed earlier fascinations with the twisted, mesmerizing rubble at Ground Zero.

The site is now nearly clear, testament to the selfless energy of those laboring there round the clock. As workers reach the bottom of the pile, they are discovering the remains of comrades trapped on lower floors and in the lobby when the towers collapsed, an awful closure. The two shafts of light seemed completely right during the time of transition from removal and recovery to the consideration of what is to come. They were a memo-rial of both power and presence, and set a high standard for future projects. That this commemoration had come about at all demonstrates the power of the informal consensus that has, for better and worse, begun to determine what can and cannot happen at this place.

For the moment, we find ourselves in a curious interregnum downtown. While no plans have been finalized, there has been intense jockeying for position, both publicly and, especially, behind the scenes. While the newly formed LMDC will have planning responsibility, the actual power to build remains dispersed and uncertain. The site is owned by the Port Authority (controlled by the governors of New York and New Jersey). It sits within the City of New York, is laced with transport and utility infrastructure controlled by various agencies, and has been leased to Larry Silverstein—a New York real estate mogul with particularly dreary architectural sensibil-ities—and Westfield, an Australian shopping-mall-management company that was to have run the huge retail complex beneath the towers.

In addition to these legal stakeholders, the public has made its sentiments known through a welter of self-organized alliances that have been meeting regularly and working hard to promulgate ideas for reconstruction. One of the most broad-based of these coalitions is New York New Visions, which recently released a preliminary report that includes a variety of sensible findings, most crucially a call to look beyond the immediate site of the towers and consider the planning of downtown Manhattan as a whole. The report recognizes a historic opportunity to reattach Battery Park City to the island from which it has long been isolated, to increase pedestrian links, to unify and augment a series of transit lines that converge but don't quite meet at the site, to intensify the mix of uses in the area, and a number of other unassailable ideas. And they are not alone; the outpouring of proposals and opinions has been bracing. At no time in my memory can I recall so many people discussing questions of planning so fervently.

As I write this, the LMDC has just released its first statement of principles for the "Future of Lower Manhattan," and its board—appointed during the Giuliani administration—has been expanded to include four directors chosen by Mayor Bloomberg. The mayor has sent out a clear message about diversity through these appointments, by placing Asian-, African-, and Hispanic-Americans (among them two women) on a board hitherto dominated by white, male plutocrats.

The new principles have been whipped into shape by Alex Garvin, recently appointed the LMDC's vice president for planning. New York City planning commissioner, professor at the Yale School of Architecture, and co-author of the ingenious and politically adroit proposal for the 2012 Olympics, Garvin has articulated a framework that is both wise and canny. Clearly Garvin has been listening carefully, and his recommendations parallel those emerging from the broader community of interests. The importance of the memorial is foregrounded, infrastructure and transportation are emphasized, mixed use is invoked, pedestrianism encouraged, open space celebrated, and environmentalism tithed.

The principles are sound and should attract wide support, but they skirt the more controversial aspects of any plan that must eventually emerge. The two major issues concern who decides the fate of the site and what actually is to be done at Ground Zero. While the report, and the new LMDC appointments, go a long way toward reassuring the public that decisions will not be reached behind closed doors, Garvin avoids taking a definitive position on the future of the site itself, listing, but not locating, uses and calling for considerable work out of sight underground. At this stage, however, the reticence is appropriate: there is still plenty of time to get it right.

The closest the principles come to a translatable declaration of design intent is in their call for the restoration of "all or a portion of" the street grid obliterated by the construction of the World Trade Center. But the plan specifically mentions only two streets that cross the site—Greenwich Street, running north/south, and Fulton Street, running east/west—not the twelve blocks that originally stood there. Of course, an open space or memorial scheme for the site (or for that matter a commercial, mixed-use development) could establish connections across it without restoring the grid as such. The question therefore remains whether there will be a city block scheme for the site—defining a series of clear development parcels— or some other approach.

Today, the day after the release of the LMDC's principles, lease-holder Silverstein revealed his own plans for the first site to be put into play, that of the former 7 WTC (which collapsed after the Twin Towers with, miraculously, no loss of life). The 7 WTC site is pivotal both because it holds an electric substation that must be replaced expeditiously and because the destroyed building had eliminated Greenwich Street, which virtually everyone now agrees should be unblocked. In the diagram of the scheme just published by Silverstein's architect, David Childs of Skidmore, Owings & Merrill (SOM), the missing street block has been restored, with the result that the footprint of the new building is considerably smaller than that of the original. Although the new tower will be higher than its forty-story predecessor, there is nonetheless a net reduction of 300,000 square feet of space.

This begs the question of what will be done with the leftover development rights, and rumors are flying that Silverstein is trying to renegotiate the terms of his lease with the Port Authority to reflect the diminished carrying capacity of the site. It has also been suggested that this may simply be the beginning of a much more protracted negotiation, to escape any potential financial liability from the consequences of the "official" plan. Indeed, rumors are also circulating that SOM is preparing studies for the entire World Trade Center site on Silverstein's behalf as part of his strategic negotiation for a new lease.

SOM has been the ubiquitous mover downtown. Marilyn Taylor, chairman of the firm, has emerged as a key player in the New York New Visions report, and is also leading a planning study of lower Manhattan's east side funded by Carl Weisbrod's Downtown Alliance, while Childs is designing 7 WTC and doing planning studies for Silverstein. Am I overreacting to the hydra of an interlocking architect/developer directorate and the fact that all the commissions doled out thus far have gone to one firm? There is a huge potential conflict between business and citizenship here, and SOM needs to lay its cards on the table in terms of its own desires and interests in Ground Zero.

The real wild card in all of this, though, is the memorial. In recent weeks the idea that the entire site be dedicated to such a memorial seems to have quietly slipped off the table. Most vocal among the supporters of such a plan have been the tragedy's bereaved survivors, although this is not a uniform position among them. This community has been disappointed at being excluded from representation on the LMDC and having only been offered a role on the memorial subcommittee. Advocates (myself included) for leaving most of this sacral site open as a civic memorial space seem to be increasingly marginalized. I get the impression that the "cooler heads" in power regard any such scheme as the victory of sentiment over reason (i.e. money) and that the dispassionate, "rational" position is for a mix of economic, cultural, and memorial activities on the site.

2002

9

Thinking Inside the Box

Admittedly, I went to the July 20 "Listening to the City" meeting at the Javits Center with visions of myself as that woman in the legendary Macintosh commercial, running through an auditorium of passive plebs to hurl her hammer at the monster screen on which Big Brother was proclaiming what a fine and orderly place the Orwellian world was. The setup seemed to confirm my worst fears for the event: 5,000 people arbitrarily assigned to 500 tables, watching speakers and images on giant video screens, each participant equipped with a remote-control keypad for "voting," each table with a volunteer "facilitator" (ours a German from Toronto) and a laptop on which to communicate with a team of compilers who would determine opinion trends in the room.

No more reassuring was the parade of the usual white men—from the Port Authority, the LMDC, the city government, and the Regional Plan Association—who extolled the importance of the process and presented the famous six schemes compiled by the LMDC and its consultants. The working portion of the event was conducted by Carolyn Lukensmeyer, a professional facilitator—who, for me, combined the more annoying aspects of Oprah and Kim Il Sung. Indeed, as the meeting wore on, I felt increasingly like a delegate to a 1950s Soviet Party Congress: the Central Committee has carefully selected this list of identical candidates for your consideration, you may now vote. (In this case, though, it was for the six schemes for street grid, office, shopping, hotel, memorial, and transit complexes all of precisely the same area). My own strained ability to participate in well-behaved Nielson-family fashion finally evaporated when Lukensmeyer ("give yourselves a nice round of applause") embellished her script with a pep talk on how the meeting was democratic as all get-out because, "in democracy, the people have a chance to speak!" Seizing upon this right, I rose to my feet to shout, "Buuuullllllshiiiit! Democracy means the people have the power to choose!"

This tiny act of insurrection went almost completely unnoticed. Inaudible over the amplified pronouncements being broadcast from the central stage, invisible in the vast hall and crowd, my outburst attracted a smattering of applause from nearby tables and not the slightest notice from anyone else. Not the first time for me, but telling nonetheless. The charade of "electronic democracy" was burst by the asymmetries of power in that room, the careful control of both agenda and process from above. With most planning, decision-making belongs to the powerful, reacting belongs to the people. At the Javits Center, original ideas were excluded because they—naturally—lacked a constituency: all the opinions that we wrote on our computers were vetted to see if enough people shared them to have them played back to the audience. Creativity was thus foreclosed by stifling the new or the unusual and by total control of what could be discussed. There was not a single mention among the alleged "choices," for example, of a scheme that would preserve the entire site as a memorial. Nevertheless, something constructive did happen at the meeting and in its aftermath. This had nothing to do with changing the underlying institutional structures—the virtually unaccountable quasi-governmental agencies that are running the process—but rather in the clarity of the audience response to the uninspiring and profoundly mediocre goods on offer. Emerging from the self-congratulatory and coercive process was a genuine act of protest: the audience consistently exercised the one planning power left in the hands of citizens: the power to say no. Given the opportunity to vote scheme-by-scheme, the crowd offered a pox on all houses.

Power had certainly anticipated this. In the week preceding the meeting, the six "alternative" schemes were released to the media by architects Beyer Blinder Belle (BBB) and were met with a fusillade of opprobrium that rained on them from every direction. Even John Whitehead, chairman and patriarch of the LMDC, mumbled with embarrassment at the press conference about this being "only a beginning." Likewise, the mayor (who has recently called for the inclusion of housing on the site), the media (including Paul Goldberger, Ada Louise Huxtable, and Herbert Muschamp), and the person in the street all responded with a raucous ho-hum. Even the governor (up for re-election in November and the man with the most power to influence events) wants to preserve the towers' footprints, arguing for a design that looks beyond the limits of the site. In the post-Enron environment, there is a growing sense that the leaders of the development community may not be the most dedicated keepers of the commonweal and that their plan simply to restore the status quo ante intolerably ignores both ethical and civic values.

While the dreadful proposals presented in this first round are the consequence of failed democracy, the avarice of power, and the imperative to make money, they are also the result of a design process that is conceptually flawed. Democracy, after all, cannot create great art, only sanction it. The essence of the problem lies in one of the cherished myths of modernity— that planning is essentially rational and objective. The LMDC has offered up a model of design by deduction, based on the idea that a "correct" solution can be derived by a hardheaded look at the facts and systematic analysis of possibilities and constraints. There's a false distinction here between planning (something on which all reasonable people should be able to agree) and architecture (the fickle realm of taste). By representing the six proposals as planning (this was not architecture, we were endlessly told, despite what we could plainly see were buildings, parks, streets, and squares), the LMDC covered its ass by acting as if the most fundamental issues of form, organization, and character were simply the outgrowth of logical thinking.

The mediocrity of the results so far can be blamed on the mindset of the designers entrusted with this project. Although the LMDC's head of planning, Alex Garvin, is knowledgeable, dedicated, and skilled, he has no track record as a friend of the imagination. Ideologically, he is squarely in the New Urbanist camp, and his vision appears hemmed by his traditional-ist sensibility. Moreover, every architectural firm "officially" working on the site shares this proclivity. And they are remarkably supine: no one from any of the architectural firms or official bodies involved in the process has publicly spoken out for a change in the office-building program, for a more far-reaching planning process, or for a competition. All are hopelessly behind the curve of public opinion.

Real decisions continue to be made behind the scenes without formal accountability, despite the pretense. The same impropriety characterizes the LMDC's design process and style of inclusion. BBB were allegedly chosen as the site designers through an "open" Request For Proposals (RFP) and stands to make a huge fee (out of a total contract of $3 million). But to call the RFP open is like saying that Trump Plaza is open to anyone who wants to live there. The LMDC's RFP—which attracted only fifteen proposals—was carefully restricted to very large corporate offices. (Firms had to have experience of at least three $100 million projects to be eligi-ble.) And at the same time as the RFP was proceeding, three other firms were already working away semi-officially without having gone through any public process at all. Larry Silverstein's architect Skidmore, Owings & Merrill (SOM) was producing plans for the site. Cooper, Robertson was master planning on behalf of Brookfield Properties, owners of the World Financial Center. And Peterson/Littenberg (a very small firm that would never have qualified via the official process) was hired by the LMDC to be its "in-house" design consultants. This particular choice was presumably based on long personal association with Garvin, their shared traditionalist taste, and collegial days at the Yale architecture school.

Before designating the six schemes for public presentation, the LMDC looked at nine plans from BBB and two from Peterson/Littenberg, as well as at the plans commissioned by Brookfield and Silverstein. The board members then voted to select two of the BBB plans, two from Peterson/Littenberg, and one each from Cooper, Roberston and SOM. This choice caused a number of people to go ballistic, among them BBB's John Beyer who—according to the *New York Post*—went to Joseph Seymour, head of the Port Authority, to grouse about the substitution of the two developer plans in lieu of similar schemes by his office.

Chastened, Seymour and LMDC director Lou Tomson agreed to replace the two developer plans with the BBB versions, a move which, in turn, caused a number of members of the LMDC task force to become enraged at the high-handed violation of "the process." Arguably, though, Seymour and Tomson's coup can be seen as restoring the process, since in theory only plans produced by BBB, the "publicly" designated architects, should have qualified.

By the end of July, the LMDC, barraged with criticism from all sides and losing its political backing from the mayor and the governor, itself came out in favor of opening out the process to smaller firms and to offices from abroad. But there's little cause for confidence that this revised process won't also be based on cronyism. Bromides about participation notwithstanding, it is clear that the architects with millions in public money to spend and with the sanction and public relations efforts of officialdom are working at an advantage. Other ideas simply cannot be heard.

Perhaps it is time for a little less management and a little more democracy. One possibility is to open the process to everyone with an idea. Let us immediately have not a competition, but an open call for ideas from around the world. Let us spend some money on a wonderful exhibition. Let us give the people some authentic choices instead of an elaborate scheme for pulling the wool over everyone's eyes. Let us have the kind of real discussion that can only come from having real alternatives.

2002

10

The Dimensions of Aura

In the aftermath of the devastation of September 11, the clearing of the site was accompanied by widespread claims for its sanctity. Everyone recognized that this was sacred ground, a gravesite, a place permanently marked by tragedy. In those first days, many of us called for the preservation of the entire fourteen acres as a memorial to the 3,000 victims of the horrendous attack. In the intervening months, this idea—most forcefully demanded by the survivors of those who died—has been quietly disappeared. The media barely refer to it, and none of the schemes proposed to date by the LMDC—all of which call for the restoration of massive amounts of office and retail space—even approach such a solution. Indeed, among those officially empowered to make choices, there seems to be a consensus that such a mode of remembering is either impractical, overly sentimental, or in some other way simply disproportionate.

It is clear though that most people consider the site permanently saturated with solemnity and therefore entitled to special consideration, not just the restoration of commercial activity. Just as the battlefields of the Civil War, the site of the Murrah Federal Building in Oklahoma City, and the African Burial Ground in lower Manhattan have been marked sacred and retain the power to arouse tremendous emotions when encroachment threatens, the World Trade Center site has an aura that must remain unbreached. The question is, what is its range and weight? What is its influence on both its immediate and extended environments? In recent months, the "footprints" of the towers have come to serve as a metonymic representation of the larger space of this tragic event. Since Governor Pataki's pledge over the summer that nothing would be built on these footprints, their preservation as the space of memorialization has become the default. Indeed, most of the plans promulgated by the LMDC have respected the idea of the inviolability of the footprints, despite the inclusion of massive construction around them.

Given that the site has now been cleared, the footprints are, however, an entirely conceptual notion: there is no longer any physical evidence of their presence. To be sure, the "bathtub"—the vast retaining wall that surrounds the entire site—is legibly clear. But the footprints themselves would have to be reconstituted in any scheme to "preserve" them. Would it make a difference if they were shifted by a few feet? Does their sanctity demand that nothing intrude in the airspace above them? Does their auratic power extend into the earth below?

A remarkable hair-splitting proposition has just been announced by the Port Authority that offers the first precise measurement of the official dimensions of this aura. Under pressure from survivor groups, the Port Authority has concluded that locating commercial space beneath the footprints is inappropriate but that retaining the alignment of the PATH commuter train (presumably a less crass, more public use) under the former south tower is okay, despite survivor arguments that the sacred space extends to bedrock.

This conundrum is deepened by a further displacement. Although much public debate has revolved around the appropriateness of a "cemetery" on the site, the lack of human remains compromises the usefulness of the model. Equally, the analogy of a battlefield seems inappropriate to the site of a mass murder of civilians, although this too is one of the widely used analogies informing the debate. Because of the difficulty in establishing agreement about the basic character of the event itself, vocal constituencies call for the memorial to be widely dispersed, while others suggest the restoration of commercial activity—including continuing demands for the reconstruction of the Twin Towers.

The city has not yet found a way to decide among these claims. Clearly, the ethical and philosophical dimensions of this question are far beyond the intellectual ken of the businessmen and bureaucrats who dominate the LMDC and Port Authority, the bodies empowered to decide on the future of the site. These agencies have further contributed to the difficulty by promulgating plans in which a "memorial" is treated as ancillary to the larger development, and not its driver. This distinction is fundamental, and is one that must undergird the serious debate that has yet to take place in the corridors of official power.

Still, the recent parsing by the Port Authority of the reach of the footprints helps define their aura in terms of space and use. After all, the question isn't simply one of how close normal life should be permitted to come, but also of what activities are to be considered respectful. Just as one bridles at the thought of a casino on Omaha Beach or a McDonald's at Gettysburg—and just as tremendous protest greeted the opening of a disco outside the gates of Auschwitz—so it should be clear that some things should not come too close to Ground Zero, wherever we decide to locate it.

In a real estate economy in which value (and meaning) is measured in inches, the care with which we discuss these questions will have tremendous bearing on the meaning of this place for future generations and on its role in the wider physical pattern of New York City. The question is whether a compromise between contending interests—finance, transportation, memorial—can yield a vision for the place. The conflict is not simply between a terribly banal politics—a little something for everyone—and a democratic process in which all voices are heard and weighed to abet a larger idea of the common good. Such matters of a collectively formed memory are not the subject for compromise but the terrain for a more spiritual consensus.

Every memorial invents the event it recalls. That "event" of 9/11 cannot simply be absorbed into things as they are: a year later it still exceeds our ability to describe it. It is only what happens now—what we do about this event and how we mark it—that will define the meaning of this horrific act. Until the endlessly "realistic" language of current discussion can be changed to accommodate this perspective, the victims of this terrible crime will not have been served.

2002

11

The World Peace Dome

Perhaps there was no avoiding it, given the pressure. And there was a certain logic to the restoration of the skyline, to patching the gaping hole. But given the growing certainty that building was going to be the "solution," we speculated about a form other than that of a tower or towers. We wanted to resist both the triumphalist phallomorphology of a bigger, higher, "better" version of the Trade Towers and to find a form that spoke to issues of harmony and peace, while still assuming some prominence on the skyline.

A dome seemed at once legible, evocative, and different. As a place for people to gather at all times of the year, it satisfied what seemed the most important activity the site should embrace—peaceable assembly. Marking and commemoration could take place with the reconstruction of the footprints and the planting of lush, year-round gardens, and people could flow across the site from every adjoining street. The big dome would serve as an enclosure for the transit center that would inevitably become part of any project. Finally, we placed a series of crescent-shaped towers within

© Michael Sorkin Studio

the dome to house other uses we thought important: a panoply of cultural institutions and a home for people and organizations working for world peace, perhaps the UN or a center for NGOs. Although the form of these structures was not strictly predictive of the style of their occupation, it did seem very important to assert that all uses were not equivalent and that reconstruction of the site had to be predicated on choosing the most appropriate ones.

2002

12

The Lotus

As we continued to look at the possibilities for the building on the site, we became more intrigued with the formal possibilities of the towers designed for the interior of the World Peace Dome.

Our next move was to remove the huge enclosure and let the tendrils grow and loosen formally, unconstrained by the formerly spherical space but still informed by it. The metaphor of a flower unfolding hovered over the project as we worked through this second iteration. Initial drawings show the buildings as a kind of Fata Morgana, unattached wisps mingling with more rooted structures. Looking back, there seems to be something both floral and flame-like in these forms that reflect both memory and ambivalence. More importantly, the paring away of the dome and the ephemerality of the sketches recall my earliest feelings about the future of the site, that it should be left untouched for a good length of time before any decision is taken about reconstruction.

Nevertheless, we pressed on to test the architectural viability of the scheme. The site organization worked well enough, and the towers were viable. There was plenty of room for the inclusion of cultural institutions below grade and within the wide bases of the towers. Aware of a private development proposal for a tower on the site of the proposed MTA transportation center on Broadway, we designed a covered galleria over Dey Street as a grand transport concourse, connecting the collection of lines converging beneath Ground Zero to those concentrated further east. The plan also included the rebuilding of the block to the south of Dey Street and the inclusion of a major cultural space—perhaps the City Opera—within it.

2002

13

Security

A recent ad for a Homeland Security Summit and Exposition bore the headline, "Grab Center Stage In a $138 Billion Market." Clearly, paranoia is a growth industry and the proliferation of conferences and meetings to discuss its implications is staggering. Since September 11, the nation has been consumed with its "war on terror" and the lens of fear refracts more and more of the meaning of everyday life. From bomb detectors at the airport to the rise in ethnic profiling to the visa difficulties of the students we admit from abroad to the Pentagon's sinister data-mining project run by Admiral John Poindexter (of Iran-Contra fame) to the new tics in our private behaviors, the culture is suffused with incitements to anxiety as the media fixates on the imminence of terror.

My own private internalization of this fear strikes me from time to time on my walk home from my studio, which takes me past a large federal building that houses, among other offices, the passport agency. As I approach this block, I often find myself thinking about car bombs. After particularly anxious days at work, I sometimes imagine I have spotted the lethal vehicle (generally some nondescript minivan) set to explode. I have walked blocks out of my way to circumnavigate the building and the impending fatal blast.

We measure the environment against our perception of its perils. Whether skirting dark streets at night, mapping and avoiding "dangerous" neighborhoods, or staying out of tall buildings, the human geography of the city entails assessments of convenience, pleasure, and risks. Our problem nowadays is that we are creating an urbanism predicated primarily on risk avoidance—one likely, in its more extreme versions, to have a terrible effect on fundamental ideas of the good city. To the degree that we acquiesce, we become complicit in a cycle of exacerbated paranoia, creating a bunker mentality.

There are both material and immaterial bunkers. The material variety—already abundant—includes the proliferation of biometric checkpoints, credentials vettings, hardened construction, defensive bollards, ditches around "high-value" targets, and so on. The immaterial fortifications are more internal and revolve around modifications to our own behavior: anxiety about leaving the house, willingness to permit prying into our private information, suspicion of people who somehow look "wrong," or demands for accelerated police action. Internalizing the means of our own repression, we risk allowing fanatics to turn us into totalitarians.

In his book *The Birth of the Clinic*, Michel Foucault describes the response of a town in the Middle Ages to an outbreak of the plague. Lacking modern medical knowledge, the town—on a signal from the authorities—adopted a state of hyper-orderliness, making personal movements geometrical and activities clockwork. This superposition of an apparently rational style of urban behavior was meant as an antidote to the evil and irrationality of the disease. Needless to say, it was not effective, although—in a typically *post hoc propter hoc* argument—the eventual waning of the plague could be attributed to the only course of action actually taken.

And this will be our delusion, too, if we acquiesce in the reimagination of our cities as battlegrounds, rushing to superimpose military order in a place that requires very different styles of discipline, hierarchy, and choice. We have all suffered the new inconveniences of the main focus of current security efforts: the air transport corridor. The time in line waiting to pass through detectors, the force of interrogators asking us whether someone has given us something to carry on the plane, the large numbers of armed personnel, the endless thresholds at which we are scanned, and our progress through space mapped step-by-step have all become part of the background of our lives. Making this process convenient by making it invisible is not something we should participate in uncritically. We may want to glide from the concourse to the gate, but I, for one, want to know when I am being electronically patted down and to whom this information is being conveyed. Given the genuine risks that we do face, however, the question becomes whether there is any meeting ground between the need for precautions and the ongoing project of urban amelioration—the construction of cities that are humane, democratic, and sustainable.

I think there are several potential points of convergence between these concerns, places where energy might be focused to make our cities both more comfortably secure and more comfortably free, a kind of "peace dividend" from a number of the measures we are likely to take based strictly on questions of security. We can begin by extracting questions of safety and security from a narrow focus on terror. So many more of us die falling down stairs or in automobile accidents than in wars or terror attacks that a little perspective is necessary, a realistic sense of proportion about the sites and organization of investment. The risk of being struck down crossing the street by an SUV is far higher than the worst bin Laden can do. I don't mean to be glib, but it is important to understand that the fear-mongering of the moment is based on a set of fundamentally political agendas.

How, then, to depoliticize the idea of safety, or rather, how to democratize it? To begin with the most obvious point, the project of making cities and buildings safer must encompass needed improvements to security from other risks. Clearly, reinforcing buildings against seismic hazards also brings greater safety from other sorts of externally induced structural traumas. Perhaps even more important is the dramatic improvement of fire safety. Many of the lives lost in the World Trade Center disaster might have been saved with better fire-abatement systems, with increased means of egress, with better internal communication, with careful attention to the presence of toxic and flammable materials. These are steps that need to be taken on an urgent basis, especially in tall buildings.

If September 11 can serve as a goad for us to address the threats mounted to buildings, this is to the good. However, even here we hazard a kind of parochialization of risk. Building safety must also encompass the effects of architecture on climate, the health-related effects of "sick building syndrome," the damage to resources in remote locations, the flat-out toxicity of many of the materials with which we build, the dangers of the building process, and the insecurities engendered by the massive consumption of energy by buildings (itself one of the reasons for the current rush to war). A national policy based on securing the means to continue the cycle of hyper-consumption has enormous and unfaced planetary and political consequences. Building security goes way beyond metal detectors and security guards.

One of the striking scenes in New York City following September 11 was a dramatic rearrangement in the movement of traffic, when access via bridges and tunnels was limited. Emergency vehicles were able to flow without impediment. Streets were preternaturally quiet. Pedestrians were predominant. Car-pooling was enforced. In the process of rethinking the city after 9/11, managing systems of movement is perhaps our central opportunity to create a synergy between security and urbanity. In New York, we have a chance to dramatically pedestrianize downtown, using Ground Zero as a point of dissemination for the network. This local greening might be accompanied by a large-scale reduction in private vehicles in the city as a whole, and the replacement of no-longer-required road space with parks, bikeways, and other public amenities. The moment is also ripe for a more rational system of goods distribution and delivery. Both security and urbanity would benefit from more rigorous management of city traffic: greater efficiency in delivering milk might have an ancillary benefit in greater inefficiency in delivering bombs.

Indeed, a general increase in architectural and urban "inefficiency" could have many positive effects. A multiplication of routes and a mix of scales would humanize cities that are too straightforward and homogeneous. Structural overdesign and redundancy could increase both safety and complexity. An architecture more integrated with the earth around it would enhance thermal performance, environmental continuity and variety of use. The sort of bottom-line inefficiency represented by European-style regulations that limit the dimensions of office floor plates to guarantee workers access to light and air would create buildings that are psychically and physically both safer and friendlier.

As Jane Jacobs has observed, strong neighborhoods are safe neighborhoods. Her theory suggested local spatial supervision based not on centralized means of surveillance but on the extension of the idea of neighborliness. Although anonymity is a prized value in city life, it is one among many, and there are styles of violation of our privacy that are more and less civic. The grandmother leaning out of the window keeping an eye on the street is a radically different phenomenon than M-16-toting guardsmen manning checkpoints downtown. It is not liberal sentimentality to suggest that building strong neighborhoods, neighborhoods with complex nets of relationship and interdependency, is an intrinsically superior style of security to CCTV on every corner. Our personal participation in the security of our cities and neighborhoods should grow from a sense of decorum, not fear.

By extension, we are now presented with an opportunity to rethink the nature of business and commercial concentrations within individual cities. The same technologies that allow corporate headquarters and call centers to grow on greenfield sites far from the pleasures and conveniences of town also allow us to adopt a policy of local decentralization based not simply on security from terror, but on the convenience of building sustainable communities—places in which living, working, education, culture, recreation (all the components of the good urban life) can be planned comprehensively: metropolitanization rather than globalization. In terms of the real economic development of New York City, for example, it would seem far more productive to apply the massive capital that is about to be squandered on unnecessary offices downtown to the reconstruction of the Bronx Hub or 125th Street.

The key to our security is neither the construction of new fortifications nor a willingness to progressively surrender our shrinking rights of privacy to the tender mercies of the national security state. Our best defense against terror lies in the strength of our democratic institutions and of our human character: armament is not a substitute for a culture of compassion and generosity. The horrible events of 9/11 are not a call to arms, but to justice, to increase the peace. Good cities, the manufactories of our civilization, are a bulwark.

2002

14

A Brief for Reconstruction

1. People must be free to gather. Uncoerced assembly is democracy expressed in space.
2. A wide range of rites and rituals of remembrance must be accommodated.
3. The need of survivors of the tragedy to come together must be served.
4. The site must be understood as a single whole.
5. The site must be easily entered and crossed. All existing streets and major building entrances surrounding the site should provide direct pedestrian access to it.
6. The literal continuation of streets and sidewalks is only the most obvious strategy.
7. The primary datum for crossing must be the grade of the site.
8. That grade should align with surrounding contours.
9. The event must be measured and marked.
10. This must include the footprints of the towers and their ramification in three dimensions, extending to bedrock and the heavens.
11. These ramifications should engage both space and use.
12. The site must permanently educate about the nature of the events that happened there.
13. The site should be a point of focus for a well-mixed urbanity downtown.
14. Any construction at the large scale must not preclude the possibility of the small.
15. The site should serve as a point of growth and spreading of green space.
16. The site should be well connected to its neighborhood, to New York City, and to the world.
17. The transportation infrastructure already below and near the site is crucial to these connections.
18. Many people should live near the site.
19. The elaboration of the site should support existing social, economic, and natural ecologies.
20. The site should be exceptional.

2002

15

Riff on Rem

I woke up to the *Sunday Times* to find the paper's architecture critic again unhinged by the object of his affections. This time, a gushing review of Rem Koolhaas's boutique for Prada on Broadway, which opened to the full Hollywood treatment: klieg lights, limos, blocked streets, and paparazzi. The *Times*'s well-timed coverage (only ten shopping days until Christmas) was bolstered by a sidebar hyping another overweight book from his firm, OMA, this one about Prada, a classic merchandising tie-in. (You've seen the movie, now get the action figure at Burger King.) The book includes lists of key concepts ("shops should not be identical"), pictures of handbags and of cardboard study models, larded with images of the master, photogenically craggy and dressed in clerical black.

I understand Prada to be an upmarket Tommy (Hilfiger, that is, whose hideous retro boutique recently opened on the other side of SoHo), an amplification of traditional shapes, styles and refinements. Prada's corporate culture is likewise geared to the shopping theory of creativity. Another tie-in piece in the *New York Times* chronicled the company's recent rapid expansion: "Over the course of its buying spree, Prada acquired controlling interest in Jil Sander, Helmut Lang, Church's shoes, Azzedine Alaia, Carshoe and the Genny Group, along with a sizeable chunk of Fendi."

The architectural haberdashery of the shop (which occupies much of the former space, and is twinned with the remnant of the downtown Guggenheim) similarly compiles brands within the brand—a boutique of received forms—from the Dan Graham light boxes to the Venturi-esque supergraphic wallpaper to the Portmanoid glass elevator, the SITE-like objects hung from the ceiling, the Diller and Scofidio video cams in the dressing rooms, the disco Mylar on the ceiling, the pulsing techno, the personnel dressed in security gray, whispering urgently into their mouthpieces. This conflation of shopping with invention is the philosophy embedded in both the shop and its massive apology. The store becomes museum and vice versa. Fabulous.

The main architectural move is sectional, a wooden wave that dips from the first floor to the basement and back, providing seating and a display surface for shoes. The wave is the Koolhaasian portmanteau metaphor and his logo for multinationalism, his "site." The architect's a surfer, the cool individualist who rides but does not pretend to tame the massive hydraulics of the system. Architecture makes multinational culture look good, all the while compiling a massive documentation of its nightmarish qualities, just to keep critical distance.

What we have here is the post–Organization Man, Madison Avenue approach to architecture, spinning the creative wheels to make the sale. In a 1991 book, *What's the Big Idea? How to Win with Outrageous Ideas*, George Lois, legendary 1960s adman, writes, "Advertising should stun momentarily . . . it should seem to be outrageous. In that swift interval between the initial shock and the realization that what you are showing is not as outrageous as it seems, you capture the audience."

The sixties were a watershed for the ad business and the formative era for Koolhaas. Hip ad people broke the mold of traditional advertising, with its stodgy formats and endless mock social-scientific and statistical research, with new "creative" approaches. The working method was co-optation: the legendary ads of the period took on the rebellious, teasing style of the counterculture; snoot cocked at the same corporations whose products they were promoting. Discarding the buttoned-down look, the ad business wore flowered shirts and ponytails, smoked pot in its boardrooms.

The Koolhaasian project merges both 1950s and 1960s Madison Avenue styles: from the 1950s, the authority of "objective" statistical information, the conflation of marketing and taste, with its barse-ackwards formulas of legitimation. From the 1960s, radical chic advertising is the crèche of postmodernity and its professionalized ambivalences, the birthplace of the multinational style. Rem becomes Rem ©. OMA spawns AMO. The idea of resistance, of friction, is lost in the go-with-the-flow. For the post-Andy generation, the subject-matter of art can only be anxiety and ambivalence, and Prada drips with it. Rem is our dark Seinfeld, producer of our Truman Show.

When Rem first began his Harvard operation, he called it the "Project on What Used to Be the City" (in a massive loss of nerve, it is now rebranded the "Harvard Project on the City"). This nominalist dodge was surely intended both to signal a fascination with the "post-urban" forms of globalization and its degraded universalism, and to put some distance between himself and the more prescriptive styles of contemporary architectural debate (eyes rolled at anyone still flogging the dead horse of humane urbanity).

The reticence is a commonplace: our legacy from utopian modernist urbanism is postmodern urban despair—suspicion and dystopia, and a fascination with weirdness. Modernity is the Taliban, something we can all oppose. Rem's fascination with this urban other may spring from formative years in colonial Indonesia: the writing presents us with the Conradian gloom of the colonizer with a conscience, helpless before the horror.

In this portrait of urban hyperbole, suspicion attaches to any optimism for the future. The association of optimism and totalitarianism is foundational Koolhaas: he's been called the most gifted architectural polemicist since Le Corbusier, and the comparison is apposite, if complicated. Koolhaas uses the epithet "optimism" to jeer at the Corbusian fantasy of power and to reveal his own deepest value: pessimism. The writing exudes it: colorfully acid descriptions of the onslaught of globalization and its weird generic architectures, couched in the prosody of enthusiasm. Backed by corporate organizational diagrams, charts of travel schedules, and a thousand neat hierarchies, the sellout becomes the marker of the ingenuity of the critique: embodying the contradiction escapes it. Architecture is performance art.

The Godardian tone of the writing—flat, ironic, Johnny Halliday voice-over as he drives through the Alphavillian night—disclaims optimism and mocks totalitarianism. Koolhaas treats urbanization like nature, a huge sweep of forces, rules without agency, the landscape of his bitter sublime.

He describes Lagos, the Pearl River Delta, and Atlanta with stylishness and insight. The prose is honed and coolly enthusiastic, like deadpan Tom Wolfe. But what actually is his position on the city? He writes,

> If there is to be a new urbanism, it will not be based on the twin fantasies of order and omnipotence, it will be the staging of uncertainty, it will no longer be concerned with the arrangement of more or less permanent objects but with the irrigation of territories with potential.

"Staged uncertainty" sure sounds like the 1960s to me. "More or less permanent" recalls the first-do-no-harm techno fantasies that yielded such product as "equipotential" space, "support structures," mega-structures, flexible modules, user-change—the last gasp of modernist urban science fiction and its pre-cybernetic technical fix. A massively noncommittal space could liberate everyone: by predicting nothing, it would accommodate everything. The city would be a series of laminations that serve its shopping subjects by smoothing the flow of traffic, allowing efficient circulation between a narrowed set of architectural certainties produced by the wisdom of the market.

After working through such post-urban paradigms as bigness, sprawl, hyper-development, and retail, Rem's Harvard (the Prada of universities) research project has turned its attention to the techniques of Roman city building, investigating especially its style of code-making. This reversion is produced by the generic city, which must inescapably turn to type for the means of its own inhabitation. Built up of standard components, the generic requires a basic gene pool of building types that can take on a variety of recombinant forms.

For Koolhaas, historicism stands in for prescription. The village green, the constructivist archive, Coney Island, Vegas, and ancient Rome are ideal postmodern enthusiasms: all understood at a distance. One as easily imagines Robert Venturi playing craps as Rem Koolhaas riding a rollercoaster. Having fun is not the point. The professional objects of Rem's sly veneration—John Portman, John Jerde, Wallace Harrison, etc.—are all big American men representing big American business, druids of a practice in which innovation is largely technical and organizational.

There's a hint of shame behind this nostalgia, the taste that dare not speak its name. Koolhaas clearly adores the actuality of postwar modernism, the repetitive blocks of the Albany Mall or downtown Stockholm, the thin curtain wall of Lever House, the 1964 World's Fair. I can understand this: I grew up on Vallingby and Scandinavian Modern. It's like liking vanilla. Ditto the thin columns, strip windows, and lifted volume of the Villa Savoie and the compulsive repetition of the Ville Radieuse. Rem's projects are darkly traditional, ironic sequels: Mies III.

The remorseless, addictive celebrity and rapier prose obscure an old-fashioned whine of alienation and a complete refusal of risk. Although he has helped open interesting territories for analysis, Koolhaas's project excludes any idea of subjectivity beyond hedonism or slavery, and any optimism for anything but the bottom line. With world-weary resignation before corporate "nature," the voluminous oversimplification, the campiness, the fogy disdain for the political, the ironic combination of criticism with celebration, all mark the larger failure to ever tell us what he really wants (so uncool).

But there must be at least one relevant urbanism somewhere between hysteria and totalization, perhaps in places to which we've turned a blind eye. The neoliberal, economic version of rationality is soulless and converts our affections to commodities. The asphyxiating environment, the grossly uneven distribution of resources, the repression of the regimes—Singaporean, Chinese, Nigerian—that run these fascinating cities, the lived lives behind the defensive walls of the compounds in Lagos or in the jerry-built apartments at the edge of the Chinese town that are replacing traditional bustling neighborhoods, the sheer stupidity of the culture of consumption—these are not to be desired. A useful urbanism needs to take a stand about what is.

2002

16

Herbert's List

In its approach to planning for Ground Zero, the LMDC has shown both a poverty of imagination and a deep desire to control the terms of the discussion. This failure has left a conceptual and artistic deficit that is being filled by individual creators and the many unofficial alliances that have sprung up in the wake of the disaster. The LMDC, however, has been deaf to their efforts, opening its inquiry only under pressure.

If there were a forum in which one might have expected to see some of the great variety of ideas and plans produced in the past year, it is the *New York Times*. Our newspaper of record, however, has provided crabbed coverage of possible design alternatives. Much of the responsibility for this stems from the gate-keeping role played by the newspaper's architecture critic, Herbert Muschamp. Muschamp has been acerbic in his criticism of the LMDC's flounderings. And his scathing commentary on the six misbegotten plans released in July was immediately echoed in an editorial headlined "The Downtown We Don't Want," which characterized the schemes as "dreary [and] leaden" and argued that no plan with that amount of commercial space would fly. It also suggested—following a proposal made by the LMDC and others— "how much better residential and commercial areas would cohere if West Street can be submerged and covered with a promenade or a park."

The very next day, though, Muschamp weighed in with a short "appraisal" in which he lavished praise on quite a different vision. Plucking one of the site diagrams published in the run-up to the LMDC Six by New York New Visions in an exemplary analytical document, Muschamp trumpeted the discovery of a scheme of "remarkable elegance" and "unmatched conceptual beauty." This turned out to be a *parti* in which the buried West Street was topped not with a "promenade or park" but by a series of developable blocks. Authorship of the plan was attributed to the architect Frederic Schwartz, who had been busily working officialdom on behalf of this diagram, now detached from the larger project of New York New Visions from which it had emerged.

While most of the July LMDC schemes had proposed to bury West Street, the Schwartz plan differed in suggesting that buildings be constructed atop the tunnel. The idea is not unfamiliar: Schwartz cut his architectural teeth in the Venturi, Scott Brown office working on Westway, and this scheme revisits the basic idea behind that project: the use of publicly funded infrastructure to create sites for private speculation. Muschamp presents this as a logical way to alleviate pressure on the Trade Center site by offering an alternative territory for development. Neither Muschamp nor Schwartz, however, has advanced any argument for the formal superiority of such a development to the creation of additional green and public space above the buried roadway.

Muschamp presents this plan as if it were the only solution to the question of off-site replacement space. Ignored are millions of square feet currently vacant downtown and the numerous unbuilt and underbuilt sites in the area (together more than enough to replace the World Trade Center twice over), as well as the possibility of replacing lost space elsewhere in the city. Although contemptuous of developer demands for immediate replacement of lost income streams—"The lease made me do it," he acidly began one of his pieces—his plan accomplishes just that, predicated on the ultimate in developer reasoning: the logic of the parcel.

The parcels, however, were also the grounds for an exercise in Muschamp's central critical operation: compiling lists of his favorite architects. Having suggested that the parceled development of West Street was the only logical way forward, Muschamp—playing Napoleon III to Schwartz's Haussmann—selected a group to implement the plan and then published their risible efforts with great fanfare in the September 8 issue of the *New York Times Magazine*. While there were a few tasty images among the proposals, the schemes were largely undercooked, with no urbanistic glue to give spatial and circulatory logic to the ensemble. Muschamp's mindless branding made Larry Silverstein look like Cosimo de Medici.

The plan, however, also suggests that the Twin Towers themselves be rebuilt—slightly southeast of the original site. But wasn't the "remarkable elegance" of the Schwartz plan that it obviated the need to replace the towers? To be sure, the buildings shown are Trade Towers with a twist: the huge structures have been torqued to resemble "a pair of candlesticks of unidentified authorship." In fact, they resemble fairly precisely a widely disseminated scheme by Richard Dattner, whose project is submerged in the claim that these buildings "enjoy a variety of sources." I am reminded of the undergraduate strategy of oversupplying footnotes to conceal a source. The week following publication of Muschamp's plan, a piece appeared in the House & Home section entitled, "At Home With Frederic Schwartz, The Man Who Dared the City to Think Again." Here, after congratulating him for his "aspirational" scheme, the writer described Schwartz's SoHo loft, his girlfriend, and his breakfast. The shelter section of the *New York Times* is, of course, obsessed with pedigree. And, given the fact that

Muschamp's list is about celebrity, the hapless Schwartz had to be made into one.

The celebrity mill received a further spin in the September 11 special issue of *New York* magazine, which included its own collection of schemes organized by its architecture critic, Joseph Giovannini. Complete designs were sought from six architects, with results that certainly raised many more interesting urbanistic issues than Muschamp's (not so) exquisite corpse, while still feeding the celebrity beast. Indeed, two of Giovannini's six designers were also on Muschamp's list. For *New York*, Peter Eisenman and Zaha Hadid produced completely different, more fully elaborated schemes. Somebody has a good agent.

Stung by the attacks on its own six schemes, the LMDC had announced in August that it was ready for some list-mania of its own and was prepared to pony up a puny sum ($40,000 per team) to sponsor six more schemes. And whom did the LMDC choose from the 400 who applied? The same people. Frederic Schwartz (already backpedaling from the idea of burying West Street in the face of rising community opposition), David Rockwell, and Rafael Viñoly—all from Muschamp's list—dominate one team. Another is composed of masters-of-the-universe Steven Holl, Charles Gwathmey, Richard Meier, and trifecta winner Peter Eisenman—Muschamp's list, one and all. Norman Foster makes the cut, as does Daniel Libeskind, our leading iconographer of trauma.

There is also an interesting, if jerry-built, team made up of a group of younger stars from the US and Europe. The final slot goes to Skidmore, Owings & Merrill, making this the fourth such commission they've received. They are already designing 7 WTC for Larry Silverstein; they've produced a site-wide scheme for Larry Silverstein (featuring an extremely tall tower); and they've devised a planning study for the east side of downtown for Carl Weisbrod (head of the Downtown Business Improvement District and member of the LMDC board). Why not just hand them the commission now?

Immediately following the LMDC selection of his list, Muschamp returned the favor, doing a full 180, writing that the LMDC—those former masters of malevolence and implacable foes of art—are now likely to "change the course of cultural life in New York." Come again? What would really change the course of cultural (and political) life in New York would be an open process, a genuine competition, in which public bodies (not to mention architectural critics) devoted themselves to promoting the widest—and wildest—styles of inclusion, not this endless, mad favoritism. And am I wrong to think that in offering his own proposal at this stage of the game, Muschamp has stepped over the critical line, compromising his future ability to judge developments dispassionately?

2002

17

Splitsville, USA: Why the Practice and Teaching of Urban Design Is Coming Apart

I've just come back from an excellent conference—"The Physical Fitness of Cities"—in Salt Lake City, then in the throes of its final Olympics preparations. Salt Lake was a heightened version of its usual dull, beautiful, weird, fascinating, and scary self. Security, needless to say, was draconian: explosives sniffers in the airport, troops with rifles over their shoulders, elaborate credentials around everyone's neck, Jersey barriers guiding traffic, the whole nine post–September 11 yards. Salt Lake has always been a well-disciplined city, with its rigid Mormon theocracy, its grid of wide streets numbered to reflect their distance from Temple Square, its rigorous proscriptions of daily life (no caffeine, tobacco, alcohol), and its cultural uniformity. And it has been a physically fit city, too. Mark Twain wrote in *Roughing It* that "Salt Lake City was healthy—an extremely healthy city. They declared that there was only one physician in the place and he was arrested every week regularly and held to answer under the vagrant act for 'having no visible means of support'."

Although the event sites were dispersed over a wide area, the Olympic Village—housing the athletes, presumably the fittest people on the planet—was designed as an autonomous town, located in a set of tacky new buildings on the grounds of Fort Douglas in the foothills of the Wasatch, overlooking the city below. The military camp was itself established in 1862, ostensibly to fight the Indians but also to keep an eye on the Mormons, cannons ready to quell any excessive behavior. The village remains highly defensible, ringed by three layers of security fencing, patrolled by armed guards, and completely self-sufficient, providing housing, meals, shopping, entertainment, and healthcare (including the hugely controversial free condoms offered to the athletes)—the ultimate gated community. However dull the new architecture or sinister the security, the village has much to say about the state of our urbanism—the good, the bad, and the ugly. To begin with the good: it's well-scaled and the old military quarters nicely preserved; it's walkable and wonderfully sited, right next to the university campus, another fine pedestrian ensemble. Moreover, the campus and the village are now served by a new light-rail line that runs down the hill to the center of town. For the athletes, the village represents an ethnic and national pluralism (if with a radically skewed median age) and a great place to party that's the diametric opposite of the city below.

On the other hand, in its combination of Radburn, Blade Runner, and *The Truman Show*, the Olympic Village is a nice reflection of the troubled picture of urban design as a discipline. It's a recombinant place that embodies many of the contending tendencies in contemporary American urbanism and the sometimes freakish results of their splicings. It's also a most cautionary place, a clear marker of the ethical depths that are associated with particular formal preferences, and an object lesson in understanding that the place where strategies of organization meet form are where the urban rubber hits the road.

The field of urbanism has never been richer analytically, nor able to draw on more diverse intellectual positions. From Camillo Sitte and Otto Wagner to Max Weber, the Chicago School, Ebenezer Howard, Patrick Geddes, Lewis Mumford, Jane Jacobs, Henri Lefebvre, Manuel Castells, Christine Boyer, Mike Davis, Peter Calthorpe, and Rem Koolhaas, the discipline teems with analysis. At this point, there is virtually no position without an extensive pedigree. Formal paradigms, however, are far fewer.

This split leaves urban design education in a parlous state. With no ideology enjoying the hegemonic sway of modernism, the field is contested and, in many ways, adrift. This reflects its own ambivalent origins. Arguments for the starting point of the discipline are both thick—José Luis Sert and Kevin Lynch, among others, are often cited as progenitors—and largely irrelevant. While the origin of urban design as an academic field cannot be clearly attributed, it is certainly the product of a particular moment in postwar American culture and reflects, in its emergence, other schisms that have characterized the practice of architecture.

The great originating rift in architectural education was the parting of the ways of architects and engineers in nineteenth-century France and the establishment of separate academies. This division of the artistic and the technical is one of the key operations of modernity, reflected both in the continuing clash between the two cultures and in various efforts to recuperate one side of the argument or the other.

A cause of the split lies in the origins of the discipline of planning. The central ambivalence here has long lain between the idea of physical planning and the set of anterior technical, social, and economic analyses that form the basis and shape the perspective of action. The conflict is not simply internal to planning, but is reflected in its fraught relationship to architecture, a product of planning's dual origins in the social sciences and social work on the one hand and the formal disciplines of architecture and landscape design on the other.

This nexus of confusion is reflected in the academy by the migrations of the field of planning within the larger structures of university organization. The planning department at UCLA (in recent years the most progressive in the country) is now split off from the school of architecture with which it had long uneasily coexisted. At Harvard, a somewhat lackluster planning department was moved out of the design school into the school of government and, in effect, replaced by the urban design program, only to be moved back and joined to urban design under a bifurcated umbrella. At City University of New York, planning is at Hunter College, urban design is in the City College School of Architecture, and many of the powerhouse intellectuals—David Harvey, Neil Smith, Setha Low, and others—are rigged into the graduate anthropology department.

This bureaucratic discomfort reflects the historical circumstances of the emergence of the discipline of urban design in the attempt by architects to recover some influence over the physical design of cities from the planners who so dominated professional urbanism in the 1940s, '50s, and '60s—the brains behind urban renewal, the interstates, suburbanization, and the paternalism of one-dimensional structures of social control. In this sense, urban design was itself oppositional; although, in another, its own position was nebulous, concerned both with questions of the rights of city dwellers (if in a crudely theorized way) and with traditional urban forms that constituted the vessel putatively necessary for the exercise of such rights.

These issues continue to run through the heart of the discipline. In many ways, this is salubrious: one thing we do not need right now is a single theory of urban form and a single style of urban practice. The best-organized candidate for such dominance—the practices clustered under the rubric of "new urbanism"—is far less influential in the schools than in the profession in general. And, happily, the internal contradictions within the group seem likely to produce more and more open schisms as the green faction seeks to free itself from the lugubrious Disneyfication-by-prescription of the historicist wing.

More influential as an academic model is the school of neo-quantification, an abstract version of functionalism that seeks to translate statistics directly to form. This group has far deeper affinities with intellectual postmodernity (as opposed to the architectural revivalism sometimes encompassed by the term), and its analysis has a good deal more bite. Unfortunately, any diagram is always at risk from the next diagram and from the pushy relativism of postmodernism, with its focus on constant shifts in perspective and the incessant interrogation of the origins of value.

Another strand in the braided taxonomy of urban design has its origins in the reformism of Jane Addams, Jacob Riis, tenement legislation, the activism of the New Deal, the oppositional practice of advocacy planning, early preservationism, and the larger movement for citizen involvement in the process of urban decision-making and design. Although I personally feel a deep affinity with this history, the problem with its current translation lies in a certain reticence about design. The emergent school of "everyday" urbanism, while distinct from the grim generic of the neo-quants and crucial for empowering citizenship, nevertheless is too suspicious of formal experiment and overly sanguine about the dispensability of architecture as an artistic practice.

Ironically, the area of urban investigation that seems to have the least influence in the architecture schools is environmentalism, the panoply of practices and investigations subsumed by questions of "green." Part of the reason is political. Unlike the European greens, our domestic variety has tended to be more delimited in its analysis, more focused on the aesthetic, spiritual, and medical consequences of deleterious environmental policies than on issues of maldistributed resources and the political effects of globalization. And part of the reason is that green architecture is only beginning to make a sufficiently compelling and comprehensible formal case for itself in this country. The upshot is that sound environmental design practice is the most under-taught subject in American architectural schools.

Every second, three people are born on the planet, two of them in cities. Urbanism is in crisis: the condition for billions of people in our cities is wretched, and we need to rapidly refit our dysfunctional metropolises for justice and sustainability and to build new cities around the globe. Urban design is a discipline—however it sorts out its relations with its professional siblings—that must be the site of a merger between social, environmental, and formal practices. If we designers are to have relevance beyond that of stylists or critics, we must produce convincing forms—as many as possible—for this coming together. While many schools of this urban joinery might and should emerge, there is no way a satisfactory urbanism can be taught that slights any of these aspects. Let a thousand urbanisms bloom!

2002

18

Urbanism Is Politics

During their recent "incursion" into the West Bank, Israeli forces were sent on a search-and-destroy mission to the Jenin refugee camp. Confronted with a labyrinth of streets far too narrow to permit tanks and armored vehicles, the Israelis elected to adopt a house-to-house approach. When a number of Israeli troops were ambushed and killed, bulldozers were introduced to topple houses and clear the site for safer access. The destruction of the refugee settlement was, among other things, an act of urbanism, Haussmannization raised to a flash-point. Although the consequences of the great boulevardization of Paris in the nineteenth century were not immediately lethal to those whose houses were destroyed to make way for Napoleon III's grand axialities, the impetus to demolish was motivated in part by military needs. The broad boulevards were meant to expedite troop movements around town and provide clear fields of fire in case of insurrection.

Nowhere today is the political use of urbanism more glaring than in Jerusalem and the West Bank. This is true of the Palestinian suicide attacks on the benign settings of urban conviviality—the murder of Israelis as they sit in cafés or shop in markets—and of the more bureaucratic styles of apartheid and occupation engineered by the Israelis. Both sides clearly understand the relationship of the patterns of the city and urban life to the politics of struggle for rights and privilege. And both clearly understand how to make cities into places of fear.

In this supercharged atmosphere, no urbanism can be spoken of outside its political dimension. Here in the US, our most pressing urban issue is sprawl, which we largely understand as an environmental question. In Jerusalem, sprawl has a different flavor. Israeli policy to "Judaize" the city has resulted in the construction of a ring of settlements—housing close to 200,000 people—that a more growth-sensitive approach would never countenance. By building beyond the boundaries of the existing conurbation, however, a ring of population has been imposed—like a wall—both to control the city and to thwart any potential division. Sitting in their arrogance on the tops of hills, the settlements represent an almost medieval style of planning, prompted by aggression and machismo.

The suburban sprawl of the West Bank settlements has been produced by the same means that generated our own suburbs. Like the cheap loans for returning veterans, the construction of the interstates, the accelerated depreciation of suburban commercial development, and the disproportionate subsidies for infrastructure, the Israeli settlements are the direct outgrowth of government policies meant to create a particular environment for particular people. In the settlements, the tools of planning produce their usual product: benign-looking clusters of Mediterranean-style, whitewashed houses with red-tile roofs, backyards, and pools. Here, too, is the idyllic atmosphere of suburbia, a rankling obliviousness that surely drives Palestinian villagers below to distraction.

But the picturesque view can only be sustained until the frame is slightly enlarged. This picture shows the barbed wire, soldiers on patrol, and a striking contrast with more indigenous styles of building and of life. In this view, nearby Palestinian villages and towns come to constitute—in their morphological and economic difference—a kind of dispersed "inner city." The familiar contrast between the city and its suburbs is played out in a tiny territory as the Israelis pursue simultaneous policies of urban renewal and ghettoization—urban renewal in the sense of the demolition and devaluation of the original inhabitants, and ghettoization not only for the Palestinians, but also for the Israelis, electively ensconced in their pleasant but beleaguered settlements.

The political sprawl of the settlements—and the murderous rage of the Palestinians—reflect the impossible physics of a situation in which two hostile populations attempt to occupy the same space at the same time. Even nominally shared space—streets and highways—becomes a battleground. The horrendous bus bombings are both murder clear and simple and an assault on the most fundamental freedom of the city, just as the construction by the Israelis of their private road networks on the West Bank are designed both to allow settlers to commute to Israel proper without passing through Palestinian towns and to divide the West Bank into a series of cantonments. Thus the traffic planner's language of convenience and speed takes on an oppressive dimension that cannot be escaped.

On a visit a few years ago to the school of architecture at Bir Zeit University outside Ramallah, I was wandering the corridor of the civil engineering department when I came across a plan for a "bypass road" around a village. My immediate thought was that this was a part of the Israeli road network on the West Bank. Closer inspection revealed, however, that it was simply a traffic-management scheme designed to avoid slow going in town for Palestinian motorists. The alternative road, in itself, is a somewhat questionable enterprise: witness the number of American towns that, bypassed by through traffic, have seen their economies wither. While the bypass may be a foolish piece of modernization, it lacks the sinister dimension of the Israeli network, which has strong parallels with the historic effect of American inner-city highways in isolating and destroying poor communities of color.

The extreme politics of planning in Israel and Palestine results in a situation that is separate and unequal at many levels. Systems of water supply, sanitation, energy, transportation, green space, and other elements of infrastructure are—despite many decades of pieties on the part of the municipal administration in Jerusalem about equalizing services—totally skewed to Israeli benefit. While Israeli Jerusalem has a reasonably integrated system of transportation, including highways, bus lines, airports, a train to the coast, and a good collective taxi system, the Palestinians are highly constrained in their ability to move, a product both of draconian and humiliating security arrangements that can extend a twenty-minute commute to hours and of a fundamental lack of transport services.

To get around, Palestinians must rely either on the Israeli systems— when available to them—or on their own network of cars, buses, and a collective taxi system of great potential efficiency, thwarted only by oppressive security delays. What is frustrating about all of this from the point of view of planning is that an efficient system for both Israeli and Palestinian Jerusalem is easy to imagine in purely technical terms. Jerusalem is a node on a linear urban system that runs from Nablus in the north through Ramallah, Jerusalem, and Bethlehem, to Hebron in the south—a classic linear city, considered in purely physical terms.

For transportation planners, the logic of a north-south system would seem clear-cut. Given the density of settlement and the relatively small distances, such a system might be both highly efficient and profitable, and an instrument of accommodation, convenience, and peace. Unfortunately, politics stands in the way.

Still, there are precedents for cooperation. There is one part of the urban infrastructure where all of Jerusalem works together: the municipal sewerage system is joined. Perhaps this is an earthy harbinger of greater possibilities should justice and reason ever prevail.

2002

19

On SITE

Modern art, born to rebel, chafes at the boundaries of its site. In the name of originality, out go easel painting, representation, bourgeois taste, the museum, the gallery system, the art academies, the anxieties of influence, Oedipus, the object. Trotskyesque, the avant-garde aspires to its own permanence. The sites and sources of innovation float. Whether embracing social revolution or simply revolutionary manners; the technical innovations of video, photography, or computing; the coalescence of abstraction; the arrogation to an "expanded field" of disciplines across such traditional boundaries as architecture and landscape; or the willful reductionism of minimalism, modern art has thrived on its apparent flouting of recent convention. The cult of the new persists.

In his prescient *De-Architecture* of 1987, James Wines points out a fundamental contradiction in this history: the disproportion between the revolution in artistic practice and any actual social change in the societies parent to this imaginative innovation. It's an observation that stems from both a particular moment in the life of art and a particular moment in Wines's own career, a crisis in meaning. Wines began as a sculptor, co-generationalist to minimalists like Judd and Serra and to more environmentally attuned figures like Heizer, de Maria, and Christo. His own sculptural work— powerfully shaped by a sense of fecundity and historicity gained during formative years in Italy—developed along strong tectonic lines, assimilating place to a powerful artistic autonomy. Little worlds.

Wines's commitment to the public nature of his work flows from this investigation of the meaning of the context of site. The dilemma of embodiment—both literally and conceptually—was crucial to someone who sought a practice infused by politics, and Wines's project rapidly took a critical turn. In this, he shared an emotional, if not formal, sensibility with the quasi-political interventions of Gordon Matta-Clark, Alan Kaprow and Dennis Oppenheim. Each of these artists begged the question of participation both by relocating the spatial and social site of art and by the explicit content of their work, whether it took the form of cheerfully subversive "happenings" or cautionary propaganda.

By moving out into the space of public life, by provoking reactions that exceeded the bounds of conventional ideas of the beautiful, and by scaling up, these artists quickly hit the edge of architecture. Architecture, after all, is historically the discipline that has combined artistic principles—style, composition—with the deliberate framing of social life. The characteristic hubris of the architect has long lain in the assumption that architecture—through its propagation of forms and spaces—actually invents social exchange by elaborating its forms and rituals.

Although this has led to much of the blithely disengaged polemic that Wines so articulately denounces, there is an element of truth in architecture's claim. Certainly, its power to oppress is brutally clear. Wines's own critique of architectural modernism and its craven universalism—most grossly in the thread running from Le Corbusier to Pruitt-Igoe—hammers a well-battered nail on the head. But Wines's muse has a mellower vibe, relishing architecture's power to please. Italy is surely the model, especially the way in which the architecture of its townscape provides rich and varied settings for both communal and private satisfaction. Up against this bivalence, Wines rapidly transferred a relatively traditional sculptural practice to building.

The fervent sixties and seventies were a backdrop. While no progressive doubted art's oppositional duty, there was much ferment about its expressive location and styles of relevance. The forms of the counterculture—happenings, squattings, demonstrations, Woodstocks, merry travels, and rural idylls—provided exuberant experiences but somewhat baroque visuals, the first real postmodern system of signification. Although stopping short of psychedelic, Wines's taste had surely been liberated, swayed by the unabashed hedonism of youth culture and by its desire to link art and life.

The "sixties" was a genuine period of popular creation, and the birth of a distinct critical practice. The art world was both stimulated and incapacitated by the outpouring, responses dividing along generational lines. The slightly older cohort—Wines's—was deep in the minimal. This might be seen as a critique of the effulgent excesses of the consumer society against which so many were in revolt. But minimalism was a dead end—further domestication of a movement with a long pedigree and a closet of grim outcomes, especially for architecture. The minimal represented nothing left to lose . . . or to do.

Minimalism's cultic purification dovetailed with that of functionalism and its worship of the idea of an asymptotic fit of form and use. The architectural reading of this ideal, the *existenzminimum* of modernity's universal worker-subject, extended this one-size-fits-all fantasy of form reduced to a core of pith, a vision that turned out to be a nightmare, penetential both socially and expressively. Artistic minimalism was a last gasp at recovering the aesthetic vitality of the sparse branch of modernism, stripping it of the social meaning that informed it in the first place, retaining only a whiff of the anti-bourgeois origins of modernism's rebellion against the over-stuffed visual culture of the Victorian and Edwardian ages. A million dollars for a plywood box.

What *not* to do was clear. The logic of the turn to architecture was clear. The logic of rebellion against pure formalism was clear. The logic of seeking sites for the reattachment of politics to form was clear. The logic of invention was clear. What was opaque was precisely what to do, what language to embrace, and what program to champion. Certainly, it had to begin with collectivity. In a declarative and optimistic act, Wines and his partner Allison Skye, with Michelle Stone and Josh Weinstein, founded SITE—"sculpture in the environment"—proclaiming their desire to unify ideas of form and place.

The architectural climate at this moment was particularly preoccupied with issues of symbolic meaning, of the expressivity of building. The seminal text was Robert Venturi's "Complexity and Contradiction in Architecture" of 1967, a work itself rife with contradiction. On the one hand, its *l'art pour l'art* defense of the prosody of architecture was gratifyingly antithetical to the devolutionary functionalism that still served as mainline architecture's threadbare theoretical cover. On the other, though, the politics was not entirely clear. Although Venturi's "messy vitality" in many ways reflected the urbanistic argument of Jane Jacobs—whose *The Death and Life of Great American Cities* was the crucial document in the critique of modernist urbanism. But Venturi's ardent formalism was also a cop-out, a distraction from the more urgent issues abroad in the streets (and the jungles).

Whatever Venturi's intent, the effect of the publication was to sanction the various historicist practices rapidly subsumed under the category of "postmodernism." America was suddenly awash in pediments and gables, not simply polluting architecture but also providing the visual and conceptual harbinger of the so-called "new urbanism," with its more explicit politics of form and function. The continuing invocation of small-town forms as a medium of political speech by the new urbanists infects the idea of content with a Disneyesque fantasy of over-determination, stifling invention by camouflaging the same old repressions with picturesque décor.

SITE's architectural beginnings were rich with modernism's own house style of protest: surrealism. The minimalist hegemon was assailed by its naughty discontents, who challenged the dour prescriptions of high modernism's Cartesianism with excess, humor, and irrationality. Because surrealism was funny, its relation to the canon had to be critical, and SITE used wit to both withering and beautiful effect. The Ghost Parking Lot (itself now under threat) of 1978 was a typically ingenious salvo—a vatic commentary, a prospective archaeology of internal combustion and its suburban spatial invention, and a place of play and assembly. Very much in the mood of Ant Farm's iconic Cadillac Ranch, the Ghost Parking Lot was a critical monument of immediate and transcendent accessibility, part of a group of projects—including the 1976 Parking Lot Showroom and the fabulous Highway 86 in Vancouver.

This research received an enormous boost from the appearance of Sidney and Frances Lewis, whose patronage allowed SITE to move explicitly into architectural territory. Owners of "Best Products," a chain of suburban department stores, and legendary art patrons, the Lewises engaged SITE to rethink the appearance of their emporia, up to that point just white brick big-boxes, sitting behind seas of parked cars. The commission was seminal, and SITE's response amazing, collapsing critique, whimsy, and identity with cool aplomb. The well-known results, which riff the most fundamental qualities of building—stability, gravitation, porosity, autonomy—are among the most indelible passages in the architecture of the late twentieth century.

Wines's research, from the start, has been explicitly engaged with questions of meaning and communication, and his "branding" of the Best stores is distinguished precisely by its legibility in all semiotic registers. Given the populism of Wines's concerns, the question of visual accessibility is both crucial and intrinsic. SITE's visual affect has always been broad, neither fey nor obscure in the historicist manner: an acerbic critique of the learned ironies of American postmodernism. Although they are clearly instances of Venturi's "decorated shed," the Best projects pose ticklish questions for the shed through a system of meaning that transcends appliqué to interrogate both the desires and strictures of the shed itself, illuminating the unconscious of the architecture of consumption.

The Best Products stores also provide a bridge to what has become the most important thematic of SITE's production: the engagement with issues of the environment and the question of "green" architecture. In designs that morph facades into terraria, that layer built and green elements, that challenge the culture of the dual categorization of architecture and landscape, SITE investigates the forms available to the operations of creating a blending of elements long bifurcated. To be sure, the immediate motives for this early work were symbolic, even decorative, but the message was nonetheless clear: the artificial distinction between architecture and its environment had to go.

Here the work hearkens back to Wines's beloved touchstone for successful public art, the Trevi Fountain in Rome. Surrealist *avant la lettre*, Trevi depicts an architectural reversal in which the ashlar of masonry is transformed into the (carefully simulated) ruggedness of a natural outcropping, which itself morphs into statuary. These meanings are instrumental in creating place, not in the sense that they are intrinsic to the function of gathering and refreshment, but inasmuch as they saturate the experience with the artistic, adding *another* layer of meaning rather than—like functionalism or minimalism—attempting to reduce all meanings to a singularity.

As a political artist, Wines quickly recognized that the dimension of argument—however artistic—was insufficient for an architecture of real aspiration that works at levels beyond simple signification. This is what distinguishes architecture: its purposive construction and its idea of service to humans is embodied, not abstracted. Here was a territory largely abandoned by the mainstream, whose formalisms and patterns of resource consumption grew increasingly empty and dangerous against the backdrop of a depleted environment in a condition of genuine crisis. For terraphiliacs, architecture had found a place to serve.

SITE emerged from a combination of taste, research, precedent, and urgency to become pioneers of planetary architecture. But there's an important distinction to be made between this globalism of environmental universalism and both its predecessor, the "international" style, and the more flexible multinational corporate stylings of today. For all the extravagance of its political claims, modernist architecture sought to generalize form as the road to political revolution. The prismatic austerities of high modernism were the projection of a very particular fantasy of egalitarianism; a style of equality that today stands in disrepute, displaced by the deeper determinations of difference. Multinationalism avers its respect for locality, but the respect is fraudulent: the Singapore Sling in the frequent-traveler lounge at Changi.

There is an architectural universal and, as SITE's work clearly suggests, it is based in the body. Rejecting the arguments of the "post-humanist" delirium of the virtual, SITE continues to reclaim the fundamentals of both art and use. In projects like the Avenue 5 "Green Wall" at the Seville exposition, for example, SITE employs its tools with rigor and mystery. Both organizational and tectonic, the wall attenuates one of architecture's fundamental constituents. It is also, symbolically and literally, a house for nature, the creation of a congenial space for plant-life, wrested artificially from an unsupportive environment and thus a means of communicating—via this inversion—a message about human agency and responsibility in the invention of the "natural" environment. Finally, it is an armature for mist pipes and therefore a comfort to the human bodies circulating in the torrid and artificial environment of the world's fair.

One of the enduring fascinations of modernist architecture is its idea of the free flow of space, the desire that the outdoors be continuous with the in. But, in virtually every classic iteration of the principle—from Aalto to Mies—the continuity is purely visual, an invisible membrane invariably enforcing the barrier between natural and architectural. SITE works hard to make that barrier obscure, to create a third way, "a fusion of buildings and environmental awareness as the raw material for a new and relevant iconography." This idea of an iconographic agenda for architecture, however, is deeper than representation, and provides a fulcrum for both expressing and creating architectures of sustainability, a medium of internal critique exposing building to the test of its own represented aims.

SITE's most recent work continues the project of blurring the distinction between architecture and environment, both technically and expressively. Certain motifs recur. The conceit of topography has long been an important element in SITE's expressive palette, visible in works ranging from the Sunset Boulevard project in Hollywood to the Shinwa Resort in Kisokoma-Kogen, Japan, from the Trawsfynydd Communication Center in Wales to the Saudi Arabian National Museum in Riyadh. Derived from the fascinating lamination of topographic models, these buildings are conceptually poised between construction and landscape, an artificial element supporting natural growth. Keenly aware of his own prehistory, Wines celebrates the groundedness in place that has been a thematic in architecture from the Egyptians to the Greeks to the Anasazi, and the idea that building not impede the flow of nature appears in project after project by SITE.

This stacked topography also appears—rotated through 90 degrees—in a series of striped or banded projects. The World Ecology Pavilion in Seville actually combines both horizontal and vertical laminar styles in a series of parallel topographic slices. The Windsor Waterfront Park takes this strategy one step further by creating a series of topographic piers, alternating bands of landscape and water, a move multiplied in the contemporaneous Four Continents Bridge, in Hiroshima. The most elaborated banding-building to date is the unrealized Museum of Islamic Arts in Doha, Qatar, in which a series of undulating laminations evokes the striated dunescape of the Arabian desert.

The Doha museum has another of SITE's signatures, the use of simple plan geometry as the medium for registering the dissolution of architecture into landscape. Here, the orthogonal system set up by the parallel walls of the building emerges in the landscape as a grid that organizes a garden which begins to wiggle and loosen as it approaches the edge of the site, lapsing finally into pure landscape. The same recurs in the Dresden Garden project and in the first full-formed version of the scheme, the civic center for Le Puy-en-Velay, France. In this work, the grid is the medium of translation between a group of historic buildings and a surrounding terraced topography, decreasing the degree of the artificial as the force of the project wanes over distance.

This technique of the graded wash between building and landscape parallels James Wines's own beautiful pen-and-wash delineations, a technique that also depends on the artful blur and controlled transition. This dissolve—rendered either as cut or fade-out—works both as blur and as seam. At the Perpetual Savings and Loan Bank of 1980, a "traditional" stone bank building changes into a greenhouse along a diagonal seam. At the San Leandro Best of 1983 and Frankfurt Museum of 1984, the joint between masonry and glass is created by a rotation in plan, one building type turning into or passing through the other, producing forms that are suave, rich, and surprising.

SITE delivers its message by merging cultural and natural landscapes to both advertise and enable a sustainable future for the earth. The embedded critique is not simply of an architecture that resists its environmental duty, but of one that fails to investigate and invent the richness of sustainability's formal palette. SITE's work is not shy about its individuality as art, re-infusing architecture with the relevance of both difference and co-determination, seducing us into a logical future.

2002

20

Who Decides?

In a phrase that can charitably only be described as disingenuous, Lou Thomson, President of the LMDC, announced that the seven new proposals for the World Trade Center site "were forged in a democratic process." If only it were so: deliberations over the future of Ground Zero have become progressively less and less democratic as layer after layer of bureaucracy is inserted between the citizens of New York and the final decision about the site.

The situation was bad enough to begin with, the most powerful players being the Port Authority—an agency of Olympian detachment from public control—and the venal Larry Silverstein, its largest lessor, who tried to claim his insurance payout for 9/11 should be doubled since, he argued, two catastrophes had occurred on the site.

In late 2001, the LMDC also entered the picture and quickly hired (through some oblique process) an "outside" planner to prepare the misbegotten, conceptually identical, and universally derided office schemes presented in July. Clearly embarrassed by the outcry, the LMDC immediately announced a so-called "competition" to elicit more "visionary" architectural proposals. And so it set up a new "non-political" committee to choose six new teams which nevertheless managed to include the architects already working for Larry Silverstein, British mega-practice Foster and Partners, a group of architects heavily promoted by the *New York Times*, and the architects already introduced through the back door by the LMDC for the first go-round.

Although the seven new schemes offer some dramatic form-making, they actually serve to make the process even more obscure and inaccessible. While more alternatives are vital if we're to reach a wise and democratic decision about the future of Ground Zero, the powers in charge are using this addition of "choice" not to widen but to narrow the options. It isn't just a refusal to consider any idea broached by the "competitors," but that virtually every scheme they do endorse serves to legitimize an even more primary lack of choice—that of the use of the site. While several of the projects do include interesting ideas for the memorial, they are all—like their roundly reviled predecessors—predominantly strategies for locating vast amounts of office space on or near the site, most offering some variation on the world's tallest building.

Two fundamentally bogus arguments are used to defend the process that has produced this outcome. The first is that the LMDC, the Port Authority and Larry Silverstein have all "listened" to the people. This is a familiar dodge of autocrats everywhere, like the Saudi Arabian princes who claim the audiences they hold, in which boons are selectively offered to long lines of mendicants, reflect some culturally specific form of "democratic" governance. Yet democracy is not simply a matter of being heard but of having the power to sway the course of events, and no amount of focus groups or sessions of "listening to the people" offer that rightful certainty of power.

The second justification lies in the similarity between the LMDC's form of decision-making and New York's indigenous style of democracy. The city's particular approach to planning lies in the "power" of individuals (or Community Boards, or civic groups) to just say no, whether through foot-dragging, litigation, demonstrations, or civil disobedience. Such democracy by negation can help curb the excesses of both elected and unelected officials but it is, at best, a gamble: no statute obliges anyone to pay attention, and initiative belongs to the powerful. Indeed, the mess we are in grows precisely out of the extralegal, back-room style of planning that has dominated the reconstruction process from the outset. It reflects the contemporary grail of efficient development as building "as of right," which is to say, without any public input.

Although planning, architecture, and democracy are difficult bedfellows—no amount of public participation can substitute for either artistic genius or genuine expertise—rebuilding Ground Zero is too important to the collective life and identity of New York to be relegated to the bottom-line mentality that is driving it. What is excluded (in much the same way that survivor representatives were excluded from the board of the LMDC) is the idea that the plan must be driven by the memorial; that commercial activity is not the invariable default; that designs might come from people other than those carefully filtered by the uninspiring leadership of the LMDC or produced in secrecy by the Port Authority or the lessor.

American democracy is not direct but representative. Such representation is least responsive when it is most attenuated, when decision-makers are furthest removed from popular recall. Downtown, decisions are being made by the appointees of the appointees of the appointees of elected officials. So perhaps it is time for a simpler strategy: let the people decide themselves. I don't suggest this as a universal formula for planning. As a general matter, direct democracy is a terrible way to plan, a lowest-common-denominator approach. But this is a special case. It is important to recognize that September 11 was an event; it happened to all of us, not to buildings or businesses or an area downtown. September 11 included everyone, and it is the extraordinariness of this fact that must be acknowledged in the plans for Ground Zero. The process of deciding becomes, in this instance, far more important than the efficiency, profitability, or even the aesthetics of whatever is finally built. The first step still remains: to find a way to ask the public about its desires for the use of Ground Zero that begins with all options on the table. The duty of a democratic politics includes the education of its citizenship, the provision of the necessary information for informed debate. The crowds that now gather in the Winter Garden to look at the new schemes testify both to the strength of feeling and depth of interest in the site's future, and to the public's ability to assimilate architectural and planning ideas.

But why just these seven choices? Why must the LMDC be interposed as gatekeeper, narrowing and coercing possibilities instead of helping us look at every idea that might (or might not) work on the site? Why can't we have an open invitation to anyone with a cogently drawn plan or intelligibly written text to post it at the Javits Center or the Winter Garden for a month or two to draw out a conversation about possibilities? This profusion of ideas (and there are thousands out there) would allow the public to coalesce around a program, to make known what they want built on this fraught site. An open process would also allow the public to make fiscal decisions properly its own, to decide how to pay for the memorial, how to compensate stakeholders, if necessary, and what transit infrastructure improvements to include. Then, and only then, can there be a genuine competition for the entire site. Such a competition would seek solutions that merge memory and moving on, and must be open to all. And would it be completely unreasonable for the public to choose the winner? Indeed, the only collectivity that has shown any wisdom in this corrupt and depressing process has been the public in its decisive rejection of the mediocre work of our mediocre public servants and private entrepreneurs.

The answer to terror is neither muscle-flexing nor the oblivious politburo style of the LMDC and the Port Authority, with their spurious and short-sighted "practicalities." The real reply is an excess of democracy: flamboyant participation. It's more than improbable (and happily so) that the public, especially with the experience of tragedy so near, will agree unanimously on a solution. But the conversation would be guaranteed to yield a more forceful and inventive solution than anything we have seen thus far. The process of arriving at the decision would be its own memorial.

2003

21

No Island Is an Island

The barrier islands off the Carolina coast are at once fragile and protective. Home to an amazing diversity of environments, ranging from ocean to dunes to maritime forests to salt and freshwater wetlands, these islands serve as habitat for a stunning range of ecosystems and a singular variety of species. Their beauty is compelling. And susceptible. Hurricane Hugo—which ravaged the coast in 1989—was an equal-opportunity destroyer, devastating both human and natural habitats with sublime thoroughness. Both, however, have revived themselves remarkably. The islands teem with alligators and deer, sawgrass, pine, and palmetto. And the houses that crowd the coast have also returned, jostling for views along the strand.

Resistance to this overbuilding of the islands is longstanding and based in several arguments. Critics challenge the crazy economics of insurance and public subsidy, the ravaging of pristine landscapes, the privatization of an asset that might be carefully shared, and the propriety of settlements in areas that participate with such regularity in a cycle of destruction and rebirth. These are the same arguments reflected in current debates about the suppression of fires in the national forests in the face of the otherwise natural rhythm of burning and renewal.

Solutions to the question of development of the barrier islands range from the default—the kind of rampant growth that has fouled places like Hilton Head—to their preservation as purely natural habitats. Each of these extremes has an ethical vector, an argument about the highest and best use of a scarce resource. And each represents a proposition about the meaning of our inhabitation on the land. The natural environment is the ultimate utopia, a realm characterized by the moral indifference of its laws and the totality of its system. This view is representative of environmental thinking in general, the idea that our moral position in the world derives—in great measure—from the way in which we define our relationship to the sum of forces in the cosmos and from our willingness to subsume our Promethean impulses to a more humble and collaborative view. This consciousness has begun to produce new patterns of architecture and settlement, and this "green" impulse is legible in a variety of incarnations along the islands. One of the more remarkable of these is Dewees Island, just north of Charleston, a place that proposes a kind of "third way," intermediate between development and preservation. The project is the brainchild of John Knott, a charismatic builder who, uniquely, gives the lie to the idea that "enlightened developer" is an oxymoron. Over the past ten years, he has transformed Dewees into a model for the possibility of building communities with a light lie on the land, simultaneously evoking both the promise and difficulties of constructing truly sustainable settlements.

Like other gated communities, Dewees is enabled by a series of restrictions and by a population that shares in their intent. Construction is confined to 4 percent of the island's footprint, leaving the rest in its natural state. Each of the 150 lots in the site plan is governed by a code that allows no more than 7,500 square feet to be developed (including the footprint of the house, driveway, septics, cisterns, and so on) and caps the total size of houses at 5,000 square feet. The code sets out a long series of extremely sensible environmental parameters for construction, and designs are vetted for conformity by a compliance committee. No cars are permitted on the island (a ferry shuttles residents and guests back and forth), and the main medium of transportation is golf carts, restricted to a top speed of 17mph. Roads are graded sand, and existing flora and fauna are rigorously protected. To reinforce the vibe, the development assumes a gently didactic role, abounding with small cautionary and explanatory labels ("boardwalks protect our dunes").

The results are very different from the typical coastal pattern. Houses are pulled back from the shoreline and roadways and are largely concealed by native trees, despite the height generated by the need to raise each structure 15 to 20 feet above sea level. The experience of the island thus centers predominantly on its natural features, which are scrupulously protected. Dewees's architecture is largely Low Country generic in flavor, and modest, rather than distinguished, in character. (Notable exceptions are a pair of lovely houses built by Charleston architect Whitney Powers.)

The island's harmonies are also produced by the homogeneity of its inhabitants, people of means with a prior commitment to at least basic principles of sustainability. Successful communities always grow from such shared interests, and the question to be asked about enclaves like Dewees is not one about shared values but about those excluded. Knott is dismissive of cavils about the lack of social diversity in the midst of the stunning biodiversity, and he is probably right. A tiny resort island cannot be expected to do the work of transforming an entire culture predicated on distinctions of wealth and class. And working on environmental amelioration is everybody's business.

My own initial skepticism about Knott's project dissipated after watching an encounter between him and two bubbas on the Dewees ferry. One of them approached Knott to ask if he could help out a friend of his, the coach for a local baseball club who was planning to move to greener economic pastures in Florida. The coach's day job was laying out golf courses, and the man proposed to Knott that Dewees would be well served by the construction of a few putting greens to give the men of the island an alternative to fishing and "watching the women swim." Although the Dewees ethos precludes a golf course (the landscape equivalent of an SUV), Knott heard the man out and suggested that he would be happy to talk to his friend if he understood that he'd have to build his green using native species, grown without fertilizer. When the man and his colleague registered perplexity at the latter requirement, Knott explained with exactitude, and without a hint of condescension, the negative effects of fertilizer on the environment. The men were clearly convinced, and Knott (whose early Jesuit education reappears in both his environmental fervor and his love of argument) had started another pair on the road to conversion.

But the real proof of Knott's commitment to social as well as environmental justice is made clear in his current project for the transformation of the city of North Charleston. The development, called Noisette after an eighteenth-century French botanist banished from Charleston proper for his marriage to a Haitian woman, encompasses both the abandoned Charleston Navy Yard and a series of neighborhoods whose population is 68 percent African-American and largely poor. Knott has partnered with the North Charleston municipality, and planning encompasses 3,000 acres at an estimated eventual cost of over $1 billion. This is projected to yield 10,000 new and rehabilitated housing units, 3 to 5 million square feet of commercial space, the renewal of thirteen schools, several new museums, and the creation of a large environmental reserve.

Evidence of the seriousness of the commitment is already visible at a variety of scales. Work has been completed on the conversion of a tiny house to a high green standard to serve as an educational center and model for work to come. Tax-increment financing is in place for major infrastructural improvements throughout the site. A nonprofit sustainability institute has been created. A waterfront park is under construction. The city has overlaid a special environmental district on the whole area, and Mayor Keith Summey has called for Noisette to be "a national benchmark for smart growth." Most remarkably, the city has promulgated and publicized a "pledge" that commits it "to practice 'no tolerance' for gentrification."

The fascination of Noisette springs both from these sterling intentions and from the amazing character and pattern of the site itself. In relatively small compass, Noisette holds one of the most concentrated collections of model communities I have ever encountered, places created with deep deliberation on the relationship of architectural form and social life. While these are not necessarily models to be emulated, they add tremendous complexity and depth to the project. Both happy and sad instances of neighborhood organization make an accidental heterotopia of wild diversity. Within the city's boundaries lie the scrupulous hierarchy and elegant architecture of officers' housing on the local naval base; the oppressive uniformities of public housing projects; the elegant dispositions of Park Circle, designed by the Olmsted brothers in 1904; the settlement of Liberty Hill, one of the first communities of freedmen after the Civil War; Century Oaks, a fantasy of tiny identical houses built in haste for workers during World War II; Cameron Terrace, a comfortable middle-class community of curved streets, green lawns, and brick rancheros; and a classic, if frayed, commercial main street, the very idyll of small-town America.

The U.S. has a special genius for the creation of such dreams of order and communality. The South is particularly rich in these fantasies, including the master narratives of the Old South and the Confederacy. And the fantasy abides, sustained by prodigies of exclusion. Just as the South romanced itself with comparisons to ancient Athens, the noble cavalier democracy was constructed (like that of Athens) on the backs of slaves. Utopia, of course, is as much concerned with the construction of subjectivity as of buildings. Ironically, the one element still lacking in Knott's vision is architecture; but this, one hopes, will come. Most importantly, the infrastructure of difference already present in North Charleston provides an extraordinary canvas for painting a portrait of twenty-first-century America as it ought to be: proud of its plurality, wedded to the celebration of non-oppressive diversity, concerned for the future of its natural environment, committed to the idea of generosity and security for all—and open to the new. This is a story I look forward to following closely.

2003

22

Obstructed Vision

The first duty of reconstruction is remembrance. Whatever design is chosen for the World Trade Center memorial, it will frame the meaning of the events of September 11 in its depiction of loss and its mnemonics of memory: what is built will convey to future generations both what happened and to whom. The second duty is healing. This must include both balm for the sufferings of the bereaved and dressing of the wound to New York. The jury for the memorial competition faces very serious issues, both in the artistic specifics of its choice and in balancing the potentially conflicting claims of these two obligations.

There has already been a de facto decision to conflate healing with restoration, to make urbanism a surrogate for lives lost. In the months since the tragedy, the idea that the appropriate response is to revive the character and uses of the site before the attack has been fixed. In the current master plan, this means both the literal replacement or enlargement of what was destroyed—huge skyscrapers, vast amounts of shopping, transit hub, and so on—and the repair of the urban damage done by the World Trade Center itself through the reconnection of several cross-site streets severed during its construction.

The thirteen-member competition jury (which includes designers Maya Lin, Enrique Norten, and Michael Van Valkenburgh) is already bridling at its constraints. Shortly after being tapped, several jurors declared their willingness to "break the rules" by entertaining submissions that ignore the announced requirements. Even the brief for the competition hedges its bets by stating that "design concepts that propose to exceed the illustrated memorial site boundaries may be considered by the jury if, in collaboration with the [LMDC], they are deemed feasible and consistent with the site plan objectives." Juror James Young put it most strongly: "Anything [competitors] might have in mind, any response, will be considered here."

It is easy to understand the jury's unease, given the constraining character of Daniel Libeskind's master plan. His scheme is not simply a proposal for the organization and reconstruction of the site, but a large-scale assimilation of the grammar of memory. Clearly the master plan is itself intended as the primary memorial, and thus dramatically deforms the scope and possibilities of this competition, much as the two rounds of architectural consultation were themselves hemmed by a program that brooked no variation on the commercial character of the project. For those trying to produce the memorial-within-the-memorial, the constricting influence of the master plan will be felt in two registers. First, the memorial site is located 30 (or perhaps 70) feet below grade and surrounded by the bloated Libeskindian apparatus of train station windows, neatly glazed bathtub, dancing waters (the wall that held back the Hudson now apparently needs protection from the rain), giant waterfall, ramps, cantilevered cultural facilities, and gigantic towers that will certainly influence the mood of the place. Indeed, the insistence on descent has already aroused strong opposition from people who live and work in the area. A recent poll shows that 70 percent of those in the neighborhood want the memorial to be approached from street level.

But it isn't simply that the one instance of sanctioned public participation must speak from a pit; it's the command of aura that offers the biggest challenge to free imaginative access. Libeskind's elaborate iconographic agenda is a straightjacket for meaning. Its most prominent component is that 1,776-foot tower, an Ayn Randian totem of patriotism as machismo. This decision to Americanize the event assures that we accept al-Qaeda's intended meaning for the attack. Never mind that hundreds of people from ninety-two countries other than the US were murdered, the object of the attack—and of its commemoration—is reduced by this mock-patriotic metonymy with its banal association with the Statue of Liberty, her torch replaced with TV antennae.

On June 12, Governor George Pataki, at a meeting with representatives of 9/11 survivors, declared his opposition to current plans to construct a bus garage beneath the memorial site. The statement refined his earlier insistence that the footprints of the World Trade Center towers were consecrated ground and the central armature for commemoration. While this strategy seemed straightforward, a parsing process had begun months ago, prompted in part by the fact that the idea of the footprints was largely conceptual, all evidence of their presence having been cleared from the site. How deep were the new prints to be? How high? Could they be moved? And what might appropriately occur in and near them without infringing on their aura?

After selecting the Libeskind master plan in February, the LMDC demanded the addition of a garage below the memorial, and the architect quickly obliged by raising the level of his commemorative pit by forty feet. But now the governor, responding to widespread public sentiment, has insisted that the footprints descend to bedrock, and has dramatically changed the terms of the current memorial competition.

If ever a commemorated event was site-specific, it is here: we are marking a killing field, a crime scene. Given the coincidence of marker and event, what special qualities are implied? This is not a commemoration at a distance, like the Vietnam memorial. That somber wall responds to the geometries and meanings of the Mall and, in its modest descent into the earth and its simple foregrounding of the names of the dead, aptly commemorates a still ambiguous but unquestionably tragic event without the usual triumphalism of war memorials. It was our first memorial to a lost war and it rightly focuses on sacrifice. Libeskind's project, by contrast— with its bellicose iconography of strength, its giganticism, and its emphasis on heroism—seems to commemorate victory.

As evidenced by Gettysburg, the USS *Arizona* in Pearl Harbor, and Babi Yar in the Ukraine—which are commemorated in situ—the symbolic finds its most pregnant source in the particulars of place. The topography of the massive gathering of armies, the submerged hull, and the painful ravine, all supply an infusion of both forms and ghosts. Like that sunken battleship, the World Trade Center footprints are a kind of readymade. And the dust of the victims abides in place. How to mark this conjunction?

In the immediate aftermath of 9/11, a highly aestheticized discourse arose. Forced to use familiar categories to assimilate an unfathomable event, many of us lapsed into the language of the sublime. Typical was the widespread call for the careful conservation of the twisted facade of the south tower as a memorial. And it was hard to resist finding it "beautiful"—a resonant icon for the event. But the domination of the debate by aesthetic categories distracted us from broader questions. The conspiracy buff in me, for example, thinks the LMDC set up Beyer Blinder Belle for its rejection on artistic grounds, enabling Libeskind to return several months later with almost exactly the same project, now wrapped in ziggy-zaggy signifiers of "architecture."

Libeskind has been widely criticized for his own favored (and seemingly universal) iconography—that of things shattered, wounded, twisted, slashed—and the objection has merit. We revere not just what we make beautiful but also the forms we inscribe in memory to stand for the events themselves. There is a difference (not to mention a choice) in remembering the spectacular mushroom cloud over Hiroshima or the muscular hardware of the Enola Gay instead of the incinerated bodies and the lingering cancers.

How to find the grounds of remembrance at Ground Zero? Thinking hard about this issue these past twenty months, I have come to believe very strongly that all of Ground Zero should remain as open, public space. Just as New York's premier expression of private property is the skyscraper, our best public spaces are our parks. It seems to me this should be the frame for a memorial, with private interests relegated to the abundant opportunities available at and beyond Ground Zero's physical periphery. Just as Central Park forms an attractor for the cultural institutions around it, so this site might be a distributor for public use and space. Passing the site several times a week, I am increasingly struck by its power and coherence as a space. No building will ever achieve the eloquence of this void in speaking of the event. We do not hallow this ground simply by filling it with buildings.

2003

23

Remembering Doug Michels

On June 14, just a week shy of his sixtieth birthday, architect Doug Michels was killed in a freak accident. It happened in Australia, at a place called Eden Bay, where Doug was consulting on a movie about killer whales and dolphins, an abiding interest of his. He died after falling from the ladder of an observation tower where he had gone to view the marine life in the bay.

Michels was that rarest and most vital of characters: a comedian. The comedian's privilege and responsibility is to create improbable but telling cultural bifurcations, to provide a comfortable home for incompatible ideas, to insist that what can be thought can be expressed. By proposing juxtapositions just beyond what we know, comedians de-center us with our own spontaneous laughter at the unexpected.

In 1968, Doug partnered with fellow architect Chip Lord (later joined by Curtis Schrier, Hudson Marquez, and a free-floating collection of collaborators) to found that greatest of American architectural counter-cultural groups, Ant Farm. Responding to comedic, utopian, and critical muses, Ant Farm produced a series of immortal projects that spoke to both the hopes and anxieties of its generation.

With uncanny clarity, Ant Farm undertook projects that darted in and out of the sites of invention rapidly reconfiguring the world. From nomadism to inflatables to car culture to theme parking to environmentalism to electronic space, Ant Farm was there before most of us had a clue.

Many of these projects were "real" in a way that was beyond jokey forms. Was it Lenin who said that irony and love were the qualities of a true revolutionary? Ant Farm was deeply committed to a revolution with a laugh track, not one of dour homogeneity and forced altruism. It was a revolution for freedom, self-expression, and joy; for sex, drugs, and rock and roll. And architecture. Ant Farm worked hard to envision architectures of pleasure and communion.

After Ant Farm broke up following a 1978 fire that destroyed its San Francisco studio, Doug simply kept going. He investigated the same conceptual edge—the band of ambiguity between official and alternative culture—designing everything from amusement parks to doll houses to bathing suits to private homes. And even as he pursued one fantastical project after another, he kept day jobs with the corporate likes of HOK and Philip Johnson. He studied at Yale, held a Loeb Fellowship at Harvard, taught at a number of schools, but was far too subversive for tenure. Fascinated and repelled by power, he hung around the scenes of its reproduction. He lived for years in Washington, DC, intoxicated by proximity to the druids of empire, impressed and appalled and engaged in his totally singular, wild and crazy way.

Dolphins were a longstanding leitmotif for Doug. His obsession with them was complicated, made magic by an early offshore encounter with one during an acid trip. Doug was intrigued by their intelligence and their language, and by the possibility of interspecies communication suggested by these attributes. Somehow, for him, dolphins embodied a contemporary version of the state of nature, a paradise lost but perhaps recoverable. His appreciation for these creatures was further deepened by the fact that they had another, darker side. Flipper could be murderous, filled with rage. And dolphins could be deeply sexual, orgiastic.

That this attraction was obsessional was clear in the way Doug's life as an architect returned again and again to the dolphin modular. It was surely the dark side of the dolphins that humanized them, kept his interest going, and led him to do his projects to accommodate them in his architecture. Among these were his scheme for a Dolphin Embassy (begun during the Ant Farm days), a floating research station meant to facilitate interspecies communication; Bluestar, an amazing space station positioned in geosynchronous orbit and housing a crew of dolphins and humans engaged in unspecified mental experiments; and a design for a new White House for a dolphin president.

Bluestar was the outstanding dolphin project, an unforgettable image designed on the model of Saturn: orb surrounded by rings. Human inhabitation took place in the rings, which were set in motion with the appropriate gravitational spin. Dolphins lived in a sphere of water (what liquids do in weightlessness) within a gigantic glass sphere (the ultimate think tank), where somehow a collectivized, harmonized brain was to be produced to roll back the frontiers of knowledge in a charged atmosphere of joy.

It was Doug's great genius that he never gave up pushing his dreams in the direction of more familiar styles of reality. At the time he did Bluestar, Doug was working at HOK and managed to persuade them not simply to let him proceed with the project, but to subsidize it. The piece later attracted the attention of NASA, and was displayed at the American Institute of Architects headquarters in the Octagon. Its final incarnation was as a video game—unique for its nonviolent subject—which, after years of development, was destroyed by a software glitch. Had Doug lived a few more years, it would surely have found another incarnation.

A more recent project was the celebrated National Sofa, Doug's entry in a competition for the redesign of Lafayette Square in Washington, DC. The sofa—several hundred feet long—was located along Pennsylvania Avenue, facing the White House. Periodically, a giant TV was to pop out of the ground to allow those seated on the sofa to interact with the president across the street. It was an amazingly incisive piece of satire, spanning questions of public space, electronic democracy, and the phony dignities of official styles of design. Classic Doug in its hilarious premise and in the ardent, deadpan style in which he promoted it.

As news of Doug's death quickly got around, an amazing electronic wake began. From all over the planet, his friends and colleagues began to write tales and testimonials. The picture that emerged was one not just of crackling intelligence and super talent but also of enormous generosity, a willingness to reply at length to students writing out of the blue, and a tenacious devotion to friends to whom he sent a miraculous stream of words and images, festooned with weird pictures from his wonderful hand and legendary rubber-stamp collection. Doug was one of the premier correspondents of the electronic age, and a revelation of the outpouring of emotion following his death was of how many of us have a stash of postcards, letters, cartoons, and projects that Doug sent out over the years.

He wrote us to the end. Many of his friends received postcards from the now too ironically named Eden Bay in the days leading up to the accident, a sad retrospective countdown. More eerie, many of us got cards even after his death had become known. And the thought we all had was the same: if anyone can communicate from the beyond, it would be Doug.

2003

24

The Avant-Garde in Time of War

All architecture is political.

By marshaling and distributing resources, organizing social space, and orchestrating encounters, architecture is the medium through which human relations are given dimension. Since 9/11, images of assaults on buildings and cities have become ubiquitous symbols of political action, surrogates—in a war without corpses—for our own corporeality. As we watch the war on Iraq unfolding in real time on TV, we are introduced to a modified, militarized, urbanists' discourse, different from our own, but filled with mirror images of architecture's techniques.

To accomplish the ends of this new "war-fighting ecosystem," cities must be stripped of their character as human settlements and re-measured. If by al-Qaeda, the city becomes Satan's lair, the habitat of devils; if by our own military, it becomes an urban space simply devoid of habitation. We see the city with the brutal objectivity of "aim points" and "target sets" for weapons so accurate they can be remotely aimed—from across the street, from Qatar, Florida, or from outer space—at windows. Because their precision is "beyond belief," in the words of Secretary of Defense Donald Rumsfeld, he can celebrate a strategy predicated on the easy technical classification of good buildings and bad (surrogates for good people and evildoers), and direct retributive fire to its targets from satellites hundreds of miles away. The clean and distant imagery—from the World Trade Center collapsing to the row of mushroom clouds rising over Baghdad—is equally depopulated for those who perpetrate and for those who observe. The message is not simply that we cannot miss, but that no one really gets hurt.

The media make use of architecture's tools as well. Each network employs global imagery from one or another simulation shop to extend its own panoptic reach. As we zoom in on Baghdad from a position in space, a fabulously detailed computer image of the landscape seamlessly morphs into an aerial photo of the city, then back to a CAD rendering of the presidential palace to be taken out. At the scale of the city, sinister installations are clearly marked—Saddam Airport, Baath Headquarters, the Planning Ministry—so we can map and assimilate both the networks and points of evil, ready for the acupuncture to be administered by our unfailing Tomahawks.

Like their civilian counterparts, military planners are experts at zoning. After the first night of Shock and Awe in Iraq, on March 20, the architectural and urban plans became more detailed. Stretching for several miles along the Tigris, a neighborhood of evil was introduced to us: a continuous concentration of the architecture of the Saddamite regime, an area of darkness, precisely redlined to become a pyrotechnic cauldron, ready for its close-up from the roof of the Al-Rashid or Palestine hotels. Dots on the map suggest that we have administered the appropriate corrective dose only where it is needed. By pathologizing in advance all that we hit, the noisome problem of collateral damage is obviated: it's just urban renewal. Indeed, according to an op-ed piece by Daryl G. Press in the March 26 *New York Times*, Baghdad is particularly well designed for invasion. Lacking tall buildings and laced—unlike Grozny or Mogadishu—with broad boulevards, the city's terrain is not, as Press writes laconically, "ideal for urban defense."

To justify the war, Bush repeatedly elided 9/11 and the attack on Iraq as cause and effect. There is something striking in the coincidence of the planning endgame at Ground Zero with the violent site-clearing and promised reconstruction underway in Iraq. Already, the *Times* had reported that the administration had invited Bechtel, Fluor, Halliburton, Parsons, Washington (successor to Morrison-Knudson), and the Berger Group to bid on billions in projects via an accelerated process. "Bechtel would be proud to rebuild Iraq," a spokesman is quoted as saying, and surely they would be proud to get a piece of the action in downtown New York City as well. Iraq will require its own development corporation, and the administration is suggesting that these contracts will be supervised by an "interim authority" (shades of the LMDC and the Port Authority), only answerable upward. War becomes the extension of planning by other means.

Our own response as architects has been uninspiring. Architecture's political voice speaks in many tongues, and there is no reason to assume that our views—never mind our styles of expression—should be uniform. To the contrary, the idea of liberty (and of its product, difference) is the repudiation of the single voice. At the same time, this expressive latitude does not mean a world of endless relativism, one in which the defense of principle is made moot by an idea of tolerance that reduces social relations to a Hobbesian jungle of pure opportunism and anything goes. In particular, we look to our avant-garde for a riposte to power, for our own targets of opportunity. Avant-gardes always harbor the political, the idea of the overthrow of the status quo. To escape mere nihilism, though, there must be some integral vision of the good, however obscure its forms at present. Unfortunately, our response to the destruction of the idea of the city by neoliberal globalization or by neocolonial warfare has produced little constructive speculation about urbanism's future. Having seen the looming disaster, too many of our most talented have simply embraced it: many architects are becoming proponents of the sprawl and the one-size-fits-all mentality that is strangling the earth.

But what ideas of the good city are truly worth defending? And how can the architectural avant-garde use its quiver of innovation and transgression to defend them? For me, the city confronts four major challenges in realizing its future, all of which have implications for form. The first of these is sustainability, the idea that numbers and resources must be balanced in order to conserve and enhance the health of both cities and the planet. The second issue is access. This entails the just distribution of global resources and the "freedom of the city" that is a fundamental right of urban citizenship. The third is the defense of privacy from the multiplication of techniques of surveillance and manipulation that prevent us from freely forming and maintaining our sense of self. Finally, valuable living cultural and physical ecologies must be preserved. No intelligent form of urbanism can neglect the defense of its historic successes.

On an exponentially urbanizing planet, the construction of new and sustainable cities is an urgent necessity, and we haven't risen to the challenge. Given the struggle between the goals I've listed and the pressures of a winnowing globalization and militarization of culture and control, the challenge is both how to build these cities and how to find the means for their individuality. Neither nostalgic visions nor the depredations of planning left to the ineffable wisdom of the market will do: not only bombs obliterate. This assault puts the premium on artistic invention, for the creation of a singular architecture that is sustainable, malleable, and beautiful.

And it is here that an engaged avant-garde becomes more crucial than ever. Two of our most celebrated avant-garde architectural firms have very visible projects in New York just now. Daniel Libeskind's scheme for the reconstruction of Ground Zero and the exhibition of the work of Liz Diller and Ric Scofidio at the Whitney Museum, *Scanning: The Aberrant Architectures of Diller + Scofidio*, are widely celebrated as the best and most truly innovative we can do. But, seated comfortably in their institutional venues, do either of these firms have the potential for either clarifying shock or inspiring awe? Is there anything new here? The final Libeskind scheme is simply conventional, its putative avant-gardism occlusive rather than innovative, offering up poignant, if familiar, symbols to "balance" the real investment to be made and the major uses to which the site is to be restored. The grid will return, there will be shops on the street and in a vast mall underground, and millions of square feet of unneeded office space will be built. The program will be just as it was. Yet for the authorities, who were so roundly castigated for previous failures of innovation, the idea that they're now actually thinking out of the box is bolstered by foregrounding Libeskind's progressive credentials (established by referring to previous "avant-garde" work), by his hip costuming and self-presentation, and by the thick camouflage of angularities shrouding the architecture whose future may or may not be in his control. At the same time, the idea that this formal experimentalism might harbor a risky politics is defused by Libeskind's sleeve-worn heart, by treacly recitations of his immigrant sagas, by the sudden appearance of an American Flag in his chic lapel, and by his grinning face as he rings the opening bell at the Stock Exchange, much like Michael Eisner or Martha Stewart.

At the Whitney, things are decidedly more promising. Diller and Scofidio have long worked with acumen and verve at the sites of crucial issues in urban politics. By addressing the rites of tourism, the media of surveillance, the rituals of domesticity, the alienation of everyday life, and the centrality of the body to architecture, their practice can be said to be genuinely critical. Canny in their combination of irony and sensuality—two of the cudgels historically used by the avant-gardes to browbeat cultural norms—these excellent designers, by responding to the threats of the virtual, continue to celebrate the prosody of the physical.

If I have a cavil with their work, it is with a certain failure to behave badly, and for their selection of targets grown long in the tooth. This is the old issue of how acceptable a message can be before it simply becomes part of the medium. Caught up in a hyperaesthetic critique, the work seems to pull its punches, dilating on ambiguity and mixed messages. But does anyone in the Issey Miyake generation actually iron (*Bad Press: Dissident Housework Series*)? Hasn't the numbness of the robotic production line been better covered by Fritz Lang and Charlie Chaplin (*Master/Slave*)? Has anyone failed to observe the homogenization of tourism (*Tourisms: suitCase Studies*)? Must we still express superiority to simple folk who love their lawns or their vacations (*The American Lawn: The Surface of Everyday Life*)? Is surveillance really deconstructed by video monitors over the bar at the Brasserie? This is work that makes me long both for the rapier and for utopia, for the out-of-bounds, for violence or hilarity or idiosyncrasy.

The power of Diller and Scofidio's project, though, is not its p.c. critique, but the form of its objectification. When the beauty is flat out—as in their tense suspension of Samsonite luggage in the Tourisms installation at the Whitney, or that stunning Blur building in Lake Neuchâtel at the Swiss Expo for 2002, or those intoxicatingly theatric choreographies (such as the Jet Lag multimedia play)—the longing for a better world finds focus. If the avant-garde is to have a utility beyond indulgence, it's time for both excess and straight talking, for the surrender of irony and hair-splitting intelligence to a frenzy of demands for a better world. The strategy of the avant-garde depends, always, on too much, on some willing form of bad behavior, on blurring old certainties. But totalitarianism trumps ambiguity every time. War is the ultimate bad behavior and the canny politicians in charge of the current carnage—by constantly presenting themselves as an avant-garde, inventors of the "revolution in military affairs" and pioneers of a new "battlespace"—try to supersede their own savagery by giving it fresh form. We must do better than this. What's needed now are clear propositions at the scale of globalizers, whole cities imagined from scratch, big chunks of alternative realities. Against the aesthetics of alienation and annihilation we must respond with fresh forms of survival and joy. Architecture must take the field.

2003

25

And Then There Were Two

The charade of a design competition for Ground Zero has now arrived at two "finalists," Daniel Libeskind and the "Think" group. Whatever one feels about the formal merits of the two schemes, they are deeply constrained by the circumstances of their production. Survivors of a group selected by the LMDC from a list that included virtually every architect on the planet, the two finalists were premiated in camera according to unrevealed standards. As many have objected, this lack of any formal accountability to the public robs the schemes of political authority beyond logrolling, all's-well-that-end's-well scenarios.

The "competition" that has yielded these two schemes arose as a cover for the disaster of the summer, in which another hand-picked group of architects produced a set of schemes of such banality that the LMDC was forced into a more design-friendly strategy to cover its beleaguered ass. The premise behind this new competition among "star" architects was simple: *architecture* would be a sufficient source of difference, of alternatives, for the site. Displaced would be any discussion about the larger questions of program and propriety, and in their stead would stand more ineffable aesthetic categories. The LMDC, as both the programmer and adjudicator of the process, has worked mightily to preserve the core of its brief: to make sure that the site reacquires its status as a hub of corporate office space. The program, to which both finalist teams have wordlessly acquiesced, demands 10 million square feet of commercial use—including offices, hotel, and retail—as well as cultural space, widely felt to be vital to downtown Manhattan's renewal. And, of course, somewhere in the mix is a memorial to the events of September 11. Indeed, the few arguments publicly proffered by the LMDC for picking these two finalists from the rest of the litter spring from their putative success in establishing an apt image for memorial.

This result, however, serves effectively to pull the rug out from under the *actual* memorial competition that the LMDC has long claimed to be organizing. So strong is the memorializing aspect of each of the schemes that a competition for further memorialization will be desperately constrained.

In the case of the Think proposal, the footprints—of interest to anyone contemplating a memorial site—are to be enclosed in the 111-story cages of their twin "cultural" Eiffel Towers. In the Libeskind design, the terrain of memorial is below ground, and any fresh intervention must figure itself against the huge slurry/wailing wall left exposed—the sole architectural survivor of the attack.

The gambit of foregrounding big architecture (both of the competitors offer structures taller than the World Trade Center towers) seems to have had the desired effect, the happy sign that big buildings are to be the outcome. Although a number of individuals and civic organizations (including the Regional Plan Association) have spurned the closed-door, non-public process favored by the LMDC, others have risen to the bait. Of particular interest has been the coverage in the *New York Times*, which has accepted the premise of the so-called competition without a word. Instead, our national newspaper of record has remained unconcerned, focusing simply on the relative merits of the two pre-chosen schemes.

On January 21, before the final two names were announced, the *Times* editorialized in favor of the Libeskind project, urging that "one of the two design finalists should certainly be Daniel Libeskind's soaring garden tower and ground-level memorial that uses the slurry wall holding back the Hudson River as a backdrop. Neither should hark to the past to recreate the twin office towers." The editorial did not suggest which other scheme might be included in the final two, but as none of the plans proposed recreating *the* twin office towers, one might assume that any plan which proposed twin towers—Foster, Peterson-Littenberg, or Think—were being ruled out. The editorial concluded with a call for the architectural and infrastructural plan to be in place before the competition for the memorial begins.

On January 28, Herbert Muschamp, the paper's architecture critic, weighed in with his choice for the winner: Think. He touted their twin latticework towers as "a work of genius, a towering affirmation of humanism in modern times." Although the humanism of placing windowless cultural facilities seventy stories up escapes me, Muschamp's choice was unsurprising since members of the team had already been central to his own attempt to design the site last summer. He had also already applauded the brilliant idea to place new construction—per the suggestion of one of the Thinkers—above a buried West Street, leaving Ground Zero free for future deliberation. The Think solution, however, has abandoned this entirely in favor of a site plan not unlike one of those so massively derided over the summer. (Although in their signature renderings, the 8 million square feet of office space they propose seems to have been coated in stealth materials, imperceptible to the eye.)

On February 4, the two finalists were revealed and—*mirabile dictu*—they were the *Times*'s two favorites, never mind that the paper had earlier published a news story claiming that the public strongly preferred three schemes, only one of which (Libeskind) made it into the finals. Things rapidly became more interesting on 43rd Street. On February 6, Muschamp derided the Libeskind project as a "war memorial to a conflict that has scarcely begun," contrasting it with the Think project, described as "a soaring affirmation of American values." Libeskind, in contrast, is burdened with the worst descriptors in the lexicon, "retro," "nostalgic," "pre-Enlightenment," "premodern," "medieval" . . . "religious." While Libeskind is certainly no slouch in the automatic piety department (indeed, he's a virtual self-igniting Yahrzeit candle, to paraphrase Martin Filler), this criticism is totally over the top.

Muschamp attempts to argue that memorial architecture has come to stand in the place evacuated by religion. In his formulation of the separation of civil and religious spheres, he argues that under the medieval system religion was exploited for political gain, whereas in our day political actions are accountable to reason. Left out of this account, of course, is the idea that political actions in democratic culture are also accountable to the desires of citizens. Muschamp and the LMDC see eye to eye in their preference for philosopher kings ("poets are the legislators of the world," as he noted in an earlier column) and both see the problem of Ground Zero as primarily representational, as if the content of the project were purely wrapped up in issues of imagery, an amazingly medieval conceit. The competition is reduced to a matter of iconography—how is a giant World Trade Center–shaped lattice more intrinsically modern, progressive, and meaningful than a hole in the ground. Clearly, these are tangled, difficult choices only to be unraveled by clerics like Muschamp.

As if to bolster this reduction of content to a purely formal matter, a kind of fashion obbligato has been played and replayed in the ancillary sections of the *Times*. In a recent story, Daniel Libeskind—a lifelong nebbish with a fresh eye for fashion—was celebrated for his habit of wearing cowboy boots. Accepting his physiognomic account of the colossal benefits to his stride, the story neglected the real reason shortish people often take to stacked heels. The piece also reported admiringly Libeskind's Alain Mikli eyeglasses, which turned out to be the harbinger of a full-blown story about the eyewear of the finalists. Here Ken Smith of Think in his Corb redux specs. Here Fred Schwartz in his horn-rims. Those Miklis on Libeskind reappear. Rafael Viñoly is seen in this signature two-pairs-at-once look. Never was vision so conflated with sight or sore eyes. Whom the *Times* would employ, it first makes *bad*. The *Times* has given the LMDC a virtual free pass as far as this process is concerned.

As a decision nears, the *Times* has pumped up the volume both in corroboration of the cynical process and in handicapping the winner. A news story the week before the decision was to be made indicated that the political powers that be were tending to the Libeskind scheme. On the Sunday preceding the decision, a guest column by art historian Marvin

Trachtenberg—appearing in the architecture slot generally occupied by Muschamp—denounced the Think scheme as "mainstream modernism," an architecture he associated with "the repression of history, memory, place and identity; the exaltation of functionalism, technology, and the machine," and a "hatred of the city." These scary attributes were alleged to be the spirit behind Think's thing, its "flayed skeletons of the World Trade Center," a description Libeskind himself used repeatedly in public to describe his competition. As if that weren't enough, Trachtenberg identified what Muschamp had called "a soaring tribute to American values" with "a model taken from the realm of totalitarianism, the famous Monument to the Third Communist International" proposed in 1920 by the great constructivist Vladimir Tatlin.

Liebeskind's design, on the other hand, was lauded for its putative lack of abstraction, its "deeply creative, organic relationship to the specificity of ground zero and its environment and meaning, as well as its accommodation of human needs and sensibilities . . . profoundly 'user friendly' on all levels." In short, it was "a miracle of creativity, intelligence, skill, and cutting-edge architectural thought; it looks to the future of architecture, just as Think remains mired in the past . . . it reminds us what it means to be human in a city." Say what?

Trachtenberg and Muschamp, looking at schemes alleged to be polar opposites, manage to adduce exactly the same meanings for their favorites. This pathetic argumentation does nothing to advance the contest of ideas and reveals—in its glib and unanalytical associationism (Think is fascist! Liebeskind is humanist! Think is humanist! Liebeskind is fascist!)—just how bankrupt, how feckless, criticism divorced from actual reasoning can be.

The day before the winner was to be announced, the *Times* took three final shots. Under the headline "Designers' Dreams Tempered By Reality," Muschamp described modifications in the finalists' schemes to meet objections from the Port Authority and the LMDC. After some boilerplate about the process having interested the public in architecture, he took a wistful dig at Libeskind, claiming that because of his particular compromise (shrinking the pit), "the design's symbolic heart no longer exists." While later allowing that Think's scheme had also been shrunk (by the removal of most of the program from within the lattice), he insisted that "the conceptual heart of this design remains intact." Lub dub.

On the same page—under pictures of the finalists surrounded by microphone-wielding media types—another article, "Turning A Competition Into A Public Campaign," appeared. This described the twin media blitzes launched by the finalists, ranging from a full court hustle of media outlets, to the hiring of two flacks (one of whom resigned over being second-guessed) by the Liebeskind camp (which had demanded air time with Larry King, Connie Chung, and *60 Minutes*), to the hot pursuit of survivor support by both teams. Indeed, the *Times* even reported on its own reporting, citing—not unsardonically—the boots and glasses stories the paper had run.

Finally, a news story reported that the site planning committee of the LMDC had come out in favor of the Think scheme while, as reported earlier, both the mayor and governor were supporting Libeskind. The decision was held to be the result of strong lobbying for Think by Roland Betts, a local business tycoon, best buddy of George Bush, and a member of the LMDC Steering Committee, itself charged with the final decision. That committee, however, is dominated by members who owe their jobs to the governor and the mayor—Port Authority officials and members of the two administrations. If I were a betting person, I would have to say it looks like Libeskind.

Either way, though, the *Times* will have called it. Having supported both projects and having piously editorialized about the fairness of the process, the paper has signaled its readiness to fall into line. The more cynical among us are inclined to see the competition as so much smoke-blowing, the real plan awaiting the culmination of multiple deals involving Larry Silverstein, the philistine leaseholder; the Port Authority, the site's owner, currently preparing its own plan in secret; the City of New York, still trying to engineer a swap of Ground Zero for the land under JFK and LaGuardia airports; and the governor, the player with the most cards. Indeed, the only dissent from all of this has come from Rudy Giuliani, who declared that none of the plans had captured the significance of the event or the place.

2003

26

Density Noodle

What is a city? They're certainly easier to recognize than to describe. Traditional definitions tend to be dense with comparison, per the useless description in Webster's: "a large town." As to a town, the dictionary has it as "a thickly populated area, usually larger than a village, having fixed boundaries, and certain local powers of government." A village is "a small community or group of houses in a rural area, larger than a hamlet and usually smaller than a town." A hamlet is, of course, "a small village."

Spiro Kostoff does somewhat better than this S, M, L, XL classification, describing nine characteristics of cities. These include, among other things, "a certain energized crowding of people"—felicitous phrase—"places that tend to come clustered with other towns, places that are circumscribed in some way, and places that have a dynamic relationship to a latifundian periphery." Arguably, each of these descriptors has a component of density but—even aggregated—none of them truly offers a sufficient definition of either a city or of the urban.

Wading through the fuzzy and inevitable tautologies of these descriptions, some consistency emerges: the city is a function of size, limits, governance, hierarchy, and crowding. Of these elements, "crowding" would seem to be the most potentially nuanced, the best candidate for further examination of the special qualities of the urban. However, before investigating the ramifications for urbanism of this notion of density, it is important to be clear about the reasons for inquiry, and why the mere thickening of settlement is an insufficient conceptual instrument with which to practice urbanism.

The study of urbanism has proceeded along two parallel tracks since it gathered coherence in the Renaissance. The initiating discourse was both prospective and reformist. The utopianism, the intentionality, of the Enlightenment's contribution to the idea of settlement manifested itself not simply in a vast set of experiments in community but—in its notion that perfectibility could be understood and instituted scientifically—in an idea of the tractability of the environment and of the authority of humanity over the planet. For well over 200 years we have been deluged with a literature that has sought to propose ideal forms of settlement, a set of paradigms for living life in collective settings.

Undergirding all was their positivism, the idea that planning represented a means of the inevitable betterment for the species and the planet. The civil religion of the Enlightenment retained the fantasy of perfectibility, but brought the city of God to earth. We still retain the idea that city-making has a teleology, a purposive component that obliges us to think not simply about the city but about the "good" city. Today, however, there's a corrosive reticence to engage the ethical instrumentality of the urban. In part, this is the result of the other great taxonomic stream in urban discourse: the analytical, social-scientific literature that has proliferated so dramatically in the last 150 years.

This analysis was itself impelled by the work of reform, by the now quantified apprehension that cities had a tremendous power to oppress, and by the parallel realization that subjectivity was both varied and created. From August Pugin to Jacob Riis to Jane Addams to Robert Park to Jane Jacobs, the idea of the city as an ecology of effects came to color views of the city's potential for pathology, and contributed to an epidemiological urbanism—an effort to isolate the causes of the widespread despair that accompanied the rise of the industrial city and the mass migrations of modernity.

Today, the situation is both parallel and fluid. The endemic critique of the totalitarian depredations of "rationality"—from Stalinism to urban renewal—has raised important anxieties about the deductive style of large-scale planning operations. At the same time, a deepening consciousness of global ecology has led to profound concerns about the contribution of urbanization to planetary degradation. This has, at once, engendered an impetus to reform and to a certain passivity in the face of forces that have been over-naturalized by the malleable evidence of statistical observation.

Despite an analytical literature of enormous vigor, the field of practice is dominated by mock-science and mock-history. The latter, with its classic *post hoc ergo propter hoc* fallacy of form-making as the producer of cultural relations, too often argues for the restoration of patterns that have ceased to carry the valence of their original production. The mindless profusion of traditional architecture as a cure-all for a culture that no longer lives in anything approaching the pattern that produced the forms into which it is being shoehorned is only the most depressing manifestation of the reduction of architecture and urbanism to consumer goods. Current fascination with branding participates in the same invert mentality of focus groups and consumer research: the delineation of choices via strategies of trivial differences and circumscribed alternatives.

The mock-scientific side participates in skewed and disciplinary priorities of the neoliberal agenda of economic globalization and its concentrations of command and control—many of the same values as the mock-historical wing of the profession with its shallow, anti-ecological style of "preservationism." The plague of data represents an even more cynical response in their born-again functionalism. Data—in its presumed objectivity—becomes the analogue of fate, a set of irresistible flows that can only be accommodated or "surfed." Thus, premise becomes conclusion and the cruel assumptions of capital are simply recycled. This resistance-is-useless attitude takes the thesis—developed most polemically by Hardt and Negri—of a system that brooks no "outside" and simply resigns in front of the multinational agenda, failing even to begin to strategize a means of attacking the beast from within.

Which returns us to density. There is little question that the densification of the planet in megacities and megalopolitan regions is the driver behind the need for radical reconsideration of the quality and strategy of contemporary urbanization. Megacities are simply apraxic, ungovernable and unsustainable. Indeed, some set the threshold far lower, per this winningly alarmist riff from Kirk Sale:

> Certainly, there is no question that the city of a million people, or even half a million, most probably, has gone beyond the ecological balance point at which it is able to sustain itself on its own resources. Cities, particularly modern industrial cities, are like colonizers, grand suction systems drawing their life from everywhere in the surrounding world, long since having gone past the point of adjusting to the carrying capacity of either their own territory or the nearby region's. A city of one million, it has been calculated, takes in 9,500 tons of fossil fuels, 2,000 tons of food, 625,000 tons of water, and 31,500 tons of oxygen every day—and puts out 500,000 tons of sewage, 28,500 tons of carbon dioxide, and great quantities of other solid, liquid and gaseous wastes. The contemporary high-rise city, in short, is an ecological parasite as it extracts its lifeblood from elsewhere and an ecological pathogen as it sends back its waste.

Ecological apocalypse notwithstanding, it is important to distinguish density from extent, and to introduce a set of qualitative criteria into the analysis. After all, there is density and there is density. We rightly distinguish the qualities of Jones Beach on a warm afternoon or the bustle on Fifth Avenue the week before Christmas from the hyper-crowding of the Warsaw ghetto or the asphyxiating black hole of Calcutta. Density can produce efficiency and pleasure as much as it can bring on the nightmare. With this in mind, density must be considered from the standpoint not only of its defining phenomenological character in the making of cities but also its management as a component of the endeavor to improve the quality of urban life. There seems little other reason to study the city.

Density ramifies as a physical, social and environmental agent. Most basically, density is the enabler of propinquity, the coming together of bodies in space. This density of encounter is the substrate of sociability and the material basis of democracy. Both depend on the face-to-face, which is, ultimately, the paramount argument for the logic of urbanity. Like all other arguments for density, the frequency, character, and controllability of such encounters define the quality of urban life and underpin the nature of the good city. The nature and availability of these meetings is under tremendous pressure from a number of directions. On the one hand, the rise of virtual networks of contact and relationship has the potential downside of estrangement, the isolation of people from each other, and the over-management of encounter. On the other, the growth of cities hopelessly large and aggressively uniform has similar alienation effects—the creation of a landscape of sameness in which the activating gap of difference is closed.

Both the social and the political life of the metropolis depend not simply on the fact of encounter but on its structure: the good city is an instrument for producing happy accidents, not simply a collision machine. The distance between predictability and chance in the conduct of everyday life is driven by the specific character of density and is a key measure of urban success. Good cities must—in both structure and detail—offer the possibility of avoidance as well as a hedge against uniformity of experience. A good city is clearly one that cannot be completely learned but must also reward the study produced by everyday participation. And a good city is one in which freedom of movement is facilitated, not impeded.

The importance of the accidental to the functioning of democratic culture is at the core of the case the legal theorist Cass Sunstein has made against the emergence of totally personalized communications on the Internet. In *Republic.com*, he writes,

> People should be exposed to materials that they would not have chosen in advance. Unplanned, unanticipated encounters are central to democracy itself. Such encounters often involve topics and points of view that people have not sought out and perhaps find quite irritating. They are important partly to ensure against fragmentation and extremism, which are predictable outcomes of any situation in which like-minded people speak only to themselves. I do not suggest that government should force people to see things that they wish to avoid. But I do contend that in a democracy deserving the name, people often come across views and topics that they have not specifically selected.

Andy Harris, a former Apple Computer executive, has stated the complaint succinctly for urbanism:

> [T]he more high-tech we become, the greater our need to come together. Teleworkers don't want to be isolated in their homes . . . their biggest

complaint is "cabin fever," physical isolation, lack of community and continued dependence on the car. What's lacking in these workers' lives is unintentional face to face interaction, the ability to just walk out the front door and encounter other people as a normal part of living, rather than having to plan and drive to every single social activity . . . Sadly, even pathologically, many daily commuters cling to their distant offices and ersatz neighborhoods, their last remaining refuge for spontaneous friendship and conversation amidst the decimated human ecosystem and loneliness of suburban sprawl. Ironically, it's the older downtowns that have the most to gain . . . It is the very low-tech, pedestrian nature of these older parts of their cities that now makes them attractive to information workers.

Encounter within the city is not simply the province of individuals, but of groups. A useful definition of the city is an aggregation of neighborhoods. While both neighborhoods and ghettoes are characterized by affinities among their inhabitants, a neighborhood is distinguished by the elective quality of life within it. Of course, not everyone can choose to live in SoHo, nor would everyone wish to live in Brownsville. As armatures of difference, the good quality of neighborhoods is partly determined by a series of elected or forced exclusions. This is the perplexing aspect of neighborhoods in cities that continue to be forcibly defined by race and class.

But a successful neighborhood also represents another style of density: a density of uses. A good neighborhood is a place in which all the necessities of daily life—living, working, schooling, playing, shopping, and so on—are available within easy walking compass of home. This suggests both an idea about "completeness" as a measure of satisfactory density and a physical means of measure. The numbers can vary dramatically but the intent remains constant. This sharing of necessity gives each of these artificial communities a community of interest and multiplies the basis for neighborhood political organization—which can only come from a degree of autonomy and a density of common desires.

Like a neighborhood, a city can be defined by a certain set of thresholds of use and population. Again, the issues are both quantitative and qualitative. The familiar ranking of cities into tiers is a function both of sheer size and of the scope of their economic activity in local, regional, and global contexts. Although this economic perspective flattens the meaning of the metropolis, it is useful to focus on the density of urban economic activity in a more qualitative manner. One of the central impositions of IMF-style globalization is the "free" migration of economic activity, unconstrained by tariffs or subsidies—which, it is held, is an effective formula for economic equality. But according to the familiar and telling critique, this can have severely negative consequences for developing economies. One of the most insistent disciplines of the global financial regime is the elimination of "inefficient" local economic activity in favor of "cheaper" goods produced elsewhere. IMF discipline has, to cite one example, forced millions of Mexican corn farmers off their land and into the cities for the dubious benefit of importing lower-priced factory-farmed grain from the US.

Anathema to this growth regime is the idea that a city, region, or nation protect its indigenous production, despite strong evidence that such strategies can have favorable outcomes for local economies. One of the rubrics under which developing economies have operated in the attempt to nurture local production is that of import replacement: the idea that growth and autonomy can be driven by the successive substitution of local products for imported goods. Jane Jacobs has suggested that import replacement is the motor that drove the original growth of cities. While I do not argue that cities (or nations) should or can become entirely self-sufficient, I would suggest that measurement of the degree of such sufficiency—a form of density—is a crucial index of the character and success of urban activity and life.

This is true at the economic level and, perhaps more germanely, at the level of the environment. In an increasingly globalized culture, the idea of accountability is ever more dispersed. In one sense, this represents a recognition of the intertwined ecology of the planet. In another, though, it's a formula for evasion and for obscuring the location of ethical choices. One representation of the degree of self-sufficiency of a city is its "ecological footprint." This idea, developed initially by the Canadian ecologist William Rees, is a method for spatializing the actual circuit of consumption of places. By examining the range of inputs into an urban ecology—energy, food, water, oxygen—as well as the consequences of their outputs—CO_2, solid waste, heat, etc.—the true dimensions of a city can be measured. This conceptualization, by modeling the total area required by a city (which, of course, entails placing a portion of the oxygen-generating capacity of the Amazon basin in contiguity with Vancouver or New York), produces an image of the city that is far different from those suggested by either political boundaries, standard metropolitan statistical areas, or the physical pattern of inhabitation. It also begins to suggest ways out of the dilemma proposed by Kirk Sale.

An expanded version of the footprint principle would take into account not simply the respiratory aspects of urban function, but cultural aspects as well. Cities would be understood in terms of different styles of efficiency than mere physical compaction, and density would acquire a fresh and compelling set of rationales. Motion, for instance, would be understood in terms of both energy and access, mapping the location of the inventory of necessary forms and activities throughout the city and its neighborhoods. Movement systems based on such principles would cease to fetishize absolute speed in favor of convenience and of their ability to abet and invent sustainable urban forms. Similarly, compiling such an expanded inventory would likely lead to a city more concerned with variety than with uniformity. The visibility of this inventory would have a didactic effect on the urban environment, coupling form with citizenship by providing the mediation of available and legible knowledges.

This city of collaborating differences would also be prompted by ideas not just of its completeness but of its singularity. Assuming we can slow the pace of global warming, it is likely that Vancouver will never have a tropical rainforest as part of its immediate footprint. The pattern of particular bioclimatic differences that logically inform the agriculture, architecture, and daily habits of Vancouver will be crucial in describing the scope of its self-sufficiency and the originality of its forms. A global order that thwarts the articulation of these differences by homogenizing culture, diet, climate, and the routines of daily life must be considered an enemy of the dynamic singularities that propel the arts of urbanism.

Although cities articulate human drives and respond to the exigencies of planetary ecology, it is a mistake to look at them as unconscious or autonomous. They may appear so because they seem to behave as organisms, because of the insistent repetitions to be found in their patterning and evolution. Schooled as we are in the relativistic effects of our observation of the physical world, we are overly eager to apply this undecidable character to social life, and despair of ever being able to sort through the blur of activity that the concatenation of consciousnesses in the city represents. This density of everyday experience, however, should not suggest that the city is other than a human artifact, or surely that, as such, it is both tractable and infinitely responsive to desire. The growth and elaboration of the city, the accumulation of its own experiential and historical density, incite us to perfection. The task of design is one not simply of accommodating subjectivity to unstoppable exigency, but of stimulating and valuing the output of the city's capacity to invent.

The critical density for the democratic city is its accumulation of social compacts about urban form and behavior. These are legible both in the patterns of everyday life—the culture of the café, of the promenade, of the furled umbrella or the neighborly greeting—and in the accumulation of historicity. We prize the uniform texture of old neighborhoods not simply out of some rarefied aesthetic sense, but because they harbor a density of agreement, the acquiescence of both those who built them and those who inherit them. Cities are public reservoirs for the production of private experience. If we revere rather than fear dense difference in life, the city that is replete with possibility has the greatest potential to satisfy our needs. Creating such cities requires a shift from recent habits and a clarity of insight into the structures of genuine difference, as well as a robust critique of the ersatz distinctions of multinational culture. The mere existence of desire is hardly a guarantee of authenticity; desire too is produced. To the degree that the city aids us in seeking our own choices, its own density compounds the genuine into the forms of its own and our own singularity.

Here in America, we are still lingering under the sway of the Jeffersonian ideal of the pastoral guarantee: the idea that individuality is most likely to flourish in an atmosphere of isolation, outside of unexpected influences. This idea is antithetical to the idea of the good city, and is reflected in an anti-urban strain that has characterized the republic from the get-go. In this reading, the city has been seen as both coercive and hospitable to the parasitisms of immigration, dandyism, libertinism, and sloth. This "bad" city is the place of an excess of mutuality, breeding the oppressive forms of cooperation which take the form of coercion. The result has been our own special American contribution to urbanism: sprawl.

Sprawl is the bastard child of the frontier, the idea of the continuous aggrandizement of nature and the universal fantasy of apartness. Reaching the end of the continent, conveniently subdivided by a uniform grid, America was forced to double and redouble back upon itself. This unfolding evasion of density was doomed to failure from the first, and it now desperately accommodates its impossibility through a spurious mobility. Instead of experiencing density as a congenial adjunct to urban life, our suburban plebs find it in their paralyzed mobility, jammed together on clotted highways, trying to get somewhere, defended by their carapaced SUVs against the contamination of the crowd. Truly, this should lead to the end of the road: dumb obedience to consumer "preferences", "we like to drive . . . we like the suburbs," is as unsustainable as it is insupportable. Wanton consumption of the world's resources reflected in this lifestyle simply cannot continue at its present rate.

The answer is density, delineability, and difference. The city is not simply an excerpted territory in the sea of the urban, but an organism grappling continuously with the limits and logic of its own autonomy. It is an open system, in the sense that it is permeable to and dependent on flows of energy, goods, and people. But its success is founded on its legibility and self-governance. Sprawl is unsustainable. Cities are the cure.

2003

27

Caveat Competitor

Why have architectural competitions? For practitioners, they offer the chance of a job without the grief of negotiation or self-promotion, and they can sometimes jump a small practice to the next level. For clients, competitions provide the opportunity to choose from many alternatives, show sympathy with architecture, and—in most cases—to do it on the cheap. For the public, competitions carry the seal of meritocracy, seemingly outside familiar cronyism.

But the process is easily corrupted. For starters, there is something exploitative about the huge amounts of uncompensated work required to keep the system going. And there are plenty of opportunities for log-rolling, deal-making, back-scratching, insider-trading and the rest. Juries can be dramatically affected by plane schedules, blood-sugar fluctuations, personality conflicts and low-common-denominator compromises: differences in taste cannot be adjudicated except by someone giving in.

Although I am a longtime sucker for competitions, a recent spate of bad experiences has given me pause. In this circumspect spirit, I offer this brief list of potential styles of abuse:

Bait and Switch

There are several styles of this scam. On the client side, there's the premiate-Danny-Libeskind-hire-David-Childs gambit, often justified by negotiations-with-the-winner-were-unsuccessful-therefore-we're-simply-hiring-who-we-want rationale. On the architectural side, there's the answer-the-proposal-with-one-team-show-up-at-the-job-meeting-with-another strategy. For instance, my office was recently asked to join a competition team by the London office of a large American design firm. I agreed. We did lots of work, sent it to them, and the "team" won the competition. Within a week, though, we had both been dropped (and stiffed), our usefulness at an end with the commission in hand.

Then there's the matter of juries advertised in promotions that fail to show up for the judging. How many have entered competitions because some sympathetic figure was on the jury only to discover that s/he never appeared or had never agreed in the first place? Competitions that enjoy high numbers of entries are often also subjected to pre-selection by the organizers, to save jurors—whose time is limited—from slogging through piles of entries that can quickly be determined uninteresting. Competition briefs seldom suggest that such procedures are likely to take place.

Selective Punctiliousness

And who hasn't experienced the ritual race to the post office to get the midnight postmark to confirm the eligibility of their entry? Although one may growl at the extra few days local competitors sometimes have to hand-deliver their projects, the logic behind deadlines, format restrictions, and so on is clear: to level the playing field by assuring that no one has more time or space than anyone else.

But the law is also an ass. Technical reviews of competition entries can eliminate wonderful schemes on the basis of some trivial infraction or meaningless variation in format. Deadlines are also malleable. We recently invested much time and money on a very promising competition sponsored by the government tourism bureau in Taiwan. Because of the summer's blackout in 2003 on the east coast—an act of God if ever there were one—our entry was delayed in transit and arrived after the official deadline. Although we had notified the organizers of the situation and sent digital copies of all the material, and although our submissions actually arrived during jury deliberations, the authorities chose to stick to the letter of the law, and our work went unseen. Such strict construction is not simply unfair on its face, it is contrary to what one would think to be the self-interest of the organizer: to be able to choose from as many well worked-out schemes as possible.

Cover Your Ass

A frequent reason for competitions is to convey the appearance of sincerity about architectural quality and to offer the image of due diligence in the pursuit of the public weal. This abuse is often particularly egregious in cases where juries lack independence or in which no actual jury is employed. The LMDC site competition for Ground Zero in New York City had a jury to select competitors but none to choose a winner, which was simply done by fiat. The current competition for the 9/11 memorial is genuinely "open," but the site and program are so absurdly constrained by planning decisions already made that the project risks being no more than a tiny fig-leaf for the giant shaft to rise to its north.

A particularly invidious form of this use of architecture as camouflage is the so-called "developer competition." New York has had several such competitions over the years as the Transit Authority attempted to sell off its enormously valuable property at Columbus Circle. The competitions they staged were not between architects, but developers, who were asked to provide combined architectural, programmatic, and financial proposals. While the decision that begat the current construction—made by insiders—supposedly took into account all of these factors, it was clear from the get-go that the TA took its fiduciary responsibilities more seriously than its architectural ones, abundantly confirmed by the outcome.

Permanent Winners

Norman Foster has been having a particularly strong run in New York lately. He was recently chosen by the Economic Development Corporation (with three other European offices, plus Steve Holl) to compete for the wonderful project of redesigning the Lower East Side waterfront. He was also invited to the LMDC site-planning competition for Ground Zero. And, he has now been approached by Larry Silverstein to do one of the shorter towers on "his" site. I do not begrudge the talented Lord Foster the opportunity to work in New York. However, his repeated presence on the list for these "public" projects speaks loudly of the constraints of the star system. It seems that the same six architects appear on *every* shortlist nowadays. This defeats another rationale for the competition system: that it mitigates the influence of both celebrity and fashion. If the same few populate every list, though, nothing new can happen.

There's another cadre of permanent winners in many competitions. Just as President Bush explains no-bid contracts for Bechtel and Halliburton in Iraq on the basis of their being the only firms with the "capacity" to undertake the work, so too a very small group of engineers, construction managers, marketing and real estate consultants and others appears on virtually every RFP and RFQ response for major projects in New York, and it's common knowledge that every team must include a heaping of old-boy chops to move ahead. A very senior official at the LMDC confided to me that the initial selection of Beyer Blinder Belle as site planners was of relatively small import to him. The real point had been to get their teammates Parsons Brinckerhoff as engineers, because that was the arena in which the real decisions were going to be made, well out of view.

Second Place Syndrome

One of our beloved myths is that the best competition entry—from the Chicago Tribune Tower to the League of Nations—always comes in second. And there is some truth here. I do not envy the task of the large jury sifting through the 5,400 entries for the 9/11 memorial competition, but I know that they will not pick the "best" project, but the best one they can agree on. There will be a vote, a learned democracy, and the appearance of fairness. Fairness, however, is not an aesthetic category. In these proceedings, though, it must substitute for one.

As a result, there will certainly be dozens of "second place" schemes that many will consider superior. This is what makes architectural competitions crapshoots. Although calling the body making the choice a "jury" suggests a legal analogy—with all its implications of impartiality and deliberation—an architectural jury lacks what is most fundamental to the real judicial process: a body of laws. Everybody simply brings their own. A "balanced" jury—that is, one representing as many different taste codes as possible—is normal operating procedure for competitions striving to seem fair and public (much as a "balanced" team is also required to get a job, even if that's not always the best formula for creativity).

But rules and regulations about sizes and dates—although they are often treated as if they were in some way comparable to the legal basis for administering justice—are no more intrinsic to decision-making than the color of the courtroom walls. The rigidity with which these laws are sometimes enforced is simply displacement. Likewise, balancing the jury by whatever formulae of demography or taste may seem "correct" does not assure a meaningful effect on the outcome, since fair play is a desirable quality only of the competition itself, not of the entries.

Although we still cling to the basic tenets of functionalism to maintain the fiction that architecture can be judged on the basis of strictly rational standards, we all know that this has little to do with what makes projects great. The discourse may provide a sense that a logical choice can be made, but logic itself only goes so far in artistic judgments. The best one can hope for is that on some jury some day, there will be someone who cares enough about a piece of our work that they'll put up the fight to make it a winner.

2003

28

(S)Truth and Consequences

The architectural photographs of Thomas Struth leave me cold. They're meant to, of course: Their voice is clinical, "analytical." Representations of a depopulated world, cities evacuated of their citizens, they join the robust sub-genre of visual depictions of urban alienation, bleak visions from Fritz Lang, Michelangelo Antonioni, Robert Doisneau, Camilo Vergara, among other artists of the last, dystopian, century. Aesthetic grimness is a trope with a tradition.

Black and white, sunless skies a uniform gray, ambiguously shadowed, Struth's photographs depict the city as the site of a particular kind of modern peril. Post–neutron bomb, post-plague, post- any number of modern styles of holocaust, people have disappeared but have left their cities distilled to pure agoraphobia and loneliness. Their space is without time or motion: vehicles stand empty and still, dawn is indistinguishable from dusk, not even the blur of accident violates the frame.

The depopulation of these photographs forces their focus on architecture and ironically evokes one of the enduring conventions of architectural photography, the idea that the purest representation of building is one purged of signs of use. Struth's work is a darker version of the received style of architectural portraiture in which buildings are meticulously groomed to look their best. For Struth, the opposite is true: the absence of life produces a distinct chill—the city at its worst, unable to sustain life.

Subjectivity is introduced into this equation by indirection and surrogacy. The photos are populated with the standard furniture of alienation: TV antennae, advertising signs, parked cars, railway lines, potholes, untended gardens, and tacky facade-lifts. The presence of the photographer stands in for the missing citizens, unable to observe the medium of their own despair. Questions are immediately begged about the time of day at which these evocative emptinesses have been found, about the recording apparatus, about the position of the photographer, about the intended meaning of the frame through which the objects are seen, about the inter-objective social and historical relations of the juxtaposed components on view. The atmosphere of rigor suggested by this inventory of questions is as inescapable as it is crucial to the desired effects.

The same might be said of the social architectures in Struth's later (human) group portraits, which also demand that the relationships among the sitters be deconstructed. As with the architectural series, the vision demands highly dramatized, rigorously controlled compositions. Indeed, the voice of the off-frame photographer commanding the disposition of his subjects is loudly audible: there is no spontaneity, no magic moment— everything is precisely diagrammed to produce deliberate meanings. Such Kirillian depiction of psychic aura is also central to Struth's "museum" photos in which the chain of observation—the photographer looking at the viewing "public" looking at the art—represents a meta-narrative of consumption and creation, generating a buzz of self-consciousness that evokes the conventions of modern seeing and being.

Struth has called his photography both "communicative and analytical," and in these urban portraits he is clearly compiling a catalogue of something. But of what? The collection is clearly of another order than the meticulously taxonomic catalogues of Struth's teachers and mentors Bernd and Hilda Becher. Their portraits of pithead machinery, gasometers, water towers, and other elements of the nineteenth-century industrial landscape are, on the one hand, critical documentaries of vanishing forms, and on the other recuperations of these fabulous objects for the architectural canon. Their willfully old-fashioned style of recording, with its bulky cameras, long exposures, and sequential depiction of motion, gives their work intense consonance, the character of having been made when these objects were new.

The work of the Bechers—and of Struth—carefully extends the documentary tradition and conventions of early photography, connections that seem especially resonant for Struth. Obliged to understand the world in shades of gray, photography invented a formal discourse that grew out of its own limitations. Slow technique required still subjects and lead to a natural preference for *momenti mori*. Photography's precise immobilizations of the subject, however, "fleshed out" earlier precision recording technologies like the death mask or the silhouette. Matthew Brady's photographs of the civil war dead are emblematic of this convergence of form and technique: unmoving corpses suited both his message and his medium.

Struth's architectural catalogue is distinctly funereal and his work pulls a clarifying strangeness from the contemporary environment by extraction and astute framing. Whether depicting decaying nineteenth-century streetscapes *à la* Atget (over-layered by the induction of contemporary meaning), the miserable housing projects of the DDR, or the weird futurologies of Houston office towers, Struth paints the city in grim tones. While he records scenes of dramatic physical distinctiveness—there's a wide gap between a phalanx of Manhattan office buildings and a nineteenth-century

German residential street—the most insistent reading is about sameness. These are pictures of what is clearly a single place.

To make this point, Struth relies on the uniform convention of central—one-point—perspective, which he describes as "a prototype of nonsubjective interest." It is, of course, a prototype that, since its invention in the Renaissance, reworked the meaning of the city by disciplining sight to conform with this newly "truthful" means of representation. But perspective—only one way of describing space—does not simply record meaning, it confers it. By assimilating the world to a particular way of viewing it, space was radically collapsed. The result is a global space signaling the end of architecture.

Struth's photographs of office buildings in the Loop, for example, are taken from a position above the el tracks. The elevated railway, that great nineteenth-century ravager of traditional forms of urbanity, runs through a canyon of modern buildings along Lake Street toward its vanishing point, a machine for commuting, bisecting the machines for working. The subtle reflectivity of the stainless steel rail cars, the meaningless dynamic of the interplay of reflections in the building windows—distorted mirrors for the conceptually identical architecture of their neighbors, which are distinguished only by the horizontal or vertical stripes of their opaque facades—the arbitrary-feeling crop, the mental merger of Josef Beuys and Jacques Tati, confer intricacy on nothingness.

Fifty blocks south on the same street, Struth photographs two buildings from a typically grim public housing complex—indeed one of the grimmest of them all, the recently demolished Robert Taylor Houses, once the largest public housing project in America. These are photographs—shot too from an Olympian elevation some stories up—without pity, and are populated by the same forlorn cast of formal characters. The grimly repetitive facades. The anorexic symmetries. The bare trees and torn turf. The randomly parked cars. The forlorn concrete pad with its spray of unused playground equipment (the presence of a few spectral kids pulls vaguely at the heartstrings). The double-decker commuter train with its long grid of dark windows immobile in the background. The flat gray sky. The remorseless emptiness. Another terrible place in a global landscape of terrible places. A confirmation—growing from formal austerity and a well-known back story—of a familiar view of the penitential character of rationalism gone wrong.

Struth photographs the two principal facades of the buildings, revealing everything necessary to understand their diagrammatic formal organization. Choosing both frontal and oblique angles, he succinctly demonstrates the degree of their architectural poverty, their loveless, pared, functionality. He includes just enough of their immediate peripheries to make clear how thoroughly their bleakness pervades their surrounding environments. In representing just two apartment buildings at once, Struth declines the standard seriatim view of the project, the image of the Corbusian stretch of slabs extending to infinity. Focusing on the increment, he suggests the nightmare of its reproduction. This dreadful place can only be more dreadful by multiplication.

For the unseen inhabitants, identity is reduced to pathology, creating them as symptoms. By extension, the absence of residents indemnifies the photos against the damage in broken lives left unpictured. The little archive becomes the retroactive brief for the destruction of the towers: you cannot "see" any reason to save them. Indeed, these buildings are in many ways already dead. They are physically fatigued and deteriorated to the point of collapse. The ideas that informed them both intellectually and artistically are in disrepute. Hope for the reformist agenda that inspired them is gone. There is no space for happiness here. For all we know the wrecking ball may be poised just out of frame, waiting to swing.

One of the most conspicuous images in contemporary architectural history is the implosion of the Pruitt Igoe housing project in St. Louis. Held by some to signal the death of modernism and the birth of post-, this image surely helped to supply the mental framework for the later destruction of many projects, including Taylor Homes and the buildings depicted by Struth. These are portraits of the condemned. Benjamin Bucloh describes the "melancholic commemoration" of Atget's photographs of a vanishing Paris, latent with their impending absence. Struth may have been unaware of the ultimate fate of the Taylor Homes when he chose them, but he photographed them like corpses at a funeral, done with life and destined to vanish.

If the scrupulous removal from view of the buildings' inhabitants and of the complex social ecologies that they supported helps make the case for an easy destruction, it also affirms the culpability of architecture in their residents' crimes, thereby both dismissing and reinforcing the original arguments for their construction—the idea that architecture (or its absence) could save souls. But such salvation is no longer on the national agenda. Housing projects in the post-Reagan reading are emblems both of the failure of the liberal social agenda and a shorthand form of racism: the idea that people simply destroyed their environments out of savagery. Struth decorously omits the black faces that inhabited this ghetto and thus returns the reading of the photographs to the culpabilities of the penal architecture that housed them. The absence of a visible community allows the buildings to be dispatched without consequences, the human effects out of sight.

There is obvious risk in this effacement. We love the images of purifying destruction represented by the blowing down of obsolete casinos in Vegas or obsolete social practices in St. Louis or Chicago (not to mention the habitats of evil along the Tigris), flattering ourselves that the problem can be solved by the well-dosed administration of violence. But the violence simply continues its attack on the symptoms in another register. The near-complete failure to provide for the new lives of those made homeless by this demolition (banished with their meager Section 8 vouchers to the poorest neighborhoods in the city) signals not simply indifference but the rage of the culture at its failure to discipline its most reviled and marginal elements.

Representation cannot be freighted with the evil it records, and these photographs must be understood for what they are not: the cause of any of this. They record architectures and read them as both instrumental and as effect. But they describe the effects of the system itself elliptically, subsuming it under the general category of alienation, modernity's special horror. It is the measure of how far the project of remediation has traveled that this should be so—that the collective desire to offer security, hygiene, and space to the poor should be so transformed. As these pictures make clear, we have suffered a grievous failure both of imagination and of conscience.

This is not the first time miserable housing has drawn documentary attention. The social polemic of photo-documentarians like Jacob Riis—and his record of big city misery—or Walker Evans—and his documentation of sharecropper life—was to expose the suffering of the disenfranchised poor and their bearing under stress. Their project was frankly ameliorative, and the photos therefore both "communicative and analytic." Riis, in particular, used his work to cudgel the construction of the kind of model housing for which the Taylor Homes represent the failed endpoint. How terrible that these places, culmination of a project of "cure," became the points of infection, housing a population that is, in many ways, as abject as the one recorded by Riis a century earlier. The medical metaphor remains the same, as does the preoccupation with symptoms rather than causes.

In this sense, the absence of inhabitants records the failure of the environment—a place that, it seems, cannot sustain life. Struth's representation of it, however, is pinioned by the divergent demands of his aesthetic and his conscience. Clearly, the images embody a component of protest in their very bleakness. But they also reassure that the wanton destruction of these homes is legitimate, that the problem was always a too crudely instrumental application of architecture to the difficulties of the urban poor. Struth illuminates the character of these landscapes of coercion with the full measure of despair.

The representation of an environment that simply cannot be saved is not, in fact, a perception shared by those obliged to live in it. Polled before their forced removal and resettlement, the majority of residents preferred to stay, assuming a reasonable level of renovation and more enlightened management. Precisely what is invisible in Struth's photographs—the thick networks of community that represent the social reality of the Taylor Homes—is what was destroyed by the demolition of these miserable buildings. The pictures preclude the idea of adaptation by withholding any evidence that occupation does anything but make things worse. And, by situating these particular photos in a global suite of similar images, Struth suggests the even more depressing idea of no alternatives.

Struth inverts Riis, whose campaign for that housing reform was fueled by exposing what tenement housing produced: human misery. The impact of his photos of the New York poor, caught unawares in their squalid homes by his early use the flash, was produced by work that, as Edward Burrows and Mike Wallace write, "broke sharply with genteel photographic conventions." With the lens focused on humanity, architecture retreats to the periphery of this work, but there is still no mistaking its effects. Struth's long exposures turn the relationship around, locating perhaps too much consequence in architecture. The sites of messy and ambiguous subjectivity, peripheralized, simply cannot be captured directly by this particular convention. We are not shocked but dulled by this work, and fascinated.

Formally compelling, these photographs literally and figuratively float above quotidian reality, blinding the eye to immediate experience (you can't even make out the graffiti on the walls) with its everyday relationship to space and detail. The simultaneous hostility and attraction to the architectural object demotes sympathy for the human subjects, all of whom become victims. Lacking compassion, the photos devolve on the hard beauty of these meaning-purged places. Assimilated both to the conventions of artistic style and to a uniform gloom, the photos take (or perhaps simply follow) architecture in the direction of its own vanishing point.

But there is also resistance in their ugliness. In the age of Benetton, in which depictions of despair are used to sell sweaters, Struth's formal detachment establishes a protected place for his observation of the self-imposed cruelties of modern city form. The remorseless accuracy of his recording of the physical details of the spaces he observes—like the blackheads and moles of a tight portrait—suggest that there may be trouble behind those opaque facades. Certainly the space in front—the realm of public participation in urban life—has become a nightmare.

2003

29

Entering the Building

1. Enter on the right.
2. The revolving door is only to be used in a counter-clockwise direction.
3. Do not speak to the Security Guards (brown uniform).
4. Do not make any sudden movements.
5. Do not make any jokes—safety is a serious matter.
6. Cameras and other recording devices may not be used.
7. Smoking is not permitted anywhere in the building.
8. Wipe your feet on the foot-wiping surface leading to the screening area prior to removing your shoes.
9. Empty your pockets into the small blue plastic tub on the table to your right.
10. Place the tub on the x-ray conveyor.
11. Place your coat, jacket, hat, shoes, and other outer garments on the x-ray conveyor.
12. Place anything else you happen to be carrying on the x-ray conveyor.
13. When the green signal light flashes, pass through the magnetometer next to the x-ray conveyor, unless you have a pacemaker.
14. If you have a pacemaker, you may not enter this building unless you undergo a full-body (cavity) search.
15. If you require such a search, take a number from either the "female" or the "male" ticket machine opposite the x-ray scanner.
16. Await your turn in the Body Search Waiting Area.
17. When your number is called, enter the curtained booth marked "female" or "male" and disrobe completely.
18. Place your clothes and personal effects in the large yellow plastic tub provided.
19. When called by the Screener (beige uniform), pass through the curtain marked "screening" into the screening room.
20. Bring the yellow plastic tub with you and hand it to the Screening Assistant (purple uniform). Your clothes and personal effects will be returned to you following completion of the full-body (cavity) search.

21. When the yellow plastic tub is returned, put your clothes on and wait for the Screening Assistant to escort you through the Pacemaker Access Door.
22. No shoes, no shirt, no entry.
23. Present the Profiler (lime green uniform) at the Profiling Desk with your profile. Be prepared to show proof of citizenship.
24. Await the green light before proceeding through the turnstile.
25. Place your hand on the biometric reader located in the console in the Biometric Reading Room.
26. Await the green light before proceeding through the turnstile.
27. Look directly into the iris scanner along the wall of the Eye-Inspection Passage.
28. Await the green light before proceeding through the turnstile.
29. After passing through the eye-inspection turnstile, sit in one of the green molded-plastic chairs in the Olfactory Inspection Area.
30. Allow the Sniffer-Dog (green camouflage uniform) to sniff you wherever he or she chooses.
31. Do not pet, feed, fondle, speak to, or otherwise interfere with the dog during the execution of his or her duties.
32. Remain in the green molded-plastic chair until notified by the Sniffer-Dog Handler (shocking pink uniform).
33. On being told to "get going" by the Sniffer-Dog Handler, proceed to the Elevator Access Corridor.
34. Maintain single file.
35. Talking is not permitted.
36. Prepare to show two forms of Government or Major-Corporate-issued picture identification, one of which must be your Building Pass.
37. If you do not have a building pass, proceed through the door marked "Temporary Building Pass Office" to secure a Temporary Building Pass.
38. No one will be issued a Temporary Building Pass without two forms of picture identification and confirmation of an appointment with a screened tenant of the building.
39. On being issued a Temporary Pass, return to the Security Foyer and present the Temporary Building Pass along with two forms of Government or Major-Corporate-issued picture identification to the Security Guard.
40. Await the word "pass!" from the Security Guard before proceeding.
41. Place your Building Pass or Temporary Building Pass in the slot of the Building Identification Card reader beyond the Security Guard Station. At the green light signal, proceed through the turnstile.
42. Select the elevator corresponding to the floor to which you are going.
43. Place your Building Pass or Temporary Building Pass on the building card reader to the right of the elevator.

44. When the elevator doors open, you will see your name displayed on the video screen above the Building Pass Scanner.
45. When you see your name, you may enter the elevator.
46. Move to the back and face forward.
47. When you hear your name on the elevator speaker, place your palm flat on the Biometric Scanner located to the left of the elevator door.
48. When the elevator opens on your permitted floor, you will have three seconds to exit the elevator cab.
49. On exiting the elevator into the Upper Floor Elevator Lobby, place your Building Pass or Temporary Building Pass in the slot of the Building Identification Card Reader.
50. When the access buzzer sounds, look directly into the iris scanner next to the Upper Floor Elevator Lobby Exit Door.
51. When the entry chimes sound (Beethoven's Fifth), you may enter your chosen floor. You will be greeted by the Floor Greeter (ochre uniform) and escorted to the appropriate receptionist.
52. Present the receptionist with your Building Pass or Temporary Building Pass and take a seat in the Reception Area.
53. Should you need to use the lavatory while waiting in the reception area, notify the receptionist, who will arrange for a Lavatory Escort (orange uniform) to escort you to the lavatory.
54. Should you leave the reception area to use the lavatory, request a "This Seat Taken" sign from the receptionist.
55. Place the sign on the seat in which you were sitting.
56. Employees must wash hands after using the lavatory.
57. In the interest of the global environment, please use no more than a single paper towel to dry your hands.
58. Please dispose of the towel in the recycling bin.
59. The Lavatory Attendant will await the completion of your lavatory visit and escort you back to the Reception Area.
60. Return to your original seat and return the "This Seat Taken Sign" to the receptionist.
61. When you are called by the receptionist, follow his or her instructions carefully. You will be escorted to the appropriate office by an Upper Floor Escort (periwinkle blue uniform).
62. Have a nice day.

2004

30

Urban Warfare: A Tour of the Battlefield

Pregnancy

Heading uptown for a panel discussion about architecture and politics, I found myself in the back of the taxi, unprepared. Looking at the passing scene, I noticed what seemed an unusually large number of pregnant women, something I had recently observed in my building as well. America was deep into Iraq and the rash of pregnancies was only natural: sending young people to the slaughter demanded that the species replenish.

Were pregnancies on the rise in Baghdad, too?

Will G.I.'s marry Iraqis?

What were the implications for urbanism?

New Yorkers focus on the home front: more people chasing fewer rooms can only have an upward impact on prices, especially now, when money is cheap. A baby boomlet would add growth pressure on schools, on recreational space, on neighborhood character and continuity. How will the relation between existing paradigms and actual uses currently being negotiated play itself out in this new growth? Will there be an adjustment in the misfit output of family homes in the suburbs for what had appeared a bygone demographic? Will we have to move to Brooklyn to make way?

Blackout

In the largest such failure in American history, a portion of the electrical grid—serving 50 million people—collapsed in summer 2003, leaving New York City in the dark for twenty-four hours. On television, gloating Iraqis in Baghdad cafés cheered that they'd gotten a little of their own back. Ours was just a mild version of the power outages endemic in Iraq since our occupation, but we briefly felt their pain.

I tend to the paranoid view. There had been a local harbinger of the blackout, clearly ominous. The day before the lights went out, a tremendous explosion blew manhole covers sky-high along several blocks of Hudson Street and produced an acrid smell that was unmistakably reminiscent of the odor of September 11. Firemen had been fighting a mysterious under-ground fire since the previous day, and it seemed to be centered on a local building that is fat with communications lines, a purported high-value target, the only building in our immediate vicinity that retains its post-9/11 concrete barriers. The same building has been the object of longstanding neighborhood complaints about the constant noise of its private generators and fear of the catastrophic explosion of the large quantities of fuel-oil—which the building owner currently seeks to increase!—that are stored within, a disaster waiting to happen.

When we heard the blast we all had the same thought, and rushed to the window. Sirens were already wailing in the distance, but it was other-wise dead quiet: police and firemen had blocked off the street. The swarm of emergency vehicles from both city agencies and Con Ed—the electri-cal utility—gathered quickly and were around for days. The too-familiar stillness after disaster settled over the neighborhood and small groups of people gathered on corners and at barricades to share information and establish momentary bonds.

The blackout the following day fueled even greater crisis conviviality. Since 9/11 we have a new paradigm for responding to breakdowns in the urban infrastructure, and we deployed it with fine results during the power outage. Pedestrians took over the streets and sidewalks, walking home and enjoying continuous linear socializing. Outside every bar and bodega a crowd gathered—it was almost cocktail time when the power went out, but the mood was upbeat. The timing couldn't have been better, and the blackout became the Disney version of the blitz. The city was "paralyzed" but we enjoyed the opportunity to display our civil solidarity, and to use the disaster to temporarily expand the territory of public space, "appropri-ating" the street like a closing for a street fair.

For many, this dramatic expansion of public space is the most indelible memory of 9/11. That attack produced the most powerful set of collec-tive emotions the city has ever known and caused, among other things, the imposition of a series of planning and traffic measures that many have dreamt of but which "realistically" never had a prayer. Suddenly, there were *severe* restrictions on motor vehicles, mandatory car-pooling, streets for pedestrians, a dramatic increase in water-born transport. The disaster opened a window for the reorganization of fundamental infrastructures, now largely re-shut.

Civil disaster—particularly the relatively benign, like a snowfall or blackout—is inconvenient rather than horrible, and has become a new form of civic event, one that binds the celebratory sense of New Year's Eve in Times Square with a dose of moral satisfaction. It is both a measure of our resilience as citizens and of our frustrated longing for concrete forms of the civility of the face to face. In some ways, these events parallel the rise of "reality" programming in the media, a way of authenticating our enjoyment by the inscription of a standard of cause and by a set of authentic emotional responses to events.

Reality is the postmodern sublime, a credible extremity in a culture of fakery. Just as the terror bombing of World War II was intended—according to the theories of Bomber Harris and Curtis LeMay—to break civilian morale but accomplished the opposite, the actuality of disaster has, to date, been likewise galvanizing. The question, of course, is one of limits. Disaster is obviously an inappropriate medium of urban design, but it certainly does function as a prompt. With victims rhetorically transmuted into heroes, we feel a dangerous frisson of moral satisfaction simply walking home when the lights go out. Good citizens.

Ramallah

During the spring of 2003—at the time of the Aqaba summit—I lectured at Bir Zeit University in Ramallah. Getting there was largely a matter of traffic, which included congestion amplified by checkpoints and the need to switch taxis at each barrier. Door to door from my hotel in Jerusalem via three taxis was under an hour. Without the occupation apparatus, the trip might have been thirty or forty minutes less.

After breezing through the first checkpoint on the way out, we changed taxis, and made our way through crawling traffic to a second barricade on the far side of town. This was very different from the first. Accustomed to the idea of being "controlled" by passing a needle-eyed security review, I was surprised to find a passage with virtually no soldiers in sight. Instead of inspection, this was controlled by inconvenience. Big concrete blocks placed in the roadway forced us to get out of our taxi and walk down and up a hot and dusty hillside—a kilometer—before passing through another concrete-block barricade to the knot of waiting taxis.

The discipline was effective, forcing people to carry their goods out in the open over a restricting distance. For the elderly, the sick—or anyone with luggage—this forced walk was more than simply inconvenient, and it had the double effect of humiliation and control. Because the gap was near the main entrance to the university, it was (as it was surely designed to be) especially annoying to students. There was a spontaneous commerce of wheelbarrow porters who carry purchases—and sometimes people—across the gap: a microscopic, adaptive transportation system.

The return trip was considerably different. While I was lecturing, an Israeli security alert had apparently taken place, based, it seemed, on information that an attack was forthcoming somewhere. Word spread quickly and the customary cell phone cacophony took on an added urgency. One message reported that merchants were shutting their gates in anticipation of a curfew, another that the Kalandia roadblock had been closed, another that Israeli troops were entering the city in force.

Moving quickly, we managed to work our way into the city center of Ramallah—where there were no obvious signs of crisis—and, thinking that it had been a false alarm, had tea at the house of a friend. We were in the midst of an automobile tour of new architectural projects when the cells began ringing again. Urged by various informants to skedaddle back across the border, we found a taxi and set off. Almost immediately, we came upon a group of Palestinians burning tires and throwing stones at an Israeli patrol. Our driver made a hasty u-turn, got on his phone—which remained fixed to his ear—and began racing through back streets to circumnavigate the trouble spot, a routine with which he was obviously very familiar.

And so we arrived at the main checkpoint at Kalandia again. Here was something more familiar. An endless line of cars and trucks was queued for inspection. Motors were switched off and drivers milled around, inured to waiting for hours. The situation for pedestrians was similar, if more compact. A huge crowd jostled to squeeze into single file for examination by Israeli troops. As at Bir Zeit, commercial activity had sprung up, but here it was contoured not to alternative movement strategies but to the exigencies of stasis. Cold drinks, ice-cream, and other merchandise were being hawked, as were cell-phone calls for those who didn't have a handset with them, and a brisk business was being done in explanations for being late.

We joined the crowd and pressed our way forward. The sun was blazing and the numbers of people were far greater than the metal-roofed waiting shed could accommodate, and so we spilled out around it. Apparently, we were either too restive, too pushy, or too disorderly, and a young soldier—who was standing on the other side of a barbed-wire barrier, perhaps two feet away from me—fired her gun. The flash and the huge noise momentarily confused me and, as the crowd ran, my first thought was "bomb." This was my neophyte inexperience, but harrowing nonetheless. Suddenly, what had been an almost out-of-body experience of looking on became much more intimate.

Brandishing my American passport I squeezed my way to the head of the line, filed through the narrow barrier and was confronted by a soldier in battle gear who asked sarcastically if I couldn't find a better place for a holiday and accused me of not having a proper stamp in my passport. Petty, needless harassment (accompanied by sharp and instantaneous violence), multiplied by tens of thousands every day, colors life in Palestine, shapes the character of its public spaces, and creates a beleaguered wartime sociability of suffering that I recognized.

And so it went for five hours. At the next checkpoint, another style. By now we were in a big collective taxi and the soldiers took our papers and walked slowly back to their jeep, parked 200 feet away. After a long wait, our names were slowly called out, and one by one we had to clamber over each other to get out of the taxi and walk to the jeep to be handed back our identification. One boy was not so lucky, and was led off by the soldiers under some unexplained suspicion.

The next checkpoint was on a trunk road into Jerusalem which intersected a smaller road, part of the parallel system built for quick access to and from the settlements. Seeing that the settler traffic was speeding through while we were backed up and immobilized, the cabbie veered into a little lane, a detour that brought us onto the free-flowing roadway. Here we were lucky and—to the great satisfaction of the passengers—made it through with a wave, although five minutes later we found ourselves in another line of cars and had to wait another hour to get by.

It is possible that the only answer to persistent "terror" is a police state. The two form a perfect symbiosis, and it is easy to understand the utility of regular attacks to the authors of the US government's "Patriot" Act, the breeders of sniffer dogs, and the private security firms that have become such a growth industry. To produce both legibility and intimidation, the whole panoptic repertoire of spatial and social control is deployed with little objection. And the powers that be keep ratcheting up the stakes. The database that Israeli (and Palestinian) security relies on is linked to John Poindexter's data mine, and produces the lists controlling who should get through "security," who should be turned back, and who should be given a hard time.

As irony would have it, the Palestinian friend who guided me through that day has recently moved temporarily to Orange County, California, and has found some of the similarities to home spooky. In the numerous gated communities that surround him, he felt something familiar from the urban language of the Israeli occupation: walled settlements. But the American security fences are transcendently commodified. These are bulwarks against danger in general, against fear itself, barricades in the absence of any actual threat. These communities are secured instead against a spectral other, pure paranoia, blossoming precisely because the threat is unknown (although people of color figure in many a fantasy).

If an effect of the Cold War—created by the perpetually invisible threat of instant annihilation—was to motivate more dispersed forms of settlement, like the suburbs in America or massive de-urbanization in China, the prospect of a perpetual state of "preventive" warfare risks extending the logic beyond a carpet of low-density enclaves to their continued fortification. The world will be divided between fortified settlements for the materially and psychically privileged and a global refugee camp in which the world's misery will simply be banked in a huge reserve army of poor-space. Palestine and Orange County (which already boasts high-priced toll bypass roads for the rich) will converge.

The Inner Checkpoint

We know that the best policeman is the one we carry inside us. Watching my Palestinian friend forbear through what was, for him, a daily experience of harassment and humiliation, I realized something about the psychic cost of this repression. If only in complicity at our own inconvenience, we are all implicated in the anti-terror network, surrendering to its demands every time we offer up credit cards or identification, every time we pass through the magnetometer in the office building lobby, every time we see a suspicious cop pulling over a truck about to cross a bridge or enter a tunnel.

In America, we have well-developed profiling skills, habits of identification and prejudice. Al-Qaeda has only increased the ambit of our gaze. Now the most likely suspect is no longer simply the African-American male, but something more alien, more vague. Post-9/11, I profiled compulsively. On the subway not long ago I was sitting opposite an elderly Muslim man (bearded and traditionally dressed) who was carrying several large parcels. The well-drilled formula *Muslim plus package equals bomb* flitted through my mind even as I judged it ridiculous. How much time every day wasted with these thoughts?

The city maps fear. Added to the repertoire of dark streets, fast traffic, rapacious ghetto dwellers, and crowd-loving pickpockets is now anxiety at beards and turbans, close reading of hack licenses from the back seats of taxis, a weird chill when reaching for the baba ghannouj at the deli. The evildoers are everywhere locked in their invisible cells, ready to explode. Preemption proceeds.

Wozniak

Stephen Wozniak, Steve Jobs's old partner from Apple Computer, has a new company. After working for eighteen months below the radar, Wheels of Zeus has presented its first product: WozNet. The technology enables the creation of a low-cost wireless network that—using radio signals and global-positioning satellite data—allows very large numbers of "people, pets, or property" to be tracked from a single base station. According to a story in the *New York Times*, "the tags—expected to cost less than $25 to produce—will be able to generate alerts, notifying the owner by phone or email message when a child arrives at school, a dog leaves the yard, or a car leaves the parking lot."

Although Wozniak suggests that the networks may have unspecified other uses, the roll-out is being accompanied by a rhetoric insisting that WozNet is strictly voluntary, that encryption technologies will keep unauthorized users from piggy-backing on such ready-made domestic surveillance data. The situation is ripe for the creation of such networks of "elective" control. Persuaded that these technologies can be disciplined to confine themselves to keeping track of Fido, we invite them in.

For the city, the WozNet adds further impetus to reorganization based on non-geometrical styles or order. With the world now reproduced as an infinitely locatable collection of points, Cartesian strategies of mapping and place-based definitions of property are freed to float without losing any operational precision or utility. Indeed, security will make place itself less relevant, make the tasks of both hiding and seeking less and less physical. The button in our ear will tell us whether to turn left or right, speeding us on our way, even as we are assaulted by a variety of immaterial networks that can place us without reference to the physical qualities of the environment.

Like the satellite navigation systems installed in rental cars and SUVs, the WozNet reflects an in many ways necessary adjunct to the pattern of sprawl. The exponentially growing expanse of the interstitial city—unresponsive to landscape, ecology, or physical clarity—can increasingly only be navigated with the aid of continuous updates and electronic maps. New technology offers the sanction of convenience and a deterrent to old styles of "freedom of the city." In the grid of infinite sameness, content must be constantly added to this stem-space to give it meaning.

The unremitting psy-ops of the advertising industry constitutes a form of warfare on the consciousness of citizens everywhere, political speech unregulated by the niceties of response and equal time. New York is more and more covered by building-scaled advertising scrims, gigantic billboards harkening the inevitability—the necessity—of consumption. The ten-story high image of Kate Moss in her Calvins is also a form of camouflage. Like more traditional strategies of disguising, the city becomes increasingly illegible in terms of its specifics of scale and location. Revisualized as a compendium of applied images, the city is re-measured in pixels or Ben-Day dots, evacuated of the particulars of place, rushing toward the condition of a pure field of top-down communication and surveillance. We eliminate our enemies by making them indistinguishable from us and, thereby, bring the entire world under suspicion.

Ground Zero

The little debate over whether or not the American government should display the bloody images of Uday and Qusay Hussein provided an interesting measurement of the relation between warfare and its representation. During Gulf War II, there had been howls of protest when Al Jazeera broadcast images of the corpses of American soldiers killed in battle. This, the media alleged, bore witness to the barbarism of the enemy. The networks seized the opportunity to replay over and over those awful pictures of dead GIs being dragged through the streets of Mogadishu.

During World War II, it was not until 1943 that the censors allowed images of dead Americans to be displayed in the press. Still, it is very hard to combat terror without a renewable supply of images of the consequences—periodical fear of the unknown has to be topped up with palpability. At the urban scale, this anxiety reproduces itself in arguments about commemoration and the city's relationship to its war wounds. Dresden attempts to reconstruct its obliterated monuments. Rotterdam renews itself with a vigorously new precinct. Paris and Budapest retain the pockmarks of bullets in historic walls. Oklahoma City clears the site and constructs a poetic memorial. The Pentagon is carefully repaired and a monument is commissioned for the lawn out front.

New York struggles with a meaningful commemoration at Ground Zero. Almost entirely co-opted by financial power, rebuilding proceeds with commercial space, as the driver and the scheme now likely to be built will reproduce the sum of activities previously on the site, add more, and devote a modest residue to formalized commemoration. A remnant of the Trade Center complex—the still useful slurry wall—will perhaps be retained as an evocatively literal presence. Throughout the argument over reconstruction, however, the focus has been too tenaciously on the site itself, on the insistence that the effects of the attack were limited, that there was no collateral damage to the city as a whole.

That damage is legible not simply in the misery of survivors but in joblessness, in relocations out of the city, in the travails of the Chinatown economy. But is it equally visible in the recoding of the landscape in the language of the bomber? As high-value targets are hardened with Jersey barriers, security cameras, armed guards, identification checks, metal detectors, and other elements of the anti-terror state, the city is remapped in terms of its potential for disaster, its strategic locations revealed as a series of target sets.

This mapping of the new landscape of fear has its effects, barely studied. For my part, I have come to identify several buildings as particularly sinister. One of these is a very large Federal Building that houses, among other agencies, the Passport Bureau, its own documents made ambivalent by the terror. For Americans abroad, the passport itself can function as a target-marker. Equipped with a barcode scanned at the ticket counter and immigration booth, it enables our own authorities to keep track of any movements offshore. For foreign passport holders, their very foreignness restricts opportunities to visit the United States and renders their bearers suspect.

I give this building a wide berth. Having identified this place as my particular target, I also invent the surrounding blocks as dangerous, and am forced into inconvenient circumnavigations and alternate routes. On days when my own reservoir of fear is high, I look at every parked car and truck near this building as a potential bomb. I have been certain more than once that some nondescript van is packed with explosives and moments from detonation. Self-conscious, I hasten away at an urgent pace, but short of an incriminating run. The anti-terror regime forces all of us to alter our repertoire of urban dangers and make many small adjustments to the way we use the city and its streets.

Recently, I heard a colleague describe design work he had been doing in Washington, DC, to help secure that target against terrorists. Asked to provide an array of physical barriers in front of strategic buildings, he adopted a strategy that he disingenuously described as "deputizing." Quotidian objects—benches, bollards, trees, kiosks, and so on—were redesigned to withstand the rushing vehicle and explosive detonation of the suicide bomber. The point, though, was to do it without the appearance of menace: ha-has for the age of terror. By providing security without alteration to their benign and familiar guise, these devices permit an unaltered view of the world to abide on the surface, the elaborate stage machinery of deterrence artfully hidden from view. Everything's fine.

Baghdad on the Hudson

When Walter Winchell originated the phrase, he had another kind of sin in mind than those we've gone to war to punish. Still, there's something apposite in the comparison. Like the Iraqis, we are tyrannized by an unremitting culture of coercive images of the desirable, by relentless panic-mongering, by shrinking civil liberties under the guise of self-protection, and we likewise adopt the Saddamite cultures of bellicosity and fear, not to mention his triumphalist style of architectural self-celebration.

It is now unexceptional to find gun-toting troops in battle-dress on New York streets, at transportation termini, and around other "strategic" locations. If there is a marker of the failure of the good city, it is soldiers in the street, and it is a failure we New Yorkers are now obliged to share with both pre- and postwar Baghdad. Here, the troops join the other population that has come to signify the failure of our polity, the homeless. My evidence is purely anecdotal, but the numbers of people living in the street in New York seems again to be growing. It oversimplifies to ascribe this to the war in Iraq, but the reduction of taxes on the privileged, the growing spasm of war-related expenditures, and a general obliviousness to the human consequences of policies driven by meanness, greed, and ignorance do have predictable effects.

Like Saddam, we celebrate our self-inflation with the stupidities of opulence. It continues to amaze me that what will stand as a memorial to 9/11 will be the world's tallest office building: disaster triumphalized. In building this way, we ape the luxuries of Saddam's collection of palaces and the hypertrophic crossed swords with which he celebrated his "victory" over Iran. But we run the risk, like Saddam, of creating shrines to the uninhabitable, opulence that cannot be consumed. Just as the despot was unable—for fear of bombing or assassination—to actually stay in these palaces (or anywhere else for more than ten hours), so many will balk at being the sitting ducks of the unsustainable, in-your-face hubris of our own architectural celebrations of death.

Invisible Threats

The discovery of "white powder" in some public place has become a regular event in the life of New York. Recently, my part of town was paralyzed by an envelope of what turned out to be talcum powder on the subway. The line was shut down for several hours in the middle of the work day, and the event attracted a gaggle of TV news vans to Canal Street, where the discovery had been made. What would have been a meaningless incident in the pre-Anthrax days was now the medium of panic and, inevitably—because of the dramatically inconvenient response—a "newsworthy" event.

Such is the style of contemporary paranoia. The flipside of crisis sociability must be the ongoing presence of some legible threat. The administration, aware that its policies cannot be sustained in the absence of fear, resorts to portentous warnings and color-coded threat assessment. Although these are much derided for the meaninglessness of their distinctions, even as objects of ridicule they do ensure that everyday discourse is infiltrated by the subject-matter of fear, if not by anything to actually be afraid of. This too becomes part of the discussion, as the fact that we have not again been attacked undercuts the urgency of the build-up and the ancillary assault on civil liberties.

Although I would not advance such a cynical view of wag-the-dog causality, it is certain that there are urgent and ongoing conversations in the corridors of power about acceptable levels of American casualties. Accustomed to a threshold that is impossibly small—per the deathless intervention in Bosnia—the now daily list of Americans killed in Iraq challenges public support of warfare with an intensity no longer low. We respond with a policy of suburbanized occupation, withdrawing troops from unquiet cities into garrisons on the peripheries, abandoning the streets to local strongmen and hastily trained Iraqi police.

The initial invasion of Iraq was designed to avoid the risks of urban warfare. Racing around cities to seek a classic engagement with an army in the field, we had no real idea what would happen when we took over the country's towns, which have now become the primary sites of resistance to the incivility of occupation. Transformed overnight from liberators to policemen, the American army becomes that vanguard of the monstrous apparatus (wielded with panache by Saddam for so many years) that turns every citizen in society into a potential other, a conceptual doubling of every person on the planet into both one with a genuine identity and a potential identity that must be repeatedly disproved.

The Airport

Over a billion people a year pass through the air transport system, and here we find the *locus classicus* of the globalized checkpoint. An emergency rule of law is in place: all who pass through it are presumed guilty and obliged to prove they are not. And so we sweat through screeners' questions, offer up our luggage for scanning and inspection, have our identities tracked against burgeoning databases of suspicious persons, surrender our anonymity at every stage of the journey. Yes, yes, for our own safety, but the awful calculus now playing out is one that weighs safety against freedom and imprisons us behind higher and higher walls.

I slip off my shoes and place them along with my laptop, keys, loose change, and eyeglasses in the plastic bin and send it all through the x-ray. I then pass through the magnetometer, trying to look harmless, hoping to avoid any additional hassle. I watch sheepish and improbable travelers—kids, the elderly, mid-western business types—being patted down or scanned by detection wands. These unlikely candidates are inconvenienced by random checks, marker of America's sense of fair play, our ostensible refusal to profile. Every time we detain some granny, we force her—and those watching—to question the system of control and, parenthetically, to invent the other for whose rights these "good" citizens are obliged to suffer. And we hate him all the more.

The airport is the primary training ground, the vanguard of the organization of the city as a space of heavily surveilled, highly managed flows. The airport is modernity incarnate. It models the city as a pure space of circulation and commerce, mapping the circuit of capital directly onto the circuit of bodies. As a classification engine, airport design is a distilled version of the segregated efficiencies of transportation planning in general, in which the grail is the separation of means and, thereby, of people and privileges. That this is managed within a space of great crowding makes airports the premier research sites (along with places like Disneyland) for the burgeoning technologies of surveillance, data processing, perpetual motion, information management, and other top-down styles of security.

The City after Clausewitz

If there has been a change is the epistemology of warfare post–Cold War, it is in the shift to plausible, long-term styles of "engagement" (destruction). The "theory" of deterrence was not simply based on the threat of extinction, but on mutuality. Binding us together by rational fear of an irrational prospect, the threat of nuclear warfare is a great equalizer, but only in circumstances in which the opponent is presumed not to be suicidal. Despite the efforts of a variety of policy crazies to find appropriate circumstances for promoting "limited" atomic warfare, some remnant of rationality kept us free of this horrific prospect. But the era of the suicide bomber is upon us.

The Cold War (which lasted through eight US presidencies and over fifty years) inured the body politic to the idea of perpetual conflict and to a titanic flow of funds in the direction of the military-industrial complex. The new "war on terror" will not simply engorge the familiar players in this sector—the Boeings and the Grummans—but will support the proliferation of an even larger complex of profit. From the architects who have become specialists in everyday fortification, to the planners for whom security will become job-one, to the Wozniak-style surveillance queens masking their efforts behind the fiction of "convenience," to the camp-following Halliburtons and Bechtels who will arrive to pick up the pieces after further acts of smart-bomb urban renewal, to the huge cadre of private security services with their armies for hire, we are moving toward a national security city, with its architecture of manufactured fear.

The basic premise of Clausewitzian strategic theory—that war was not an aberration but an activity conducted by states in pursuit of rational aims—is now obsolete. As the importance of nations and their armed forces continue in parallel decline, the political, economic, and military role of cities is likely to increase. Filled with a plethora of actors—drug entrepreneurs, jihadists, local liberation fronts, animal rights activists, abortion abolitionists, and the rest—the future will be increasingly one of small, sharp conflicts in defense of positions that have only a marginal relationship to territories and boundaries. Whether the congeniality and citizenship that represent the legacy of our best urbanism can prevail against this remains to be seen.

2004

31

Sex, Drugs, Rock and Roll, Cars, Dolphins, and Architecture

Of the true faiths that multiplied in the sixties, the most subsuming was trinitarian. As a basis for cultural production, sex, drugs, and rock and roll was surely a more stimulating formula than the anhedonic strictures youth was struggling so hard to overturn. The times, after all, were not purely about rupture but also about rapture, about submitting the cultural and physical landscape to the revaluing of altered vision.

That vision was diverse. The rainbow world of acid and magic mushrooms, the liberated coupling, the gentleness and universal collegiality, the disdain for materialist striving, the ubiquitous soundtrack, the *Aquarian* strain—all contributed both to the project of invention and to the larger epistemology of seeing. Among the watershed events in this history, the shock that greeted Bob Dylan's switch to electric guitar in 1965, yanking folk music into the age of rock and roll, symbolized the paradigms at play. The move beyond Joan Baez, Woody Guthrie, and Leadbelly was not just acoustic but deeply political, combining electric tech with new styles of joy, eschewing suffering for abandon, and begging the old Bretchtian question of a mass authentic.

When Dylan took the stage that fateful night at the Newport Folk Festival, architecture was also at a moment of tremendous perplexity. The reductively styled mass architecture of modernism was in disrepute not simply for its boring formal endgame but, more important, for the ravages wrought in the name of its Cartesian lusts, the purifying orders of urban renewal and the pat, thoughtless, verities of the suburban consumption machine. Architecture's rebellious youth declined to sign on to the project and began to search for alternatives in the cultural grab bag of the sixties. Some chose the resistance of advocacy planning and community defense, carrying on the identification with the oppressed that was also the legacy of folk and the blues. Some repaired to the dour climes of historicism. Many took to the woods, back to nature, to study communitarianism and to live a life of virtuous simplicity. Others wondered about the architectural equivalent of rock and roll. From this matrix, Ant Farm emerged in our *annus mirabilis*, 1968.

It wasn't just the music that was inspirational; the rock *group* also emerged as a model of practice for Ant Farm and others, reflected both in the organizational routines (sleep late, drop acid, brainstorm, and riff), the spirit, the road trips, and the nomenclature: calling their collaboration "Ant Farm" is to immediately signal that the work is to be of a different order to that produced under the gray-flannel imprimatur of Skidmore, Owings, and Merrill (whose nerdy button-downomie Ant Farm so brilliantly parodied in the deeply deadpan *Chevrolet Training Film* [1978–81], done with Phil Garner). To stretch the analogy, the Ant Farm sensibility— synthesized in post–Summer of Love San Francisco—was a combination of the Beach Boys and the Grateful Dead. From the Dead came the trippy spontaneity and zapped transcendence; from the Beach Boys, the genuine fondness for pop culture—car culture in particular—and an incredibly smooth technique.

If Ant Farm was the Beach Boys (albeit a Beach Boys in which everyone was Brian), Archigram, in England, was the Beatles, and, I suppose, Frank Lloyd Wright was Elvis, a synthesizing genius, protean, multiply perioded, the King (and the Dad). The role of the Stones was shared by a variety of Europeans, especially the group of Austrians including Haus-Rucker-Co. and Coop Himmelblau, with their scintillating but ultimately sour aestheticizations of rage. Ant Farm was simply too cool to allow a traditional formalism to emerge from this opposition. The group well understood that the object was nothing without its performative aura, and their high-theatric events—*Media Burn* (1975) and *The Eternal Frame* (1975)—were characteristic of their edgy hilarity and deliriously twisted appropriations.

Indeed, the brilliance of Ant Farm's irony was ever the guarantor of their integrity. They were—and are—among the preeminent comedians of architectural culture—not Serlio parsing of the mood of the city, but Lenny Bruce or Rodney Dangerfield: "Take my architecture . . . please." Genius practitioners of the carnivalesque, the Rabelaisian world that Bakhtin so persuasively associates with insubordination and the rejection of cultural constraint, Ant Farm engaged the most powerful aspect of the joke: the possibility of splicing things that in conventional atmospheres would be considered impossible to join.

In the expanded field of their enthusiasms, the homage paid to both Harley Earl—the avatar of baroque automobile stylings—and Bucky Fuller, the Dymaxion man (and subject of a bizarre and hilarious "kidnapping" by the Ants), the group sought to unite apparent disparity through the genuine generosity of affection. Countercultural *bricoleurs*, they created a graphic and architectural style that joined the streamlined fantasy of Norman Bel Geddes with the funky delineation, sexual obsession, and dark worries of R. Crumb. Theirs was an architecture of the era in which comic books aspired to the weight of Dostoyevsky.

Bifurcation is the manufacture of surreality, and Ant Farm must be honored for being ever true to the surreal. Theirs, though, was a post-surrealist surreality: they revered the technique but not the anxiety. The French surrealists fetishized the unconscious and sought authority in the weird commonplace of dreams. But there was always something effete about them: on the one hand, the purest strain of narcissism, and, on the other, a snootcocking at the artistic establishment. The surrealists were self-identified, above all, with the world of art, and their media were those of those whom they sought to overthrow. Ant Farm was never snobbish, recognizing that dreams were chemical, and that fun was the ultimate affront to the authorities, who preferred youth to be quiescently shipped to Vietnam.

The post-modernist architecture that emerged during Ant Farm's fateful decade represented—inter alia—a kind of post-televisual surreal. Watching television, the most powerful everyday experience of surreality ever devised, was formative of the cultural outlook of anyone growing up in America in the fifties and sixties. With its endlessly strange sequence of splicings of commercials and programs and channel switchings, television was and is the ultimate "exquisite corpse," a juxtaposition engine that produces a completely weird artifact at any given watching. Postmodern architecture, in all its branches, was predicated on the idea of a post-universal style, the idea that style could be freely borrowed, and that creativity lay in a recombinant operation—the production of sequential freaks.

Unfortunately, most of the postmodernist heroes lacked the courage (or the brains) to truly pursue the insight, their own bad taste masquerading as populism or theory—unable to truly participate in culture's seismic shifts as they stood on the sidelines with their Nikons. Thus, the contributions of postmodern architects from Robert Venturi to Philip Johnson to Rem Koolhaas have been less in their modest formal inventions than in their "ironic" denunciations of the larger field of culture to justify their own conceptual embrace of the worst excrescences of corporatism—branding and image control, a resort to the authority of historical forms and practices, cynical elitism, and sell-out.

Ant Farm would have none of this, and besieged the dopiness of the profession with their lusty nonconformity. One must remember that "freak" carried a positive valence in those days. Freaks opposed the regimentation of the suburban orders of consumption and celebrated the possibility of self-invented singularity. Their defense of the creativity of difference continues to be a bracing model of architecture and its politics. In today's climate—in which the social irrelevance of architects is exacerbated by a retreat into formalism, arcane theorizing, and supine co-optation—the idea of a practice motivated simultaneously by private enthusiasm and public critique is tonic.

It would be a mistake, however, to think of Ant Farm as simply canny gonzos. They were genuine researchers, and their contribution not only anticipated the strategic polemics of the current "Dutch School," with its weighty, resistibly stylish tomes, but set the agenda for contemporary research in environmentalism, advanced building technologies, electronic globalization, public art and space, and post-industrial flows. That this research flourished outside conventional academic sanction was also the realization of a desire to see knowledge loosed from privilege. The ultimate avatar of this style of inquiry was surely our great flower-power Diderot, Stewart Brand, whose *Whole Earth Catalogue* literally and figuratively encapsulated the potentially liberatory capacity of *things*, wresting them from the authoritarian style of the market and the hyperconsumption of the suburbs. The Ant's lovely *AUTOMERICA* (1976) was a clear precipitate of this inventory of the good stuff.

That subject-matter was no coincidence. The Ants' project grew from a foundational enthusiasm: cars, our national icon. The reasons are over-determined. To begin, the Ants were all boys whose susceptible youth was spent in the 1950s, the high-water mark of the American car. Those were the days of exponential growth, of a dizzy potlatch of styling, weight, fuel consumption, pollution, lethality. It was the era in which the car became the instrument and the emblem of the American project for the reorganization of planetary space, the endlessness of freeways and suburbanism, the Ozzie and Harriet world of consumer docility and the strange constrained pleasures of the brand—how *did* they persuade millions to eat Chef Boyardee ravioli from a can? The fifties were that time when "What's good for General Motors is good for the country" became our national mantra.

But there's necessarily ambiguity in this automotive cathexis. The car both symbolized and enabled a pure cultural and physical mobility that lay at the core of the cultural desires of sixties youth. It was an agent of expression, the emblem of class, rebellion, creativity, and freedom. The counter-culture sought access to the diversity of cultural experience—whether in the romance of African-American culture, the Thoreauvian idyll of nature, or the spirituality of all those pilgrimages to the East—and was confident of the possibility that an authentic experience of the other was simply a matter of hanging out.

For the first generation in which wanderlust had truly continental—and intercontinental—dimensions, the car became the means of access to an unfolding space. The ultimate countercultural vehicles were the Volkswagen vans and converted school buses (e.g. the psychedelic transport of Ken Kesey and the Merry Pranksters), self-effacing but communal vehicles designed to enable the gathering of the tribe, but also, critically, genuinely mobile homes for the realization of the wildest dreams of hippie nomadology. Prototypes of a universal architecture, a gestating idea that had vexed modernity from the get-go, alternative automobilization outdid the hemmed-in thinking of conventional modernity by freeing itself from the constraint of site. Ant Farm's inflatables—portable, affordable, cut loose from the walls of the academy—were the extension of the car by other means.

Parallel to the investigation of "free" celestial-terrestrial space, Ant Farm worked to imagine and articulate the relationship of such a liberated style of physical space with the mesh of media that were simultaneously respatializing the planet. Moving beyond machine-in-the-garden basics, Ant Farm invested in a Hefneresque vision of private multimedia environments, such as their 1971 Newman Media Studio, and in media "software"—the videos, performances, and cautionary fables that served as both investigation and critique of a burgeoning phenomenon.

The sense of the complex relationship of these social and spatial networks gives the work of Ant Farm unusual prescience and links their efforts across a variety of media. TVTV (Top Value Television) was typical in that its core of electronic communication was supported by the groovy roaming van, the instrument for projecting the Ants into the space of observation and encounter, the territory for their own mediations. The insistence on the centrality of the physical design of the roaming home was advanced still more elaborately in the Dolphin Embassy project (1974–78). Whatever one thinks about the importance of interspecies communication, the Dolphin Embassy was both a completely realizable scheme and a recapitulation of the ideology of the movable feast, here at the service of an encounter with the most priapic of beasts.

Stylishness was always central as both a strategy and a conundrum. For Ant Farm, customization was the vehicle for insinuating radical difference into the market, the locus at which folklore and mass culture merged, and an analogue for an architecture-to-be. Their image bank is loaded with loving variations on the conventional automotive envelope, and they were certainly in the right place to study the subject: California was an incubator of the car as an artistic medium, the recontourings of standard product into private fantasy. Whole schools of customization flourished, ranging from the iconic low-riders of Mexican-American culture to the panoply of wacked hippie refurbishments, those shingled vans now composting in the woods outside Mendocino.

Ant Farm's eternal emblem is Cadillac Ranch (1974), that primal icon of gathering. Its Stonehenge quality precisely suggests the work of a cult willing to go to absurd lengths in worship of an object of totally strange character. The learned Darwinian assembly of the ascending ontology of the tailfin is at once a living catalog of a transcendent artifact and a sly riff on the utter meaningless of consumption-driven style. And the interring of the cars—the immobilization that turns them into architecture—suggests the inevitable doom of the entire project of the automobile.

Ant Farm's series of car concerts and the Media Burn Phantom Dream Car continued to expand the car's expressive, self-critical range. A Caddy customized into a hyperconcept car, the Phantom Dream Car was designed to enable a short-lived event symbolizing its own futility (being driven into a flaming wall of televisions) and to mock received futurist fantasies of speed and the glories of mass destruction. However, Ant Farm's most biting piece of auto critique, and their most brutally direct mating of form and place, was their reenactment of John F. Kennedy's assassination at Dealey Plaza in Dallas for *The Eternal Frame*. This dark, affectless event (would anyone presume to reenact the fatal crash of Dodi and Di?) was not simply a provocation addressed to the necrophiliac frenzy of the assassination industry and its endless flow of conspiracy theories, mawkish images, and premature hagiography; it was about the *car*, the Lincoln Continental and its fatal backseat, evoking Ed Kienholz's own legendarily fetid groping of this site. Sexualized in the fifties as the make-out room for millions, the backseat had been transformed into the cockpit for the politics of murder via the Zapruder film, the omega of low-budget American porn.

Which brings us to sex. Ant Farm, under the libidinous blanket of their gaze, made heroic contributions to the sexualization of architecture long before it was taken up by academics for its revealing ramifications of difference. This was the product of the amazing liberations of the sixties, but also a sign of the eruption of the post-Freudian, post-Norman O. Brown atmosphere that identified our daily relations as suffused with sex, whatever the nature of the acts. Ant Farm was thus squarely post-Kinsey (*Sexual Behavior in the Human Female* and *Sexual Behavior in the Human Male* were surely the *Whole Earth Catalog* of sexuality), in the sense that their professionalism dilated enthusiastically on the precise dimensions of sexual behavior. From Doug Michels's legendary coupling with a girlfriend under an American flag outside the Paris *Biennale* in *Make Love Not War* (1969), to the immortal House of the Century (1971–73), iconographically poised somewhere between oikema and schnozz, to the abiding fascination with dolphins, known for their cross-species appetites, to their high-testosterone-car-fetish-displaced male sexuality, theirs was an architecture that can be truly said to have gotten it on.

Architecture, invariably social, was not simply politically but also conceptually fraught during the Ant Farm era. However, that Ant Farm's work happily and continuously owned up to the rubric and practice of architecture is central to its heft. The Farmers' indelible contribution was not abandoning the centrality of the idea of building, despite the assaults on its meaning resulting from its dissipation in the "expanded field" of landscape, art, and consumption. Here is the root of the Ants' abiding optimism. Despite the irony in which much of their work is shrouded, the project was always one of both social and physical reconstruction and never ceased its flirtation with the practical. Such playing it relatively close to the bone is the key to the idea of an oppositional architecture. Given conventional architecture's locked embrace with the power that produces it, the contest must be fought in the formulation of alternatives with a chance of replacing the mire of the present.

Walking the fine line between the impossible and the practical was Ant Farm's stock-in-trade. Beginning with their first inflatable projects, Ant Farm rode the wave of political and cultural enthusiasms that sought a new architecture that could be realized outside the intentions of the Man. The idea of the inflatable, lightweight, and nearly immaterial joined notions of nomadology and ephemerality to create spaces that were freely inhabitable by routines outside the cellular orders of offices and families. Supported by air, they were at once gentle and evocative of the fragility of the threatened biosphere. The dome, recurrent in their work from the inflatables to Convention City (1972) and Freedomland (1973), was a crucial totem of the liberty of undifferentiated enclosures to support free styles of inhabitation. Hostile to hierarchies and phallomorphologies, the dome was a stab at the death of patriarchy. Finally, responsible propagandists, Ant Farm also authored the 1970 *Inflatocookbook* to share and promulgate both technology and vibe, the pneumatology of freedom. The point wasn't simply form, but access too.

Looking back at the amazingly fertile oeuvre of the Ants—produced in a ten-year sprint that would have left lesser artists burned out for life—one is overwhelmed by their vision and their generosity, their interventions in the range of practices and issues that set the contemporary agenda for architecture. Performance, video, public sculpture, architecture, and polemic were all wielded with huge skill and massive aplomb. The Ants' rapier sliced and reconfigured mass culture, the automobile, environmentalism, professionalism, the shifting fields of architectural and artistic practice, and did it with hilarity, discipline, brilliance, and beauty. And, shunning the geriatric antics of rock bands living on their endless reunion tour, they snuffed their candle when it was still burning bright. Long live the Ants!

2004

32

Displacement

In 1989, after a protracted struggle, the federal government removed Richard Serra's *Tilted Arc* from the plaza in front of the Jacob K. Javits Federal Building in lower Manhattan. The brief against the sculpture had been its alleged disruption of the public space in which it sat. Although I had no particular love for *Tilted Arc*, I argued at the time that the rage against it was in large measure a displacement of anger that should have been directed at the awful architecture that formed its backdrop—serenely ugly and, in its hugeness, minimalist to the point of idiocy.

Two similar displacements are being enacted in Manhattan today—one at the southwest corner of Central Park and the other all the way downtown. The first centers on Columbus Circle, where a heated controversy is ongoing over plans by the Museum of Arts and Design (MAD), formerly the American Craft Museum, to re-skin its new home in the former Huntington Hartford Gallery of Modern Art, designed with confectionery panache by Edward Durrell Stone in 1964. This odd building has become a cause célèbre for preservationists, who argue for its historic and formal consequence. I have always been very fond of this quirky, bright little folly, and strongly agree that it should be saved. Articulating the argument is problematic, though.

While I love the building, defending it on the narrow grounds of its aesthetic importance requires a grain of salt: this is not a "great" work in the sense that the Guggenheim is or Penn Station was. Defending this building requires a somewhat more expansive—if equally compelling—interpretation of the idea of preservation. It should be saved because many hold it in deep affection for whatever private reasons, because it is a very good building, and—perhaps especially—because it contributes so strongly to defining its site. The gleaming white marble punctuation visible down Broadway, the polka-dot frou-frou of its corner apertures, the legendary lollipop columns at its base, all vitalize Columbus Circle indelibly, *represent* the place in mind and memory.

This is a gray area in landmarking, one which must recognize that artistic and historic arguments engage only a limited range of meanings. Where, in this construct, do we fit singularity, familiarity, identity, difference? Landmarking is a form of consent, a compact about what is collectively valued in the city. In its focus on the physical and the artistic, landmarking always risks the neutron-bomb approach, preserving the object but insensitive to the cultural setting in which it acquires its meaning. A more expansive view of landmarking sees it like rent control, a subsidy (or a "taking," as lawyers would say) that enables neighborhoods to "preserve" their diversity. This approach, though, would require a different style of consensus, one that goes beyond form to embrace lived life.

The importance of 2 Columbus Circle exceeds the categories through which its future is being argued: we simply do not have a legal basis for saving nice old friends. As with *Tilted Arc*, however, the displacement at Columbus Circle comes in the poignant absurdity of the intensity of the debate when far larger battles have already been lost and when issues so crucial to the future of the place are on nobody's agenda. It becomes even more imperative to save this building because of the monstrosities that surround it and loom over it, including the just-completed Time Warner Center, which sets new lows in original design moves per unit volume.

The result of a developer competition in which the Metropolitan Transit Authority auctioned off the site to the highest bidder, the Time Warner Center is far too large, a problem dramatically exacerbated by the scalelessness of its smooth, unperforated, black skin. Looming over Central Park and holding down a crucial corner of its architectural envelope, the building is whimsically dark, in contrast to the generally pale color of the structures around the park. From a million angles it appears to be a rude lump on the cityscape, faceless after the manner of the corporation that rents it and the corporation that designed it.

The major experience of Columbus Circle for most people, however, is in the encounter with the subway station beneath it, busiest in the system and one of the most unspeakable, filthy and labyrinthine, totally degrading to travelers. And here is the main displacement: the complete failure to deal meaningfully with the most profound urban question on the site. Patting themselves on the back for the building's curved base, twin towers, and front door at the end of 59th Street, the project's boosters tout its civic presence and formulaic "urbanity." And a good time will doubtless be had by the media executives and hyper-rich who sport in its boardrooms, condos, and upmarket hotel and restaurants. Meanwhile, like the slaves in Fritz Lang's *Metropolis*, the masses will continue to sweat and toil below in a zone visited by no nicety whatsoever and with no meaningful influence on the architecture above. This is the income gap literalized in steel and glass. And this is the context in which the haste to destroy the last winning and familiar thing on the circle becomes especially ludicrous, as the place is sucked dry by the vacancy of the cultural forces behind it.

But the most grotesque displacement in town has been recently revealed in the results of the competition for a memorial at Ground Zero. This is surely the most managed displacement ever, a virtual Ponzi scheme, revealing—like Columbus Circle—a set of priorities that are realized precisely backwards. From the start, the LMDC has made craven use of architecture in a classic instance of what magicians call misdirection. We are distracted by the ridiculous travails of David Childs and Danny Libeskind trying to agree on the shape of the world's tallest office building in order to avoid the question of precisely why the world's tallest office building (as well as its shrimpier kith) must be built on this hallowed ground.

And now we are vilely distracted by the act of hallowing. The finalists in the memorial competition have been almost universally criticized for the generic character of their submissions and the abstracted quality of their iconography. Again, the heat is being taken for a problem that—at the gargantuan scale of real estate development—is simply glanced over. Look at what has been decided for them in advance: adjacent 1,776-foot-high office building, abstracted representation of Lady Liberty's arm, wedge of light, lines of access, site below grade (but not to bedrock!), glazed slurry wall, giant waterfall. The competitors have done nobly to struggle through this pious fog of representation and constraint with any form of integrity, knowing that whatever they proposed will have chamfered buildings flying over it and will sit in a hole at the foot of the humongous building that will—in its preening supersize and banal iconography—usurp memorial duties in the service of the egotistic ambitions of our governor, the leaseholder, the LMDC, and the architects.

I say, let us keep one of the memorials—how shameful the cries to set aside the competition process when we finally have an open one—and forget about the clutch of needless buildings that will engorge the coffers of Larry Silverstein, the Port Authority, and the architects. The astonishing eloquence of the void—which has the potential to become a matchless urban space—will never be equaled by slick styling and enormity. It is our last chance to save this place for everyone, to create a site for conversation and contemplation, a terrain for additional memorials and expressions from the diversity of voices—so movingly expressed in the aftermath of the tragedy, but now subsumed in the uniformity of form and intent that threatens to destroy this place once more.

2004

33

Crippled in the City

We cripples see the city a little differently. Where two months ago I bestrode New York like a colossus, roaming freely, scampering up stairs, jaywalking with the best of them, I now find the city reorganized as an obstacle course. The accident that precipitated this was the result of what turned out to be a needless trip uptown. It had been snowing and my wife cautioned me as I left home about slipping on the ice. This is a frequent wintertime comment of hers, signifying both familial concern and a critique of the fact that I feel that Top-Siders are appropriate year-round for flâneurs like me, assuming sufficient care and grace are displayed.

Her cautions also had more serious credit in that we had both suffered fractures from falls on the ice the previous two years, hers most recent. To cut to the chase, I slipped as I was heading down 145th Street to the A Train and badly broke my ankle. As I lay on the sidewalk, looking at my dangling foot and at the bone poking at the skin, trying not to pass out from the pain, I knew things were going to be different for a while.

Two passersby dragged me to an adjacent stoop and spoke comfortingly. Cell phones were whipped out up and down the block and 911 was quickly dialed. Within five minutes an ambulance had arrived and I was being loaded in. The first truth of the experience emerged: faced with the suffering and incapacity of a stranger, most citizens behave with kindness and appropriate dispatch, although there are still those who let doors slam in my face or who honk impatiently as I've struggled out of a cab.

Mobility is, of course, the primary issue for a disabled person negotiating the city. I got my first dose of the fresh contingencies I now experience on the ambulance ride to the hospital. While delays in traffic were no surprise, the pain transmitted to my leg from the rutted roadway of the East Side Drive was awful: what is annoying on a cab ride can be torture in an ambulance. As I came to learn, the unevenness of surfaces is a major issue for urban mobility. This can be encountered riding in the street; walking down the sidewalk and negotiating curbs; or within buildings where loose stair treads, missing tiles, unsecured carpet, and a thousand other perils present themselves.

The range of barriers is great. Heavy doors are tough. Revolving doors are too fast and too small. Narrow spaces are challenging. Even the office of my crack orthopedic surgeon is filled with obstacles, especially for those in wheelchairs. The sharp and narrow corner between the receptionist and the waiting room is daunting. The bathroom door is too heavy to be easily opened with one crutch-holding hand while balancing on one foot. Even the entry to the building—filled with orthopedists— requires descending a series of steps with no handrail, risky in rain. Only on my second visit did I discover the handicapped ramp. As it turns out, these are often installed in a spirit that is short on convenience, longer on the letter of the law. At the surgeon's building, the ramp is located so far off to one side of the entry plaza as to effectively double the distance from the curb to the front door. What is gained in easy inclination is lost in the extra exertion of length.

The instruments of mobility are themselves fraught and amazingly underdeveloped. My lightweight Chinese-manufactured aluminum crutches are well made and easily adjustable. I am now pretty fast on my foot but sometimes forget to be vigilant about watching the ground in front of me for obstacles, which are profuse. The nightmare, for me, is at the end of the day when I return to our fifth-floor walk-up apartment. Climbing up is slow and tiring, and it's all I can do to propel myself to the horizontal when I finally arrive. To keep my balance on the stairs, I hold onto the railing. This raises the question of what to do with the second crutch. I have learned, when on the stairs, to hold the unnecessary appliance in the same hand as the crutch being used. Indeed, I have now become sufficiently adept to hold the mail as well. Might it be possible to include a crutch clip on each crutch to enable its mate to be carried during one-crutch excursions?

At the other end of the spectrum of mobility are the cabs that are now central to my movement in the city. The standard-issue American backseat is extremely unfriendly to those of us with boots and casts, who lack the ability to turn our feet or ankles to fit into the contracted legroom or to get down to or up from low-lying seats. As I wait for a cab, I mutter my silent appeal that one of the new "stretch" cabs—a few extra inches make a tremendous difference—or a minivan will come my way. That after all these years—with the vanished example of the Checker or the sensible London taxi in mind—our cabs remain so poorly designed is a tribute to the stupidity and greed of the auto industry and the indifference of public regulators. In a city where the cost of a taxi medallion approaches $200,000—and their number is artificially limited—it would seem a slam dunk to require accessible design (and let's add safety and zero emissions to the basic package).

My ankle, however, has become a fabulous piece of design. As I was wheeled into the operating theater to have my bones repaired, I noticed a wonderful drawing on the wall. It had been done by the surgeon on tracing paper, laid over an x-ray of my fractures. The sketch depicted the various screws and plates he was intending to implant, a working drawing. As I succumbed to the anesthesia I remember a couple of thoughts drifted into my head. First, that the surgeon was a kindred spirit, designing in the same representational medium we do. And second, wondering what was going to happen when I first confronted an airport magnetometer.

A couple of weeks ago, I found out. My ankle, previously no more than the connection between my leg and foot, had been transformed into an object of suspicion, and I joined the queue of the lame, halt, and blind who were getting the extra once-over from security, immobility compounding itself, insult added to injury. My scar was probed with care lest I were carrying an ankle bomb. The airport was a giant ordeal, partly overcome by a wheelchair. Of course, one would not ask for a wheelchair if the infirmity were not highly and legitimately visible. What, I wonder, will I do when the boot comes off and a cane substitutes for crutches. I will certainly walk the concourse miles, bucking crowds and distance as I slowly make my way to my connection.

The plane itself is even worse. My injury had forced the cancellation of trips to Taiwan and South Africa (my not wanting to risk deep vein thrombosis, infection, and various other ailments) and my maiden journey was a shorter one, although requiring a change. The seat pitch was impossibly narrow, and I began the dance of stretching my bad foot out in the aisle and removing it for passing passengers and flight attendants and their drinks trolleys. Having put my crutches in the overhead bin, going to the bathroom became a big issue. The crutches unavailable behind piles of luggage, I was forced to hop my way to the back of the plane on my good foot, risking a fall on every turbulent bump.

In the great scheme of things, my injury is not so serious, and I will eventually resume walking. But my designing and my reading of the accessibility of the city will be affected permanently. Looking at the Americans With Disabilities Act infrastructure with which the city is being retrofitted, I can't help feeling that all of this is generally treated as an afterthought. Of course, it *is* an afterthought and a necessary one. But the spirit appears equally in refits and new construction in which fitness remains the default for participation. The idea of reducing barriers is simple and elegant, one that should spark invention, not snide remarks or resentment.

I will also be cautious about the appealing surgical metaphor for our profession. My excellent surgeon reflected the doctor's view of the body, formed from the inside out, ending at the membrane of the skin. Architects, to successfully house us, must come from the other direction, and along the seam of capacity the two professions meet. Our job, after all, is accommodation—and that means everyone, not some statistical modular or formal abstraction. The profession needs to overcome its indifference to this very real difference among us. Architecture will be better for it.

2004

34

The Limits of Tolerance

In early May, Arnold Schwarzenegger made his first official trip abroad. Among his stops were a visit to troops injured in Iraq recovering at a military hospital in Germany, a meeting with King Abdullah in Amman, and a ground-breaking in Jerusalem. This last was for a "Museum of Tolerance," a franchise of the existing Museum of Tolerance in Los Angeles, which combines exhibitions on the Holocaust with more diffuse installations designed to teach principles of tolerance in general. Schwarzenegger has been a generous supporter of the LA museum, which is known for its high-tech, interactive exhibition technology. And the museum has returned the favor, rising to Arnold's defense when he was tarred with the Nazi past of his father.

The Jerusalem branch of the organization has been designed by Frank Gehry and may cost something north of $200 million to build. It will include not simply a museum but a congress hall for meetings on tolerance, a movie theater for films about tolerance, a library of tolerance, and a restaurant. The museum, however, will differ from its LA counterpart in not including its central element: displays devoted to the Holocaust. Although this was originally intended, Yad Vashem, Jerusalem's historic Holocaust memorial, museum, and archive, objected to this invasion of its proprietary territory, and the Museum of Tolerance agreed to exclude it from their exhibitions. Which massacres, one wonders, will they include to prick the consciences of those attending the conferences on tolerance? The LA museum has recently been criticized by the Armenian community for slighting their suffering to avoid offending the Turks. Will its new branch include Sabra and Shatila? Deir Yassin?

The Museum of Tolerance arrives with high hopes and the strong support of the right-wing Likud government, most prominently Ehud Olmert, former mayor of Jerusalem. The reasons exceed tolerance; the museum's sponsors avow that it "is forecast to become a stimulant for economic, cultural, and educational growth, as well as a boost to tourism resources." Indeed, according to Rabbi Marvin Hier, director of the Simon Wiesenthal Center, the umbrella organization for the Los Angeles museum, with the completion of the Israeli project, "the hotels and streets of Jerusalem will be bustling once more with millions of visitors from around the world, many of whom will come especially to see our Center as they have come to see the Gehry-designed Guggenheim Museum in Bilbao, Spain."

This so-called Bilbao effect has captured the imaginations of municipal authorities around the globe, who understand the phenomenon—with its dramatic economic impact—to be almost entirely the outcome of flamboyant architecture, the actual content of the project seemingly secondary. The easy slide from an art museum to a museum of mass murder is accommodated by foregrounding the envelope, emphasizing its meanings over those within. Presumably those millions from around the world will come for the uplift of Gehry's design, not the horrors depicted inside.

The project's reception in Israel has been, to put it mildly, mixed. As the distinguished historian and former deputy mayor of Jerusalem, Meron Benvenisti, wrote in the Israeli daily *Ha'aretz*:

> It is difficult to imagine a project so hallucinatory, so irrelevant, so foreign, so megalomaniac as the Museum of Tolerance. The mere attempt to stick the term *tolerance* to a building so intolerant to its surroundings is ridiculous. Others have already referred to the extravagant arrogance expressed in the geometric forms that can't be any more dissonant to the environment in which it is planned to put this alien object. There's no need to waste words on the absurdity of a Museum of Tolerance planted on part of an ancient Muslim cemetery, some of which has long since been turned into a parking lot, and will now be topped by spaces in which people are meant to learn about tolerance, mutual respect, and religious coexistence.

Benvenisti's skepticism is echoed by Esther Zandberg, the architecture critic for *Ha'aretz*, who wonders why Kikar Hatulot, "a highly popular urban plaza" that currently supports an ethnic market and a range of informal social activities on the site, is being eliminated for the building. Zandberg takes special umbrage at the Wiesenthal Center's refusal to make plans and images of the project public—despite their having been published in early 2002 in the Japanese magazine *GA*—an embargo she claims is designed to forestall opposition and humor potential funding sources. Zandberg also shares Benvenisti's sense of the irony of erecting a "temple of tolerance" in a city so seemingly dedicated to fanaticism, brutality, and repression.

What better place, it might be argued, for a museum of tolerance. Certainly, the architectural component of Benvenisti's argument is disputable, a matter of taste, especially given the stultifying monotony of so much of modern Jerusalem. Indeed, there was a faction in Bilbao that took the same line about the Guggenheim's aesthetic impropriety. But the center of Benvenisti's objection is telling: can this building have anything to do with promoting understanding between Israelis and Palestinians? That the answer might be "no" was dramatically reinforced for me during a visit to Jerusalem in April, when I visited the Israeli "security fence" where it passes through the Abu Dis neighborhood, less than a mile from the site of the new museum. Here was intolerance materialized, a thirty-foot-high wall of concrete barricading Palestinians from the center of the city, from jobs, from friends and family, from medical care, and enclosing Israeli Jerusalem in a terrible illusion of security.

The two expensive constructions cannot be separated: their conflict is clear. A community cannot simultaneously repress its neighbor and proclaim its love of tolerance without hypocrisy. By identifying tolerance with an enormous building with a vaguely defined program, tolerance becomes an object of consumption rather than an act of conscience. More, the idea of constructing a beautiful center in which people—those invited by the institution—can discuss their differences short-circuits obvious matters of the inequality between those building it and those with whom they might have discussions, furthering the imbalance of power and rights that fuels the conflict. As Herbert Marcuse observed, tolerance can also repress, an effect literalized in the substitution of a controlled environment for an existing public place, a place of both accidental and elective encounters rather than the scene of purely orchestrated and mediated events.

This museum, above all, is a rhetorical project in which a building is substituted for the harder processes of bridge-building, for the myriad acts of fairness that characterize a tolerant society. Gehry's building, in particular, with its familiar fragmentary style, evokes the "deconstruction" of Yasser Arafat's headquarters in Ramallah into a pile of rubble by Israeli security forces. The painful contrast between these two places makes the absurdity of the new construction (we build shining monuments to our sense of tolerance while we blast your institutions to bits) so much more profound.

But my questions are for the architect. Will an extravagant building advance the cause of tolerance or simply stoke resentments? Is any sectarian attempt to co-opt the idea of tolerance for its political armamentarium worth supporting in an atmosphere as riven as Jerusalem's? What is the real purpose of this project? If it is to try to heat up the Bilbao effect with a museum of genocide, is this really a project an architect of conscience should participate in? Does Gehry think that describing the central hall of the complex as being "like a mosque" will really establish the tolerant credentials of this project?

Although Gehry is generally gnomic in his political utterances, an interview in *GA* revealed that he is not altogether unaware of the political geography of this undertaking. He speaks of his satisfaction that the project was moved from its original site in a more peripheral location because it was opposite a proposed Israeli jail. The new site is opposite a courthouse, a distinction probably lost on most Palestinians who pass through the system, the same Palestinians who will be prevented by the wall—their permanent jail—from visiting the Museum of Tolerance erected to stimulate friendly conversation.

Many will recall the old saw: "When you want to build a bad building hire a good architect. And when you want to build an outrageous building, hire a distinguished architect." Eminence has a responsibility that extends beyond the realm of professional practice: we have high expectations of our best artists because their work and words carry special weight in the world. It is not possible to build this project without an opinion on larger issues—issues of tolerance—in the region. What is Gehry's? This is not a question of the use of titanium versus Jerusalem stone. It is one of justice.

2004

35

When Good Architects Design Bad Buildings

The first architectural protest demonstration I remember joining was organized by a group called The Architects Resistance. It took place in front of Skidmore, Owings & Merrill in New York and was aimed at their work on a mixed-use office tower in Johannesburg. I don't remember much about the event itself, but the leaflet that was being handed out asserted that, somewhere in the drafting room above, there was an architect designing two sets of bathrooms, one for blacks and one for whites.

The ethical case seemed very clear: here was a piece of architecture that—in the most nitty-gritty part of its program—was racist. But architects are rarely confronted with an ethical dilemma as sharp and functional as this. Our dilemmas tend to be either more ambiguous (ideas about appropriateness) or more general (supporting the machine that allows us to consume our disproportionate share of planetary resources). And the whole thing is contaminated by an habitual distinction between the ethical and the imaginative—posed as if they were in opposition, a zero-sum deal.

The core of the ethical performance of building lies in its program, and we must take responsibility for a building's behavior as well as its artistic performance. Indeed, "good design" is often a cover for the ethically questionable. The most outstanding recent instance of this tactic is, of course, Ground Zero, where "distinguished" architecture has been used to con the public into supporting the massive office scheme. But there are many other examples. Suddenly, after years of disheartening indifference, the city is awash with proposals by global star architects, and a majority seem to be involved in leveraging projects of dubious ethical provenance.

To be sure, none of these projects houses a program—like apartheid— that rises to the level of the truly reprehensible. And, it is also true that recent theorization of architecture tends to locate ethical content in places too small to support it, belaboring expression while taking too little interest in effects. Most of the infractions today are sins against neighborliness and comity, in which the presumed vision of the architect trumps (and often Trumps) any sense of obligation to existing communities and compacts.

This is murky territory. We all agree that we shouldn't be designing concentration camps. And we all agree that an architect is obligated to the safety of the occupants of his or her project whether by assuring egress, avoiding toxic materials, or resisting seismic loads. We are also agreed, in more general terms, about our duties to the planet, however they may be fulfilled in the form of lip service and window dressing, like those windmills KPF has put on the hulking proposal for the Jets Stadium in Manhattan, or those that David Childs may or may not intend for the ridiculous Freedom Tower. Of course, no one discusses the energy savings that might be realized by not building these two white elephants.

Architecture does not create community, but it can provide a setting conducive for the playing out of collective values. Historic cities like New York—despite fatuous claims that the genius of the city lies simply in its wanton dynamism—are records of consent, public agreements about values worth preserving (or dissenting from), whether in single buildings, neighborhoods, or the security of individual members of the commune. Here, as in many places, architecture acts within a dialectic between gentrification ("development") and our historic rent laws that seek to codify and defend diversity, in which the market takes no interest. In many communities—including my own—these laws are the only thing preserving a mix of people from varying incomes; without them, market forces would push out the diversity in favor of an upper-class monochrome.

Where should we draw the line on the architect's complicity? The big planning argument in my neighborhood these days is over a dramatic upscaling of the Hudson River waterfront. The poster children for this are two (soon to be three) apartment buildings by Richard Meier, whom many activists identify as Public Enemy Number One. I am less disturbed than many by the sleek white towers, which—focused on the river view—do have fairly brutal concrete elevations to the neighborhood out back. I am less enthusiastic about their lack of sun control on their glassy western elevations (just add a few more tons of a/c) and don't quite see why there need to be three. The point, though, is that these buildings embody a proposition about the scale and character of place, on which the architect has implicitly signed off. I believe that this entails, at the very least, a burden of explanation, an argument why this transformation is a good thing.

About twenty blocks south of the Meier towers, Norman Foster has proposed an apartment building that sits between two much-used neighborhood parks. Here, scale is also an issue, although for very different reasons. Because of its size, the building will cast shadows on these parks, some sports fields, and three schools—one side in the morning and the other in the afternoon. Given the scarcity of public open space downtown, this is a very serious matter, one on which a conscientious architect should have an opinion. Of course, it may be that the big tower is a stalking horse, providing wiggle room for scaling back to something more "reasonable" when public protests arise, much as Frank Gehry's overly dense scheme for Bruce Ratner in Brooklyn looks likely to shrink due to community push-back. But should architects facilitate such gamesmanship? Should they ever produce projects that, if built, would have a clearly deleterious effect on a neighborhood?

The same question arose not long ago over a project by Jean Nouvel for a hotel in the Meatpacking District, not far from the Meier condos. The issue was the great height of the engagingly slim tower in a district whose relic texture—key to its character—is predominantly two stories. While this was a prima facie violation of context, the argument made—a classic of the false ethical/imaginative opposition—that the tower was sufficiently exceptional to excuse treading on the existing convention of scale. Fortunately, public opposition shot down the too-big project, much as it did a particularly awful one by Philip Johnson/Alan Ritchie fifteen blocks south of there. The developer of the overbearing Johnson project tried to sell it by papering the community with posters describing it as a "vertical work of art," the mantle of artistry again conferring the right to its narcissism of scale.

Over in Queens, design is well advanced on New York's first project by Richard Rogers, a building for the Silvercup Studios, a motion picture production facility. Located on the East River, directly south of the beautiful Queensborough Bridge, this building—a Beaubourg-like podium housing the film studios with three very tall towers on top—will irrevocably destroy the bridge's breathing space. A handsome span now visible in its all-at-once-ness will forever be placed in ensemble with this big new structure, which—however elegant it might be on some other site—will eternally alter (*ruin* is perhaps a better word) a view that has been part of our civic imagination for a century.

The same effect is produced by two unusually mindless buildings—one by KPF, the other by Kevin Roche—recently completed by New York University just south of Washington Square. The KPF item—an addition to the law school—sits directly behind McKim, Mead and White's fabulous Judson Church. The giant, new, redbrick lump—for which a house once occupied by Edgar Allen Poe was torn down—has now also destroyed the beautiful profile of the church spire against the sky. The horrible Roche building (what *has* happened to this man's career?) both contributes to the dramatic upscaling of its street (a process begun years ago by Philip Johnson's mammoth university library) and has the same effect on the Washington Square Arch as the KPF building does on the Judson Church. From far up Fifth Avenue, the beloved arch (just restored) is overwhelmed by the lumpy limestone mass of the Roche building, which arrogantly insinuates itself into a stirring and measured public space.

Jane Jacobs' new book *Dark Age Ahead* describes the way cultures forget their own values, and offers a cautionary tale of how quickly this can happen. The projects I've mentioned all contribute to this texture of forgetting. Cities are civilization's mnemonic, a contract in stone between past and future. The preeminent value of the good city lies in its neighborliness, its respect for the other, for existing and historic patterns of life. In my last piece I wrote of the difficulty of imposing collective symbols on communities in fundamental disagreement. The ethics of architecture require loving your neighbor, not dictating to her. This means some circumspection about casting shadows in other people's gardens.

2004

36

Advice to Critics

1. Always Visit the Building

A photograph is not worth a thousand words, although many millions have been generated from them. There simply is no replacement for prowling the premises. Use all your senses. Be intrusive. Open doors and windows, climb to the roof. Circumnavigate. Look at the thing from nearby and from afar. Knock on the walls. See what people are doing.

2. Style Is Seldom the Issue

Style is what architects and editors generally prefer you to write about. Not that expression is unimportant, simply that it often conceals more than it expresses. Architecture is utility made beautiful. Connoisseurship risks buggering flies, tiny valuations of tiny things based on narrower and narrower criteria. God may reside in the details, but people tend to live in the house: wallpaper will not put the wall back in plumb or block the sound of the neighbors' arguing. Indeed, Halliburton headquarters (or Saddam's *palazzi*) may be gorgeous, but that isn't exactly the point. Don't get caught defending the indefensible by too much fascination with form.

3. Credit Effects, Not Intentions

Architects always tell a good story. And, certainly, one should listen with care and take note of any worthwhile ideas. But the recent history of theorizing and criticism of architecture is overloaded with the phony authority of intent. Architects read philosophy and attempt to make form from it. Not a problem—inspiration comes from wherever you find it. But sources confer no special blessing: no amount of special pleading on behalf of a fantasy of philosophical immanence can overtake the greater importance of how a building behaves. Strangeness can be a virtue and is often a leading characteristic of the new. A critic, however, should arrive on the scene with a quiver full of her own values and take her best shot, not be a conduit for someone else's delusions.

4. Think Globally, Think Locally

Architecture is deeply implicated in the world's environmental crisis. It consumes more energy, uses more materials, and radiates more heat than anything else we do. To fail to note this particular effect of building is to abrogate one's critical duties. A good way to think about this is in terms of a building's "ecological footprint." How much of the earth's resources does it consume, and to what end? How many degrees does it heat the air around it? How much energy is required to produce all that titanium? How much of the jungle disappears to line those elevator cabs with mahogany?

5. Safety First

As physicians are counseled first to do no harm, so too must architects. The primary legal responsibility of builders—codified from Hammurabi down—is to assure the safety of those who use or encounter their buildings. This should be taken in the broadest possible sense. Buildings can kill in fires and earthquakes, but also in the carcinogenic off-gassing of toxic materials, in construction accidents, in the preparation of materials on far-off sites, and in the depressing effects of excluded sun and recirculated air. The effluent and heat produced by a building and its operation have dangerous potential far away, and all buildings have a duty to those at risk downstream. These issues are not trivial but central for critics, and they should equip themselves to inventory such effects.

6. Who Profits?

In our beloved capitalist system, buildings are generally not acts of charity. Private engorgement is what produces most of our built environment, and profit is not known for its generosity. A critic is obliged to name as many names as possible of the real shapers of any work of architecture. These include the bureaucrats who conceive and institutionalize degrading workplace relations, those who endanger the quality of the public realm by outright hostility or miserliness, those who do not understand the inevitable civic dimension of building, and those for whom all larger issues of the commonweal recede before matters of the bottom line. Numbers are important. The critic has a duty to cut through the mystification that conflates economical and cheap. Architecture must look beyond the depreciation cycle to understand its true worth. Real criticism is too important to be put in the real estate section.

7. Consult the User

By user, of course, I mean in the first instance those who most regularly inhabit the building. Their opinions count and should be counted. Which is not to say that their taste should trump the critic's. However, inhabitant happiness is primary and their unhappiness truly significant. How is this to be assessed? To begin, people are to be given some credit for understanding the terms of their own comfort, convenience, and taste. Our consumption system, though, is founded on the provision of illusory choice; a million brands of soap, all the same. The suburbs, for example, may not be the unmediated expression of user desire. They are, rather, the collusion of many interests—many of them suspect. Our preferences are produced, not "natural," and a critic should make the case for real choices. I, for one, do not believe that obesity, diabetes, automotive pollution, highway mayhem, alienating commuting, isolation, segregation, and sprawl, represent the freely considered and chosen wishes of the people. This, rather, is the "wisdom" of the market.

8. History Is Not Bunk

All building stands in context. Our architecture and settlement patterns represent a history of social agreements—entered with varying degrees of complicity—that physicalize human relations. Such compacts demand respect. There is, however, history, and there is history. I remember a panel discussion ages ago where the virtues of the Lincoln Memorial were being extolled and classical architecture identified—in standard-issue Jeffersonian style—with democracy itself. An African-American architect demurred. Those Corinthian columns reminded him not of freedom but of the Big House on the plantation. History is written by its victors, who generally prefer to see its progress as positivistic and singular. But culture writes many histories all at once, and the critic must be acute in unraveling whose history is being served, and whose is being suppressed.

9. It's the City, Stupid

Critics should be careful about imputing too much meaning to the object of architecture. Since we love it, we tend to exaggerate its consequence as a repository of social and philosophical codes, and its power to set agendas for human interactions. This devolves frequently into angel-counting irrelevance. While our building practice does tend to ossify living and gender relations, and to reproduce the strictures of class, the big picture can only be observed by looking at the big picture. To understand America (or India or Russia or Ancient Rome), it is crucial that small patterns be tested against large and vice versa. Our convention (after Alberti) is to understand the city as a big house, but this is wrong. Scaling up, more meanings are absorbed and more perspectives available: the city *emerges*. Just as our own personalities are formed in interaction, so architecture is forged in the crucible of collectivity.

10. Defend the Public Realm

The most important single task for architectural criticism is to rise in defense of public space. Threatened by the repressive sameness of global culture, contracted by breakneck privatization, devalued by contempt for public institutions, and victimized by the loss of habits of sociability, the physical arena of collective interaction—the streets, squares, parks, and plazas of the city—are, in their free accessibility, the guarantors of democracy. Particularly now, as we are browbeaten with the threat of terrorism into the surrender of more and more of our rights, the freedom of the city and the freedom of assembly, enshrined in the First Amendment, are in desperate need of all the friends they can find.

11. Keep Your Teeth Sharpened

Courtesy is an important value, but a critic should prefer to be fair. Judiciousness should never trump candor, however, and a critic often needs to shout very loudly to be heard over the din of interests that surround the building process. The rapier will always defeat the noodle, and almost always produce a better prose style.

12. Play Your Favorites

This can, of course, get out of hand: a critic should not be a publicist or a slut. The point is that unbiased criticism isn't ever: the critic is out there to describe and defend a set of values in which s/he believes. If there are designers, builders, politicians, activists, or manufacturers who well embody these same values, they deserve special treatment. They also deserve to have their feet held to the fire if they falter in advancing them.

2004

37

Liberty Square

One of the basic rights enshrined in the First Amendment to the Constitution is that of "the people to freely assemble." Free assembly is the primary expression of democracy in space, the physical embodiment of liberty. This relationship far predates the American experience. Cities, in particular, have long been seen as especially conducive to freedom, as exemplified in the famous motto of the Hanseatic League: "City air makes you free." The just city is one where citizens move unimpeded and gather in many different forms for self-expression. In modern times, social progress has been directly linked to the variety of rallies, demonstrations, marches, and insurrections that have had as their arena the streets and squares of the city. From women's suffrage to civil rights to union organizing to anti-war protests, the power of bodies together in space has been crucial to the defense of our rights. In real democracy, the streets belong to the people.

In city after city, certain places have become linked to these gatherings, institutionalized by repeated use. While the street is the bedrock of the popular right to the city—the conduit of association—it is only part of the necessary infrastructure of assembly, which includes privatized spaces such as bars, cafés, lecture halls, stadia, and stoops, as well as bigger public spaces: the parks, plazas, and town squares that remain fundamental to sound urbanism. Whether the Zocalo in Mexico City, the Mall in Washington, or Tiananmen Square in Beijing, these great sites are zones of focus, the common property of those dedicated to the struggle for free association. Indeed, the right of the public to gather in these places continues to be defended in blood.

Such matters have been much in the news in the current political season. The protest cage at the Democratic Convention in Boston—a prison-like enclosure surrounded by razor-wire—suggests a sinister elision of the war on terror with the control of popular assembly. The frustrations of those seeking to demonstrate against the Republicans in New York have also provided ample evidence of the constraints on the popular right to make use of its own spaces. They also point up something else: the lack of enough suitable places for mass political rallies. Our main rallying spots in New York—whether Central Park, Times Square, or Fifth Avenue—all depend on the disruption of some other activity, whether traffic or recreation, and are thus subject to negotiation with the authorities who, as the present situation so vividly shows, can be recalcitrant. Other venues, like Union Square with its rich historic association with protest, are too small. Still others, including City Hall Park, have been fenced and "improved" to prevent gatherings.

The organizers of the largest New York demonstration, a group called United for Peace and Justice, originally applied for a permit to gather on the Great Lawn in Central Park. This was denied on the basis of the alleged fragility of the grass. The city offered as an alternative the West Side Highway, which the demonstrators refused, electing instead to march more visibly in the streets near Madison Square Garden. Insubordinate assembly is a crucial element both of democratic discourse and of the character, location, and political valence of the space that's crucial to such expression. Speech demands its audience and its places of transmission and reception.

© Michael Sorkin Studio

This problematic lack of suitable space comes at a critical moment as the nation rushes breakneck to restrict freedom of movement under the guise of fighting terror. While vigilance is necessary, these restrictions also represent a victory for the enemies of freedom, both at home and abroad. The attacks of 9/11—the initiating event in this cycle—were both an act of murder and an assault on our freedom to assemble. The World Trade Center replacement project, however, contains remarkably little non-programmed gathering space. The major component, of course, is a memorial, but that is park-like and solemn, not the spot for mass rallies. Remaining spaces of nominal assembly—such as the Wedge of Light—are residual, scarcely more than enlarged sidewalks. The proposed cultural facilities may be public, but they are decidedly not political or about large gatherings. Ironically, the World Trade Center contained a larger plaza than anything currently proposed. It was, however, so inhospitable and its associated meanings so commercial that it never functioned as a place of assembly, simply as a windswept expanse to be crossed or avoided.

Instead of useful forms of assembly, the Ground Zero plan substitutes an iconography of freedom that slights its actual expression. The "Freedom Tower," for example, is an office building, doubtless one in which free access will be heavily circumscribed by security demands and sky-high rents. Its vague asymmetry is meant to evoke the Statue of Liberty, a devoluted icon for an icon, abstracted beyond recognition. The memorial is centered on the symbolism of the Trade Center footprints, which are to be water-filled and uncrossable. The Wedge of Light—should it actually be realized—calls for passive solemnity. The yet-to-be-conceived Museum of Freedom, however important it might become, will be a largely individual experience.

What has happened downtown is the creation of a plan that is essentially about recreating what was there before, validated as appropriate by a laying on of sacral iconography. Everything receives its label—Freedom Tower, Wedge of Light, Park of the Heroes—to create a nimbus of occluding piety. If anything points up the fast-and-loose style of reverence of the rebuilders, it is the recent announcement by the LMDC and Larry Silverstein that—given the flat office market and the failure to obtain a double payout from Swiss Re—they are likely to build "taxpayers" on the eastern portion of the site, an area (on either side of Santiago Calatrava's fine train station) that amounts to more than three city blocks. These proposed low-rise commercial buildings would be intended as placeholders for future office towers, which might not be constructed for decades. If this goes ahead, a shopping center would line the rebuilt Greenwich Street, facing the memorial and the two cultural buildings that the LMDC is currently developing.

Clearly, this is not the highest-and-best use for New York's most significant urban project. However, it does present a remarkable opportunity. These blocks might become the great public plaza that the city lacks.

Surrounded by a strong edge of building, highly accessible, and located on a site of remarkable resonance, the space might become not simply a symbol but the scene of liberty in action, a zone of free assembly and free speech. It is also in the heart of things, at the center of our institutions of governance and commerce, an apt and visible site for public expression. And, instead of managing remembrance through a series of themed activities that offer little opportunity for spontaneity or collectivity, it would truly belong to the people, an embodiment of our nation's greatest ethical and political power.

It is time to build Liberty Square.

2004

38

Bush in Space

"Only Christians have a place in heaven."

In early 2004, George W. Bush—invoking the two-hundredth anniversary of the transcontinental voyage of explorers Lewis and Clark—announced his plans to colonize the Moon and go on to Mars. "We'll build new ships to carry man forward into the universe, to gain a new foothold on the Moon and to prepare for new journeys to the worlds beyond our own."

Why this sudden proposal? The United States space program has been floundering for years without clear objectives, and no longer stirs the public passion that carried it forward in the era culminating with the landing on the moon. For our most incurious chief executive, claims of the disinterested pursuit of scientific knowledge strain credulity. Indeed, the only technological investigations suggested by either Bush or NASA involve developing the means of getting there, not what might be learned or done on arrival. While seemingly spacey, Bush's space proposal is deeply emblematic of a range of more general environmental, geopolitical, and theological agendas of his administration. And there are surely photo-ops aplenty waiting for the Astronaut-in-Chief (whose penchant for appearing in flight gear is well known) to help prove he is full of the "right stuff."

For the filially pious Bush, the space program is meant both to secure his visionary credentials (his father was reviled for lacking "the vision thing"), and to deal with the contradictions between a world that has become increasingly borderless (to capital and arms at any rate) and the belief that America must remain central. In his effort to preserve this planetary architecture, Bush has embarked on a project of old-fashioned colonization in which the landscape—including America's—is seen primarily as a site for the extraction of wealth. Confronted by the rapid depletion of earth's natural resources, the resistance of much of the rest of the world to our plundering them, and the exponential growth of non-American populations, Bush has fallen back on the idea of perpetual expansion as the driver of our national project. And, running out of earth, he has turned his eyes to the stars.

Bush's "visionary" rhetoric insistently invokes that ancient trope of American expansionism: the frontier. According to this thesis—which once dominated American historiography—US culture was driven by the relentless dynamic of a seemingly perpetual western expansion. The closing of the continental frontier in the second half of the nineteenth century, however, shifted America's growth to another register: its own territory exploited, the US embarked upon a colonial mission with newly imperial energies. The invocation of the frontier—as in JFK's "new frontier" or the Boeing Corporation's current slogan, "forever new frontiers"—reasserts the idea of American "manifest destiny," a special planetary proprietorship understood to be our mission and entitlement. This semi-religious notion that America is the global chosen one forms the ethical and political substrate of the US's current "mission" in Iraq, among other places along its axis of interference. But as America's terrestrial territorial expansion is arrested by competing powers, and as its global hegemony is threatened by the demographics of the coming Asian century, the redirection of America's expansion is logically toward more distant conquests, presumably unpopulated and therefore less resistant to its agenda.

This lack of any known resident population on the Moon or Mars is significant. As Bush never tires of telling us, he has been born again: his policies are informed not simply by everyday rapacity but by divine mandate. Bush's fundamentalism does not simply shield his fanatical ignorance ("the jury is still out on evolution"), but—in its absolutism—suggests that he shares the creationism of his core constituency, and with it the conviction that we are alone in the universe. We're definitely not going back to space to look for little green men! Bush's "pro-life" stance—with its rejection of stem-cell research, strident defense of embryos, and endless efforts to control the inner space of women's wombs—has its roots in this theological presumption of the complete uniqueness of terrestrial life, of which American life is surely the highest instance. This excludes another possible motive for W's excellent adventure. Without a history of life, there can be no oil on Mars or the Moon.

This does not mean there are no resources to be had. The Moon is considered a possible site for Helium 3, crucial for the expansion of "clean" nuclear power back home. Lunar ice is contemplated as a source of hydrogen, which in turn might possibly fuel the trip onward to Mars. The presence of other such mineral resources is a likely, if distant, rationale for the expansion of the frontier to other planets, which are seen—like early America—as an infinite abundance ripe for the taking: for colonists, the point is not to learn but to acquire. Bush—foe of Kyoto, creature of the petroleum industry, free-trade bully—blithely believes in a national sense of entitlement. For him, America's piggish exploitation of resources (let's drill in the national parks!) has no wider implications for the planet, and so we consume and pollute in insane disproportion to our numbers, as if by divine right. This planetary gluttony only extends the frontier mentality, with its push across the continent destroying forests, animal species, and those sub-human red people who once presented such a noisome obstacle to white America's pale fantasy of paradise.

Like so many of his projects, Bush's Moondoggle would result in a gigantic transfer of public money to a small number of very large corporations. The US aerospace industry, in particular, has been suffering from serious contraction due both to increasing competition from abroad (Airbus now sells more passenger planes than Boeing, America's last surviving manufacturer), to its own inefficiencies, and to a slipping dependency on the Cold War defense economy, which Bush struggles manfully to restore under various guises, including the so-called war on terror. This epic and growing corporate hand-out—to protect the "homeland" (to use the favored, creepy, fascist-tinged locution)—is the residue of the enormous Reagan "Star Wars" project with its cowboys and Indians vision of national security in outer space. The "paranoid style" that suffuses Republican Party culture has found its perfect embodiment in Bush 2: America must get into space for its own protection. The back-story of the Bush/Cheney planetary agenda holds an unspoken military objective, an impetus stoked by the announcement that the Chinese intend to pursue manned exploration of the Moon. The suddenly renewed interest in space is just more "preemption," the cornerstone concept of the Bush foreign policy, an assertion of America's right to rule anywhere according to its own self-interest.

Bush's imperial project and his defense of the *Heimat* have taken a particularly sinister twist with the recent announcement of a massive project to create a "virtual border." As Bush continues to stiffen America's defenses against global terror and alien ideas, he has begun to compile an enormous data bank and surveillance network so that "terrorists" and other undesirables can be identified while still abroad and intercepted before they are able to enter sovereign American space. The declaration by White House spokespeople that the program will extend our borders beyond their physical territory is an unusually frank declaration of the elasticity of Bush's sense of boundaries, of a piece with his invasion of Iraq, and with the creation of the global gulag of secret detention centers for sundry evildoers and thinkers. This space between America's physical territory and a limitless virtual border is itself a kind of frontier, and a haven for the twisted norms of a place outside the system. Like "frontier justice," in which self-appointed guardians of the peace lynched those perceived to threaten it, so Bush plans to mete out rough justice in a space beyond observation or sanction.

The contract for the multi-billion dollar-project for a virtual border has just been awarded to Accenture, successor to Arthur Andersen, famous cooker of the books for the corporate thieves of our recent go-go economy. In a further wrinkle in this neoliberal spatial order, Accenture is headquartered in the tax haven of Bermuda, that most virtual of nation-states. Like the shadowy legal protocols and draconian surveillance that the new virtual-geographical system will implement, those tasked with its creation occupy another island in this extraterritorial archipelago, a place designed to frustrate accountability, to reinforce the elision of the corporate and the national, and to encourage the "free" movement of capital.

Bush's expansive sense of American space reflects his own privileged experience, a life spent entirely in a series of near-utopian environments, each coded to affirm his wealth, authority, and license. A patrician childhood of big houses and summer homes, part passed in Midland, Texas, a get-rich-quick oil-town complete with Yale, Harvard, and Princeton Clubs. All male Yale, which Bush relished as frat-boy heaven, culminating in his anointment (as his forbears had been anointed) to the Skull and Bones secret society—legendary prep school of the CIA—with its wanker-kitsch clubhouse and adolescent rituals of ruling-class self-affirmation. Harvard Business School. A stint playing jet pilot, zooming through the clear, unthreatening skies of Texas. Under these same skies—on proving his incompetence in the oil business—he was set up by family cronies with a stake in the quintessential field of dreams, a baseball team. Sporting among the boys of summer, he makes a fortune doing next to nothing, watching his players run around the neon green of the diamond. He buys that huge ranch in Crawford, moves to the Governor's Mansion, thence the White House.

Bush spends a lot of time on the ranch. Four thousand acres means that the spread is effectively boundless, its edges distant: pure property. While Bush plays cowboy, wife Laura commissions an environmentally sensitive house, rendering her husband blameless as he quashes Kyoto, eviscerates environmental legislation, opens national reserves to exploitation, kills housing programs, and trespasses on other people's territories. The arrogant spatiality of the Bush lifestyle is only reinforced now that he is in the White House, attended hand and foot, traveling the world in a bubble of space in which nothing is ever out of order, and in which he is the proud possessor of the biggest corporate jet on the planet. And it has all been so easy. Bush simply cannot understand why everyone doesn't have it so good and—in his breathtaking ignorance of the world—why so many billions hate America for electing a man so thoroughly oblivious to the dire and uneven distribution of wealth and space. Bush has simply never been in a place where the lunch wasn't free.

And so, it seems, he has decided to take another helping, another country, another wilderness, another planet. For Bush, space is not legacy but opportunity. Like the western frontier, the planets are not encumbered by recognized ownership. Given the primitive state of the laws governing human behavior in outer space, the universe is there for whomever has the means to grab it. On planet Halliburton (it was Cheney who actually drafted the new space program), we will again be able to indulge in qualm-less exploitation, remote from bleeding-heart environmentalists, or from the claims of the suffering on earth. The sacred mantra of property rights will be invoked over every pebble and crater, and the pockets of the multi-nationals (or, prospectively, the multi-planetaries) will be lined ever more thickly as our empire expands to the boundaries of the universe.

In Bush's world, the point is not simply to get rich; it is to assure that the right people get rich. His massive redistributive scheme confers rewards on those who are worthy, on true believers, on those whose manifest destiny is to rule. Like the "rapture" at the end of days, these faithful will be swept up to heaven while the rest of us gruesomely suffer and die, victims of our fail-ures to comprehend God's plan. Bush's heaven—like his earthly idyll—is a strictly gated community, an Eden of exclusion. And so he seeks to reshape America and the world, to keep the wrong people out, to reward those with adequate faith in Jesus and the market. Bonesmen and businessmen and the sons and daughters of money sit secure in their entitlement because they know that it isn't the meek that will inherit the earth, the Moon, Mars, and all the rest. In the paradise of privatized space, borders are not expected to be a problem. In the infinity of space, there's always more for the taking.

2004

39

Architecture and Revolution

Every revolution has a creative half-life. The Russian Revolution begat constructivism before its slide into totalitarianism. In France, the architecture of Boullée and Ledoux represented a moment of confidence that was too soon displaced by the Terror. In Cuba in the late 1950s and early 1960s, a brief halcyon day of intense architectural and artistic creativity soon gave way to dreariness as the country's economy collapsed and politics became increasingly repressive.

Architecture and Revolution in Cuba, a show at Storefront for Art and Architecture in New York City, curated by Eduardo Luis Rodriguez, documents the efflorescence of architecture in Cuba following the overthrow of the Batista regime. This was a time when Cubans embraced the optimistic promise of bread *and* roses, reflected both in the range of programs encouraged by the new government—schools, housing, cultural centers, hospitals, ice-cream parlors—and in the flamboyance and freedom of their architecture.

Perhaps the best-known and most magnificent of these projects is the complex of art schools—for music, drama, modern dance, ballet, and the plastic arts—begun immediately after the Bay of Pigs invasion in 1961 as a cultural riposte to Yankee designs on the island. Personally initiated by Fidel Castro and Che Guevara, and sited on the grounds of what had been a posh country club, these buildings—designed by the Cuban Ricardo Porro and Italians Roberto Gottardi and Vittorio Garatti—embody the best of a compassionate revolution, one in which artistic expression is seen as indispensable to human development and success is marked by expressive freedom.

The buildings themselves are sinuous, complex compositions—each an urbane little village—laid out with tremendous sensitivity to the lush, undulant landscape, and built in a common materiality of brick, tile, and concrete. They share, too, a technology of hand-built Catalan vaulting—supervised by an elderly Spanish master of the art—that yielded an amazing Xanadu of domes and arches. Both individually and as an ensemble they represent one of the great architectural creations of the century, rich in influences but ultimately *sui generis*. A piece of good news is that portions of the complex—much of which is in a state of ruinous deterioration—are slowly being restored.

The star of the Storefront show is Ricardo Porro. He holds center stage not simply because of his leadership of the Art School project and his astonishing architectural work (continued in Europe after his exile from Cuba in 1965), but thanks to his beguiling appearance in a film of interviews produced for the exhibition. Porro (whose students and colleagues affectionately nicknamed him Porbusier and Porromini) is an enthusiastic and articulate sensualist, and his sexualized and ethnic description of his work is unabashed. In the art schools, Porro sought to express the Afro-Cuban culture he thought held the island's soul. Unfortunately, this sensibility was at the core of the project's fall from favor. As the revolution grew more Stalinist in its suppression of diversity, the schools were charged with a variety of bourgeois crimes: individualism, irrationality, idealism, luxury, and the rest.

But in the beginning, what a time it was! Porro describes this "utopian" period as "mas surealista que socialista," and the sense of adventure throbs from accounts of a moment when all seemed possible. Utopia is the ultimate erogenous zone of architecture, and the merger of the discourses of revolution and pleasure was one of the great promises of the time—certainly part of the initial ideological equipment of the long-haired, cigar-chomping progenitors of the Cuban revolution, before their slide into puritanism and homophobia. Indeed, the cover shot for the exhibition (a 1959 photo of an elegant group of architects in suits and ties mingling with bearded revolutionaries in baggy military fatigues) suggests a conflict that was to return.

Describing the Art Schools project, Porro recalls the "victorious and almost epic atmosphere" and the directive from Fidel to create "the most beautiful art school in the world." He speaks of making a symbol of fertility and evokes Ochun—the Afro-Cuban fertility goddess—as the muse of the building, and female sexuality in general as intrinsic to the Cuban national character. "Cuba es una mulata," he declares, and the three (albeit male) architects of the schools deliver on this description of the feminine in terms that, however regressive they may seem to us nowadays, were the conceptual medium for producing work of curvaceous sensuality and often frank symbolism (including Porro's famous water-squirting papaya sculpture).

Those happy days were all too brief, and the schools were never fully completed and only partially occupied. Porro describes the discouraging atmosphere engendered by what was to become a permanent political and economic crisis. There is a striking moment in the film when Porro describes the arrival of Soviet panelized housing as the death-knell for the creative period that produced the art schools. (In 1964, the Russians sent a gigantic factory for production of the "Gran Panel" system as a gift to the Cuban people.) As Porro speaks, the camera angle widens to reveal a terrible—and terribly out of place—panelized building for student dorms looming in the background. In its grim rectilinearity, mindless siting, and shabby detailing, the building is the antithesis of the organic, humane approach of the schools.

The art schools were not alone in representing this approach. A striking revelation of the show is the numerous examples of post-revolutionary Cuban architecture embracing progressive design practices that were international in their appeal, and very much parallel to directions contemporary in the US and elsewhere. Experiments in modularized housing, cement-asbestos prefab pods, standardized school construction, and integrated housing developments have a wonderful familiarity to those of us who were in US schools back then.

Although the narrative of a small island caught in the rivalry between two colossi is by now the standard issue, it was crucial in shaping Cuba's architecture. A visit to Cuba nowadays is filled with awful contrasts. There are few places where the gap between education and income is so great. Terrible scarcities of goods and services (public transit, for example, is in ruins) dominate the island. This is an economy in tatters because of bad and authoritarian choices, sclerotic bureaucracy, misplaced alliances, and, of course, unending US pressure.

Ironically, the dire situation has had some fortuitous effects. Crumbling Havana—one of the most beautiful cities on the planet, with centuries of wonderful buildings—remains relatively unscathed by development, because there isn't any. But once Fidel departs the scene, there will likely be a new set of risks. However much one wishes the Cuban people to enjoy lives of freedom and prosperity, the onslaught of US-style urbanism—with its domination by the car, its fast-food effluvium, its insensitivities to history, its suburbanization—will likely put at risk the coherence of the city and its very public atmosphere and vibrant, if stoic, solidarity.

Although Porro may be the star of the film, the best line comes from Mario Girona, architect of the fabulous Coppelia Ice Cream Parlor. Girona recalls that, in designing the project—a wonderful and complex prefab dome—he was struck by a program that asked for a place where "a thousand people could eat ice cream." *That's* my kind of revolution.

2004

40

What Can You Say about the Pritzker?

The Winners[1,2,3,4]

1979 – Philip Johnson	- 73	USA
1980 – Luis Barragan	- 78	Mexico
1981 – James Stirling	- 55	UK
1982 – Kevin Roche	- 60	USA
1983 – I. M. Pei	- 66	USA
1984 – Richard Meier	- 49	USA
1985 – Hans Hollein	- 51	Austria
1986 – Gottfried Boehm	- 66	Germany
1987 – Kenzo Tange	- 74	Japan
1988 – Gordon Bunshaft	- 79	USA
Oscar Niemeyer	- 81	Brazil
1989 – Frank Gehry	- 60	USA
1990 – Aldo Rossi	- 59	Italy
1991 – Robert Venturi	- 66	USA
1992 – Alvaro Siza	- 59	Portugal
1993 – Fumihiko Maki	- 65	Japan
1994 – Christian de Portzamparc	- 50	France
1995 – Tadao Ando	- 53	Japan
1996 – Rafael Moneo	- 58	Spain
1997 – Sverre Fehn	- 72	Norway
1998 – Renzo Piano	- 60	Italy
1999 – Sir Norman Foster	- 63	UK
2000 – Rem Koolhaas	- 56	Netherlands
2001 – Jacques Herzog	- 51	Switzerland
Pierre de Meuron	- 51	Switzerland
2002 – Glenn Murcutt	- 66	Australia
2003 – Jørn Utzon	- 84	Denmark
2004 – Zaha Hadid	- 53	UK
2005 – Thom Mayne	- 61	USA

Pritzker Prize recipients by age group

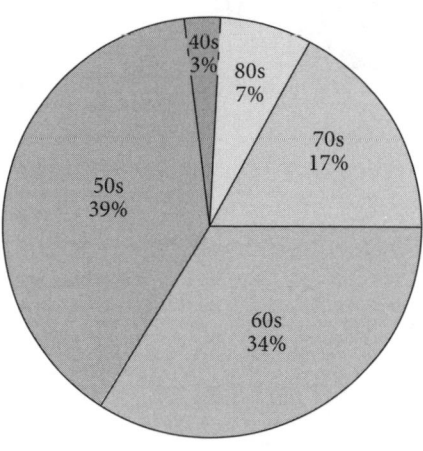

Age of Pritzker Prize recipients in the year of award

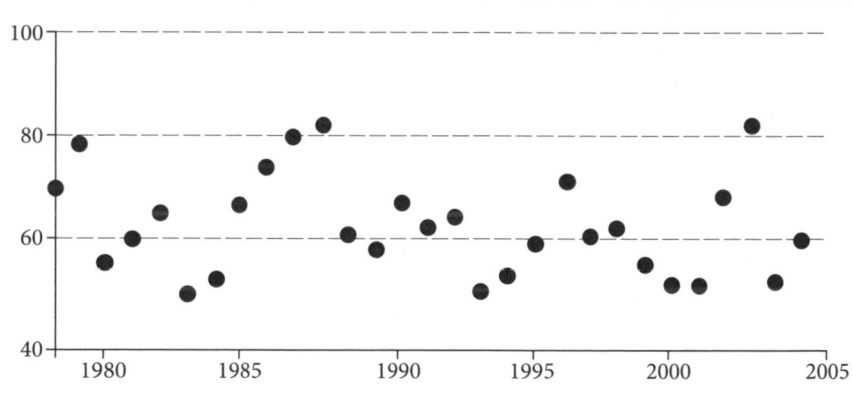

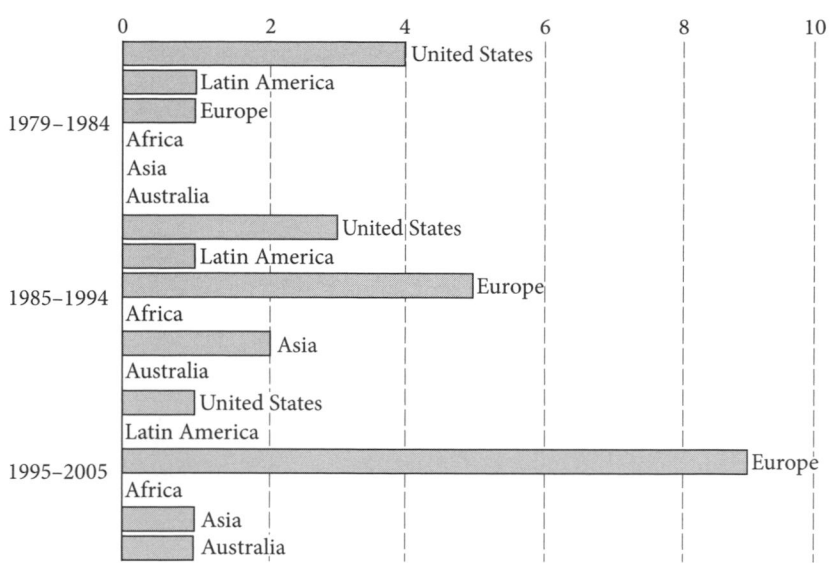

Pritzker Prize recipients by region of origin

[1] A cursory glance at the list of winners reveals the self-evident: as in so many areas of life, it helps to be a white guy. Which made 2004 a banner year: a woman of Arab origin became the twenty-eighth laureate. Of the previous twenty-seven winners, all were men; of those, twenty-one were white, four were Asian, and two were Latino. The twenty-ninth winner was yet another white male.

[2] Age distribution is well spread, with substantial numbers of winners in their fifties, sixties and seventies. There also seems to be a cyclical quality to this recognition, with no special priority given to working down from older to younger practitioners.

[3] Only one collaborative practice—Herzog & de Meuron—was recognized as such.

[4] The American hegemony in the early years of the prize has been decisively replaced with European domination. Before Thom Mayne won in 2005, the last American recipient was Robert Venturi in 1991. Indeed, the prize has been strikingly negligent in recognizing the younger cohort of American architects, though younger Europeans have done very well.

Composition of Pritzker Prize Juries 1996–2005 [5,6]

Gianni Agnelli, Industrialist
J. Carter Brown, Curator
Charles Correa, Architect
Balkrishna Vithaldas Doshi, Architect
Rolf Fehlbaum, Industrialist
Frank Gehry, Architect
Ada Louise Huxtable, Critic
Carlos Jimenez, Architect
Toshio Nakamura, Editor
Victoria Newhouse, Historian
Lord Palumbo, Parton
Lord Rothschild, Banker
Jorge Silvetti, Architect
Karen Stein, Editor

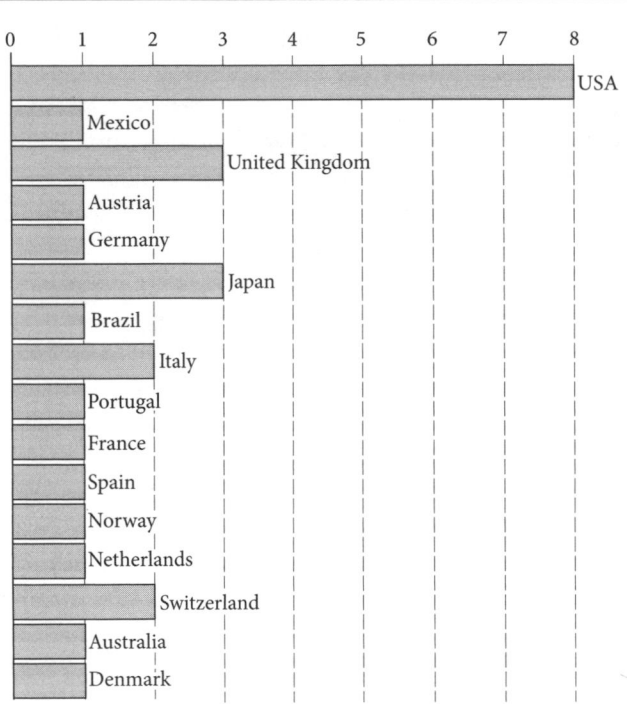

Pritzker Prize recipients by country of origin

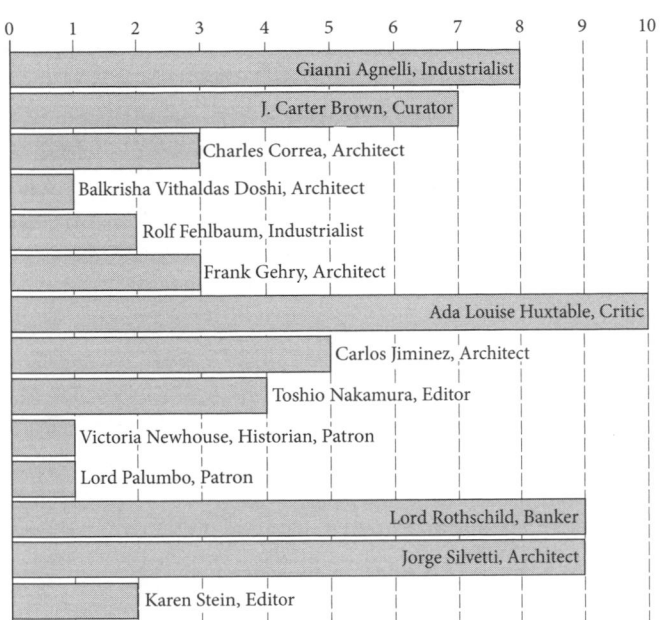

The Jurors by numbers of years served 1996 – 2005

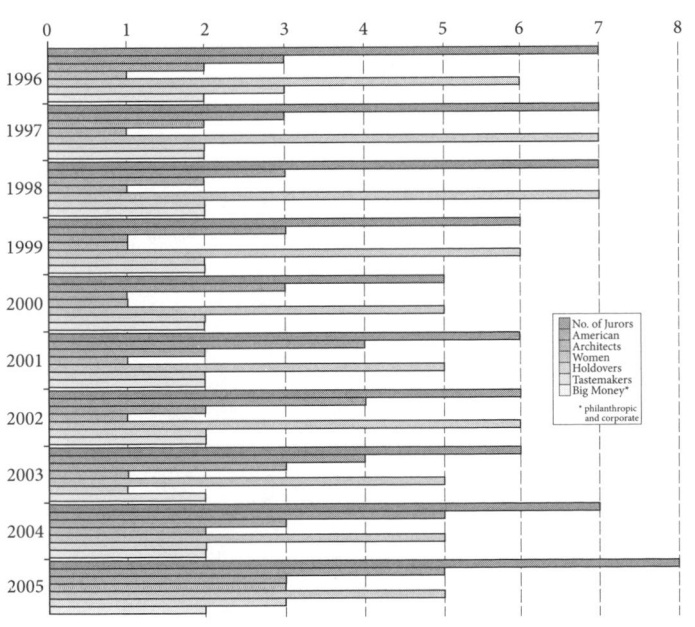

Composition of Pritzker Prize Juries 1996 – 2005

2004

[5] The constellation of jurors is generally of similar configurations from year to year, with practitioners in the minority. Architects are balanced by approximately equal numbers of tastemakers—critics, editors, and curators—and juries always contain at least one representative of big money in the form of a recognized patron. Women stand a better chance of serving on the jury, although only in the tastemaker category, and there is a significant bulge of Latin males that defies ready explanation.

[6] The jury tends to be not only structurally comparable from year to year, but to be composed of the same members, suggesting a single standard of taste. In the ten-year period from 1996 to 2005, for example, Ada Louise Huxtable was present for ten consecutive years, Lord Rothschild and Jorge Silvetti for nine, and Gianni Agnelli for eight. Of the total of fourteen jurors to serve during this period, seven were Americans.

2004

41

A Trip to Tijuana

Not long ago, after a lecture in San Diego, I paid a visit to Tijuana. Among those along for the ride was my friend Omar, a Palestinian architect who had just begun his Fulbright at Irvine. Omar was depressed. Lost in the invidious sprawl of right-wing heaven, he was having a bad dose of suburban agoraphobia. Carless, he was stuck in his apartment, forced to walk for miles to buy a quart of milk.

We collected him at the San Diego station and headed south as Omar recited his tale of woe. Orange County was, for him, both completely alien and terribly familiar. The tile-roofed gated communities—fortified against some unspecified other—were of a piece with the Israeli settlements in their architecture of exclusion, and made him feel the more a second-class citizen. His despair was palpable as we tried to cheer him up with promises of camaraderie, seafood, and tequila.

As we joined the checkpoint queue to cross the border, though, his mood lightened measurably. The scrutiny of armed guards cut through his home-sickness and he felt suddenly at home. Laying eyes on the city itself, on the thick pattern of life, on the graffiti daubed along the fence, he began to smile. Arriving at a seaside bar, he became positively delighted. "I love this place," he announced. "It could be Gaza."

2004

42

Seven Chairs

Modernism revolted against the sentimental distortions of representation. Every representation pares and distorts, proposing a way of seeing as well as a vision of its object. Modernism bridled against this, understanding representation as constraint, and produced the idea of abstraction, conscientiously diversifying this methodology by steady degrees. Cubism broke down the object through conceits of simultaneity and geometricization. Surrealism abstracted by the free interchange of object and context. The Russians assaulted optic prejudice through the representation of geometry, itself an abstraction. But even abstraction always represents *something*, if only the idea of representing nothing.

This crisis in modern art stemmed in part from the press of technical events that fell increasingly outside its purview. Art was challenged by the proliferating, deadpan expression of engineering and science, a system that grew increasingly hermetic and bold in meeting its own needs. The dazzling technological artifacts of the past two centuries conjoined to produce a vast system of visuality that was largely indifferent to received formal criteria. This was a tremendous challenge to the enterprise of art, which was forced out of its role in the vanguard of cultural expression. What was easel painting in the era of the Great Eastern or the Brooklyn Bridge or the movies? What was the relevance of history in the face of such enormous ruptures as the world wars?

Duschamp's "discovery" of the ready-made insisted that the act of *seeing differently* was a sufficient definition of artistic practice, with the power to "turn" objects from one thing to another. Whether this meant a urinal brazenly hung on a gallery wall or a deft bike-part bull, this mode of art-making used the mass-produced consumer object as its medium. However, its critical relation to this means depended on devaluing its useful status to convert it to mere contemplation, bringing it in line with traditional styles of artistic valorization. Art's crisis was one of both meaning and use.

Early modernism coincides with the origins of the discipline of industrial design. Such design depends on the prior representation of the object to be produced *ad seriatim* by machines. This relocation—with its separation of designing and making—was taken up in the discourse of the appropriate form of the industrial object and of the manner in which it was to be judged. While the mythic rhetoric of functionalism provided and continues to provide the main means of judging such production, it was clear from the outset that this was not nearly enough. In this sense, both William Morris and the Bauhaus represent similar styles of resistance to the anonymity of the mass-object—dosing it up with craft or style that far exceeds the simple requirements of use.

Abstract art seethes with both represented meanings and their denial. In mainstream architecture, this contradiction offered an especially intractable dead-end, and by the 1960s the gigantic vacancy of corporate minimalism that had come largely to dominate the sanctioned face of architecture was ready to take a fall. The assault came from many competitors, including historicists, sentimentalists, and ironists, as well as from the free-for-all visual convulsions of the counterculture with its tooth for depiction—however mind-altered—and its political critique of the oppressive forms of late capitalism.

In this re-creation of the art of design, there was (and is) no greater figure than Gaetano Pesce who—as no other practitioner of recent times—recaptures representation for both politics and pleasure. To a degree, this is accomplished by a strategy of "turning"—resituation—if not precisely the kind favored by peers like Ant-Farm or Archigram, with their affectionate capture of mass-consumables from cars to cozy-cottages. Pesce has instinctively understood something a level deeper: that the creation of images—in particular images of the human body—is a fundamental property of the way we behave as a species and also a means of defending the body against the threats of "post-human" culture. His work—at all scales—is suffused with body images, artfully abstracted to retain an energetic balance between media and message.

But if this friendly inclusion of the human image were the end of it, Pesce's place would be misunderstood. His genius has been to unite his frank and idiosyncratic representational style with a vivid politics of craft and meaning and with an enthusiastic, adept, and brilliant use of new technology. While the majority of his cohort continues to work out the model of the rigid, metal machine (however cowled in voluptuous shape or soft skins), Pesce has understood that the organic is a concept that far exceeds loosey-goosey forms, that organisms are both hard and soft, that matter appears in different phases and guises, and that the human body is the eternal subject of architecture and domestic design.

"Serie Up" (and particularly the "Up 5/6" chair) is a vivid example of Pesce's precise embodiment of meaning and technique in useful and artistic objects. In the late sixties, when foam was a material of considerable fascination for designers, Pesce had a transcendental insight: foam is largely air. With B&B Italia, he designed a system for removing the air from foam furniture and vacuum-packing it such that the volume to be shipped was a mere fraction of the volume to be used. Thanks to foam's own "shape memory," chairs squashed to pancake proportion rapidly—on being liberated from their packaging—resumed their shape and rigidity. This is surely one of the most astonishing innovations in the history of furniture design.

In many ways, this "inflatable" technology inverts a preoccupation that was very prevalent at the time. While designers around the world produced endless variations on the balloon—inflatable objects as mere air-supported membranes—Pesce was the first to produce an inflatable *mass*. This nearly alchemical transaction is breathtaking both in its innovation and in the fundamental simplicity of the observation that inspired it. The reanimation of the chair by exposure to the air is miraculous.

"Up 5/6" takes this innovation another step, layering the image of the body to support the body-to-be-seated. But not just any body, a woman's. To say that the female body was contested territory in this era—of *The Stepford Wives* with its docile robot-women, of pneumatic, hyper-objectified *Playboy* bunnies, of inflatable sex-toys, and of the raging, liberating reaction of the women's movement—is to gravely understate the situation. Pesce responded by carrying his design a little further, providing an "ottoman" (another colonization) for the chair/woman in the form of a ball and chain. The meaning is clear: the woman objectified is a prisoner.

But there's ambiguity as well, and this, too, is part of Pesce's brilliance. The chair is beautiful and, consequently, so too the represented woman. Her oppression seems so much more drear because the victim is so robust and generous. In Pesce's mind, the image of the woman's body could—at that historical moment—only be recuperated for artistic representation with appropriate critique. This contradiction—that an appliance designed to serve the body could only represent it with visible qualifications—captures something central to the struggles of that time and the present. In the work of Gaetano Pesce, a chair acquires astonishing eloquence.

2004

43

A Letter to Bob

Dear Bob,

I've just returned from a weekend at MIT, my first extended visit in years, had a good look around, seen new buildings and old colleagues. I also happened to read your column while I was there and I couldn't disagree with you more.

To begin, what is this anxiety with the idea of the metaphorical or, more properly, symbolic role of architecture? Do you really believe that architecture should be purged of directed meanings? Do you think that Chartres Cathedral makes a mistake in its heavenward aspiration and slathered iconographic agenda? Do you wish that the Einstein Tower was just a little more boxy? That Legal Seafood leave portholes alone? Indeed, do you really think that the domes, stairs, and classical columns of the Bosworth plan are simply a neutral "brown" wrapper because they're a little more butch than the Pantheon? Clearly, you do not, because you describe this architecture as "denotative" of the "commonality of the present and the past," as well as, presumably, of strength and tradition, civic consequence, ruling-class solidarity, and deep roots in the western canon.

Your cavil seems to be not with the idea of symbolic content but with the expressive particulars of those new MIT buildings, which you see to be the content of their metaphorical message. But really, why shouldn't a building in a place that is the virtual Vatican of ingenuity seek to express itself through works of architecture that are themselves formally ingenious? Holding aside questions of more direct functionality, I can see—reading between the lines—that the issue might be a more general one of the apt modesty of the technical mind and its disdain for the peacock end of the narcissism spectrum. We like our scientists with chalk on their pants and elbows poking through their jacket sleeves. We liked the old tumbledown and temporary Building 20, a wooden barracks dating from World War II, better than its expensive and formally elaborate successor, just as we prefer the studiously casual uniforms of the American general staff of the era to the over-the-top, drag-queen outfits of the Germans.

Actually, though, both are rich in meaning, equally connotative of attitudes toward hierarchy, tradition, and warfare, dramatically evoking the difference between Germanic *Soldatentum* and our own reluctance to militarize (talk about nostalgia!). One might well question the message, but not the mechanism: taste can be bad but not wrong, certainly not in terms of a logical category like fallacy. Ex-president Charles Vest—as leader of the institution—is certainly within bounds to express his hopes for the environment of the university he directs in aspirational terms. Would you have been happier if he'd said "great" architecture befits a great university? Would that have left us in a more tractable place than looking to architecture for signs of "ingenuity?"

True, symbolism can be craven and dopey, and there are plenty of instances of poor and misleading translations of meaning into architecture. The Dr. Evil pinkie sticking up from the Freedom Tower to evoke an expressively shriveled statue of liberty. The green roof on the Ford Rouge plant, a good idea in and of itself but finally a monument to craven hypocrisy, camouflage for the environmentally nefarious product being produced underneath it. Or the moribund neoclassicism of the swagged and symmetrical memorial to World War II vets and victims on the Mall. But none of these failures really rebuke the idea of the architectural embodiment of specific meanings. Nor does our current preference for forms (like the work of Gehry's billowy period) that—like clouds—beg but do not specify their metaphorical gloss, although we prefer this for the more respectably abstract character of their iconography.

However, I think you most misread the new buildings not at the iconic level but in performative terms. You favorably contrast the original MIT complex to the new additions by calling it "corridor positive." This is a nice observation, one that foregrounds the importance of the network to the meaning of the campus. Both Stata and Simmons are *extremely* corridor positive and each makes a serious effort to expand the meaning of the corridor. This is something of a tradition at MIT where Aalto's Baker House— the greatest building on campus, indeed in Cambridge—offers that glorious straight run stair, a rising corridor that functions as a social condenser as well as a sublime means of ascent, comparable in its way to the towers of Chartres.

The same effort to extend the meaning of the corridor to a role beyond horizontal circulation is clear at Simmons where the "corridor" ascends through those troglodyte multi-story common spaces, allowing residents to overcome the tyranny of floor-based affinities by producing a more three-dimensional space of interaction (and the kids love it!). Stata is structured around a complex interior street, a clear expansion of the idea of the corridor to embrace a variety of forms and functions and to initiate a complex (but surprisingly clear) system of circulation that proposes a more irregular, "medieval" pattern that has the a capacity to generate spaces of accident and encounter that are just as capable as the grid-scheme of the Bosworth buildings. These provide a wonderful network but—in the efficient uniformity of their section—little opportunity for repose.

You are right to admire the loft-style flexibility of the Bosworth buildings but wrong, I think, in your identification of the idea of loft space with large, simply configured, undifferentiated spaces. If the goal of a loft is to accommodate diversity of use, the almost parodistic variety of activities in Stata would seem to satisfy the requirement. Disciplines from linguistics to philosophy to cybernetics and from computation to guided missile design (this is MIT, after all), and uses from auditoria to seminar rooms to labs to offices to cafés are all well and compatibly housed. Of use, there is no environment more mixed!

Your idea of loft space is very much a product of the sixties, of the idea that flexibility grows from maximum generality, a set-up for the "equipotentiality" of subdivision. But flexibility can also be the outcome of assembly, and this is surely the message of both the larger aggregation of the MIT campus and the assemblage that underlies the elegant plan and exciting section of the Gehry project. Here malleability is the byproduct of variety rather than uniformity. A change of use requires the search for an appropriate space or series of spaces rather than the serial redesign of big rooms. And, to cite another paradigm of academic paradise, there's a lot to be said for the near-neural patterning of the Oxbridge model, with its panoply of engaging eccentricities. Indeed, the brain seems a considerably more interesting model than the factory for this virtual age. And this, you are right to observe, has nothing to do with the style of the hat that keeps the grey matter warm. Who wants to wear the same Fedora as everyone else, anyway?

Finally, what's this about the lack of an iconic outdoor space? It's true that the campus plan doesn't congeal into a singular, instantly comprehensible, metaphorical space like Harvard Yard or the Piazza Navonna, but it has, instead, a particularly urban quality, with a premium on elaborate networking and extensive distribution of commons spaces. This produces both strong set-pieces and the amazing labyrinth of connections that ground campus character. Among the former are the plaza in front of Catalano's student center and the two beautiful Saarinen buildings, Bosworth's great lawn on the Charles, and the emerging Vassar street corridor. While these may not evoke the pastoral feelings of privilege and prestige evoked crossing the Yard on a crisp winter morning, to say that these spaces play "little role in the life of the inhabitants" is absurd. The network (and its useful diversity) is both the icon and the space of use and interaction. Indeed, the greatness of the campus is the result of a stimulating collision of paradigms, not the domination of one.

MIT has a particularly high per capita provision of athletic space, and it occurs all over campus. To be sure, there is no giant football stadium à *la* Harvard, but I see this failure of traditional campus iconography as a strength, a far more useful attitude than the puerile spectacle of drunken Saturday afternoons in the stands watching somebody else exercise. As I was walking along Vassar Street, I passed a track meet and a baseball game with huge numbers of kids participating, not simply watching. Here, well-expressed, is the embodiment of the hoary academic ideal of *mens sana in corpore sano* and the informality of distribution of these spaces of participation (an energetic game of capture the flag was even in progress *inside* Simmons when I visited) is at the core of the *genius loci*.

The series of peripheral dissolutions from the formal central campus to more fragmented surroundings has long been a core problematic for campus expansion, whether it be into mixed-scale industrial and residential surroundings to the west and south or the burgeoning high-tech theme park to the east and north. The MIT campus is so remarkably urbane precisely because it is formed in reaction to the unpredictable and unfolding complexity of its surroundings. I find the work of particularizing these interactions far more potentially stimulating than, for example, the megalomaniac uniformity that is likely to result from the Harvard expansion into Allston, a move that has the potential to annihilate the winning propinquity that makes the Cambridge campus so singular.

Funny that your concluding quip about typography so directly evokes Victor Hugo's claim that the book had become the assassin of the meaning of the public communication of the cathedral. Setting aside the history of manuscript illumination and expressive typography (I assume the "modern" sans serif face used in *Record* does not dissolve your intended meanings) and appreciating your indirect reference to the precious illegibility of the posters for the lecture series at Yale, I believe you founder on the old *langue/parole* distinction. The question of expression does not really devolve on typography but on your writing, the real medium for the expression of your ideas. Sloppy execution by the contractor can harm architectural expression but it isn't the source of it any more than Charles Vest's metaphor of ingenuity really speaks to what's going on in those projects you so dislike.

By the way, do you wear a tux when the event calls for black tie? Do you find that people take your ideas more seriously if you do?

Hope to hear from you soon.

Best,

Michael

2004

44

Into the Woods

Lebbeus Woods is the world's greatest living architect. While we are rich in form-makers and technicians, Woods's genius is to combine visionary tectonics and a staggering imagination with a deepening and insistent ethical imperative. Indeed, his research examines the fundamentals of embodiment and the ways in which architecture absorbs and expresses the nature of the political, particularly at the margins.

For Woods, politics is ambient. As a manifestation of culture, the political accretes all the styles of knowledge and media of expression that surround it. In a political architecture—by which I mean one that actively propagandizes—there is an expressive supplement to the programmatic, the site of architecture's most intrinsic understanding of social relations. In this sense, Woods creates an architecture of persuasion.

The work of Lebbeus Woods proposes a kind of epistemological unified field theory in which architecture is responsible for a content that articulates its character in both mind and matter. Woods's work has had a long and intimate relationship to physics and cosmology, particularly phlogiston theory and chaos. The trajectory of his projects recapitulates the history of celestial mechanics, beginning with a Copernican interest in the cyclical behavior of bodies and now absorbed with more notional—more invisible—behaviors and particles. This analogous system provides Woods with a medium capable of combining the social with the material at a precisely controlled conceptual level, and the results are breathtaking and mysterious.

A marvelous exhibit of Wood's work now at the Carnegie Museum of Art in Pittsburgh shows the range and development of his thinking as well as the prodigious and growing span of his technique. His Centricity project of 1987 speculates about an intertwining of urban form and the concentric shells of the atom. What is striking about this work—aside from the amazing delineation—is the way in which the metaphors function reciprocally. Architecture becomes a tool for investigating physics and vice versa. Of course, this is not a technique for uncovering primary physical attributes, but for organizing our imperfect knowledge of such events for comprehensible expression as part of the everyday.

The Aerial Paris project of 1989 extends this inquiry. Here Woods confronts architecture's most compelling physical constraint: gravity. Utilizing some mysterious and pervasive energy—one we know to be there but are presently incapable of tapping—he creates a series of habitations that float and dance in the sky above the city, housing a magical endo-atmospheric circus. What better place for a band of performers whose "practice" defies both physical and social gravity.

Beginning in the early 1990s, Woods's work takes a more demonstrably and localized political turn. The Berlin Freespace project of 1990–91 invents an architecture of parasitic insinuation, a system of spaces that burrow under the city and inhabit existing buildings. The spaces themselves—complexly described but imprecisely, "freely," inhabited—propose the propagation of freedom by means of an autonomously acting spatial eruption, an expression of the spread of choice that assaults the received architecture of sameness and constraint. A large part of the project's fascination—as with so much of Woods's work—is the precision of the design. His work is only "un-constructible" because of the limits of our ambition, not of our technology.

Shortly after the Berlin project, Woods began a long relationship with the city of Sarajevo, one that brought him there repeatedly, even during the worst of the violence. His speculation focused both on the destruction of the city and the nature of future redress. Throughout, his concern was with the institutions of civic life after the war and with the meaning of repair. Confronting a default of simple restoration, Woods directed his work to a transformation that paid appropriate respect to the reality of the trauma. Here, he introduces an explicit biologism—long part of his often organic formal palette—to structure his investigation of healing. Buildings, however humble or damaged, are assigned a compassionate subjectivity and mend as the body might, with scabs and scars, transplants and patches. Woods recuperates from the mesmerizing horror of war not by juxtaposing some mawkish image of the benign but by co-opting—turning—the result in another direction. What he does not do is glamorize or aestheticize destruction; rather, he looks to the effects of war for the seeds of reconstruction.

In 1995 Woods produced a project for Havana (represented by a fantastic model in the show) that is startling in both its form and its practicality. The proposal lines the Malecon—the Havana seafront—with a series of giant moving plates that can be raised during storms to prevent the flooding that is a persistent problem for the city. The project is as canny as it is beautiful. By creating a work that has a single and unassailable function, one that traditionally belongs in the realm of engineering rather than art, Woods both celebrates the beauty and tenacity of the city and challenges the long history of official stricture on "pure" expression in building. It is altogether brilliant.

At about the same time he undertook his Havana project, Woods designed a series of structures for San Francisco under the rubric "Inhabiting the Quake." These buildings continue several ongoing themes, including recovery from and acknowledgement of disaster, architectures of shards and pieces, and the ways in which the new finds its home. More important, however, is the positioning of the project in relationship to the primal tectonics of slipping plates. Like his ongoing tango with gravity, this absorption with the nature of the terrestrial speaks to architecture's most abiding fundamentals: earth, space, gravity, and society.

In his latest turn, Woods has been investigating another boundary between abstraction and representation. In a series of installations—in New York, Paris and Pittsburgh—Woods has constructed fields of bent metal rods, blizzards of tangled linearity. These installations have a sibling relationship to many of his current drawings, likewise greatly abstracted, in which compositions made up of angular lines coalesce to limn a building in becoming, not yet clearly recognizable. There is incredible dynamism in his work that dazzles simply as form.

However, these projects resonate harmonically with the longer history of Woods's preoccupations. Like the trails of particles in a cloud chamber, the rods embody a primary, almost religious observation about the order of things. They also suffuse the spaces they occupy with resistance and ambiguity, impossible to inhabit in any conventional way. Finally, they represent the irreducible core of the act of architectural invention: the making and consolidating of line, the representation of boundaries. Our own have been immeasurably enlarged by the work of Lebbeus Woods.

2005

45

Cardinal Points

The National Mall is the lodestone of our national geometry. From its inception, it has been freighted with metaphor and a weighty job of symbolism. The L'Enfant plan—in which the Mall forms the central space—was a paragon of rational abstraction, a description of both the meaning and organization of power. It formed the great lawn on which the deliberately separated powers are joined, a void through which democracy might flow and be collectively activated.

Over the years, the flanks of the Mall, as well as its center, have accumulated structures that have celebrated and marked our national project and have—in their differing ways—described the limits of an official consensus about the meaning of architecture and its metaphorical expansiveness. At one end, the Capitol with its baroque dome and hilltop authority embodies the re-expressed classicism that was the official architectural expression of the early Republic. At the other end, Lincoln sits in a classical temple. The mid-point is marked by Washington's giant Masonic obelisk.

Neoclassicism has been Washington's official default for most of our history, whether handsomely expressed in the National Gallery, grotesquely overblown in the House Office Building, or variously stripped in the undercooked stone symmetries of buildings all over town. Of all American cities, Washington is the most rigorously homogeneous, whether enforced in its mandated height limits or the strictures of the Fine Arts Commission or two centuries of habit.

But there have been important exceptions. The foundational other is James Renwick's 1842 castle for the Smithsonian Institution. Constructed of red brick in the then-popular Gothic Revival style, it differs—in color, in style, and in poking into the Mall—from its successors and predecessors both. It also sets a benchmark for difference. The building is charming and beautifully made, and has for years been one the city's most emblematic landmarks, beloved in its eccentricity.

As the center of Washington was increasingly built out, the mall too moved toward completion, as all its sites were consumed by structures from the triplet of governance, collection, and commemoration. The republican treasure houses (shrines both to rationalist taxonomy and to massive accumulation) of the Natural History, History and Technology, Air and Space Museums, the Hirschorn, Freer, National Galleries, and the Botanical Garden dominate the eastern end of the Mall. To the west of the Washington Monument's Masonic pivot, memorials predominate, including those dedicated to Lincoln, Roosevelt and—nearby—Jefferson.

However, the great turning point in the meanings associated with this space came with the construction of the Vietnam Veterans Memorial, commemoration of a tragedy and a defeat. This marked both a militarization of the Mall—it was followed by memorials to both the Korean War and World War II—and a renewal of the simmering culture of architectural exception. Although it cleaved to the spirit of abstraction embodied in Washington's originating plans (like the overrated I. M. Pei gallery with its Baroque slicing), the memorial was dark—polished black granite—and excavated into the earth, not standing triumphantly upon it. It was somber, not celebratory.

This Vietnam memorial was soon followed by another project that dramatically reconfigured the meaning of the Mall: the United States Holocaust Memorial Museum. Although a block away from the Mall proper, it irrevocably altered its mood and its style. While its architecture was outwardly cut from the longstanding classical cloth, it introduced another mode of understanding to the official repertoire: this was not a museum about collecting, but "interpretation" and a kind of redress, a form of accounting for a tragedy yet incomprehensible, like the war in Vietnam.

This is a prism through which the new National Museum of the American Indian (NMAI) must be refracted. The building—and its program—resume the project of architectural and thematic exception embodied in both the Vietnam memorial and the Holocaust museum. The move to Washington was initiated in 1989 when the Smithsonian took over the extraordinary Heye collection of the Museum of the American Indian, then located in New York City. Under the new arrangement, the museum was to maintain a branch in the old Customs House in lower Manhattan, move the bulk of its holdings to a new archival building in suburban Maryland, and build a centerpiece museum on the last remaining building site on the National Mall.

The choice in 1993 of Douglas Cardinal to design this new structure was a natural one. This gifted Canadian architect had long understood his work in relationship to his own Blackfoot roots—expressed in built form, in a dedication to aiding indigenous communities, and in a series of writings that attempted to capture the value and spirit of Native American space. Cardinal was also the designer of the Canadian Museum of Civilization in Ottawa, completed in 1989, which marked the expressive maturity of his work and was a project of comparable intent (and even greater scale) to the National Museum of the American Indian.

The process of programming the NMAI building was heavy on consultation with Native American communities, and was conducted at a deliberative, iterative pace, very consonant with Cardinal's style of design. Indeed, from what I'm able to observe (buttressed by the analysis of Trevor Boddy, author of an excellent 1989 monograph on Cardinal), his work is best when the process allows him space for testing and contemplation.

Over several years, a design for the building emerged that was clearly an extension of the language of the Museum of Civilization and, in many ways, a refinement of its formal premises. However, in 1998—in a dispute over fees and creative direction—Cardinal was sacked from the job. Brought in to investigate the conflict, the Polshek Partnership emerged with the commission to finish up. Although I am not able to comment on this skullduggery, it left Cardinal embittered, so much so that he accused the Smithsonian of "forgery" and declined to attend the 2004 opening. For its part, the Smithsonian has treated Cardinal as a near non-person, listing him low in its credits and hyping the "collaborative" nature of the process.

Although replacing the lead architect midstream makes it impossible to assign responsibility for many details of the project, the parti, plan, and basic design expression are clearly Cardinal's. Closely following the Museum of Civilization, the building is expressed via a geologic metaphor, a set of laminated, curvilinear, stone strata. Constructed of a lovely, buttery, Kasota limestone, dressed adroitly in bands of varying dimensions and roughness, the building wisely chooses to evoke a natural setting of wind-carved rock rather than any particular Native American architecture.

This conceit of stratification in stone poses a fundamental formal issue: transparency. How to introduce light and permit views in what wants to appear as a stone mass. One possibility is to top-light in the manner of the Guggenheim, which allows the walls to remain closed. Another is to puncture the building with apertures, revealing mass and thickness. Cardinal's choice is to use alternating stone and transparent bands. This begs its own tectonic issues. Is the transparency a kind of shadow? Are the stone strata floating? Is the dark glass meant to evoke a similar solidity to the stone?

The NMAI has glass bands that undulate in the same rhythm and proportion as the stone—as if a geological stratum of another material—and divides them with a very regular pattern of mullions. This close spacing gives the glass strata the look of a structural solution—bearing the weight of the slab above—not simply of the membrane itself. While the solution basically works well, the detail lacks a final measure of elegance, and the smooth, artificial stucco soffits beneath the overlapping laminations are a little unsatisfying.

The real structure of the building is columnar and lies within, largely uninflected by the wall/skin. The interior holds almost nothing of the governing metaphor of stone carving—its own default Sheetrock—although it often opens to well-calibrated views of the Mall. The main move is a full-height, domed, cylindrical rotunda that forms the entry space of the building. This faces east toward the Capitol, and its placement at the end of the building—rather than on its long street or Mall facades—sets up both a logical processional and a rife dialogue with the domed rotunda up the hill, topped by a statue of a Native American, a perverse symbol of conquest.

Entering the building, one descends a ramp to the grade of the rotunda, which turns out to be grand but curiously vacuous, undercooked. The dome itself—a low copper roof on the exterior—is resolved in a tacky-looking, non-structural Sheetrock corbel within. The (slightly sub-) ground floor is devoted to auditoriums, a cafeteria, and, most visibly, a gift shop. The ramp down, however, has the (unintended?) consequence of lengthening the stair up to the second floor (where yet another gift shop awaits at the landing). The would-be grand stair—grafted to one side of the rotunda—feels ancillary in a space that calls for a more refined and dramatic means of vertical ascent.

But, for me, the least successful aspect of the museum is its content. Not simply does one feel that the exhibition spaces are not nearly adequate to the subject or the collection, their design is uninspired at best. The lighting—one passes into the galleries from circulation spaces that are successfully day-lit—is lugubrious. There is an excess of television. Organization is confusing and the didactic intent is made more so by a curatorial approach that puts a theoretical emphasis on inclusion but winds up producing a mish-mash of materials, lacking any persuasively cogent point of view.

Perhaps most disappointing is the amazing paucity of actual artifacts. For a rich continent of cultures that has left such an amazing material legacy over the millennia, the shortage of *things* (there are more in the two shops than in all the galleries combined!) is a huge disappointment. This is not some regressive complaint based on a disreputable nineteenth-century view of the museum, but a deep disappointment with the didactic approach adopted: it is not simply inadequately celebratory, it distrusts the eloquence of the objects themselves, absent some situating gloss or overly composed presentation. And where is the architecture!

Of course, there is no denying the politics of this institution, its vital duty to reclaim this rich history from centuries of erasure and distortion, its obligation to teach, and its crucial role as a gathering place and point of pride for Native Americans. But it's too much in thrall to the Holocaust model, too eager to see its contents simply as evidence, and insufficiently attuned to their resonance and beauty as art and expression. It is in this register that the depth of Cardinal's vision becomes clear. The power of this building lies in the exceptional character of its presence on the Mall, an assertive other in our civic holy of holies.

The NMAI is visibly a different kind work. It is yellow in a field of white—a building of color. It is rough-dressed in a sea of smoothness and mechanical precision. It is curvilinear in a context of unremitting orthogonality (one Native American observer described it as "the first female building on the Mall"). It is surrounded by specimen biotopes rather than traditional "formal" landscaping. And it commands its own spiritual and practical orientation—a modest, if meaningful, bit of resistance to the alien, "rational" organization that so devastated Native America. Symbolically, it couldn't be any better.

2005

46

My Last Philippic

The past year has seen the demise of two major figures of American culture, filmmaker Russ Meyer and architect Philip Johnson. Although Meyer was the purer talent, both made enduring, seminal contributions to the ironic, vaguely pornographic, and deeply kitsch sensibility that has become one of the major markers of our contemporary creativity.

Meyer—the celebrated soft-core "King Leer"—began his career as a combat photographer during World War II, and went on to make industrial films and take photographs for *Playboy*, leading to his cinematic break-through in 1959 with *The Immoral Mr. Teas*, a film which *Time* magazine suggested had "opened the flood gates of permissiveness as we know it in these United States." The film was Meyer's Glass House: it put him on the map by exposing almost everything. His oeuvre went on to include such legendary works as *The Supervixens*, *Beyond the Valley of the Dolls*, *Beneath the Valley of the Ultravixens*, and *Faster Pussycat! Kill! Kill!*—the latter described by John Waters as "beyond doubt the best movie ever made." Meyer himself responded to the film's cult status by insisting that "too much emphasis is put on it being significant."

The critic Roger Ebert—author of the screenplay for *Beyond the Valley of the Dolls*—described Meyer as having "a sensibility somewhere between Andy Warhol and Al Capp," a succinct appreciation. Meyer's legendary attachment to big breasts (often described by him in such architectural terms as "cantilevered," "superstructure," etc.) is strongly analogous to Johnson's feeling for architecture, which might, in its sensibility, be described as somewhere between Andy Warhol and Walt Disney. Both Meyer and Johnson were professionally inspired by a deeply felt connois-seurship of the chosen objects of their affection, and both devoted their lives to inventing forms of representation that were worshipful rather than inventive. Both also displayed a critical relationship to their own work that consistently refused to treat it seriously according to the canonical theories of the day. And both were clearly enabled by the sense of liberation that grew out of the styles of consumption that blossomed in the 1950s.

The central mass-cult figure of the period was certainly Disney, whose project suffuses the work of both Meyer and Johnson. For Johnson, the kitschy creative geography of Disneyland, with its recombinant approach to form and style, was the foundation of his own practice. By liberating the juxtaposition of nominally discrepant, phony mimetic architecture in space—Main Street, USA terminated by Ludwig's Castle—Disney anticipated the temporal trajectory of Johnson's career, which in due course managed to superficially ape virtually every known architectural style and, in turn, free a legion of hacks to do the same.

Because Johnson and Meyer so succinctly embody the sense of excess that is central to kitsch, both are likely to be remembered less as auteurs then as exemplars. Both represent the entertaining but vapid core of American mass-cult, the complete disengagement of form from constructive systems of meaning, amusing inducements to stop thinking. Although Meyer was well grounded technically and Johnson was unable to draw two parallel lines, neither proposed any purpose for his project other than self-entertainment (in Meyer's case, what used to be called self-abuse). Both were flacks for the kind of confident American styles of hyper-consumption that were spawned by postwar prosperity, and that morphed over the succeeding years into the unsustainable Bushian greed ravaging the planet today.

Both men had, to put it mildly, problematic politics. Meyer foundered on his "*Playboy* philosophy" approach to women. If he was less self-conscious than Hugh Hefner, who made endless claims to be a leader of liberation, Meyer nonetheless shared the same stupid core of unremitting objectification, never mind efforts to invent him as a kind of proto-feminist. Johnson, whose writing is vastly overrated by his coterie of sycophants, was purer in his evil—although, like Meyer, he did contribute, through his utter cynicism, to the anything-goes assault on the era's hypocritical puritanism. The generation of his postmodern admirers (themselves using Johnson to justify a social indifference that pollutes the profession to this day) worked hard at ignoring (or excusing) the fact that Johnson was an out-and-out Nazi. This was not the youthful indiscretion that many suggest, but a dedication of years, and one for which Johnson never fully accounted.

Johnson's fascination with fascism deeply informed his work. Just as Hitler's vision for the world was deeply couched in an aesthetic vision of uniforms, redemptive violence, and racial purity (and just as Walt Disney's seemingly benign project concealed his own racism and anti-Semitism), so Johnson's emptily aestheticized world-view conceals a politics of privilege and indifference. In a life of nearly a century, Johnson never interested himself in any of the registers through which architecture and its philosophy can help enfranchise; never showed much, if any, concern with housing the poor, with the environment, with the fate of cities. His own philosophy was rooted in a schoolboy Nietzcheanism of supermen and the will-to-power. Indeed, his major contribution to the intellectual history of architecture is probably his early, largely successful effort to introduce modernism to the United States (via the famous 1932 Museum of Modern Art *Modern Architecture* show) in a way that thoroughly sheared it of its founding commitment to social betterment, reducing its content to nothing but form.

My only regret over Johnson's shuffle from the coil is that he never wrote an autobiography (unlike Meyer, who left *A Clean Breast*, published in 1992). How fascinating it might have been to read his own account of his meetings with Kingfish Huey Long or Father Coughlin, his ride into Poland with the Wehrmacht, his appreciation of the décor at the Nuremberg rallies, his real opinion of the younger generation of architects who devoted so much time to sucking up to him, his take on the so-called sexual revolution. Unfortunately, all that's left is his mediocre body of work and his lavish contribution to the politics of narcissism. The end of an era, let us hope.

2005

47

Gulf States

How to comprehend the disaster of cities destroyed? It begins with the rush of analogies: the 9/11 attack, Baghdad, Dresden, the Chicago fire, Johnstown, Pompeii, the San Francisco quake. We assemble fragments and screen them on our own neighborhoods, imagining the high-water mark on our own streets, grappling with what would be lost here, speculating about the frayed ties and deepened bonds that a flood would produce. How would we deal—personally and collectively—with the lost commerce; the failure of public services such as power, water, and sewage; the unleashed misery; the greed?

Living through 9/11 shapes my ability to assimilate the horror. Four years later, Ground Zero remains unreconstructed and controversial, a magnet for bad behavior. Only recently, ground was "broken" for the new transportation center designed by Santiago Calatrava. Just a few weeks ago, the city coughed up an enormous package of tax breaks to induce Goldman Sachs to build its new headquarters near the site. Architects and developers preen. The memorial is un-started and its features still contested, caught in arguments that continue to bring out the worst in people, focused now on how much free expression is to be permitted in the shadow of the "Freedom Tower," itself distilled to an imaginatively shriveled, heavily fortified symbol of triumphalist paranoia and real estate go-go.

Much of the early reaction to Katrina seems eerily familiar. Billions are appropriated for incompetent agencies of our government-hating government. Halliburton is to be further fattened with public funds, and money-grubbing lobbyists queue to the horizon. The *New York Times* runs a photo of a model of a house someone in Libeskind's office roughed out to try to get a piece of the action in Sri Lanka: the architect hero is ready to save us once again. Accusations fly about intelligence failures, starting with the refusal of the federal government to take seriously study after study that pointed out the jeopardy to coast and levees from major storms, maliciously cutting the budget for reinforcing the system year after year in blithe denial. Coastal wetlands—indispensable barriers and biological engines—are disappearing at the rate of fifty square miles a year, ravished by development secured by taxpayer compensation for those vacation houses that predictably get knocked down again and again. Bush continues to deny the impact of global warming, which everyone else on the planet acknowledges is contributing to the frequency and energy of hurricanes, to rising water (seven inches in the last century, eighteen to thirty-six predicted for this one), to the decomposing heat.

Recriminations are important, and important now. Like the Trade Center attack, it was an unnatural disaster that doomed New Orleans. The city came through Katrina's wind and rain relatively intact, and citizens were already returning to the streets, relieved, when the levees were breached by the risen water of Lake Ponchartrain. Bring on the media spectacle. Sensitive celebrity reporters tear up and jabber endlessly about the *stench*, as the screen shows creepy subtitles proclaiming "State of Emergency" and armed troops pass in the background. Bill O'Reilly and his cohort of evil talking heads mount their high horses over the immorality of looters (Fox-speak for black folk), depicting them as part of a culture that simply awaited a hurricane to liberate them from constraint. But no one in the media questions his or her own fundamental role in the manufacture of the array of unsustainable longings that figure in the American dream. Their moral parsing is sanctimoniously fine: one pair of sneakers might be justified because of nakedness, the second pair proves the intrinsic immorality of the poor. After all, if these "people" had gotten the message of the commercials that helpfully punctuate the TV coverage and owned cars like the rest of us, they would have been easily out of there.

Now we must really help. The huge appropriations coming out of Congress must be used deliberately, wisely, expeditiously. Urgent needs for food, medicine, shelter, and repairs must be quickly and compassionately met. But Katrina has not simply created a need for compensation; the storm has raised crucial questions about how we've lived, how we will live. Reconstruction is not enough, not a sufficiently capacious category to guide the mass action that will both produce and define recovery. This is even more true now than it was after the 2001 attacks. While that disaster was enormous, its site was remarkably small, given the scale of the havoc. Reconstruction was charged with a huge weight of symbolism, but never allowed to raise fundamental questions about the nature of New York's form and development.

Biloxi and New Orleans do not have the same luxury of a little-questioned return to business as usual and a focus on the aesthetic niceties of a lavish program of commemoration—of simply tearing down the Superdome, as if it were a Republican Party Bastille. September 11 caused death on a massive scale, but little homelessness. Many lives were lost, few jobs. For the planners of the future of Ground Zero, the issues are circumscribed. Much of the energy of the post-9/11 debate has been liberated by the artfully narrowed parameters of the reconstruction, which never exceeded the apportionment of proper ratios of office and civic space and the apt forms of symbolic commemoration of an event of frighteningly and deliberately Manichean clarity. And even this cannot, it seems, be accomplished.

Rebuilding and renewing our Gulf will be much more difficult. Calls to bring on the bulldozers to complete Katrina's remarkably focused urban renewal are irresponsible. New Orleans and Biloxi are treasures to be saved, not erased or reprocessed as Disneylands. And the ripped fabric is not simply architectural. New Orleans has the highest proportion of native-born citizens of any American city, and these connections in and to place down the generations are at the core of its genius. While it would be callous to talk about 9/11 or Katrina having "silver linings," both have wiped slates clean. To reflexively reproduce the status quo ante without vigorously questioning both its values and its defects would slight the disaster and obscure the urgency of the opportunity. Reconstruction must be modeled at all appropriate scales, and the complex ecologies of regions, cities, neighborhoods, and architectures harmonized with art and care, slighting none. Coastal development must be dramatically regulated. Wetlands must be massively renewed. The levee system must be rebuilt to a standard raised to the level of experience. The social fabric of neighborhoods must be mended and people restored to comfortable and familiar surroundings, to re-established continuities. Buildings must be repaired.

But this is not enough. The easy theodicy of justification and blame must be put aside in favor of work that focuses not simply on restoration but on making life better, more responsible, more attuned to the realities of our prosperity and to a renewed sense of our shared project as Americans. The discourse must become high-minded, not merely high-flown, and the opportunity to shape truly sustainable communities immediately engaged. This is ultimately a strategy not just of renewal but of survival, the question Katrina most vividly begs. There's a powerful juxtaposition of the offshore city of glistening oil rigs (and the fantastical refinery metropoles it supports)—all surely to be back online in no time, thanks to resources of a level never available to protect the public—with the stricken city ashore. This is the time to question the relationship radically, to reflect on the intimate connections between the fossil-fuel economy and the future of urban development.

Rebuilding must meditate decisively on sprawl and density, engage the role of renewables in powering our cities and lifestyles, act dramatically to expand public transportation, and revisit planning and building codes for sustainability and self-protection. Strong, careful, and comprehensive planning is an imperative—the only way to mitigate the effects of outrageous poverty on the fabric and organization of the city, to recast urban organization along lines informed by twenty-first-century knowledge. It is the only way to deal with new pressures like the relocation onshore of the casinos that float along the Mississippi coast and the need to create new neighborhoods from scratch. Neglecting this is an affront to the dead and to the survivors.

And hope itself must be restored by making victims into collaborators in the creation of their own better futures, not simply spectators or consumers. A wonderfully encouraging moment in the midst of all the bleak coverage was a brief interview with a small contractor in New Orleans who was taped standing in front of a damaged house, visibly straining to get to work. Pleading for plywood and shingles, he put the urgency eloquently: "The faster we can build, the faster we can wake up from this nightmare." Time for us to help.

2005

48

People Who Live in Urban Glass Houses

What can this image possibly mean? The huge billboard—now obscured by the rise of the building it hypes—appeared on Spring Street some months ago. I recognized the Philip Johnson brand, but who was that on the right? Had Philip (now with Liberace, Hildegard, and Elvis in mononomial nirvana) posthumously evolved into a woman? The sign had the desired effect: I checked the website, and it turned out the second face was Annabelle Selldorf, the architect doing the interiors.

The big glass box acquired its bulk via the transfer of air rights from the tiny 1817 Federal house next door (home of the beloved Ear Inn), creating expansive millionaire's views of the Holland Tunnel ventilation tower across the street. While this seems conclusive evidence that the evolution of modernist luxury hasn't exactly led to intelligent design, there is a certain survival-of-the-fittest aspect. The Urban Glass House replaces an earlier Johnson effort to build a cartoonish thirty-six-story "habitable work of art" on the site, hooted from the scene despite efforts by the developer to whip up community support for the giant zoning variance required by suggesting that resistance to the project was simply philistine.

The art hype continues. According to Johnson's partner Alan Ritchie, "the discipline and Modernist principles of the New Canaan house were consciously applied to the final design for the Urban Glass House." Key word: *applied*. The building is being skinned with panels that represent a clear devolution in functionalist tectonics. Instead of frame and infill or its descent into the Miesian curtain wall, these panels use the implicit assembly of mullion, window, spandrel as decorative devices, part of a cladding sandwich meant to signify joinery and mark structure, but having nothing to do with either. Like those fake Louis Vuitton handbags sold a few blocks away on Canal Street, it's just code.

But the code's genetic and much reproduced. The Johnson project is one of a number of glassy buildings that have gone up in the last two years in an area of only a few blocks. While ranging enormously in quality—from a cool, curvaceous building by Winka Dubbeldam to a pair of Soviet-style boxes from Handel Associates—all boast facades that are almost entirely glass. There's something striking about this (most of the surrounding context is masonry), and I think it has to do with styles of both consumption and paranoia. The original glass house became iconic not simply for its architecture but as a medium for self-exposure. In a masterstroke of celebrity, the house made the career of its creator by putting not simply itself but himself on display. Like David Blaine suspended under London Bridge (or Eichmann boxed in Jerusalem), the work of architecture was made meaningful by the visible character of its inhabitation. Indeed, the Glass House combined the transparency of Blaine's box—simply a window on his stunt—with the doubly protective quality of Eichmann's, which at once sequestered the monster and defended him against the potential violence of his victims.

The raft of new glass buildings down the street share this bivalent quality. Like the Johnson tower, all of them (the majority of which face west) have windows that are either sealed or barely operable. In an era of raised environmental consciousness, in which cross-ventilation would seem to be the minimum level of architectural common sense, there is something perverse about this attitude. It is, however, perfectly attuned to the post-9/11 culture of anxiety, the contemporary phenomenology of safety. As the media endlessly alert us to the risks around us and increasingly identify surveillance with protection, this glass architecture seemingly satisfies the nominally contradictory demands for both isolation and exposure.

Such architecture sees the environment as pathogenic and gaskets itself away from it. The glass house next to the tunnel extract fan is metaphorically precise. Here, windows should not be opened for fear of filling the room with carbon monoxide (or the avian flu, or sarin gas). And yet the activities within remain visible. If safety is identified with panoptic transparency, the willingness to expose oneself becomes a medium for the reduction of risk. More and more of daily life is governed by the management and manipulation of fear. A trip to the airport obliges surrender to close vetting and intrusive examination as the price of protection. (Have you been through one of those air-puff explosives sniffers yet?) The police can now check any bag and pat down any rider in the subway. Public service announcements caution us to be on the lookout for people who dress unusually, which covers just about everyone around here. The result is a shrink-wrapped city, designed for the pleasures of danger.

The rise of such actuarial aesthetics has become very pervasive, and it's making me nervous. While it is the duty of architects to protect the public from danger and the hard-fought history of health and safety codes marks our progress as a society, a line must be drawn between sensible protection from risk and hyping the morphology of fear. Although we seem to have largely gotten over the mimetic anxiety of decon and its vapid celebration of trauma, the pervasiveness of "terror" as a driver for architecture and urbanism grows by the day. A recent exhibition at the Museum of Modern

Art called "SAFE: Design Takes On Risk" deals with the assimilation of various countermeasures to the discourse of "good" design, scrupulously refraining from passing judgment on their meaning. The architectural press constantly publicizes the high-tech ha-has that are being installed everywhere to protect us from truck bombers. We are being swept along in a frenzy of the fear of fear and look for reassurance in the wrong places.

A society can surely be judged by the risks to which it chooses to respond, the dangers it values, the targets it gives high priority. Katrina shocked us not simply for its elemental ferocity but because it peeled back the layers of indifference and concern we so selectively apply. The "news" paused in its usual preoccupations to reveal something it habitually obscured, and we saw not simply the failure of the levees, but the horrible poverty and inequality their collapse suddenly made visible. In the numbers game of lives and dollars, we were forced to wonder why our priority was the weekly expenditure of dozens of lives and billions of dollars in Iraq when our own citizens were so miserable and our own infrastructure so lacking. And we could clearly see that the "better" people and parts of town disproportionately enjoyed the tools and resiliency to recover.

I have been spending some time on the Mississippi Gulf Coast, working with my students on a reconstruction project. Everyone is waiting for FEMA to determine the new legal topography, to come up with a cogent strategy for managing hurricane risk, dangers to the homeland that demand at least the same level of attention as terror. There will certainly be restrictive zoning, new building standards, a shake-out in the insurance industry, including some revisiting of the federal flood insurance that makes building on such dangerous shores feasible. At a minimum, the federal government must stop subsidizing risky behavior, stop being the fiscal enabler of the wanton development of our fragile coasts.

Unfortunately, the solution may make things worse. One dangerous possibility is that new regulations will lead to dramatic upscaling, the building of "safe" high-rise buildings to replace more susceptible houses: Class A construction rode the storm out well. In this scenario, risk becomes a privilege, and higher insurance and mortgage rates, coupled with more restrictive building codes, will exclude the poor from these areas forever. Declared dangerous, life at the shore will only be enjoyed by those who can afford to defend themselves against nature (although the rest of us will keep on picking up the tab for infrastructure). The Gulf coast might quickly become very much like my corner of Manhattan, defined by a lavish, overscaled architecture of self-protection, and marked by unassailable exclusivity, by habitable, hurricane-proof, high-rise works of art.

2005

49

Ten Better Places for a Football Stadium

The fight over the city's attempt to build a stadium on the West Side of Manhattan was never about football (other than the political kind) or, for that matter, the Olympics: it was over where to put the stadium and who should pay for it. The West Side project has now gone down in flames because the administration chose one of the worst places available and then asked us all to pay, largely (and transparently) in order to jack up real estate prices in the area for the usual cohort of salivating developers. Not only did construction depend on building a platform—an artificial ground—over an active rail yard, a proposition that would have added as much as a billion dollars to the cost of the project; access to the site is awful. Bringing the number seven subway from Port Authority would have cost additional billions. Automobile access from the West Side Highway or from the avenues would have been nightmarish. Structured parking would have been expensive and could never have allowed the tailgating so beloved by fans.

The enormous object also sought to extend the blocks-long barrier to the waterfront created by the Javits Convention Center; their combined lump would have obliterated connections to the Hudson River from the island and permanently disfigured the scale of the West Side. In choosing to move the site for the Olympic proposal to Queens as part of a new Shea Stadium, the city has been forced to settle on a site that makes sense for such a project. Indeed, Flushing is one of the best places in the city for a stadium from the perspectives of automobile and mass transit access, of potential synergies with surrounding athletic and public facilities, and of the minimal effort required to prepare the site for construction.

The wave of projected stadium-building in New York—for the Mets in Queens, the Yankees in the Bronx, the Nets in Brooklyn, as well as for the Olympic bid—is a symptom of a larger phenomenon. Sports stadia have come to be represented not just as premiere emblems of American civic culture (all hail the steroid-bloated millionaires at play!) but as drivers of urban economic revitalization. Here, they join that other instant panacea, gambling casinos, as leading markers of the decline of public planning, as the development paradigm shifts decisively to so-called public-private partnerships. What this means in practice is that private business—including such fatted enterprises as sports teams, gambling cartels, and office developers—are given giant public subsidies as an inducement either to come to or to remain in cities. Public benefit from such investments is allegedly returned in the form of jobs, taxes, or other more elusive outcomes of "development."

In New York this model has become the virtual default, and every major project proposed by the Bloomberg Administration—from Greenpoint to Ground Zero—follows it. Indeed, large-scale planning has shifted from the Department of City Planning—which has been reduced to an urban design role—to the office of the deputy mayor for economic development, whence the big "visions" come. These, predictably, tend to be calculated to enrich the Ratners, Silversteins, and Steinbrenners of the city, civic paragons who need to be bribed to stay in town to trickle-down on the public. Of course, it is a hopeless, evil ploy, another contribution to the yawning income gap, welfare for plutocrats who, it is hoped, will throw the rest of us a crumb or two.

In fact, study after study has demonstrated the folly of this approach. Virtually none of these subsidies is ever recouped, and such subventions for the powerful always rob the poor—those at the bottom of the list of municipal priorities, for whom housing, education, transportation, and healthcare are of somewhat greater importance than football. Moreover, the only good jobs generated by these projects are in construction (permanent jobs tend to be few in number, seasonal, and low-paying) but these would also be provided through building apartments, clinics, or subways. Indeed, these projects may be the least efficient expenditure of public funds imaginable, and one of the highest hypocrisies of the self-celebrating laissez-faire thieves who run the country.

Setting aside the fiscal foolishness of public support for this private enterprise, the city's initial proposal also relied on a distorted view of the nature of large sports facilities and their capacity to add amenity to cities. A football stadium is not a neighborhood-friendly object but an industrial one, and the criteria for siting such huge constructions resemble those for choosing a spot for a factory or power station (the proportions of which are perfectly reproduced in the stadium design proposed for the Jets). Receptacles for enormous numbers of people briefly gathered, stadia are assembly lines for intermittently pumping them in, pumping them full of beer, and pumping them out.

Because of this industrial character, huge stadia have little to offer directly to viable neighborhoods, although their energy does have the potential to benefit places that cannot be used otherwise, are derelict, or lack a community in place to suffer any adverse impacts. Likewise, a stadium can add élan, jobs, and secondary commerce to neighborhoods that are struggling for economic help (as a number of European stadiums have done). On the Far West Side—a neighborhood at the point of booming, as recently reported in the *New York Times*, football or no—the stadium would clearly have been a liability, reinforcing the large-scale developer-driven urbanism favored by the administration and thwarting the more intimate grain that viable neighborhoods demand and deserve.

Although Mayor Michael R. Bloomberg, Deputy Mayor Daniel Doctoroff, and the rest of the anything-for-the-Olympics crowd insistently represented the Far West Side as the only viable possibility (until it was voted down), at least ten other sites in the city would be far more advantageous and suitable for such an infusion of energy and cash, assuming that any public contribution for the greater good can be more persuasively argued. One of these is Flushing, and it may attract the Olympics yet. The odds, however, seem long for 2012, which suggests that there is time to consider additional sites for 2016, for the Jets, the Giants, and for the big public gatherings that are important to our collective life. Here are ten worth thinking about.

1. Hunts Point/Port Morris/Mott Haven

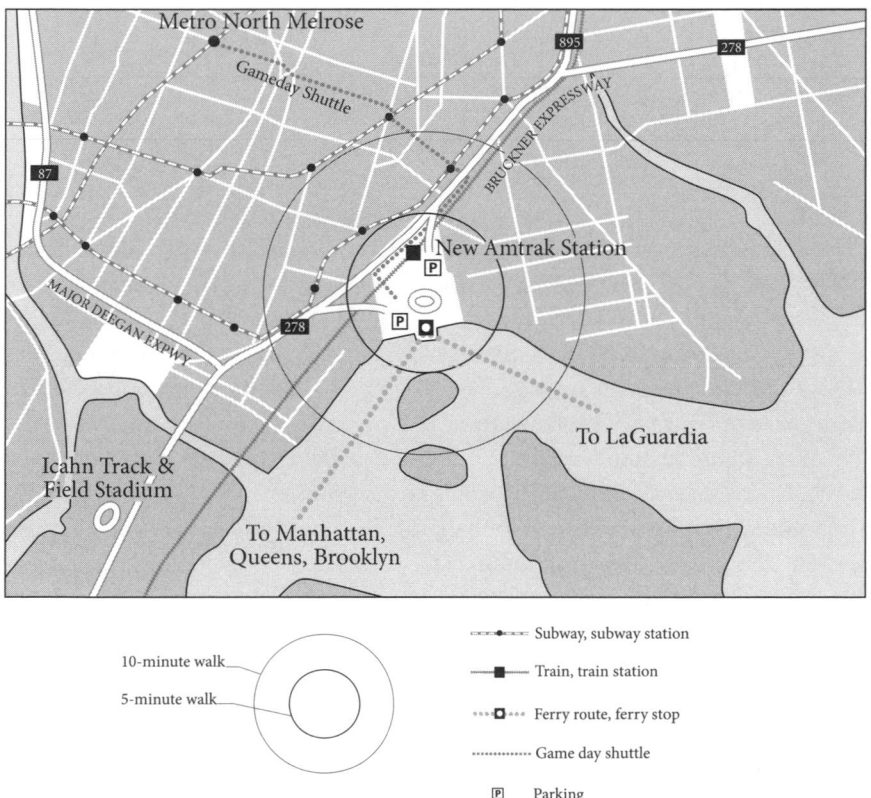

A huge site adjacent to the Bruckner Expressway (from which cars could be directed to parking without hitting the city grid), astride the Amtrak line, close to the water, and easily served by both subways and Metro-North, seems to be all plusses. Not simply would construction be minimally disruptive, it would provide a strong symbol for neighborhoods that are among the city's poorest. The easy relationship with the athletic facilities on Randall's Island would also be a positive should the city win the Olympics. A second potential site in the same vicinity is the nearby intermodal railyard opposite Manhattan.

2. Yankee Stadium/Bronx Terminal Market

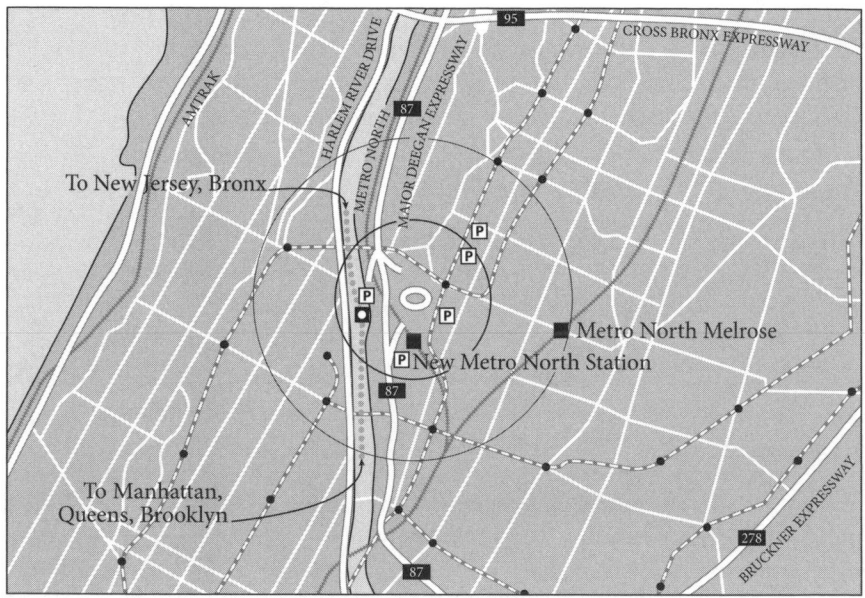

If Yankee Stadium is to be replaced on a nearby site while the house that Ruth built continues to host games, it is clear that the neighborhood has room for two stadia. Transportation is excellent, an infrastructure of bars and other support sites is profuse, and the prospect of the redevelopment of the Terminal Market and the Harlem River waterfront would add greatly to the area's atmosphere. A football stadium could also help anchor the revival of the central Bronx from the Concourse to the Hub. In addition, the relationship between new baseball and football stadiums would make the neighborhood one of the premiere sports sites on the planet.

3. Sunnyside Yards, Queens

A superb place for a stadium. As the city presses ahead with plans to create a fourth commercial core around Queens Plaza (to join midtown and downtown Manhattan and downtown Brooklyn), a stadium could form a powerful centerpiece, especially if it accreted a series of additional uses, such as housing and big-box retail. Transportation is excellent and is projected to improve with the construction of a multi-modal station under the Queens

Boulevard Viaduct. And with modest new construction, cars could be routed to parking directly from the LIE, parking that could also serve commuters into Manhattan. To be sure, additional costs would result from the need to build the stadium above the railyards, but the payback in convenience and non-disruption of neighborhood life would more than compensate.

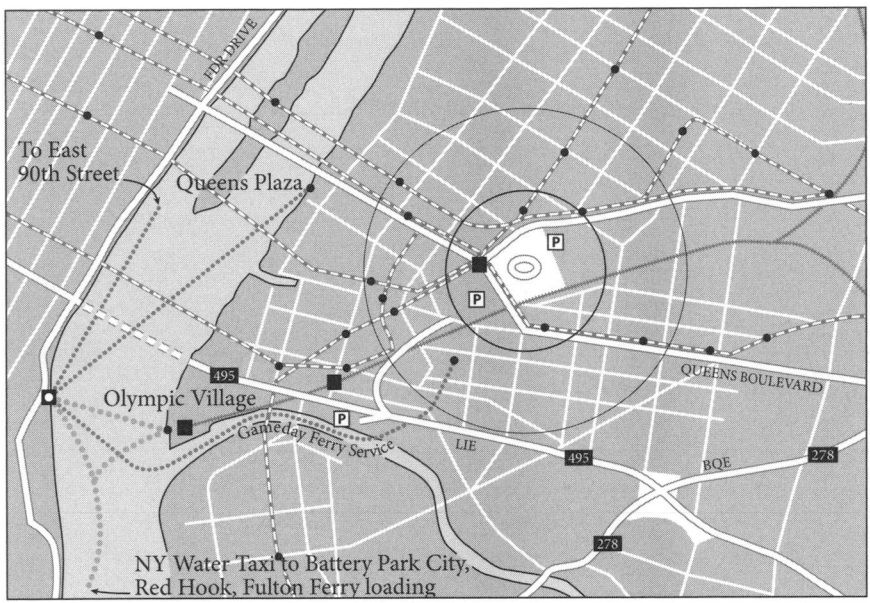

4. Brooklyn Navy Yard

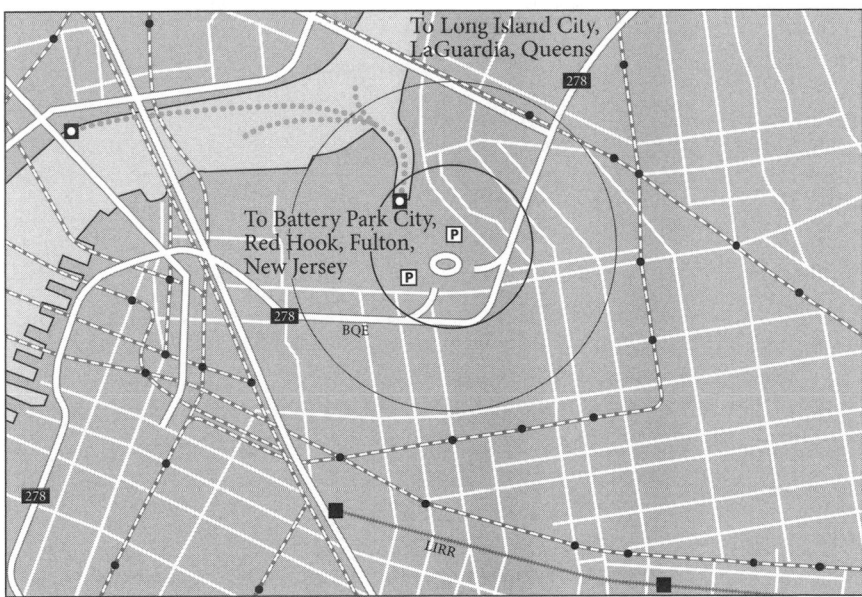

Although this site has obvious access issues, they are not materially worse than those on the West Side and are more cheaply solved. Like a number of potential locations, this one could be made to work by improved water access, by special shuttles from surrounding subways on game day, and by direct access to parking from the BQE. The site commands marvelous views of the Manhattan skyline, and the industrial character of the stadium would blend well with that of the Navy Yard.

5. Sunset Park/Bush Terminal, Brooklyn

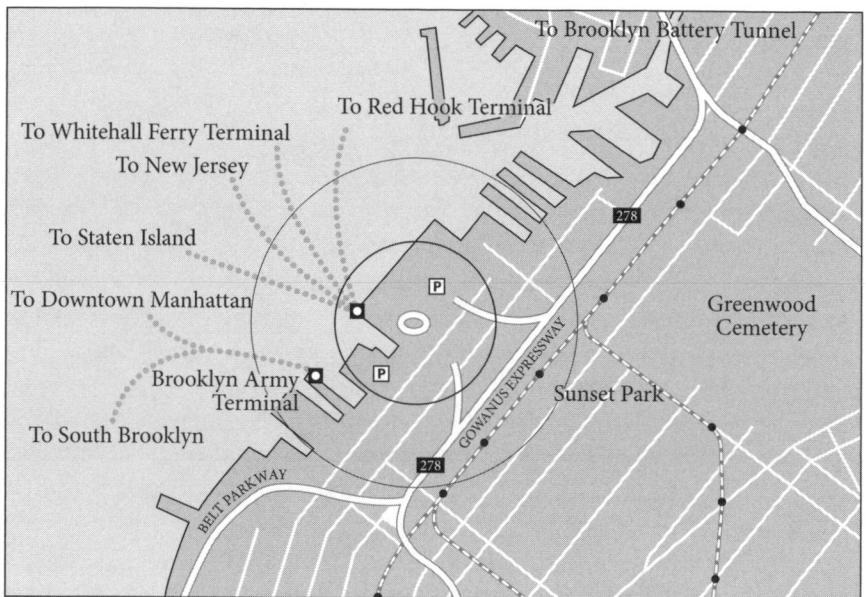

The largely derelict waterfront between the Bush Terminal and the harbor is an extremely tasty possibility. This is one of the last living industrial areas in the city—with over 33,000 jobs—and it could profit from what, in other circumstances, are negatives. The stadium's own industrial character is compatible with existing uses which also support a population of potential sports fans. Moreover, a stadium could help save Sunset Park from the likely fate of Greenpoint under the city's just announced re-zoning plans. Their implementation threatens existing neighborhood character both by their upmarket, over-scaled ambitions for the waterfront and through a mixed-use policy that is likely to see remaining industry displaced by gentrification. The Sunset Stadium—combined with a planned park, nearby cruise ship terminal, recycling plant, and automobile port—could create unique synergies.

6. Hunters Point, Queens

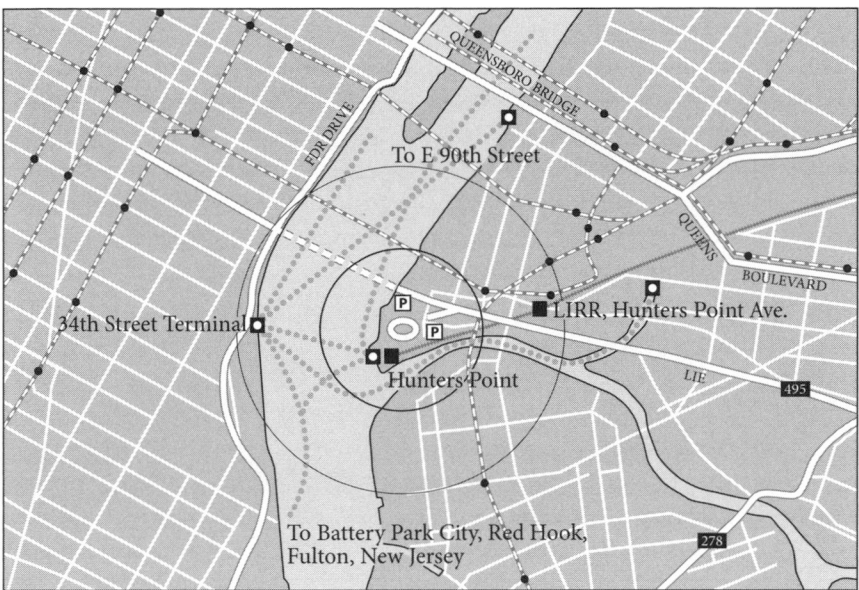

Assuming that New York is not the winner of the 2012 Olympics, the site of the proposed Olympic Village at the mouth of Newtown Creek would be very good. This generously scaled, unbuilt area would allow a stadium surrounded by housing and parks and could become a driver in the rehabilitation and remediation of the fetid Newtown Creek. Access is excellent, including all rail modes, water movement, and a possible direct link to the LIE and BQE. The site also enjoys the kind of elastic relationship to its surroundings that would allow such a huge facility to be both near enough for neighborhood access and far enough to be buffered against the risk of overwhelming what remains a relatively fine-textured community.

7. Flushing/Willets Point, Queens

Perhaps the most self-evident site of them all, this location next to the new Shea Stadium would plug into a tested area at the convergence of four freeways (perhaps the best served spot in the city for cars) and to the LIRR and subway stations already on site. Adding ferry service would benefit both the athletic complex and the burgeoning neighborhoods of Flushing and Corona, which are now isolated from each other. The convergence of stadium building, buoyant neighborhood growth, the reclamation of the Flushing River, and the relocation of the Willets Point automobile shops (perhaps within the site, perhaps within the stadium) make this a slam-dunk (if you'll forgive

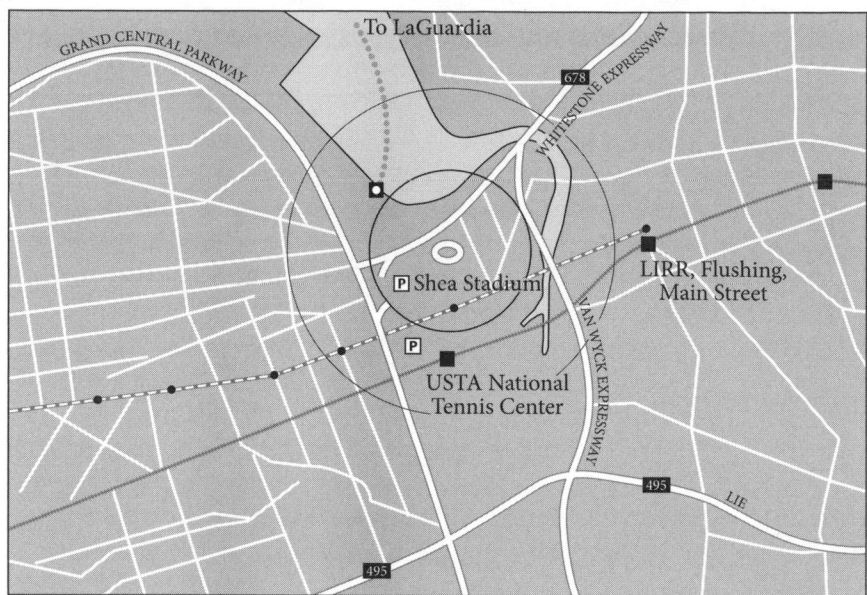

the metaphor). And, nearby LaGuardia would again make sense of a team called the "Jets."

8. Coney Island, Brooklyn

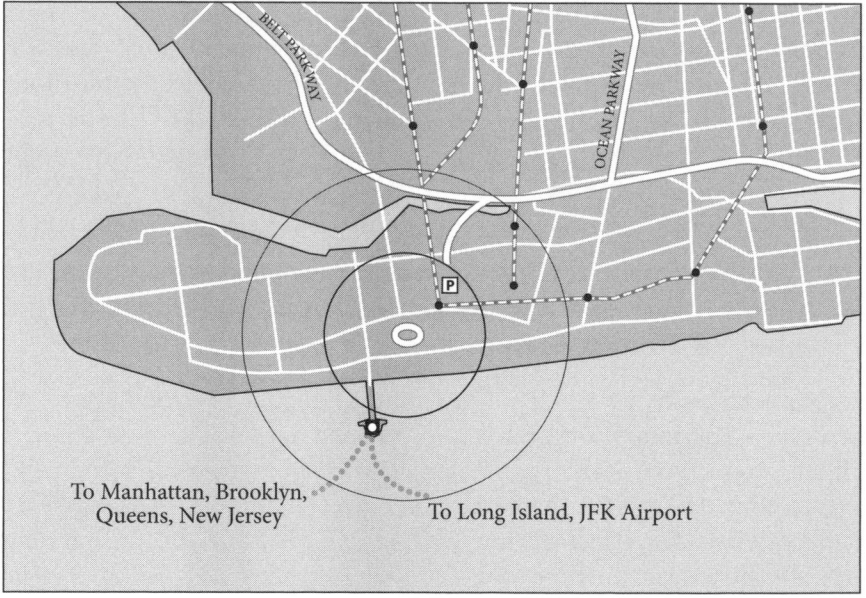

The revival of Coney Island has been announced for years but proceeds at a snail's pace. Some hopeful signs: Keyspan Park, a minor league baseball stadium, is enjoying great success; the city has just completed a massive renovation of the Stilwell Avenue subway station; and use of the beach is on the rise. Moreover, Coney Island is a virtual synonym for urban recreation, and locating the stadium adjacent to Keyspan Park, Astroland, and the beach would take it to the next level of attraction, luring other sports, entertainment, and related uses. The nearby Belt Parkway and ample opportunities for water transport round out a very pretty picture. And what more logical neighbor for Nathan's!

9. Fresh Kills, Staten Island

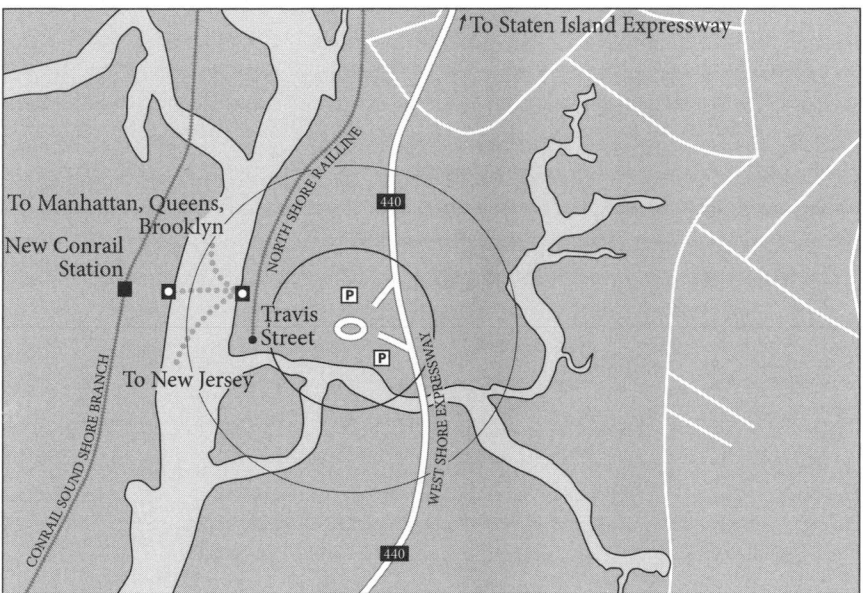

The closing of the municipal dump at Fresh Kills has been followed by a proposal for a park that takes a delicate, naturalizing view of our garbage Himalaya. But this landscape of industrial and residential waste is also ideal for a use that simply caps a portion of the site for stadium building and parking. There are obvious accessibility challenges, but both the Staten Island and West Shore Expressways skirt the site, Arthur Kill provides passage for water transit, a disused rail line leads to the St. George Ferry Terminal, and a link to the Perth Amboy/Elizabeth branch of the New Jersey Transit line on the opposite shore is easily imagined. So too is a stadium that sits within and utilizes our municipal mountains.

10. Governors Island

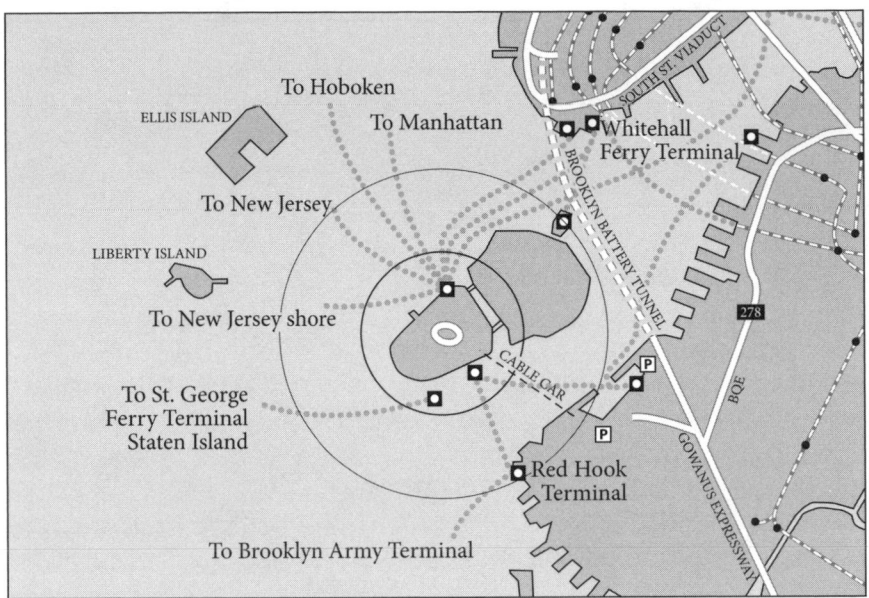

Simultaneously unlikely and perfect, Governors Island currently languishes in indecision, awaiting its big idea. Perhaps it can accommodate two. The island itself embodies two conditions: the original "natural" island as it existed until the beginning of the twentieth century and its large southern extension, built from fill excavated during the construction of the subway. By re-dividing the island into northern and southern islands, the historic northern half could become an extension of the space-challenged United Nations, the perfect site for the pursuits of peace. Appropriately isolated, the southern island would be a glorious and secure site for mass gatherings and big games. The challenge of getting there could also be turned to advantage. Unless a pedestrian bridge or tramway were built from Red Hook (not a completely illogical pair of possibilities), all access would be from the water. But this is less daunting than it otherwise seems. To begin, Governors Island is very close to both Manhattan—with its existing infrastructure of ferry terminals—and Brooklyn, with its capacity to lead cars from the Battery Tunnel and the BQE or Gowanus Expressway directly to shore-side parking. Moreover, given that football is played on Sundays—when service on the huge Staten Island ferries is reduced—a dedicated boat or two making round trips from South Ferry could efficiently deliver very large numbers of people to the island in minutes. Finally, the proximity of the stadium to the Statue of Liberty raises the prospect of a view of that great symbol through the uprights of another, from the new Freedom Bowl, America's stadium.

Stadium Scorecard

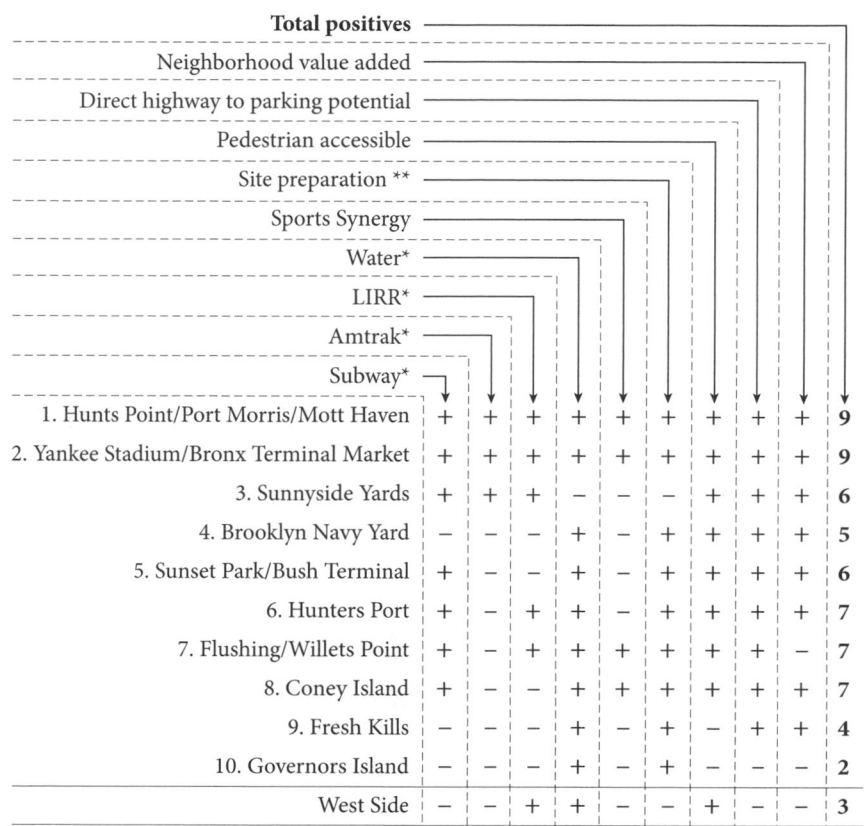

Stadium Scorecard

	Subway*	Amtrak*	LIRR*	Water*	Sports Synergy	Site preparation **	Pedestrian accessible	Direct highway to parking potential	Neighborhood value added	Total positives
1. Hunts Point/Port Morris/Mott Haven	+	+	+	+	+	+	+	+	+	9
2. Yankee Stadium/Bronx Terminal Market	+	+	+	+	+	+	+	+	+	9
3. Sunnyside Yards	+	+	+	−	−	−	+	+	+	6
4. Brooklyn Navy Yard	−	−	−	+	−	+	+	+	+	5
5. Sunset Park/Bush Terminal	+	−	−	+	−	+	+	+	+	6
6. Hunters Port	+	−	+	+	−	+	+	+	+	7
7. Flushing/Willets Point	+	−	+	+	+	+	+	+	−	7
8. Coney Island	+	−	−	+	+	+	+	+	+	7
9. Fresh Kills	−	−	−	+	−	+	−	+	+	4
10. Governors Island	−	−	−	+	−	+	−	−	−	2
West Side	−	−	+	+	−	−	+	−	−	3

*10 minute walk   ** Indicates special site work is required (e.g. rail platform)*

2005

50

Finding a Dramatic Home
for a Political Football

After years of promoting a West Side stadium for football and the Olympics, the Bloomberg administration—stung by the defeat of its plan in Albany—quickly regrouped and proposed to build in Flushing Meadows, Queens, piggybacking an Olympic facility on a new Shea Stadium for the Mets. The new site is vastly superior in practically every way: public transportation connections, automobile access, and adjacency to other sporting venues. And, unlike the West Side location, which would have required construction at public expense of a huge platform over an active rail yard, the Queens site is largely parking lots. Mayor Bloomberg was wistful in giving up the West Side, however, claiming that his tenacity in defense of the site was largely motivated by its spectacular relationship to the Manhattan skyline, visual drama he thought apt for the Olympics. While the location was ridiculous from virtually every other perspective, this idea was not. An honorific gathering place for large-scale public events—such as the Olympics, football, rock concerts, political rallies—does suggest a compelling locale. This city offers no site more suited to the task than Governor's Island. Sitting in the middle of the harbor opposite the Lower Manhattan skyline, East River bridges, the Statue of Liberty, and Ellis Island, the former military base (holding, among other things, two spectacular War of 1812–vintage fortresses) awaits a new use and is currently in the midst of a developer-focused Requests-for-Expressions-of-Interest process. This narrow, real estate–driven approach is depressing. The city has certain assets of such transcendent value that ideas of use must precede financial strategies to realize them.

A Double-Island Design

After conducting an analysis of ten alternative sites for the proposed stadium, my studio reached a double conclusion: the Flushing site is the most logical from the point of view of existing infrastructure, but Governor's Island is the most spectacular. And so we decided to work on a scheme to see what

© Michael Sorkin Studio

a harbor stadium there might look like. The first decision was to split the island in two with a new canal. This is not unprecedented. Until the early twentieth century, the island was approximately one-third its present size. It grew only when contractors dumped fill from the excavation of the IRT subway line. As a result, all of the island's historic architecture lies on its older, northern section, and this would remain in our scheme.

The double-island configuration accommodates a double use, and our proposal calls for the stadium, a public park, and a marina on the southern island and a United Nations enclave on the northern one, with the conversion of the existing Fort Jay into a "diplomatic arena," a location for intense negotiations over the beating of swords into plowshares. This doubling into an island of free assembly and an island of peace is intended to carry apt symbolic weight. Indeed, given the floundering plans for Ground Zero and the largely commercial program proposed for it, these uses seemed especially meaningful to both time and place. In analyzing the suitability of the site for large-scale gatherings, the primary issue is that of transportation; the island is currently accessible only by water. In many ways, this is crucial to the compelling character of the place, which stands dramatically apart from the city. A visit takes one to another world of greenery, views, and breezes—a purely pedestrian realm. This isolation has an additional useful aspect in assuring the security of the site, an issue that is inescapable for both of the intended uses. For everyday purposes, existing docks and ferry systems are essentially adequate, with only small modifications needed to allow berthing and drop-offs on both islands and to provide dedicated service to UN headquarters in Manhattan. The major traffic generated by games and events—which might attract as many as 70,000 people—would require additional means of access. Primary among these would be the construction of new slips capable of docking the existing Staten Island ferry, which sails across a narrow channel from South Ferry at the southern tip of Manhattan. Deployed as a shuttle on game days (typically on the weekend, when the ferry schedule is dramatically reduced), these huge vessels could easily transport the necessary numbers in an hour. This movement might be further assisted by the construction of a pedestrian bridge over Buttermilk Channel to Red Hook in Brooklyn, where parking and bus connections could be provided. And new lots here would logically network with others—in New Jersey, Flushing, Staten Island—and link to Governors Island via smaller ferries.

© Michael Sorkin Studio

Energy Independence

The stadium itself would be located within a craterlike earth berm, constructed from the fill re-excavated to form the canal. Covered in greenery, the berm would minimize the impact of such a large piece of architecture in this very visible place, blending it with the parks that would surround it. The dominant visual element would be a large wind farm that would form a stately and kinetic field of objects. Joined with a system of tidal generators in adjacent Buttermilk Channel, these windmills would form a system robust enough to supply all the energy for the two islands. This assertion of complete energy independence is intended not simply to attenuate demands on an overloaded system, but to address one of the principal factors in America's international political crisis. Now that the International Olympic Committee has selected London to host the 2012 games, what better way of priming the pump for New York's 2016 bid than by offering this utterly spectacular site? And the Jets still need a home.

2005

51

The Great Mall of New York

All cities laminate many models of spatial organization and use. Inscribed within New York are fragments of medieval, Georgian, industrial, suburban, modernist, City Beautiful, and other urban patterns that, meeting the grid and its exceptions, coalesce to ground the contemporary city. These spatial arrangements are activated by an even greater range of styles of use and inhabitation that power New York's dynamism and self-transforming energy. A constant stream of immigrants—people and ideas—and their shifting habits and desires takes the physical defaults with which they are confronted and morphs them to accommodate their skills, ambitions, and need for the familiar. The market—whether the speculative gyre of real estate that drives so much of the local economy, the long-wave shift from production to service employment, or the growing dominance of globalized retail operations that increasingly mark every city—subjects New York to constant revision to accommodate the insatiable needs of capital.

Is the city growing suburban? Perhaps. But searching for the evidence requires some sense of what it means to *be* suburban, and clearly demands proof beyond the odd McMansion in Queens or shopping mall in Manhattan: the city has always thrived on anomaly. Widespread anxiety about suburbanization suggests bigger fears, that some annihilating principle threatens to sweep across our protective rivers and torque the thick and sociable city—with its sacred architectures and comforting rituals—into something we no longer recognize. This portrait of the city at risk presupposes a particular idea of suburbanism. These suburbs are not the symbiotic dependencies of the street-car era, nor the genteel Ardens in Westchester and Fairfield that continue to serve as ruling-class dormitories, points on the power triangle of Yale, Wall Street, and New Canaan. Nor is the threatening suburbia that of the deteriorating "inner ring," a zone lapsing into a syndrome long-associated with the city itself, the complex of unemployment, drug-use, bad schools, collapsing infrastructure, and failing public facilities—everything the middle class once fled the city to escape.

Rather, these dangerous suburbs are more recent, part of a toxic compound of spatial and cultural forces that afflict all the space of the contemporary environment. Such suburbs originated in the post-war years, the result of the most deliberate project of national redesign since the imposition of the Jeffersonian grid. Like that universalizing instrument, postwar suburbia has been a force for homogeneity masquerading as choice. In the endlessly (but trivially) recombinant brandscape that has become America's emblematic pattern of settlement, daily life is designed to maximize consumption—of goods, of time, of energy, of processed information. And so we produce the sprawl of Orange County or Atlanta, those dream-worlds of super-sized houses, super-sized cars, super-sized people, super-sized habits of getting and spending. Lurking darkly in the ideological background is the panoply of secular humanist anxieties, the Republicanism, the religiosity, the tightly bound psychopathologies that produce Columbine, Jon Benet Ramsey, and the bland violence of the American nightmare. Bush country.

What are the origins of this suspect place? The instruments that created and organized this sprawling territory were spatial, financial, and political. The paradigm of the individual house in an individual yard on a street of identical yards and houses was multiply engrained in the culture. The fantasy of ownership, historic marker of enfranchised citizenship and traditional home of the American dream, became postwar policy via the easy availability of FHA loans to (white) veterans, accelerated depreciation for suburban businesses, gigantic subsidies for infrastructure (led by the vast project to construct the interstates, their cloverleaf access points managing suburban space with the precision of the mile grid), and by the Manichean counterpoise of city and suburb with greenfield rancheros for the anointed classes and urban renewal public housing complexes for the noisome, mis-colored poor.

These suburbs were also the operating system for the radically reconfigured style of consumption that now dominates world culture. In the postwar suburb, everything to be had was taken into the realm of mass consumption, re-modeled as a consumer good, rolled out with the maniacal replicability of our wartime production of the arsenal of democracy, cars replacing tanks, split-levels, high altitude bombers. The animating, transitional object was the automobile, the key for unlocking the system as a whole: the suburbs simply could not be inhabited without a car at each domestic unit's disposal, and the automobile was the touchstone of the "what's good for General Motors" mentality that had—since the high Fordist era—ratcheted up the scale and intensity of the social necessity of things. The need for multiple cars, the meaningless, style-driven, keeping-up-with-the-Joneses, incitements to trade in last year's for this year's version, and the willful profligacy of gas-guzzling, long-distance driving, created a sector of expenditure that represented a new and habituating idea of consumer necessity.

The automobile system permitted and modeled a similar mass-market approach to spatial products. Here, the paradigms are Levittown, the strip, and the shopping mall. The ticky-tacky, all-look-the-same boxes of sprawling suburbs were simply real estate iterations of production and marketing techniques perfected in the automobile industry. The same superficial inflections of difference, the same segmentations of the market with its pressure to constantly move up, the same potlatch of energy and spatial consumption, the same branded aura, and the same predication in and reinforcement of nuclear family, woman-at-home lifestyles, moved both products and linked them inextricably. Where once mobility had been a leveler—a social encounter on foot or in a streetcar—movement now atomized, accelerating the podification of the American subject, isolated in a two-thousand-pound prosthesis, breathing refreshed air, radio on.

Of course, the big-ticket items could only function via a logistics chain that constantly replenished, repaired, maintained, and improved them. This produced two characteristic sites of consumption, the strip and the mall, both of which grew from precedented formats, greatly attenuated by their adaptation to automotive culture. The strip was the logical scaling up of Main Street to accommodate the speed and habits of shoppers in cars, calibrated to quick in-and-out trips for gas, groceries, fast food. The mall—from its initial incarnation as shopping center to it apotheosis in the universal big-box of Wal-Mart—offered a centralized, park-once, shop-many-times format that, like hub-and-spoke air transit, offered the icy dogmatism of an efficient diagram. In both of these formats, the epistemological glue was provided by the brand, whether in the institutional semiotics of K-Mart, Costco, Esso, McDonald's, Taco Bell or Chuck E. Cheese, or in the universally branded (and bar-coded) goods on offer within—Tide, Crest, Green Giant, Cheerios, Martha, Calvin, Nike, Panasonic, Sony—with their endlessly disciplined uniformity and "quality." This suburban mode of consumption was driven by the endless transfer in an infinite stream of Chevys, Buicks, Hondas, and Fords of branded goods from these centralized emporia to the waiting closets, freezers, walls, and garages of home—the penultimate link on the global logistics chain that ends in Alpine landfills.

New Yorkers are not exactly slouches in the consumption department and we are, like many suburbanites, crippled and confined by a distorted economics of habitat. For many in the city, however, the suburban horizon continues to reflect a dream world of spacious houses, clean streets, and cheap shopping. Indeed, surprising numbers of the city's poorest citizens make their way—by car-pool and bus—to outlying malls to enjoy their low prices, disciplined sociability, and one-stop convenience.

While city policy continues to vigorously resist the construction of big-box stores within residential and commercial neighborhoods, the debate over their benefits is in no way resolved. Questions of displacement of local businesses, of traffic generation, of out-of-scale building, of the hegemony of the corporate way of doing business, of upstream consequences for workers in sweatshops abroad, affect cities and suburbs alike. Many New Yorkers take comfort in the apparent fact that these places have yet to arrive in serious numbers, at least not in their original suburban form.

And yet they have found their own way in. The city has been infused with a nearly ubiquitous infrastructure of multinational commerce, which has, to a remarkable degree, fitted itself to existing commercial settings, spatial scales, and ethnic and class organization. Like the suburbs, we are awash in McDonald's, Starbucks, Gaps, Staples, Old Navies, Blockbusters, KFCs, Toys R Us, and other familiar multinational retailers. Indeed, our native retailers—from Bloomingdale's to Barnes and Noble—are themselves now part of the portfolios of corporations larger still. Far from proving resistant to this commercial rationalization, its penetration of the city has been greatly enabled by historic spatial formats that have proved remarkably adaptable, and by a real estate market that constantly ratchets prices upward, creating a legendarily hostile environment for small and low-margin businesses in general. The issue for the city is thus whether the literal content of these places is so inimical to traditional urban styles of commerce and sociability that the city is itself transformed in some fundamental and irreversible way. The picture in Manhattan is not promising, as the following cases suggest.

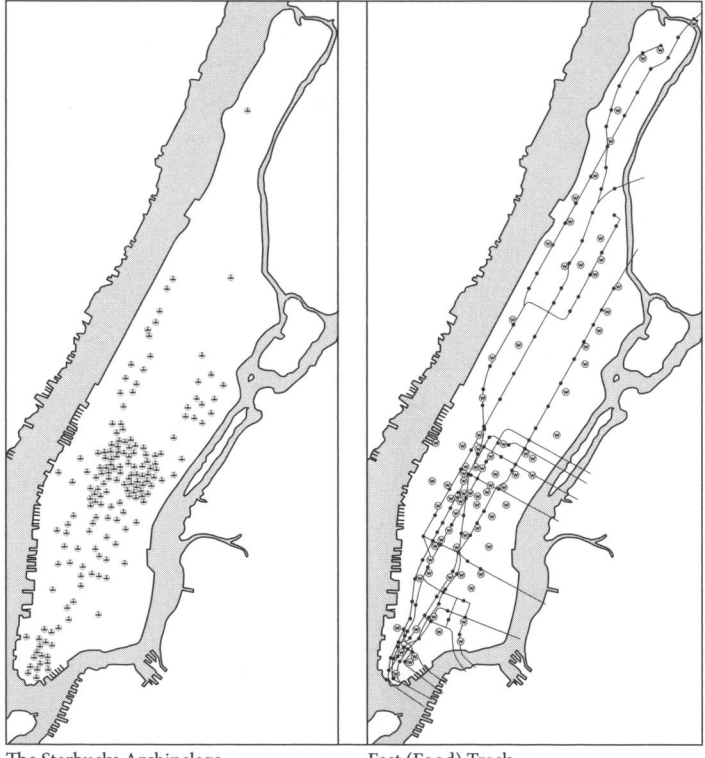

The Starbucks Archipelago   Fast (Food) Track

Finding Fast Food

The location formula for fast food outlets is constant for cities and suburbs: traffic. Just as suburban branches of McDonald's are attracted to strips, malls, and highway interchanges, their urban relations are closely correlated with subway stations and high-volume institutions. Reflecting the station density of the subway itself, this leads to a predictable clumping in business and shopping districts. There is, however, an egalitarian quality to the borough-wide pattern, with a relatively evenly spaced distribution of outlets in the poorer neighborhoods of upper Manhattan. While consumption behavior may vary according to income and other social factors, the locational pattern in Manhattan does not correlate with either poverty or obesity. The ubiquity of these outlets reflects a more crucial pervasiveness, the universal presence of television, the main instrument for the incitement of structured consumption. Television is the too little acknowledged enabler of suburban life, a cultural point source that paradoxically both immobilizes leisure activity in couch-potato mode, while at the same time converting it to a school for the more energetic pattern of a daily life focused on shopping. Television is the great elider of city and suburb, creating spatial equivalence for every living room and priming the shopping reflex to be activated by remorselessly encoded signals. Have it your way. Freedom of choice. At McDonald's.

1	Taco Bell	50	Starbucks
2	McDonald's	51	Cingular
3	KFC	52	Carver
4	Subway	53	Chase
5	Amalgamated Bank	54	T Mobile
6	C Town	55	Rite Aid
7	Carver	56	Body Shop
8	Dunkin Donuts	57	Apple Bank
9	Domino's Pizza	58	Pathmark
10	McDonald's	59	Sleepy's
11	Chase	60	Washington Mutual
12	Old Navy	61	Popeye's
13	Magic Johnson Theater	62	DR
14	Commerce Bank	63	The Children's Place
15	Popeye's	64	McDonald's
16	Radio Shack	65	Payless Shoes
17	KFC	66	Cingular
18	Rite Aid	67	Bank of America
19	North Fork Bank	68	Radio Shack
20	Foot Locker		
21	Lane Bryant		
22	The Children's Place		
23	Champs		
24	White Castle		
25	Aerosoles		
26	DR		
27	Subway		
28	Apollo Theater		
29	Banco Popular		
30	McDonald's		
31	Bank of America		
32	Citi		
33	Sprint		
34	Verizon		
35	Studio Museum		
36	Burger King		
37	H&M		
38	Blockbuster		
39	Staples		
40	Planet Fitness		
41	Washington Mutual		
42	CVS Pharmacy		
43	Dunkin Donuts		
44	Subway		
45	Con Edison		
46	H&R Block		
47	Washington Mutual		
48	Taco Bell		
49	Pizza Hut		

Labels on map: Broadway, Frederick Douglass BLVD, Lenox Ave, Lexington Ave

The Starbucks Archipelago

The distribution—and numbers—of Starbucks correspond closely to the pattern established by McDonald's. There is a close relationship between Starbucks and subway stations, as well the same attraction for major institutional locations—hospitals, universities, and so on. However, there is a dramatic absence of Starbucks in northern Manhattan, with only four locations north of 110th Street (two of these adjoin Columbia University). Unlike McDonald's, Starbucks is a close predictor of neighborhood income. Nor is the chain café phenomenon exactly a fresh intrusion: although product and price point differ, Starbucks joins an historic pattern—notably the Chock Full O'Nuts brand—that has legs as an urban phenomenon. Unlike its aggressive down-market competitor, Dunkin' Donuts, Starbucks represents more than a necessary jolt of caffeine stimulation: it carries an aura of "lifestyle," an invidious pre-packaged formula of self-authentication. Part of the genius of the Starbucks brand is its suburbanization of a quintessentially urban phenomenon—the coffee house—and its reinscription in the city as a generic, branded commodity. While I am agnostic about the product, the distribution of Starbucks maps the push of uniformity and the fetish of universal commodities that represent the suburbanization of everything.

The 125th Street Mall

One-Hundred and Twenty-Fifth Street is the main street of Harlem and, by extension, of African America. It is the historic home of cultural institutions like the Apollo Theater and the Studio Museum, and has long held a mix of small shops and street vendors aimed at a local clientele. Over the years, control of commerce on 125th Street by white and Asian, non-neighborhood owners has been the subject of considerable contention, even violence. Today, the situation has changed dramatically. As the gentrification of Harlem proceeds at a rapid clip, the character of 125th Street has itself been transformed, marked by the brisk penetration by multinational chains. Indeed, 125th Street has effectively become the urban analogue to a suburban mall, cleansed of locality. Anchored at one end by a multiplex theater in a building that also houses several national chain stores and at the other by a major supermarket (a considerable rarity in Manhattan), the street's once singular, if frayed, character is rapidly tipping into the generic. The politics of this transformation are vexed. While the global chains are an even more incendiary accelerant for the departure of local shops, driving out small-scale retailers and sending real estate prices skyrocketing, they also constitute a form of acknowledgement for a community long ghettoized and neglected, a kind of welcome into a larger community. The complicated relationship between brand and identity—which plagues us all—has, as is widely noted, become ingrained in the consumption habits of African-American youth. While this is not the place to deconstruct the importance of Tommy Hilfiger and Nike to the self-definition and social currency of this community, it is clear that this is a decidedly "suburban" phenomenon, part of a more general convergence of national values of aspirational consumption. As can be seen all over the city, the shopping mall—which has the street as its prototype—simply re-adapts itself to its originating source. With subway stops in the position of mall entrances, 125th Street is seamlessly initiated into the multinational system.

Vegas Fifth Avenue

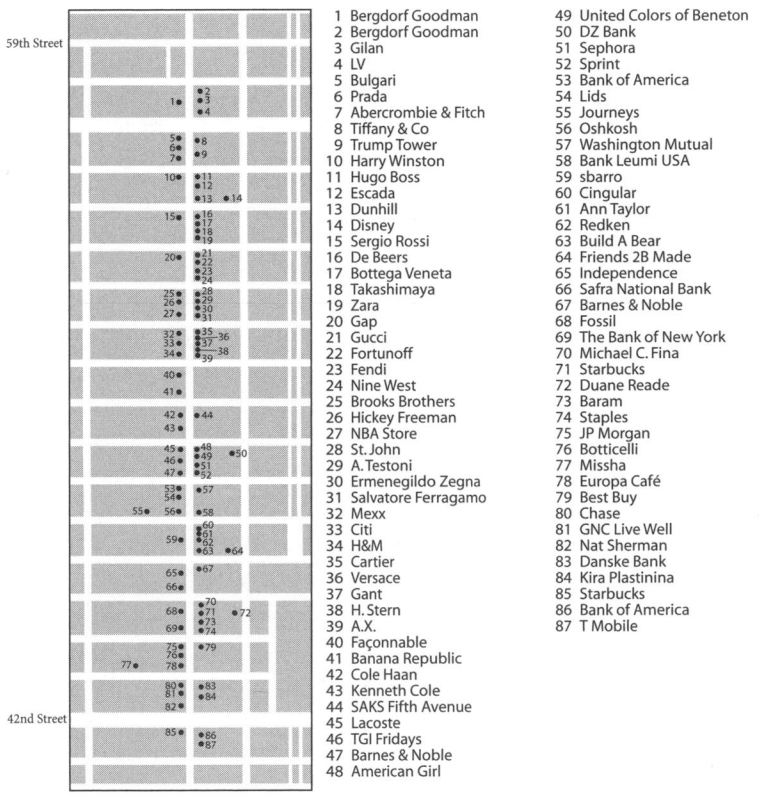

1 Bergdorf Goodman	49 United Colors of Beneton
2 Bergdorf Goodman	50 DZ Bank
3 Gilan	51 Sephora
4 LV	52 Sprint
5 Bulgari	53 Bank of America
6 Prada	54 Lids
7 Abercrombie & Fitch	55 Journeys
8 Tiffany & Co	56 Oshkosh
9 Trump Tower	57 Washington Mutual
10 Harry Winston	58 Bank Leumi USA
11 Hugo Boss	59 sbarro
12 Escada	60 Cingular
13 Dunhill	61 Ann Taylor
14 Disney	62 Redken
15 Sergio Rossi	63 Build A Bear
16 De Beers	64 Friends 2B Made
17 Bottega Veneta	65 Independence
18 Takashimaya	66 Safra National Bank
19 Zara	67 Barnes & Noble
20 Gap	68 Fossil
21 Gucci	69 The Bank of New York
22 Fortunoff	70 Michael C. Fina
23 Fendi	71 Starbucks
24 Nine West	72 Duane Reade
25 Brooks Brothers	73 Baram
26 Hickey Freeman	74 Staples
27 NBA Store	75 JP Morgan
28 St. John	76 Botticelli
29 A. Testoni	77 Missha
30 Ermenegildo Zegna	78 Europa Café
31 Salvatore Ferragamo	79 Best Buy
32 Mexx	80 Chase
33 Citi	81 GNC Live Well
34 H&M	82 Nat Sherman
35 Cartier	83 Danske Bank
36 Versace	84 Kira Plastinina
37 Gant	85 Starbucks
38 H. Stern	86 Bank of America
39 A.X.	87 T Mobile
40 Façonnable	
41 Banana Republic	
42 Cole Haan	
43 Kenneth Cole	
44 SAKS Fifth Avenue	
45 Lacoste	
46 TGI Fridays	
47 Barnes & Noble	
48 American Girl	

A much-observed marketing trend is the emergence of "experience retail," which amounts to the merger of shopping and entertainment in explicit, "themed" fashion. Themed retail is a strategy for extending the authority of the brand by taking its meanings into ever more diffuse territories of association, a displacement of object by aura. The origins of experience retail are complex, but can certainly be associated, in the near term, with the creative, imaginative geography of the theme park and, in the longer term, with the rise of the larger social category of luxury within the context of the

mobile aspirations of bourgeois culture. Much of midtown Manhattan—
the experiential ground zero for New York tourism—has been co-opted as
the locus for a set of "destination" stores that might be found in Las Vegas,
Orlando, or Dubai. These include the Disney Store, the Warner Brothers
Store, the NBA Store, the NBC Store, the Museum of Modern Art Store,
the Metropolitan Museum Store, and Planet Hollywood, as well as a plethora of high-end retail chains.

The local genius of cities lies in their marshalling of a wide diversity of
experiences and in the particular patterns with which these experiences are
deployed. Every city represents a compendium of places, and the pleasure of the city lies in both the special qualities of neighborhoods and the
circulation between their differences. The mosaic of New York has long
been a particularly dynamic and variegated instance of the energy of difference, and the array of its distinctive places—Harlem, Chinatown, Little
Italy, Greenwich Village, the Lower East Side, Atlantic Avenue, Flushing,
etc.—has derived from self-organizing aspects of each of these localities
and their embodiment of the cultural communities that make up the city.
They remain, nevertheless, distinctly of New York, inhabiting a range of
physical space and architectural types that is specific to the city, adapting
imported cultural patterns to native spatial typologies.

If suburbanization—or globalization—threatens the city, the main
danger comes not from the physical side of the equation, the introduction
of specific alien architectures from suburbia—big boxes, ranch houses,
shopping malls, and so on—but from the content side, which has proved
adaptable enough to remain relatively independent of the constraints of
its setting. To be sure, Trump Tower and the Time-Warner Center are
interiorized malls, but are not effectively different from traditional urban
department stores, themselves frequently organized into a series of
designer boutiques. The issue, rather, is the uniformity of content—the
same Sephora, Armani, Victoria's Secret, Sharper Image, and Talbot's as
anywhere else on the planet.

Incredible amounts of ink have been expended—pro and con—on the
transformation of Times Square into a corporate amusement park, particularly the concessionary arrangement that made a once-raunchy block of
42nd Street into a Disney fiefdom awash with franchised fun. Here is the
Disney effect succinctly achieved. As at the Disneylands themselves, each
entered through a generic "Main Street" housing a variety of multinational
establishments, the trick is to house an identical content behind a hollow
locality. Thus Fifth Avenue—the city's premier retail address—remains
stately, and 42nd Street glitters with neon extravagance, even as each is
stripped of its meaningful particulars. De-localized in content, Manhattan's
sites are free for promiscuous global recombination, to reappear in Beijing
or Vegas or LA or anywhere. It isn't that the city is becoming *physically*
suburban, simply that it's becoming the same as everyplace else.

The Return of the Ladies Mile

By the years following the Civil War, the blocks of Broadway from 14th Street to 23rd Street had come to be the city's premier high-end shopping district, known as the "Ladies Mile," a predecessor of Fifth Avenue's current status. Enabled by the invention of the "safe" space of the department store, by a solidified middle class and its creation of women's leisure and the shifting mores that offered them greater independence, New York underwent a shopping revolution. The result was this tight district, continuously lined by department stores and other dry-goods shops. This district was itself mobile, having been first established further downtown and later migrating to midtown, reflecting both the northward movement of population and the energetic real estate speculation that has always been the core driver of spatial location in the city.

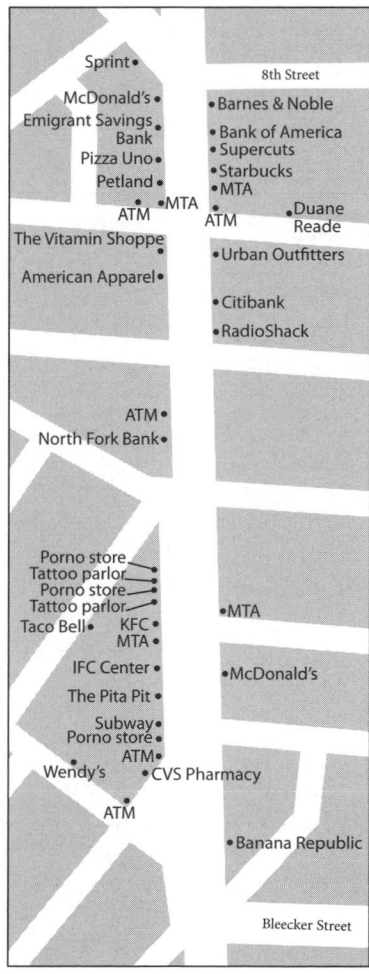

Toward the end of the century, as department stores first reached their maximum scale and as an elevated rail-line was constructed on Sixth Avenue, a second retail spine grew to the west of Ladies Mile, also between 14th and 23rd Streets. This was lined with enormous, marvelously designed department stores, many a full block long, and the growth of this complex paralleled a decline in the Ladies Mile, squeezed out by the development of skyscraper office buildings, the presence of sweatshops with their "unfashionable" workers, the continued northern migration of the better classes, and the competition from the dramatic growth of retail into ever larger establishments. A similar fate was to befall the department stores of Sixth Avenue in turn, as the major emporia—like Macy's, Altman's, and Lord & Taylor—built new stores further uptown.

Two proto-suburban organizational patterns are clearly visible in this nineteenth-century story. The Ladies Mile was anchored at either end by Union Square and Madison Square, themselves surrounded by commercial activity. If the scale was greater, the dumbbell *parti* closely resembles the classic organization of the suburban shopping mall developed a century later: the idea of a back-and-forth circulation induced by strong magnets is mall design writ. Likewise, the finitude of classic shopping streets—in both their small-town and big-city incarnations—reflects the combined demands of patience, fatigue, and variety. Indeed, the parallel development of street-based shopping and its interiorized variant has been in play for centuries. Shopping malls *avant la lettre* are surely visible in the arcades of Paris, London, or Milan, in the souks of the Arab world, in covered market halls, and a variety of other architectural armatures.

Both the Ladies Mile and Sixth Avenue reflect an organization characteristic of suburban malls, their careful response to market segmentation. This division into up- and down-market malls, high- and low-rent shopping streets, and upscale and downscale stores, is a fact of shopping that transcends spatiality and adapts with ease to a wide variety of formats. Finally, the finite duration of the commercial lives of the Ladies Mile and its Sixth Avenue double have a comparable life in the suburbs. Witness current concerns with the proliferation of "dead malls" and the devastating comings and goings of Wal-Mart in the pursuit of superior locational demographics and better taxation and subsidy deals. The permanence of commercial arrangements is not a product of sentiment, but the bottom line.

In the past decade, the old department stores of Sixth Avenue, long considered dysfunctional for most contemporary uses, have undergone a remarkable revival. Preserved from demolition by landmarks designation, inefficient for conversion to residential use, and demandingly large, these buildings were long thought to be dinosaurs, immune to re-use. But then the suburbs arrived. In a short span of years, the district has been revived as a shopping nexus, now populated by the ranks of global retail. Bed, Bath, and Beyond, Old Navy, Barnes and Noble, Staples, Filene's Basement, the whole panoply of mid-range mall standbys. Is this a sign of suburbanization or simply the return of a phenomenon of distinctly urban origin? Both, probably. Sixth Avenue is newly lively, thronged with pedestrians, and this activity certainly helps local shops on adjacent streets, and the old department store spaces are again in use. Perhaps this is the best we can hope for.

There Goes the Neighborhood

My own block lies in the center of Greenwich Village, quirky, historic bohemia, dense with students, tenaciously liberal, preservation obsessed, and scaled for intimacy and chance encounter. This romantic view, however, is belied by certain facts on the ground. I live near the West Fourth Street subway station—a major transfer point which runs like a grotty, detached, shop-less mall under Sixth Avenue—ten blocks south of the reborn retail corridor described above. Like 125th Street, a thoroughfare that was once distinguished by the particulars of its locality is now a strangely (contested) mix of multinational franchises and more local businesses. To be sure, Sixth Avenue is not a local street but a highly trafficked north-south axis. Moreover, the Village remains an entertainment destination for a very wide variety of people, and houses a huge number of students, a population of temporarily limited means.

The blocks of Sixth Avenue near me represent an extremely fluid intersection between a great number of interests which range from the most distinct to the most generic—a vivid seam between suburban homogeneity and urban resistance. Here, I think, is encountered the most graphic and decisive difference between city and suburb: the influential presence of the street. The sometimes oppressive raffishness of this stretch of Sixth Avenue is secured by three particular presences that are decidedly problematic components of the suburban landscape. The first is a two-block row of sidewalk booksellers, mainly homeless black men, who offer used magazines and books from folding tables that line the sidewalk. The second is the regular presence of several political activists and advocates who distribute literature and raise funds from smaller tables. And the third is a garish row of sex shops and tattoo parlors clustered in another block.

The triple configuration of chains, local shops, and these "exceptional" activities operate in strange concert. The combination certainly serves as a curb to the gentility that abounds on many surrounding blocks, both through its insistent diversity and by its "dangerous" content. Despite the plethora of fast-food shops, cell-phone stores, and chain drugstores, this is a place that is not like the mall, with its rigorous exclusion of undesirables, its prohibitions of the exercise of free speech, and its G-rated content. Indeed, the attraction of this space with these marginalized activities can be seen as an urban coping mechanism, in which an array of powerful urban antigens are drawn to the site of multinational malignancy. And, once again, the unyielding spatial character of a neighborhood with strong preservation protections assures that the upward spiral of scale that characterizes so much suburban retail is frustrated. Once again, the inconvenience of the historic city becomes a bulwark for the protection of the very possibility of diversity and the local.

But if these porn stores and tattoo parlors help retain the louche credibility of the Village, they function as the theming elements that give this particular mall its distinction as a destination and "experience." Without a doubt, Sixth Avenue has been taken over by the usual globalization, becoming a compendium of familiar brands inscribed in the yielding tissue of historic scales and architectures. Daily, the tour buses roll by, and visitors from Omaha or Toronto can point out the local Starbucks or Uno's Pizzeria, just like the one back home, only different somehow. If suburbia is all about packaging uniformity to create the limited and malleable differences of branding, then the suburbs are here.

Suburban Nation

I often have trouble sleeping and find myself sitting in the living room, reading or watching TV. In a dozen windows across the way, I can see the flicker of cathode tubes as students and insomniacs burn the midnight oil, whether purposefully or desperately. If there is a growing reciprocity between suburban and urban patterns and behaviors, it is clearly mediated by the great equalizer, mass electronic media, and by the commercial universalism of the brand. While one worries about the destabilization of physical space under the regime of the virtual, this anxiety has diffuse results. Thinking about the annihilating effects of suburban organization on great cities like New York, the risk seems only marginally formal. The city has been active and effective in defending its treasures of architecture and texture. But this defense has been dangerously narrow—a kind of neutron bomb of aesthetic consideration. We save the facades of our buildings, but have little concern for their human content. This is not to slight the importance of maintaining physical continuity, respecting the achievements of past generations. However, as rampant gentrification, the elevation of shopping and mass entertainment to the center of cultural activity, and the triumph of branding and multinational economic arrangements become pervasive, the specific character of the city and its ability to multiply differences risks being reduced to an empty shell—the decorative "experience" that frames a life too uniform.

2005

52

The Bounding Mayne

For years, the media, ever eager to narrow our understanding, have been describing Thom Mayne as rebellious, countercultural, a sixties hangover. This characterization sets up an ongoing story that seeks to explain how this insubordinate character winds up with a giant project list of court-houses, government agencies, banks, academic buildings, and other facilities that might otherwise arouse the suspicion of someone so steeped in the politics (and architecture) of opposition.

Two divergent accounts are offered. The first is that Mayne has sold out, surrendering his tortured soul for celebrity and big bucks. This is nonsensical. If one thing can be said about Morphosis, it is that its path has been both clear and uncompromised from the get-go. The firm has reached its present level of accomplishment by tenaciously keeping faith with its own investigation: three decades of dedication, research, and consistent ethical values. These principles—which have never sought to de-link desire from form—remain the basis for the singularity of the Morphosis project.

The second explanation for this straw-contradiction is that Mayne's values have triumphed, that his politics have infused the work. This is much closer to the truth, and I would simply add that Mayne—at sixty—is now dealing with clients from his own cohort, that a lot of the hippies, yippies, friends, and fellow students who once wanted no future in the system are now judges, doctors, scientists, bankers, and bureaucrats. These clients—far from being recalcitrant philistines—have been exemplary in their curiosity, engagement, and support, ready for the adventure of authenticity.

It's also true that a "progressive" position within the field of archi-tecture has moved its location: values that once produced pure resistance have now found forms of advocacy with which they can proceed with a clear conscience within the system. The most important of these is the defense of the environment: our reds have become green. The environ-mental movement has reread historic struggles against inequality in a new planetary frame, and the project of sustainability has emerged as a crucial medium of social redress and amelioration. Although this has produced much green architecture as window-dressing and camouflage, it has also resulted in the growth of a dedicated cadre of architects with a truly global view of justice.

Morphosis arrived at its powerful environmental sensibility via a long and careful trajectory. Of course, Los Angeles helped, a climate benign enough and a culture body-focused enough to demand easy communication between inside and out—the aethetic flow of nature though the house—as a fact of life. The transplanted European modernism of Schindler and Neutra, the native styles of Greene and Greene, Gill, and Wright, and the elaborations of Ain, Soriano, Lautner, Elwood, and others of the "second generation," as well as the still flavorful impact of Gehry and those inspired by his formally liberating practice, were powerful antecedents. Their influence—so strongly articulated by Esther McCoy, John Entenza, Reyner Banham, and others—helped foreground the object *in place*, in its interaction with surrounding visual, cultural, and natural ecologies. From all of these, Morphosis received ideas about permeability, about the simplicity of the envelope, and about the endless expressive possibilities of detail. With these cues, the firm developed an ethos that productively located intensity downward. That is, the smaller the detail, the more susceptible to high elaboration. This acknowledged both the importance of the hand of the literal maker (something that grew out of longstanding relationships with a series of local fabricators) and the nature of eccentricity in relation to the scales of public and private.

The ethical valence in the work of Morphosis is thus multiply sourced. From the first, the firm has been devoted to that old modernist jones: honesty of materials. This has entailed the direct use of materials in their "raw" condition, their modification into a sympathetic tectonics (being what they want to be), their legible, frequently mechanical joinery and connection, and the visibility and celebration of their structural role. It has also—as with other practitioners of the Los Angeles schools—involved the reduced use of concealing finishes and a penchant for self-cooking patinas. Each element seems clearly motivated by its nature as a part—not functionalism exactly but an artistic version that expands its overly reflexive principles to a broader, but still highly controlled horizon.

All this has also led to a clear attitude toward the key metric of embodied energy, a richer reading still of the particularity of the element. Although the sense of the integrity of materials has been lifelong with Morphosis, it has become clearer—as we all become greener—that renewable wood worked on site or that steel fabricated nearby are in a different class from aluminum, plastic, or long-traveling exotics. In this sense, Morphosis has used what is effectively a "native" palette at global scale, substituted embodied intellectual energy for thermal or kinetic varieties. The result is not the quasi-folkloric insistence on straw bales or adobe but a much more nuanced understanding: Morphosis is flourishing in the "official" culture because they are creating conditions that are simply sensible and that extend the visual and conceptual resources these clients bring with them.

Morphosis grew into its leadership in sustainable architecture from this fundamental preference for "simple" materials and from a taste for minimum technology in their use. In such recent projects as the Caltrans Headquarters in LA or the Federal Building in San Francisco—enormous undertakings both—Morphosis has ingeniously understood and designed solutions to thermal performance that are predicated on a rigorous and learned application of the philosophy of less-is-more to the use of energy. This has yielded very sophisticated strategies for passive cooling and ventilation in climates that are, to say the least, challenging. The San Francisco project, in particular, is meant to run—on most days—with no air-conditioning whatsoever, and this is at the core of its importance. Within a formal envelope recognizably that of the "office building," Morphosis has produced work that advances the state of the urban workplace by miles.

This achievement lies in the ability both to scale up a set of passive strategies developed in smaller projects and to integrate these strategies into an artistic vision of building that has rarely proved compatible with them. Just as the practice's architecture has long been associated with the art of the screen, with the layering of both space and its defining elements, so treatment of energy systems smoothly enters this discourse of combination. Both literally and conceptually, this understanding of the "space of flows" in buildings has enriched the work—especially in section—at the scales of both the wall and the whole.

Morphosis was born with a love of the mechanical, not merely its representation. In the formative work with Michael Rotondi, this was expressed in a rich eccentricity of joinery and contrivance. Projects were filled with moments of constructed intensity, sometimes in the form of useful objects—chairs, tables, cabinets, doors, and so on—and sometimes in the form of mechanisms that simply exceeded any clear description of use, the machine for machine's sake, an abstracted representation of the formal quintessence of purposive construction, like the explosive object in the big dining room at Kate Mantilini's restaurant.

The addition of the idea of flow to this ubiquity of mechanism forms the basis for complex strategies of modulation. And a clear identification between the social and the environmental has produced a merger of tectonic and mechanical means that marks the originality of Morphosis's synthesis. Dramatic spaces rising through buildings do not simply manage air and act as chimneys, they serve as visual connectors and describe a public grandeur, sited in the buildings' commons. By setting up powerful regions of intercommunication, this architecture serves as an agent of community, reinforcing the collective identity and social contact of those working within these buildings both by creating spaces of encounter and by associating those spaces with advanced environmental action.

This comes together very beautifully in San Francisco. The circulation armature is remarkable, making the right-angle turn from horizontal to vertical via careful spatial modulations that begin street-side with an entry plaza (holding a freestanding public cafeteria) and canopy, leading to an atrium and elevator lobby, and opening again in a three-story "sky garden" on the eleventh (of eighteen) floors, again public. This complex but legible social space is further activated by a skip-stop elevator system that obliges the interaction of the stair, attenuating the "unprogrammed" space of exchange in the vertical axis.

The San Francisco building is a slab, quite thin, which permits the deployment of most workspace along its perimeter and a resulting access to views, natural light, and fresh air from operable windows. The slab configuration is also crucial to the energy-saving strategy. By radically reducing reliance on mechanical air handling and artificial lighting, the firm estimates that 70 percent of the cooling load can be dealt with through natural ventilation and energy for light cut by one quarter. A series of passive systems is topped off by extensive computer management that will automatically turn lights off when natural levels reach a certain point or when spaces are determined to be unoccupied, and that will open and shut vents in the building's "living skin" to keep temperatures comfortable.

Such "active passivity" is increasingly part of Morphosis's style of working and, in many ways, represents the essence of its project. It reflects and extends the attitude embodied in the earlier work and its strategy of intensified detail. Its recursive quality allows big systems to learn local sensitivity, to respond not simply to the particulars of use and occupation but to the uneven behavior of climatic effects over the course of a day, season, or year. Such a distributed, small-element system opens a strong dialectic with Morphosis's growing taste for bold envelopes. In both the San Francisco building and Caltrans, the interdependence of small and large elements does not simply reformulate the historic conceptual rift between envelope and systems, it brings the buildings alive—a genuinely organic strategy.

How well this works in practice will soon be seen. Certainly everything is technically as it should be, the result of research in collaboration with leading scientific experts. The huge multiplication of automated moving parts that enables the active passivity of the system—the hundreds of servos and pistons to open and close the windows and shades—will inevitably perform unevenly, testing the redundancy of the system and its maintenance protocols. As with the mechanical irises on the south facade of Jean Nouvel's Institut du Monde Arabe in Paris, dysfunctional victims of their own elegant delicacy, preserving the robustness of the simply conceived but complexly installed system is likely to be a challenge. And this begs a key question for the ongoing realization of truly green architecture, which must have, as its grail, ever simpler solutions, and which must also live with new, more relaxed styles of imperfection.

The wonderful headquarters for the National Oceanic and Atmospheric Administration (NOAA) outside Washington, DC, adds an additional element. Like much of Morphosis's work, this project studies the relationship of building and ground, an old concern most formatively expressed in the underground Cedars-Sinai cancer pavilion of 1988, where the insulating earth is used to protect human vulnerability by creating a calmly embedded space focused on the light. By reading the earth not simply as mass but as a series of laminations, the firm has arrived—along with other architects in its formal ambit—at the conceit of the earth as a folded plate, able to detach itself as necessary from the "ground" to form a building envelope or to enclose one. The masterful sections that characterize so many Morphosis projects often carve into the earth to displace a too-dogmatic grade, blurring the line between the built and the found. Other projects deal with the earth/building seam by disengaging the elements, allowing topography its autonomy beneath lifted slabs and fragments.

Morphosis deploys metaphors that logically grow from the nature of NOAA's activities, the use of satellites to study the earth and its atmosphere. Reflecting this, the building elevates a long bar, filled with control rooms and topped by the antennae by which NOAA communicates with its orbiting satellites, above a large, partially submerged element that houses the agency's office and service spaces. The disengaging void between bar and berm penetrates the wide lower element, carving out a large courtyard to introduce daylight into the earth's depth. The effective section of the structure thus extends from outer space into the earth, precisely parallel to the axis of observation of the agency itself and to the vision of the architects.

By joining the calming logic of Euclidian space to the invisible and immaterial flows that give architecture its reason for being, and by closely identifying the prosody of detail and organization of building to clear social and environmental agendas, Morphosis has created a way of building that is both *sui generis* and rich with implications for architecture in general. This is an architecture of tremendous hope, planetary in its implications. Unlike architectures that fetishize the difference between the "natural" and our own intelligent design, the work of Morphosis pioneers a new negotiation, a weave of form and behavior that neither slights architecture's long accumulation of original shapes and habits nor forgets for a moment its complete dependency and dramatic influence on the fate of the earth.

2006

53

Drowning in the Gulf Again

The recent report by the Congress for the New Urbanism (CNU) on the reconstruction of the Mississippi Gulf coast is impressive for the speed of its execution, its voluminousness, and its sound recommendations for transport infrastructure, neighborhood consolidation, and the eleven towns it examines. But, like so much CNU product, these useful ideas are weighted by a concrete kimono, an overwhelming fixation on *architecture*, a unitary fantasy of perfection that seeks to prescribe the precise character of every stick and stone in the state. Grafted to the collection of town plans (and promulgated in an accompanying "pattern book" being distributed in the tens of thousands at local Wal-Marts) are reams of model architectural and planning code—generic CNU boilerplate specifying correct forms of architectural behavior, including styles, setbacks, window types, plantings for the front yard, color schemes, gazebos, picket fences, *ad nauseam*.

The disproportionate prominence of prescription renders suspect many of the appropriately sketchy planning suggestions by implying a necessary connection between the logic of light-rail or centered neighborhoods and an architectural uniformity designed to render every shotgun house, corner store, and casino stylistically the same. This relentless specification is purely formal: almost completely absent from these "smart" codes is any real attention to the issues of natural systems so crucial in the wake of a disaster whose effects were founded in willful environmental ignorance. While the report groans with morphological instructions, it is virtually mute on mitigation strategies for the inevitable future storms and floods, and offers next to nothing about energy, cooling, materials, waste management, durable structures, wetlands restoration, barrier island protection, or flood-zone policy. To be sure, there is a brief laundry list of environmental proposals (generally no more than a sentence or two each) attached to the "regional framework" plan (build *one* certified green building in each town, promote energy efficiency, start recycling, use rubble for fill, etc.), but the weight of the CNU's interest is clear. Lip service to environmental and social issues smothered in piles of maniacal detail on traditional styles acts as a nudge and wink to the people who pay the group's bills. What a pity that so much good effort is rendered ridiculous by being immunized against interpretation, by the dogmatic insistence that intelligent urbanism must always be subservient to the stylistic peccadilloes of a single imagination and its uptight tastes.

Because of this narrow fixation, the CNU project has become increasingly undemocratic in both style and content, advocating a way of building that is constantly defended as the people's choice—as if any such unitary version of "the people" exists in our marvelously diverse country—but posed in a way that offers only the most superficial and exclusionary options. As with environmental questions, the CNU report offers a dozen vague recommendations for "social issues" (planning should accommodate diversity, low-income housing should "look good," there should be rental and for-sale housing, only the private sector can produce what we need, and so on), but even these are ghettoized in their own separate—and easily ignored—report. Bromides to the contrary notwithstanding, the CNU—*in its actual practice*—has become the corporate advocate for monochrome, strictly residential, single-class, automobile-based, visually homogenous towns and suburbs that increasingly camouflage, with hypocritical piety, the larger failures of policy—economic, social, and environmental—that they are allegedly designed to redress. By serving as the *architects du roi* for Haley Barbour and his clique (a marriage brokered by Mississippi real estate developer Leland Speed), the CNU functions as a fig leaf and advocate for Republican big business programs and policies—including massive casino construction, upscaling of coastal development, environmental negligence, repression of diversity, dictatorial planning, the exile of the poor, and Disneyland culture—that their sanctimonious official line allegedly opposes. CNU pattern books have nothing to say about the rigid patterns of segregation that their smiley-face architecture so blithely reinforces.

By coincidence, I happened to be in Biloxi during the CNU charrette that helped guide the development of the group's plans for the Gulf, and I found it both impressive and horrifying. The CNU is nothing if not well organized, and was able to summon more than 100 of its members from around the country to brainstorm in Biloxi. They arrived, took a bus tour, and got down to work, organized by the leadership into teams (each under the supervision of a trusted apparatchik) that dealt with individual towns and with common issues, including regional development, transportation, and architecture. Outside participation appeared limited to a small number of politicians and business types, well-intentioned and dedicated local architects standing in for actual grass-roots groups or "inexpert" local citizens and organizations. Of course, the media were there in droves, and Andrés Duany circulated majestically among the teams, accompanied by a film crew to record his every pearl. What's a movement without a cult of personality!

The charrette, an important and effective planning instrument, is an excellent medium for rapidly getting a large number of ideas on the table and for testing them by looking for the synergies and compromises that help professionals understand and incorporate the needs and desires of those they seek to serve. CNU charrettes, on the other hand, seem to be media for the recirculation and validation of ideas that are already decided, for *telling* people what's best for them. It is clearly not possible for a CNU charrette to produce a plan that is *not* based on Traditional Neighborhood Development, on old-timey architecture, on the whole range of self-evident and uniform truths that they seek to instigate with minimal inflection everywhere. Thus, the town teams find the sites for the Celebration-style "neighborhoods," while the architecture teams add stock schtick from headquarters to flesh them out. The outcome of these charrettes is never in doubt.

Something very similar appears to be happening in New Orleans. Planning initiative there has been placed in the hands of the Bring New Orleans Back Commission, which has just released its report. The Commission is a mayorally appointed, big-business dominated group whose leader and most influential member is Joe Canizaro, a real estate developer and major Bush fundraiser, who heads the Commission's planning committee. Canizaro, a past president of the Urban Land Institute who has been called, among other things, the Donald Trump of New Orleans, is notorious for his 1990s role in fomenting the demolition of a large public housing project adjoining a seventy-acre parcel he was seeking to develop. To advance this scheme, Canizaro facilitated hiring the ULI—a non-profit developer "think tank"—as consultant, and it, in turn, produced a plan that ultimately resulted in the demolition of the project, the removal of most of its tenants from the neighborhood, and an ensuing deluge of gentrification, including abundant neo-traditionalist townhouses and a giant Wal-Mart. This construction redounded to the immense profit of both Canizaro and crony Pres Kabacoff, a leading local CNU backer and the developer of the project that replaced the destroyed public housing (and drove up the value of Canizaro's adjoining property).

Soon after its formation, the Bring New Orleans Back Commission turned, *mirabile dictu*, to the ULI to formulate a plan for the city as a whole. This was duly completed in late November, to gales of protest. That plan, which has effectively framed debate since its release, was predicated on triage—the idea that certain parts of the city must be abandoned as too expensive to save. This structured disinvestment strategy—the inevitable *realpolitik* of the invincible bottom line—is nothing less than the return of the 1970s-style "planned shrinkage" so vehemently denounced then as code for an assault on the poor. As with its previous effort for Canizaro, it's no surprise that the places the ULI proposes to abandon are disproportionately the homes of low-income African-Americans: the plan is nothing less than a strategy for ethnic cleansing.

The commission's own plan (like Mississippi's or Ground Zero's—a citizen-circumventing end-run around the checks and balances of more conventional planning processes) simply amplifies the ULI recommendations, reflecting, as well, the position of the Louisiana Recovery Authority (which has recently hired the CNU as its planning consultants), the RAND Corporation, and other groups that insist that New Orleans must contract by as much as 40 to 50 percent of its pre-Katrina population. Although the commission plan suggests that citizens be "allowed" to rebuild anywhere in the city, it simultaneously undermines the possibility. Not simply does it suspend permitting for another four months—frustrating individual rebuilding—it gives destroyed neighborhoods only a year to get it together and reach an unspecified threshold of viability on their own. The intended effect is clear. By offering little or no public assistance for the effort, and suggesting that if people are not able to find the wherewithal to reconstruct by the deadline their neighborhoods will simply be bulldozed, the plan continues Katrina's assault. In Canizaro's words, "If a neighborhood is not developing adequately to support the services it needs to support it, we'll try to shrink it." It is clear which neighborhoods he is referring to. In the words of ex-Mayor Marc Morial, who is the current president of the National Urban League, the commission has offered a "massive red-lining plan wrapped around a giant land grab."

What, one wonders, is the position of the CNU on this matter? To be sure, it will want any reconstruction to follow its conformist architectural taste and will praise the new light rail. But what about the real issues— those of justice, equity, responsible environmental stewardship, and diversity? With the volumes of publicity the group has been receiving (not least in this magazine), where are the ringing calls for state and national policies that are fair and sustainable? Where are the demands for citizen empowerment? Or the protests against the Catch-22 of "allowing" people to return and simultaneously making it impossible for them to collect insurance, get financing, or receive public services? Where is the heart? Where are the stirring words of the great Charter? I am not the first to observe that the CNU—as an ideological and organizational construct—is remarkably (and deliberately) similar to the modernism it so acerbically criticizes for cruel formalist monomania and self-important manifestoes. Like the Congres Internationaux d'Architecture Moderne (CIAM), the CNU entered the world calling for spatial reform as an instrument for creating a better society, espousing principles both admirable and succinct. And like CIAM, the CNU is adamant in insisting that these goals can only be accomplished by the universal application of the right style of architecture, prescribed down to the clapboards and mullions.

The issue with such prescription is not the superiority of one uniformity over another, it's the uniformity itself. Modernism, informed by a dreamy utopian socialist ideology, was grounded in the idea of producing a universal subject—a "new man"—and in architecture's potential to help model these reborn citizens, happy workers in identical flats set in a sunny, salubrious landscape. But that god failed when it became totalitarian, when equality was transmuted into identicality. The New Urbanist's ideal subject may be a happy consumer committed to traditional family values, but the fallacy is the same: the idea that architecture is not to be designed for people in all their messy, squalling, and delightful variety but as a means of assuring that they converge into behavioral sameness. Instead of towers in a park, CNU citizens will happily inhabit their Dryvit Taras, rocking rhythmically back and forth on their obligatory porches, ears cocked for the tinkle of the approaching Good Humor man.

The core problem of New Urbanist dogma is neither its stated principles nor its architecture per se—there's room for plenty of styles in a democracy—but its pious simulation of consent. While we can all be grateful for the restored interest in the textures and adjacencies of the traditional walking city that the CNU has helped to promote, there is something deeply wrong in the attempt to distill these relations into a uniform, replicable set of forms, to insist that any one architectural interpretation of "tradition" represents the accumulated wisdom of the species. In the effort to codify the architecture of the Gulf—or New Orleans—in narrowly fixed and eternal normative patterns, this slim set of "correct" generalities yields both architectural Muzak and laws that insist you listen to nothing else. Get those damn pink flamingos out of the yard before the taste police arrive! Fixated on perfection, New Urbanism dreams of spotless cities resistant to patina and eccentricity, the soul-numbing sameness of multinational consumer culture. In its neocon brandscape, "aesthetic" considerations always trump social forms of variety, denying the real genius of urban growth and transformation: the power of the city to be its own social and morphological laboratory, its ability to define its singularity through the adventure of invention, conflict, and agreement. New Urbanism founders not on an excess of affection for the city, but on an excess of fear of its uncontrollable diversity.

2006

54

Sincerely, Jane Jacobs

Jane Jacobs will forever be remembered as the woman who stopped Robert Moses in his tracks. When the city's planning czar set his sights on Greenwich Village, with designs to bulldoze a boulevard through Washington Square and an expressway across Canal Street and to replace blocks of vibrant life with his beloved towers-in-a-park, Jacobs proved his deft antithesis, an indefatigable organizer of local fight-back. Her success came from knowing both what she was attacking and, more crucially, what she was defending. *The Death and Life of Great American Cities*—her first masterpiece—is not simply a screed against the ravaging simplifications of urban renewal but a brilliant account of the intricate ecology of good neighborhoods. Like no one else, Jane Jacobs was able to understand and describe the interaction of the social and physical components of rich community life, the dialectical bulwark of the good city.

Over the years, the idea of a Manichean struggle between Jacobs and Moses has become a fairly sorry trope. As New York passes through a long period of brisk prosperity—much of it focused on the very historic neighborhoods once considered so blighted—the relationship between the city's social and physical architectures has been transformed for both better and worse. Although preservation has emerged as the planning equivalent of motherhood (tellingly, Moses had dissed Jacobs and her cohorts as "nothing more than a bunch of mothers"), its spawn—gentrification—has become the soft form of urban renewal, still removing the poor but lovingly restoring their former homes. And the hard version of the big plan is making a major comeback in a new wave of jumbo projects emerging on sites of more ostensible dereliction—or at least with smaller populations. These enormous initiatives include the reconstruction of Ground Zero, the redevelopment of the rail yards on the West Side of Manhattan and in downtown Brooklyn, and the transformation of the Brooklyn waterfront in Greenpoint-Williamsburg.

The presence of Jane Jacobs in all of this is very palpable. Paradoxically, the design rhetoric of these mega-schemes invariably now ritualistically evokes principles Jacobs so strongly defended—the importance of the street and its life, the advantages of short blocks, the need for a mix of uses, for density. Urban design—a discipline born in rebellion against the received wisdom of modernist planning—derives many of its central formulations from their foundational articulation by Jacobs, if too often dumbing them down to fit more neatly under the bottom line or max out bulk. But Jacobs's influence is also—and far more genuinely—present in the vociferous opposition to these projects; in the grassroots defense of threatened textures and prospects for local life; in suspicion of big, single-sourced plans; and in anger at the unyielding imperatives of profit in a city that seems bent on running its poor and middle class out of town.

Mutatis mutandis, the riposte of city officials, developers, and their architects frequently brands dissenters as misguided and obstructionist, as enemies of "progress"—the same claim Moses so reflexively retailed. A classic: Frank Gehry suggested recently that opponents of his humongous Atlantic Yards project "should have been picketing Henry Ford." In the past year or so, there has even been a marked rise in criticism of Jacobs herself, more and more widely denigrated as a relic of an outlook that's outlived its relevance. The terms vary slightly, but almost invariably evoke the standard Jacobs/Moses duality. The former director of the Manhattan office of the Department of City Planning (now an operative for the developer The Related Companies) assails both Jacobs and Moses as evil twins, thwarting the enlightened operations of today's post-planning "third way." Rem Koolhaas snidely dismisses Jacobs as an obstructive anachronism, out of touch with the global urban inevitable. Even Nicolai Ouroussoff, the *New York Times* critic, in a commentary entitled "Outgrowing Jane Jacobs and Her New York," published following her death, suggested that Jacobs's influence had "distorted the public's understanding of urban planning," and offered that we might want to "mourn a bit for Mr. Moses as well."

This opposition is both dangerous and misleading, suggesting a false dichotomy between modernity and community and casting Jacobs's arguments as irreducibly antithetical to vision. There's a confusion of categories here. Jacobs's beef wasn't with any particular style, and her formulations were not those of an architect; it was never her intention to fix the particulars for the design of new cities, but to locate, in the fabric of the old, a more general set of values that were conducive to community, and that might be extrapolated to many different urban situations. Jacobs was an advocate for choice, not someone to insist that everyone live in any one way—including hers—and she argued against the imposition of one-dimensional planning ideas on living urban tissue. The depth in her critique grew from the way her close and sympathetic reading of a beloved and familiar place excavated issues that extended far beyond it. It's just wrong to convert this revelatory particularity into a deficit in her analysis. Hers was too fine a mind to think that the empty reproduction of forms, traditional or modern, could be the vehicle for creating community life, which depends on a slow buildup of relationships and agreements. She spent her life opposing the myopia of all such prescriptive singularities. Jacobs's famous comment that "a city cannot be a work of art," far from suggesting that cities not be beautiful, was her way of insisting that *any* uniform reading of the city imposed an order that obscured a view toward its true complexity.

Jane Jacobs spent over half a century making New York neighborhoods better places to live, not trying to preserve them in amber. Among her many achievements was the work she undertook on behalf of the construction of the West Village Houses, a series of small-scale (and modernist!) apartment buildings with a total of 420 units, dotted through her old neighborhood. Although their architecture is perhaps modest to a fault, the apartments are spacious, and the project as a whole—quite large in aggregate—fits unobtrusively within the intimate weave of its surroundings. It's a model piece of urbanism because of this careful integration; because its architectural expression is not treated as a big, determining deal; and because it grew out of the self-organized impetus to provide new and better housing for people of modest means, for whom the market had little empathy. The lesson for planning and design is both about basic physical harmonization and about the clarity and value of the social interests embodied in these buildings. Every project, whether in the historic city or out on its fringes, embodies a compendium of such interests. Too often, architecture is complicit in obscuring the worst of these, through preservation that reveres old buildings extravagantly while driving out their inhabitants, or by hyping the art-for-art's-sake pose of new developments that—however fab their stylings—press the same upmarket homogeneities all around them.

Jacobs may not have been a conventional connoisseur of the fine points of architectural history and form, but nobody had a keener eye for architecture's effects. A little over a year ago, she wrote a letter to Mayor Michael Bloomberg to protest the city's plans for a massive makeover of a stretch of the Brooklyn waterfront with luxury high-rise apartment buildings. Her objection had nothing to do with tall buildings facing the water per se (the city is rich with brilliant examples of winning morphologies of view, like Riverside Drive), but with their likely consequence for the ecology of the community behind them. She was worried about their *effects*. And she wrote as an advocate, as always, for the right of communities to steer their own destinies. The following letter, an eloquent summary of Jane Jacobs's life and values, was published in *The Brooklyn Rail*. Like everything she wrote, it is passionate, clear-eyed, and gets right to the point.

Dear Mayor Bloomberg,

My name is Jane Jacobs. I am a student of cities, interested in learning why some cities persist in prospering while others persistently decline; why some provide social environments that fulfill the dreams and hopes of ambitious and hardworking immigrants, but others cruelly disappoint the hopes of immigrant parents that they have found an improved life for their children. I am not a resident of New York although most of what I know about cities I learned in New York during the almost half-century of my life here after I arrived as an immigrant from an impoverished Pennsylvania coal mining town in 1934.

I am pleased and proud to say that dozens of cities, ranging in size from London to Riga in Latvia, have found the vibrant success and vitality of New York to demonstrate useful and helpful lessons for themselves—and have realized that failures in New York are worth study as needed cautions.

Let's think first about revitalization successes; they are great and good teachers. They don't result from gigantic plans and show-off projects, in New York or in other cities either. They build up gradually and authentically from diverse human communities; successful city revitalization builds itself on these community foundations, as the community-devised 197-a Plan does.

What the intelligently worked out plan devised by the [Brooklyn] community itself does not do is worth noticing. It does not destroy hundreds of manufacturing jobs, desperately needed by New York citizens and by the city's stagnating and stunted manufacturing economy. The community's plan does not cheat the future by neglecting to provide provisions for schools, daycare, recreational outdoor sports, and pleasant facilities for those things. The community's plan does not promote new housing at the expense of both existing housing and imaginative and economical new shelter that residents can afford. The community's plan does not violate the existing scale of the community, nor does it insult the visual and economic advantages of neighborhoods that are precisely of the kind that demonstrably attract artists and other live-work craftsmen, initiating spontaneous and self-organizing renewal. Indeed, so much renewal so rapidly that the problem converts to how to make an undesirable neighborhood into an attractive one less rapidly.

Of course the community's plan does not promote any of the vicious and destructive results mentioned. Why would it? Are the citizens of Greenpoint and Williamsburg vandals? Are they so inhumane they want to contrive the impossibility of jobs for their neighbors and for the greater community?

Surely not. But the proposal put before you by city staff is an ambush containing all those destructive consequences, packaged very sneakily with visually tiresome, unimaginative and imitative luxury project towers. How weird, and how sad, that New York, which has demonstrated successes enlightening to so much of the world, seems unable to learn lessons it needs for itself. I will make two predictions with utter confidence. 1. If you follow the community's plan you will harvest a success; 2. If you follow the proposal before you today, you will maybe enrich a few heedless and ignorant developers, but at the cost of an ugly and intractable mistake. Even the presumed beneficiaries of this misuse of governmental powers, the developers and financiers of luxury towers, may not benefit; misused environments are not good long-term economic bets.

Come on, do the right thing. The community really does know best.

Sincerely,

Jane Jacobs

2006

55

Are You Now or Have You Ever Been?

I felt a certain disquiet at *Architectural Record*'s recent coverage of the Richard Rogers flap. As the magazine reported, Rogers was threatened with the loss of two giant commissions in New York—the $1.7 billion expansion of the Jacob K. Javits Convention Center and the $1 billion Silvercup Studios project (sound stages, offices, and apartments on the Queens waterfront)—for his (guilt by) association with Architects and Planners for Justice in Palestine (APJP), a small British organization which had its first meeting in Rogers's London office in early February. Convened by Abe Hayeem—an architect and old friend of Rogers—the group (around 60 people, many of them Jewish and Israeli) agreed on a statement of principles:

> We share the international condemnation of the continuing annexation and fragmentation of Palestinian land through the expansion of illegal settlements and outposts and the construction of the Separation Wall in defiance of international law. We hold all design and construction professionals involved in projects that appropriate land and natural resources from Palestinian territory to be complicit in social, political and economic oppression, and to be in violation of their professional ethics.

Although it has not yet adopted a specific course of action, APJP has been discussing a variety of targeted moves—including boycotts—aimed at the design and construction communities. Boycotts—embargoes or sanctions as they're called when governments apply them, as the US currently does against the Palestinian Authority (also embargoed by Israel) and Cuba, among others—are a widespread and often effective means of political expression. Most of us have probably participated in a boycott at one time or another, forgoing trips to apartheid South Africa, eschewing grapes on behalf of California farm workers, or skipping Dixie Chicks concerts in support of Bush. The risk in the tactic is that the brush can be too broad, leading to unanticipated downside consequences; there was, for example, much discussion during the South Africa boycott of its potential economic effects on ordinary people.

In the case of Israel, such actions are especially troubled. For years, the country was the object of an Arab boycott that extended to companies doing business with it. The craven acquiescence of many American corporations in this ban is a sorry, if scarcely unusual, chapter in the history of big-business ethics and one of the reasons that legislation was passed in the 1970s to stop such collusion in assaulting Israel's fundamental right to exist. A current attempt to organize a general academic boycott of Israel by British academics is being resisted for being both undiscriminating in its target and an affront to academic freedom—feelings I share. It is also being tarred (by Larry Summers among others) with the charge of anti-Semitism, in an overworked reflex that effectively aims to shut down any criticism with its disingenuous conflation of "effect" and "intent." While such claims may impugn the motives of many critics by pointing out the hypocritically disproportionate opprobrium heaped on Israel by groups and media that take far less interest in the behavior of other regimes in the area—which include some of the vilest on earth—they do not gainsay the substance of the criticism. And the exclusive defense of Israeli academic freedom sidesteps the question of an appropriate response to the widespread Israeli denial of Palestinian academic freedom, which has included the closure of eleven universities for varying periods, the longest four years.

Whatever the difficult issues of balance, people of conscience have a responsibility to act with vigor, intelligence, and compassion, to confront situations with which they strongly disagree. The right to speak out unimpeded is a cornerstone of the US Constitution: dissent makes democracy go. For architects and planners—whose work inevitably concretizes social relations and meanings—there is always a question of where to draw the line. Should we take part in development projects that destroy existing homes and communities? Design nuclear power plants? Build in fragile environments? Block someone's view? If we refuse to be involved with such ventures, do we have an active responsibility to try to stop others from participating, to try to stop the projects themselves? When does the right to make our feelings known become a duty?

Although the idea of some form of directed boycott was simply *discussed* by the APJP, it was enough to generate a chorus of outraged calls from New York officials, including Sheldon Silver, Speaker of the State Assembly, Comptroller Alan Hevesi, and New York Congressman (and recent mayoral candidate) Anthony Wiener, among others, to dismiss Rogers from the Javits job and to withdraw tax credits from the Silvercup project should Rogers continue as its architect. At the same time, Rogers was hastily summoned to New York by his client, Charles Gargano, chair of the Empire State Development Corporation, to account for himself. The publicly offered reason for this extraordinary step was that Rogers, by hosting the meeting of APJP, had supported an "illegal" economic boycott of Israel. Lurking behind this charge was a much uglier one: the thinly veiled suggestion that Rogers, by lending his weight to "bigoted" criticism of Israeli policy, was anti-Semitic, an especially pathetic accusation given the fact that Rogers's Jewish father was forced to flee fascist Italy to escape persecution, and that his wife is Jewish.

In the third paragraph of the *Record* story, several names—including mine—are listed as belonging to the suspect "group." Although I have not attended any meetings or paid any dues, I have been in regular contact with Hayeem, a British Iraqi Jew who lived some years in both South Africa and Israel before settling in London. Hayeem and Rogers have a history of shared activism, and campaigned together against apartheid, advocating the widely supported boycott (perhaps the origin of the reflexive assumption that Rogers was simply at it again). If sympathy can be conflated with membership, then I am clearly a "member" (no cards have yet been issued to be carried). APJP is an affinity group, and I have deep affinity with its point of view, which is neither unusual nor extreme: the route of the separation barrier has been declared illegal by the International Court of Justice and the United Nations, among other bodies. These are positions I've expressed in a book, *Against the Wall*, published in 2005. Still, seeing my name in print as a member of group considered so dangerous that having anything to do with it would disqualify an architect from public projects in New York gave me a chill, and I began to hear faint echoes of certain phrases in my mind's ear. "I have in my hand a list of names . . . Are you now or have you ever been . . . ?"

And not for the first time. The issue of *Record* covering the Rogers matter also contained an item about the Frank Gehry–designed Museum of Tolerance in Jerusalem, which reported that the project's construction had been delayed because of the discovery of graves during the excavation of the site, part of an ancient Muslim cemetery. I had written skeptically in this column some time ago about what I felt were the museum's hypocritical politics, and was vehemently attacked in a subsequent issue by the project's sponsor, Rabbi Marvin Hier of Los Angeles, who said my position "reeks of McCarthyism" for wondering about Gehry's thoughts on the undertaking. He claimed that I was proposing a political litmus test as a precondition for selecting an architect, much as HUAC might have tried to prevent one of the Hollywood Ten from making movies because of some prior association with communists or their suspect ideas. Of course, this smear entirely missed the point. I was not asking about Frank Gehry's politics in general, nor his opinion on any matter unrelated to the meaning of that building which embodied, I thought, a deeply problematic message.

The difference in the two situations is fundamental. Rogers's commissions are not in Israel or Palestine but in New York City, and the two projects have nothing to do with Middle Eastern politics, nor has anyone suggested that Rogers has in any way attempted to politicize them. Indeed, there has been no discussion whatsoever in all of this of the designs themselves. Rogers has been subjected to an obscene piling-on by grandstanding local politicians—playing to New York's "sixth borough"—who have attempted to disqualify him from these jobs for his alleged connection to positions that have absolutely no relevance to the work, save the shabby accusation that the man for whom the convention center is named—the late Senator Jacob Javits, a strong supporter of Israel (and, one might add, of the First Amendment)—would have been affronted. Where does the logic of this witch-hunt stop? Will everyone in Rogers's office be obliged to sign an oath? How about the contractor? The caterer? The chain of phantom associations is the very essence of McCarthyism.

It is also part of an increasingly pervasive assault on free expression and association in the city. Performances at a local theater of a play about the young American peace activist Rachel Corrie—crushed by an Israeli bulldozer while attempting to defend a Palestinian house from demolition—have been cancelled under pressure. The Freedom Museum and Drawing Center have been banished from the reconstruction of Ground Zero out of fear that, in the exercise of their expressive rights, these institutions *might* sometime in the future support articulations offensive to our self-proclaimed guardians of political correctness. Such actions are more worthy of the Taliban than of American democracy. And the growing fortification and surveillance of both public and private realms—whether through ubiquitous security cameras, unwarranted wiretaps, or the insane bollardization of the cityscape—represent a dramatic and growing threat to the freedoms of association and assembly that are the main expressions of a democratic polity in physical space.

To save his commissions, Rogers, admired by many of us for both his remarkable building and his previously forthright politics, launched into a monumental and humiliating grovel, orchestrated by New York master flack Howard Rubinstein, whose defense of Rogers (referred to in press releases as "Architect"—never "Lord"—Rogers) included publicizing the tidbit that he had honeymooned in Israel with his first wife and trumpeting his readiness to accept commissions there. Rogers immediately denounced the group he had recently hosted ("I am not now nor have I ever been a member"), declared himself against boycotts "of any kind" (never mind his vocal support of the anti-apartheid boycott), called a press conference to denounce Hamas, offered his ringing support for the separation barrier, and generally did what it took to obey H. H. Richardson's famous First Law of Architecture: get the job. While there may be no shame in saying what one must to escape an inquisition, Richard Rogers had the power and prestige to stand up to it, and his lightning cave-in has bolstered the enemies of free speech. Rogers isn't quite in the Elia Kazan league—though he did "give up" the APJP—but the disgrace is real.

Good career move, though. Rogers has just been hired by Larry Silverstein to design one of the new office buildings at Ground Zero. It should generate enormous fees and will offer excellent views of the Freedom Tower.

2006

56

Stuyvesant Town

Of all the concepts dear to modernist urbanism, perhaps the most uniformly reviled is the notion of "towers-in-the-park." This idea, which descends from Le Corbusier's "Radiant City" plan (a late spawn of the marriage of rationalism and pastoralism that produced its immediate predecessor, the garden city), is heavily identified with the failures of urban renewal and public housing, with a deadening, penitential, environment—the very antithesis of the good, diverse, city. The most focused and devastating attack on such planning was surely that of Jane Jacobs, whose advocacy of the rich and variegated ecology of urban neighborhoods like Greenwich Village or Boston's North End forms the substrate for the way most of us think about successful cities today.

Among the places that came in for Jacobs's most seething opprobrium were Stuyvesant Town and Peter Cooper Village—adjacent developments covering eighteen square blocks on the East Side of Manhattan—which she excoriated for their uniformity and deadly effects on the lively, economically mixed life of the street, her gold standard for urbanity. To be sure, the phalanx of 110 red-brick, minimally detailed slabs, designed by Irwin Clavan and Gilmore Clarke in 1947, do look like a typical—and, at 11,000 units, especially enormous—"project," and Jacobs's observations about their lack of commercial activity remain largely valid. But the well-maintained and very green enclave is beloved by its residents, many of whom have lived there for years. And in a huge city configured as a mosaic of neighborhoods and districts, its exceptionality, its interruption of the grid, is more than supportable, it's downright pleasant. New York has many such successful enclaves of exception—including Forest Hills and Sunnyside Gardens, Washington Square Village, and Penn South—that suggest the city can be enlivened by occasional large-scale departures from the short-block default.

Stuyvesant Town and Peter Cooper Village were the vision of Jane Jacobs's arch-nemesis, Robert Moses, and embody the sweeping, authoritarian way of doing business that allowed him to remake the face of the city like no one before or since. Moses conceived the project in 1943 as a home for veterans returning to a housing-strapped city, and turned to the Metropolitan Life Insurance Company to build it—a classic "public-private partnership." MetLife was already a major developer of large-scale urban housing, including the Parkchester complex in the Bronx (Clavan and Clarke were also on the design team), constructed from 1938 to 1942 for 40,000 residents. Both projects were aimed at middle-class families, and the historian Samuel Zipp has described them as "urban Levittowns." While this is an apt comparison in terms of their social and formal homogeneity and their ambition to tackle big problems at big scales, there is one crucial difference: Parkchester, Stuyvesant, and Peter Cooper were rentals—in a city that regulated rents.

Moses, however, offered MetLife a sweet deal. Not only would the city acquire all the land via eminent domain and throw out the 3,000 poor families living in the "Gas House" neighborhood, it would "de-map" and convey all the streets on the eighty-acre site (one-tenth the size of Central Park) to MetLife. More, the city agreed to freeze property taxes for twenty-five years at the value of the expropriated land before development. Finally, it turned a blind eye to MetLife's exclusionary practices, which banned blacks ("Negroes and whites do not mix," said the company president), unmarried couples, and single parents, until the issue was forced by protests and legal actions in the fifties and sixties. The story was the same at Parkchester, segregated until the city's Human Rights Commission intervened, leading to its sale in 1968 to Helmsley-Spear Inc. which, in stages, converted the complex to cooperatives.

This last bit of history is in the process of repeating itself. In August, MetLife put Stuyvesant Town and Peter Cooper Village on the block, prompting a frenzy of interest from potential buyers ranging from real estate companies to investment banks to the usual unidentified financiers from Qatar. However, while MetLife's announcement was greeted by the real estate community with salivation and lust, it struck fear into residents, who have been growing anxious about the sale of the property for several years, sparked by a $300 million upgrade undertaken by MetLife and by newly vigorous efforts to get rid of tenants not listed on leases. Anxiety is focused on rent: about three-quarters of the apartments in the two developments are protected by the city's rent-stabilization law, which limits increases to a level fixed annually, presently in the neighborhood of 4 percent. The law covers about a million units in the city and is a defining factor in shaping New York's demographic character, and a large part of the reason we still have a middle class. Loss of protection would be a disaster.

Apartments can now be removed from the stabilization regime under two circumstances. When monthly rent passes a threshold of $2,000—via regular mandated increases or pass-along expenses for "major" improvements—any vacated apartment leaves the system of controls and floats to the market rate. And tenants of apartments with rents over $2,000 face a means test; those with incomes in excess of $175,000 for two consecutive years lose their protection, and their apartments permanently exit regulation. Due to such "natural" processes, 27 percent of the units in Stuyvesant Town/Peter Cooper Village now rent at market rates, which currently top out at $3,800–$5,850 for the biggest units versus $1,500–$1,600 for those still stabilized—two very different "markets."

Recognizing the immense potential in this difference, bidders for the complex surely calculated actuarially—examining the age and income of tenants, the frequency of turnovers, the number of apartments nearing the de-control threshold, the possibility of further renovations to drive up rents, the prospects of enticements or harassment to stimulate turnover, the number of young couples in small apartments likely to have children and move on, and the vigor of the market in general. The strategy is to get apartments de-stabilized, converted to condos, and sold to tenants as quickly as possible. The arithmetic looks promising. According to a real estate investor quoted in Crain's, "Rent stabilized apartments in New York City are one of the best risk-adjusted real-estate investments in the country." The sales literature put out by CB Richard Ellis, MetLife's marketer, hypes the complex (already festooned with banners advertising "Luxury Apartments") for its potential to become the "city's most prominent market-rate master [sic] community," and predicts that by 2018 fewer than 30 percent of the units will remain stabilized.

Manhattan—where the middle class is the smallest by percentage in the country and the income gap the largest—may be the extreme case, but in city after city across America it is more and more difficult for the core of our citizenry—teachers, nurses, fire fighters, service workers, technicians, and cops—to find decent and convenient places to live. The Census Bureau has just reported a dramatic national rise in the burden of housing costs. In New York, over half of the city's residents pay more than 30 percent of their incomes for housing, and percentages are soaring in suburbs and cities from coast to coast, with the biggest crunch in Southern California. Recognizing this crisis, the Bloomberg administration has declared its intention to create or preserve 165,000 "affordable" units by 2013 and is pursuing the goal with some success through a variety of subsidy arrangements, including zoning bonuses, tax exemptions, forgiven interest on city loans, and other indirect strategies. But, as the scale of the Stuyvesant Town/Peter Cooper Village sale makes dispiritingly clear, market forces are winning invisible-hands-down and the net decline in affordable apartments is only accelerating.

Tenants organized—with labor-union and local political backing—to bid on the project themselves with an offer of $4.5 billion and a proposal that would have retained 20 percent of the apartments as affordable rentals and sold another 20 percent to tenants at below-market rates. Their case was greatly bolstered by the tremendous public subsidy that supported the project in the first place (although MetLife claims that its twenty-five-year legal obligation has long since expired). It also reinforced the original idea behind the project: the provision of rental apartments for middle-class residents at a time of shortage. However, while there should be no question of tenants' rights to remain in their homes free from fear of displacement by spiking rents or coerced purchase, even a successful bid would, like any other condo conversion, eventually transform Stuyvesant Town/Peter Cooper Village into a largely luxury estate, simply delaying by one cycle the departure of the middle class—and the evisceration of the rental market—and constructing the city as a place with a small middle class, dependent on some form of affirmative action for its survival.

Unfettered, laissez-faire is not capable of providing decent housing for everyone, nor of making the kinds of locational decisions that conduce the cities of diversity and mix extolled by Jane Jacobs. If the market must be regulated to assure public benefits—as it is, one way or another, in virtually every sector of the economy—the question becomes how and where to apply public intervention. As an idea, subsidy is a constant—benefit and equity are the variables. The suburbs, symbol of the American dream of private property "rights," were built on the back of gigantic tax-payer subventions and the vast provision of public infrastructure—from sewer lines to interstates—in arrangements that are, compared to the efficiency of such systems at urban densities, disproportionately expensive. New York offers enormous tax and other benefits to corporate operators—to Goldman Sachs or Barry Diller—to encourage them to build in the city.

As a culture we prefer our subsidies to be diffuse, oblique, disguised as incentives whenever possible, rather than regulations or "hand-outs." But the complex of vouchers, tax breaks, zoning bonuses, and infrastructure funding is subsidy all the same, and it just isn't doing the job for those who need help the most. Claims that the real problem lies with rent regulation are simply disingenuous. It is time to face up to the magnitude of the housing crisis in the US, which includes a squeeze both on middle-class incomes and on immigrants packed illegally four-to-a-room in urban apartments and suburban basements. It is time for government at all levels to intervene massively and directly. There's no shortage of strategies, and they all require subsidy. The question is to whom and for what.

Jane Jacobs proposed encouraging affordable housing through "guaranteed rent," a subvention to landlords on behalf of tenants, based on a cost-plus system in which rates of profit are fixed, not so different in kind from current rent regulations but potentially more precisely tailored to specific circumstances and fairer to small landlords. Inclusionary zoning—the current silver bullet—allows a developer to build more luxury housing in exchange for including some affordable units. Here the subsidy takes the form of a hit to the public environment through the loss of light and air and added strain on services from the larger project. In the case of tax incentives, the subsidy comes as a sacrifice in general tax revenues. Rent vouchers, often fixed below affordable rent levels, hand public money to individuals to spend in the private market.

In October, Tishman Speyer Properties and the Blackrock investment bank bought Stuyvesant Town/Peter Cooper Village for $5.4 billion, the largest real estate deal in US history. The city administration, to the disappointment of many, stayed on the sidelines: "MetLife owns it, and they have the right to sell it," said Mayor Bloomberg, and his powerful Deputy Mayor for Economic Development rejected the tenants' sought-after tax subsidies as an inefficient use of public funds. The day after the sale the city announced a purportedly more economical plan to build several thousand affordable units across the East River, in Queens. A worthy project, but not enough to staunch the loss of New York's affordable housing nor effect the transformation of Manhattan into the world's largest gated community.

2006

57

How I Invented Asia

One of the inviolable rules of architecture is never to design for an unvis-ited site. This stricture cuts to the heart of the meaning of the architectural act, embodying ideas that range from the practical to the ethical. At one level, the site visit represents fundamental due diligence, required to assess the soil, to look for unforeseen obstacles, to take careful measurements. At another, walking the site is crucial to understanding a somewhat more abstract idea of *genius loci*, to picking up the vibe, to channeling a sense of place that will ultimately govern form, expression, orientation—all the components that set the terms of the relationship between building, land, and the other "scapes" in which it sits.

While this framework may be sound as a general matter, its operation is deeply subjective, depending on the values and techniques of observa-tion brought to bear on the goals of any transformation, and, of course, on the very meaning of the idea of site. All places are necessarily collusions of climate, culture, history, ecology, economics, and politics, and each can only be comprehended relativistically, as an evanescent concatenation of values and meanings channeled through an observing consciousness. While we may—especially in an age of heightened environmental and cultural sensitivity—ask the site, as Louis Kahn asked the brick, what it wants to be, I'm afraid the answer will always be underdetermined and imprecise. A good thing, too, for the usefulness of architects.

Although some still subscribe to a shopworn dichotomy between tradi-tion and modernity, it does seem more useful to look at their mutual embedding. After all, that site visit is a means of understanding both possi-bilities and constraints, and tradition and modernity weigh on each side of this equation, similarly located in contexts that continue to shift. Tradition and modernity find expression through both arbitrary and instrumental signification, themselves situated at various removes from their origins and requiring different styles of authentication. Southerly exposures in north-erly latitudes have a consistent logic of insolation that abets the conserva-tion of energy. The thick walls of traditional desert building are superbly adapted to their climatic circumstances. In cases like these, traditional and modern responses embody identical standards of economy and value. The preferred eastern orientation for entrances in Vastu geomancy, on the other hand, springs from a somewhat more ineffable relationship to orientation, one in which the symbolic trumps—or is folded into—the functional. Current efforts by the late Maharishi Mahesh Yogi's operatives and others to demonstrate Vastu's social and physical efficacy "scientifically" may well yield measurable experimental results—but, most likely, of the placebo effect.

I do not mean to be dismissive: placebos are, in many ways, the highest form of medical practice. They activate the triumphant management of body by mind and—being no more than a bit of sugar—are loyal to the physician's law: first, do no harm. But, in the end, Vastu, Feng Shui, Koran, and Bible all regard architecture through the same instrumentalism as modernity, proposing that the form of building is not simply a record but an actor in shaping social and individual behavior. Functionalism—which remains the unassailable mother tongue of our architecture—may be broadened in terms of the way in which its effects are read, but the same test of purpose inheres in both modernist and traditionalist ideologies. The transparency of a glass house to nature and the transparent relationship of a house of worship to the deity are completely homologous. And, in both architecture and theology, the degree and medium of this transparency has been an ongoing object of contention and schism.

However, for the ready production of meaning, tradition has a leg up on modernity in several key respects. Although it is completely appropriate to speak of the tradition of modernity, at this point deep in its history, this very question of longevity locates a quality that is particularly pivotal for urbanism. Traditions endure by consent. The importance of cities is not dumbly instrumental—as necessary sites of production and exchange—but lies in their role as armatures of agreement, the physical register of accumulated compacts and memories. All cities are sited at the nexus of innumerable traditions, embodied in form, ritual, and habit. Over time, these traditions produce the specificity of both the city and its citizens. Without tradition, the city is inconceivable.

Tradition is inherently slow: its authenticity lies in the depth of assent that supports it, in the way in which it is learned and internalized, and in the particularity of its institutions. This is what distinguishes it from branding—the rhetoric of hypertradition—however congenial the product. In a globalizing culture rich with media of instantaneity and transportability, traditions predicated in slowness and locality are at obvious risk. The threat comes not simply from rupture and replacement but from co-optation, from styles of incorporation—like the neo-traditionalist New Urbanism so prominent in the US and its mental satellites—that claim that de-contextualized meanings are transmissible at the level of form, that building a suburb that looks a bit like an eighteenth-century agrarian village will produce all the imagined happinesses of another time and place, never mind the Hummer in the driveway (or the witches being stoned just out of frame).

If the authority of duration is not transportable, its forms obviously are. This is the condition of tradition in the context of modernity, and it means that access to the imaginative product of millennia is now universal. From glass pyramids in Kazakhstan to Eiffel Towers in Vegas to Dutch villages in Japan or Mediterranean ones in Beijing, the work of recombination and hyperbole is everywhere underway. In the era of television and the internet, the conceptual latitude for the juxtaposable is infinite, and we have plenty of reasons to fear the blizzard of instability that circulation at the speed of light enables. But we can also take heart at a new potential for creativity, for the kind of dynamic splicing that can produce unimagined architectural forms as well as the miracle of a polyglot metropolis like New York or London.

As a member of a class of architects whose frequent-flyer miles have reached the equivalent of multiple round-trips to the moon, the confrontation with unfamiliar sites comes, as it were, with the territory. The issue, begged by my initial citing of the rule of visitation, is how such a practice can be ethically pursued, how deeply the particulars of site must—or can— be imbibed, and what responsibility that encounter imparts. Some of this is easy. Bio-climatic sensibility is the core of sustainability—perhaps the key location for the ethics of architecture—and no building can any longer be appropriately designed that ignores the precise environmental character of its site. Such sensitivity reverberates throughout the building process, engaging questions of orientation, ventilation, minimum direct and embodied energy, "neutrality" in the emission of pollutants, self-supply of water, and a range of other critical components of "green" architecture.

There are, of course, cultural ramifications. For example, one of the canons of sustainable design is the use of locally produced materials and techniques. But this is not the straightforward matter suggested by either reflexive traditionalism or reflexive environmentalism, but always assumes other tests—the fact that an aluminum plant or a virgin stand of teak is just down the block does not, *ipso facto*, suggest the automatic propriety of using them. Nor, for that matter, should a tradition of unreinforced masonry construction be persuasive in a seismic zone. Nor a tradition of exploitative labor practices. Nevertheless, there should be a strong prejudice for the living aspects of locality in any design that purports to be sustainable.

While the memory of tradition may inhere in particular forms, its life does not necessarily. Tradition is a set of practices that are weighted, as Yi-Fu Tuan has pointed out, by constraint, and it is clear that traditional societies live in symbiosis with both the fact and idea of their boundaries. This is an extremely fluid concept. Following Edward Said, Janet

Abu-Lughod has pointed to a kind of postcolonial diffusion effect in which the idea of tradition is re-circulated as an instrument of domination by the colonizer, setting the boundaries from without rather than within. And Nezar Al-Sayyad has joined others—including Arjun Appadurai and Ed Soja—in hypothesizing the idea of a "third place" in which traditional constructions are roiled by the buffeting flows of globalization, producing a variety of hybridities by which the local seeks to mediate the un-placing force of multinational culture. This is the space of Michael Hardt and Antonio Negri's "multitude," the living and subversive democratic alternative growing in the maw of empire.

These arguments are obviously crucial as a critique of the dumb bivalence of received wisdom: tradition is at once potentially the product of a kind of enduring empiricism—tested by time—and radically uncritical. As a signifier, though, tradition is particularly buoyant, especially now. The folding of tradition into the various insistent discourses of identity that characterize contemporary politics means that every "tradition" on earth, once marked, is inescapably contaminated by *somebody's* gaze, if only by that of those operating "within" the tradition who consciously seek to protect it from the baleful influence of those without. We live in a world in which everybody is constructed as somebody's other, and the force of tradition, increasingly taken up in an idea of the political, is more and more directed outwards.

This predicate of otherness is central to any workable definition of tradition. However, just as Eric Hobsbawm and Benedict Anderson have pressed the argument for the invention—and imposition—of tradition, so too must we look at the ways in which otherness and alterity are continuously produced and at the reasons and values behind them. And we must look at the context—in the age of globalization, nothing on the planet is immune from its spreading implications. One of the byproducts of a globalized environment is, of course, what is called multiculturalism, which I choose to understand simply as the fact of a constant and accelerating process of juxtaposition of genes and memes, of people and understandings.

The resulting hybridities—however evanescent—are tossed off by the global system at a rate of zillions an hour, a constant production of new forms of otherness, a system of difference that increasingly resists ready taxonomy and which, as Hardt and Negri have famously observed, nobody can stand outside. Resistance to this system is, in one reading, completely futile: always already within it as we are, there is simply no prospect of penetrating its elastic membrane. On the other hand, the world is filled with struggle against this hegemony, however Quixotic or reactionary, and the spaces of wiggle room—even if pinioned *within* the system—are themselves part of a process of constant creation and adjustment, a marathon between diversity and hegemony, multitude and empire.

Whether or not any of these responses—traditionalist, avant-gardist, or whatever—can be considered genuinely subversive, many are undoubtedly both creative and satisfying. Their powers of resistance take three forms that are relevant to the argument about the future of cities, each with its upsides and downsides. The first is the reinforcement of existing classifications and taxonomies. At the most primary level, the idea of the city as a bounded singularity is urgent in creating an alternative infrastructure to the metastases of megacities and sprawl. This leads to arguments for increasing local autonomy as a democratic hedge against a neoliberal planet of powerful transnationals and weakening states, for growth boundaries to reduce regional predations, and for the creation of new cities as a more logical way of accommodating an urban population that's growing at the rate of a million people a week.

The second is the defense of specific morphological traditions. On the one hand, this implies tenacious, but discriminating, preservation of urban heritage. This is our collective memory—repository and mnemonic—and we abandon it at our peril. But the re-creation of these morphologies in contemporary contexts and spaces is more problematic—not just in terms of the promiscuous reassignment of meanings and of the use of vibe to certify contested authority, nor in the risk of repression to spaces of creativity by filling their enabling void with exclusionary repetition, but also in their inability to accommodate shifting styles of life and to address the parlous state of the planet. Resistance is an unfailingly mixed bag, after all. As ever, it's a matter of where to draw the line: even the Taliban make a good point or two.

A third fulcrum of difference is found in the movement to a condition of universal otherness, in trying to keep ahead of the system through the constant output of singularities. The endless recombination of genes and memes is a factory for accelerating the production of freaks, a renewable exotic. If we take natural selection as a conceptual model, the eternal refreshment of possibilities can be seen as the necessary condition of successful adaptation to exigency run amok. Viewed culturally, this means that resistance will often privilege non-conforming behaviors. Many of these may be plucked from the repertoire of "traditional" patterns that themselves become portions of recombinant organisms hitherto unseen. Bin Laden works out the logistics of jihad via GPS while wife number two relaxes in a back corner of the cave with the Victoria's Secret catalogue. Guido Googles kiddie porn while sipping a latte in the Piazza Navonna. My plastic surgeon refashions my nose to the precise dimensions of Cosimo de Mèdici's or Johnny Depp's.

Orthodoxy tends to look at all cross-fertilization as miscegenation. Most of us, however, are not so averse to dating the other. I'd now like to describe something of my own experience in trying to make architecture and urbanism that is responsive to the "context"—the traditions—of Asia. To paraphrase JFK, I am an Asian and so, to an ever-increasing degree, are we all. I'd therefore like to construct a kind of primitive taxonomy of embodiment, to look at a series of responses to the idea of an alien site that will, I hope, suggest some sources of nuance for both global operatives descending into unfamiliar territory and for local actors beset by anxiety over the waning influence of the *genius loci*, robbed of its authenticity by the tsunami of hypertradition. The idea of inventing a "private" Asia is meant to argue both that mediation is inevitable and that it may be necessary to radically invert the etiology of the traditional by fixing its origins in individual invention and private fantasies, which then potentiate the accumulation of consent that gives them public validity.

For me it begins in Japan. As you know, Japan was, during its long boom in the eighties and nineties, the architectural promised land. The extravagant sums, the fashion for imports, and a craving for the new combined to make an amazingly fertile terrain for building, and the business class cabins of every flight from the US to Narita were chock-a-block with American architects eager to cash in. Watching this spectacle from afar, I wanted to be a part of it but, as is often the case with my practice, no client stepped forward to share this enthusiasm. I've never found this to be a particular impediment, and so decided to design a very large building for Tokyo, sight unseen.

Never mind the mantra earlier invoked about the ethical obligation to visit any contemplated site; it is also true that there's value in not doing so. Framing a design problem is always a matter of both inclusion and exclusion, and holding certain orders of observation aside is necessary and stimulating—a way of locating issues of interest and of situating a project epistemologically, of generating self-consciousness about knowledges invoked, whether in their presence or absence. I knew things about Japan and Tokyo already and took them as sufficient. Included in this inventory were stories told by a panoply of Japanese friends and colleagues, a cover-to-cover reading in college of an English translation of the *Tale of Genji*, as well as of many contemporary novels like *Some Prefer Nettles* and *The Box Man*. There was an architecture school course with Gunter Nitzchke about Japanese traditional architecture and ritual that left indelible images of the Ise shrine cycling side-wise, of boulders bound with rope, and of candles floating downstream. There was my addiction to sushi, the paper koi hanging in my childhood bedroom, 1950s boy's war games fought against an alternating cast of depraved Nazis and Japs, activism on behalf of nuclear disarmament, the shame-guilt binary of Ruth Benedict, an appearance at the age of thirteen in the title role of *The Mikado*, a penchant for the megastructures of the Metabolists, a text- and image-learned fascination for the density and irregularity of Tokyo and its convulsive visual style (reinforced by the pithy commentary of Roland Barthes), and hundreds of hours watching Japanese movies, including not just elevated work like *Sanjo the Bailiff*, *Woman in the Dunes*, or *Rashomon*, but such mesmerizing, over-the-top gems as *Mothra* and *Godzilla*.

Godzilla

Indeed, it was this latter that became the inspiration and eponym for this skyscraper. Placed on an invented site, the project was meant to suggest an intensification of Tokyo-ness, an eruption of its density, and mix up the z-axis, a verticalization of an existing horizontal order. Its tripartite sectional organization both reflects a traditional skyscraper morphology and is the instrument for achieving a rich mix of uses, with large public facilities—department stores, theaters, etc.—in its base, offices in its middle range, and residences floating above to command the view. Godzilla is also intended as a point of horizontal dissemination. The radiating tendrils of its plan, which systematically interfere with and reorder the system of streets, recapturing that space from the automotive system to create an island of pedestrian priority, a reversion to a more "traditional" style of occupying historically narrow street spaces. Finally, the project represents what might be seen as a symbol of Japanese post-nuclear anxiety, inscribing the core message of the Godzilla films. It must be noted, though, that that message, like many traditions, morphed dramatically. Although the initial 1954 film by Ishiro Honda—who had witnessed the aftermath of Hiroshima and Nagasaki—was clearly intended as a cautionary tale about the unbottled genie of atomic power, by 1964 the monster, matured through numerous sequels, had become a good guy: defender of Japan against monsters more alien.

Godzilla © Michael Sorkin Studio

Sendai

A few years later, when I landed an actual commission in Japan, the result was also a kind of monstrosity. For a large municipal incinerator employing an advanced zero-emissions technology to be built on a green field site outside Sendai, a largely unconscious collation of hillocks, segmented armor, and cruising swans appears to undergird the design. The towering chimney—glass to make clear the plant's benign output—also cathedralizes the structure to celebrate its inescapable prominence on the landscape and its importance to the municipality; and gathered around it, in medieval fashion, is a little village devoted to small-scale recycling and re-use industries. This welter of referents tries to add up to something that is simultaneously singular and familiar, deploying elements of traditional form and organization to achieve a set of effects that are not uncanny or *unheimlich* but, on the contrary, are both legible and accessible.

While I would stop short of describing Godzilla or Sendai as simply mimetic—a concept that is surely crucial to a theory of hypertradition—their component of representation is obviously central. The relationship of traditional architectures to the idea of representation clearly depends on local anthropologies and appears in various forms of ornamentation, abstraction, and ritual in many cultures. Today, however, many of these—in both the developed and developing worlds—are busy with the nominal recuperation of traditional spaces and architectures through styles of mimesis that conform fully with the simple Aristotelean idea of nature imitated, depending, as with that formulation, on an observing position outside the field of what is being observed. Nature—or tradition—is thus recuperated for a work of art or architecture by an artist or observer standing at some critical distance from what he or she surveys, and who values it precisely for its alterity. The skyscraper pagoda in Taipei, the ersatz mud shopping mall in Dubai, or the little *palazzi* of the American suburbs, all trade on ideas about the value of continuity; but their meanings are defined by their distance from their sources, by the bearing capacity of their grafted iconographies, and by their problematic relationship to the other ideas of creativity that also inform them. Shopping malls, skyscrapers, and suburbia—or giant garbage incinerators—are not "traditional" morphologies.

What these examples have in common is not simply appropriation, but the glomming of forms that are already architectural. Two later designs for tall buildings, one in China and one in Malaysia, are frankly mimetic—direct imitations—but seek to establish their credentials of locality by reference to forms that are architectonic but not architectural. Each refers to a physical thing that has the proportion, structural character, and spatiality of a building, but which is not itself one. The Chinese skyscraper is derived from a "philosopher's stone," a traditional object of contemplation that struck me as having amazing potential as a habitable form, and

Sendai

that might—given the possibilities of computation to translate almost any shape into building—undergo the transformation with relative ease.

The second project has a more familiar source. The metaphor of the inhabited mountain has a long history in the literature and imaginary of skyscrapers but, as with any metaphor, the particular expressive qualities of any given translation are bound up with the attenuation of the object from its source. For example, these skyscrapers from 1920s Manhattan have a clear affinity with the prismatic shapes of the mesas of the American west but are, in fact, also mediated by the kind of mountain-making that abounds in many traditional societies. Here the influential intermediary is Mayan, and the interaction of the famous 1916 New York zoning law— which called for tall buildings with a sequence of stepped set-backs— clearly sent architects scrambling to investigate morphological precedents for such forms. That the Mayans also incorporated a highly abstract system of ornamentation—widely influential in so-called Art Deco—was only, as it were, icing on the cake.

Penang Peaks

Antonio Gaudí's famous project for a skyscraper hotel in New York is clearly also highly mountainous in proportion, but at a further remove from specific observation. The proposals of Bruno Taut for an Alpine architecture were both inspired by the glassy, glacial, and prismatic character of mountain peaks and imbued—like so many traditional architectures—with a sense of the sacrality of the mountains. This exhilaration in altitude is something that cuts across many cultures, and the natural land-scape abounds with literal and conceptual ready-mades for inhabitation—many of our families found their first homes in caves—and I have a long relationship to two in particular: the inhabited cones of Cappodocia and the kinds of vertical formations that so mesmerize at places like Guilin in China or Ha Long Bay in Vietnam. This project in Malaysia and another in Shanghai seek both to capture the formal elegance of these shapes and to look at the ways in which an essentially vertical object can be covered in greenery as part of the logic for creating a more sustainable idea about building, particularly in matters of climate control and CO_2 mitigation.

Globalization—and its discontents—might indeed be said to produce a more universal referent, with the right heft to offer the authenticity of traditional building in circumstances in which its meanings are unrecoverable, save museologically. As our building practices are increasingly engaged by global issues of sustainability, the place-bound bio-climatic inflection of architecture and urbanism offers the possibility of both a meaningful and legible localism and an agreeable universalism founded on ancient wisdoms. If the rationalist modernity of the eighteenth century can be said to have invented nature as the ubiquitous other in an anthropocentric universe, rejecting the "superstitious" integration of natural forces into the cultural fabric of traditional societies, it might be said that rationalism has now brought us full-circle, back to an appreciation of our own deeply contingent position on the planet. While this refreshed view is utterly vital, we must still be wary of distortions that grow from modernity's long and guilty romance with the "primitive." As recent revisionist accounts of Native American habits of consumption make clear, much received wisdom about the superiority of traditional arrangements is simply fiction.

The translation of this new universal tradition predicated on the scientific and economic certainty that our settlement practices are increasingly a formula for our own extinction offers both a vitalizing opportunity for the design of new urban patterns and a goad to reacquire the sound formulations of traditional arrangements. In particular, I believe this suggests two particular orders of arrangement. Here are some images of an imaginary city somewhere in Asia, along a line from Hong Kong to Hanoi. Their inspiration came from my first actual visit to Japan, to attend a conference in Osaka. On my first day, I was driven around the city by a local architect. In the course of our tour we came upon what was, for me, a completely arresting sight. Between two bleak concrete towers, there was a tiny farm, occupying a piece of real estate that one would have expected the invisible hand to have long since crushed.

The farm had survived because of both a cultural reverence for agriculture and a strong impetus to self-sufficiency (particularly in the production of rice) and, more specifically, because of inheritance laws that allow farms to escape taxation if they are maintained in use. This artifice in defense of traditional values—a form of protectionism rather than preservationism—strikes me as a bracing model for the creation of the kind of global tradition I have alluded to. One of the clear lessons of sustainability is a powerful prejudice for the local, for a continuous ratcheting up of the idea of autonomy at all scales, from building, to neighborhood, to city. As a morphological matter, this militates for a certain clarity of each increment—from the legibility of neighborhood centers to rational boundaries for cities as a whole—as well as for the constant vetting of local self-sufficiency as a means of accounting for demands on the planetary environment. We face a tremendous crisis of overdevelopment, exacerbated by a blithe failure to moderate our asphyxiating greed. The simple fact is that if everyone on the planet were to consume at American rates, the surface area of two additional planets would be required to fulfill their needs. By making legible the actual operation of demand and supply, that little farm—however impossible under the current regime of irresponsible extraction—begins to model a way of thinking about the city that, by restoring legible relations between city and country, offers valuable lessons for the future.

Neurasia

In the imaginary city of Neurasia, you can see a certain reversion to what might be described as traditional qualities of settlement. Green and agrarian spaces are abundantly inscribed within the texture of the town. Cars are banished in favor of movement on foot, augmented by a tight lace of public transport for longer-distance movement. Buildings are low to support human locomotion in the vertical as well as the horizontal axis. Neighborhoods—the fundamental constituent of any successful urbanity—are made in village-like form in order to conduce the community of the face-to-face and to offer a more familiar environment to immigrants from the countryside, the population that is so swelling the cities of Asia. Finally, the city has a clarity of edges to help harmonize growth and resources. By sitting in a system of new cities, the logic of expansion beyond a certain point lies with the creation of *another* city, rather than the endless extension of an existing one.

Hin Heup

These qualities are also present in this small town designed for a site in Laos. Although the town—developed by a timber company and housing a large sawmill and wood products factory—is a kind of classic nineteenth-century mono-economic construct, we've attempted to make it particular and sustainable by many of the same means deployed in the potentially richer fabric of Neurasia. Connections to the strong existing landscape are carefully considered. The pattern of settlement includes both a strong

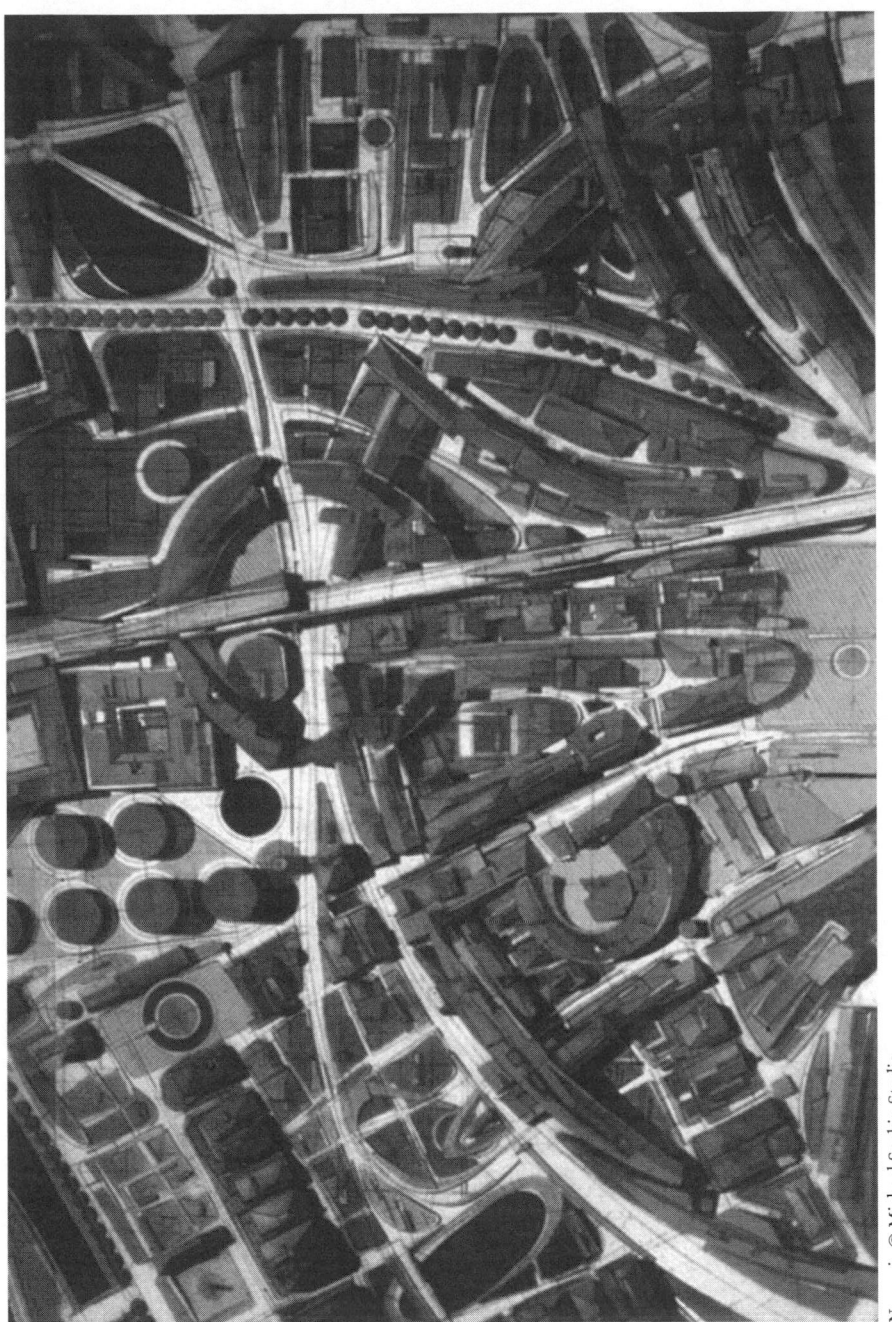

Neurasia © Michael Sorkin Studio

central place and a series of village-like neighborhoods. Agriculture is closely integrated within the structure of the town. Internal circulation is by foot or bicycle. The architecture is constructed of local materials and expands upon existing dwelling types. Strong consideration is given to the local production of energy. And yet, the aggregation as a whole does not attempt to ape some de-contextualized "traditional" morphology but find fresh forms on the basis of still lively ways of living.

In developing the project at Penang, the same basic process of harmonization lies at the core. Again, I don't want to tie the idea of traditional

Hin Heup © Michael Sorkin Studio

environments too closely with ineffable connections to the rhythms of "nature," nor to suggest that such environments are the repositories of ultimate wisdom about sustainable best practices for today. However, I do want to argue that there are powerful values associated with delimitation which I, like others, take to be the hallmark of traditional cultures. While these values are not absolute—save bliss, there's no special profit in ignorance—they are radically important economic models and crucial means for measuring the physical dimensions of cultural and productive relations. They are touchstones for the restoration of the values of scale, so assailed by global culture and its much remarked annihilation of space by time.

Penang Peaks

Although the forms of the buildings at Penang Peaks are not deeply engaged with traditional local architectural morphologies—which are, in any case, historically diverse—they are intended to evoke a prominent feature of the landscape and are assembled in an urban structure organized around streets, arcades, courts, and parks that are at the core of familiar understandings of the city and form keys to its tractability. Equally important are the project's responses to the particularities of climate—there is a very elaborate effort to use every possible resource for cooling and shading—and much attention has been paid to the balancing of the development's inputs and outputs: the whole is designed to be self-sufficient in waste treatment, energy generation, water collection, employment numbers, educational opportunities, recreational facilities, and CO_2 sequestration. I firmly believe that the future of architecture and urbanism is vitally bound to the nature of their boundary conditions and to their collaboration in producing ever higher levels of local environmental autonomy.

A possible, if arguable, description of traditional environments lies in the physical contiguity of their ecological footprints. That is, the boundedness

Penang Peaks © Michael Sorkin Studio

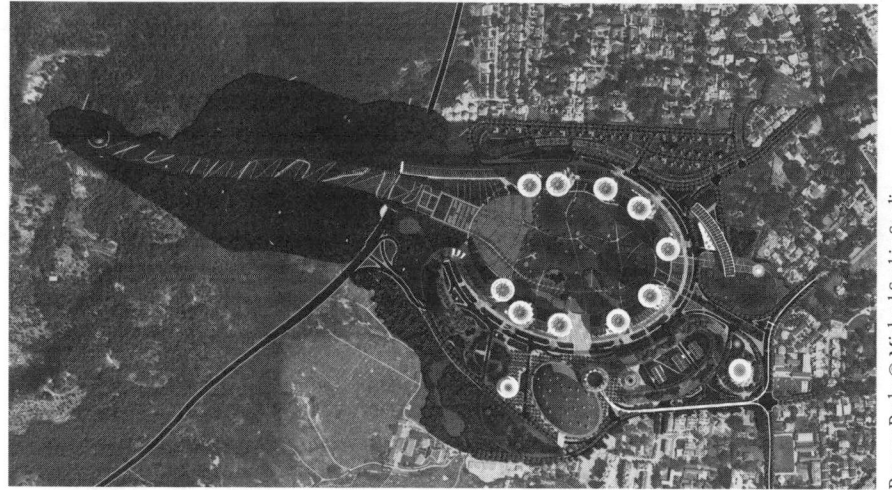

of traditional societies is not simply cultural but also environmental. Even if not fully hermetic, such societies might be calibrated comparatively via the measure of the hinterlands of their survival. One of the reasons that the planet is in such dire straits is precisely the loss of the kind of ecological accountancy that is obliged by narrower forms of self-reliance than those promoted by a fully globalized circuit of capital and production. In this sense, I am arguing for the necessity of a return to a radical variety of traditional values, to a conception of cities as responsible for the necessary elements of their own respiration. And I believe that, in an era of weak states and powerful transnational corporations, this style of independence will ramify both environmentally and politically, that cities will come to form the necessary bulwark for the future of democracy, our own multiply-inflected tradition.

Chungcheong New City

The final example I would like to show is another city designed from scratch, a proposal for a new administrative city in South Korea. Here, again, arises the issue of creating ideas and practices of locality that will induce an accumulation of tradition and identity. To this end, the project deploys the triple repertoire of radical environmental autonomy, recognizable urban morphologies, and artistic invention, to create a framework of transformative inhabitation. The project begins with an inventory of the prospects for self-reliance, and its elaboration proposes strategies for achieving neutrality—or balance—in eight particular areas of autonomy. The result is intended to be a dramatic shrinking of the city's ecological footprint—its required resources—as well as a strong attempt to situate their production in direct contiguity with the city.

The city is structured around a series of distributed stimuli meant to gently induce a structure of neighborhoods, and is only loosely regulated by use. It does, however, deploy its densities prescriptively to promote compaction, variety, and a walkable scale. In terms of its evocation of values specifically Korean, the city anticipates the vibrant, contingent variety and convulsive graphic environment that typifies modern Korean cities. In the complexity and irregularity of its street system, it likewise seeks to retain the characteristic texture of cities that have grown and found their character through the accumulation of fabric over time and through the efforts of many actors. Finally, it seeks to address the contemporary dynamic—the mass production and use of automobiles—that threatens to eradicate the future of such wonderfully variegated urbanism, and that is rapidly turning contemporary Korea into one of the world's largest examples of the Radiant City run amok. By the redirection of the prodigious energy of the Korean auto industry to the production of the next form of vehicle—the small, slow-moving, soft, non-polluting New Urban Vehicle—and by the banning of conventional cars, the irregularities of the city become supportable, as does the traditional primacy of people on foot. Technology can be friendly to traditional arrangements, not their nemesis.

These projects represent the way Asia looks to me, and frankly acknowledge the transformative and inevitable character of the gaze. They reject the idea of an economy of mediation that seeks to evade the usefully critical potential of distance. Valuing tradition is not to reduce its components

Chungcheong © Michael Sorkin Studio

to pictures at an exhibition, or so many zoo animals. Nor is it to seek an asymptotic approach to the signifier-degree-zero of the hypertraditional. It is, rather, a rigorous and respectful process of reciprocal assimilation by each of us of the other based, in the case of the city, on a necessary mutuality in defense of our survival and our difference.

2006

58

Everybody's a Critic!

There's an ad on American TV—for a home alarm system—that depicts a comical burglar in a striped prison uniform, sitting behind bars as he's interviewed by an off-screen voice. The burglar describes the overgrown lawn—a "sure sign"—that led him to conclude the inhabitants were away and attempt a break-in. But, asks the interviewer, didn't you see the obvious medallion of the home security company? The embarrassed burglar responds in high annoyance: "Jeez! Everybody's a critic!"

For architecture, everybody actually is. We are always in and around architecture and cannot escape its influence—coercive, delightful, useful, or compromising—and it has always been so. It is part of what marks us as a species, something, like the highly developed use of tools, intrinsic to our identity. The press has just announced an effort to unravel the Neanderthal genome, which will surely affirm that we humans share most of our genetic character with this ancestor (much as we do with chimps and nematodes and our other carbon-based cousins). This activity of tracing back also seems an irresistible aspect of our singularity, encoded in the structure of our curiosity, whether we account for it through our innumerable theisms, or more scientifically through the search for the evolutionary alpha-point, the moment when some primordial slime was energized and realigned to become "life."

Architecture too is built up from its origin tales, the taxonomy of its lineages, always argued backward from some privileged present. We insist on beginnings, on being little gods who labor to create our universes (and then take a break). The famous primitive hut, the first habitation, establishes the myth of architecture's rationality: the idea that shelter was, for us, something motivated by experience, not simply doing "what comes naturally." We don't imagine a conference of swallows or beavers from which descended—through their analysis of the mode of production of foodstuffs, the family, the protection from predation and inclemency, the need to live in exclusive communities, or even from a spontaneous moment of conviviality—the idea of the nest or the dam. We, on the other hand, demand such a moment to establish the idea of our agency and our capacity for transformation. It seems teleologically impossible simply to think that we were always already sheltering animals.

The same patterns of filiation dominate and defend the way we do our critical business. If we look to writers on architecture and the visual world—including Marcus Vitruvius Pollio from the first century BC; Johann Joachim Winckelmann, Marc-Antoine Laugier, Immanuel Kant, and Georg Wilhelm Friedrich Hegel from the eighteenth and early nineteenth centuries; John Ruskin and William Morris from the nineteenth century; as well as Heinrich Wölfflin, Ernesto Rogers, Bruno Zevi, Gilles Deleuze, and Jacques Derrida from the twentieth—it's all remarkably patrimonial: a tribal anxiety about influence. Indeed—unlike Vitruvius, whose fantasies were for the *hut*—we nowadays seek to understand and (if we can) to justify our ways with less reference to the object of our gaze than to the techniques of our own observation, fixated on our telescopes but losing sight of the stars. This relentless narrowing to a belle-lettristic or academic paradigm—the paradigm of writing—has served to distance us both from architecture itself, by inventing it too narrowly, and from its primal scenes: the interaction of space and habitation.

A distinguished psychoanalyst once usefully observed that you don't need to be an architect to hit your head against the wall. Nor, one might add, to be a critic in order to shout "ouch!" The volume (about architectural criticism in the Islamic world) in which this originally appeared is full of lamentations: as critics, we gather to collectively bemoan our meager reach and to produce ourselves as victims of animus or (worse!) indifference. From the West, we hear about the baleful impact of big money, the superficiality of "starchitecture," the corruptions of hyper-consumption, and the sheer philistinism of it all. From the East, we hear about confrontations of tradition and modernity, old-fashioned styles of authoritarianism and censorship, the lack of a critical culture, and a poverty of resources. What I would like to suggest, though, is that criticism is flourishing everywhere, and that our task is not to deny this but to identify, channel, and amplify its manifold messages.

The appearance—the look—of buildings is at once both the least and the most interesting thing about them. The least, if it is the hinge by which architecture is reduced to sculpture, to a "pure" form described in private languages: something self-referential, hermetic, detached, and canonical. The most, though, if it offers an opening to architecture's multiple possibilities for representation, its rich and shifting dialectic of form and content. This ultimate resistance to abstraction, this intrinsic multiplicity of meanings, results from architecture's literal inhabitation, and is what distinguishes it from other artistic expressions. The social is not the *context* of architecture but its substance. And this is the reason why everybody can—and does—read it, from the most effete *kunstwissenschaftler* to the infant crawling across the cold floor toward the warming rug.

Architecture's own polyvalence should also remind us that its critical tradition is highly diverse, that the codification of the architect's responsibilities in the eighteenth century BC by the Babylonian King Hammurabi is as consequential as the dismay expressed about the nineteenth-century industrial city by the architect A. W. Pugin, or the defense of contemporary neighborhood ecologies by the late, great urbanist Jane Jacobs. This interweaving of architecture with the social life that produces it and that it, in turn, supports has produced the formal tradition of architectural commentary and critique, which dates back millennia, and assures us that it has always come from multiple perspectives and has been embodied in multiple discourses. The task of criticism is surely not to "resolve" this polyphony in a single approach (like the fine arts style dominant today), but to enable more voices to be heard.

We all come from countries in which architectural activities are conducted under the framework of building codes, planning ordinances, and other legal instruments that define, sometimes with overwhelming specificity, an idea about "good" architecture. Setting aside, for a moment, questions of the legal manipulation of matters of appearance—requirements to design in historical or "contextual" fashion, or to include a portrait of the President, Dear Leader, Dictator, or Sheikh in the lobby— it is clear that both the utility and forms of our buildings and cities have been dramatically influenced by the legal frameworks that site, organize, and judge them; frameworks that, however fraudulently, rest their authority on an idea of social benefit.

Contemporary architecture is very much the product of a series of innovations that were conceptualized performatively and only later worked out morphologically. Demands originating in movements for social transformation and equity were translated into laws requiring daylighting, ventilation, heating, sanitation, and protection from fire. We know something about the disastrous consequences of the *evasion* of seismic regulations in Japan and Turkey, and it is the general recognition of the importance of those standards that makes flouting them so scandalous. Only because of the existence of an enormous body of criticism—some of it from the community of architecture—are we able to take the necessity of these fundamental qualities of our building for granted: the imbrication of architecture with an idea of the common good.

Today, we are passing through a period in which the shape of buildings and cities is in desperate need of reconfiguration—a continuation of the historic process of re-describing architecture in terms both of how it must act and how it must be: what its fundamental qualities are. Just as many of the reforms that established the parameters of building today are the direct outcome of specific disasters—fires, earthquakes, cyclones, and epidemics—radical transformations in architecture (for both good and ill) are being produced by more contemporary crises, by situations that are the logical focus for the work of architectural criticism, a practice in which some form of advocacy must always be embedded.

The first of these crises falls under the rubric of "the environment," and inevitably will alter virtually every aspect of the way in which we design. The acceleration of climate change is very real, and our buildings, cities, and transportation infrastructure are directly implicated. Although the United States is the disproportionate champion in producing greenhouse gasses, consuming energy from non-renewable sources, and setting an unsustainable model for overdevelopment, it is joined by the rest of the world in increasing degree. China currently has a level of car ownership comparable to that in the United States in 1912, and seems determined to match our ridiculous overdependence on the automobile. Recent studies of air quality in India—the first such to be undertaken comprehensively—reveal levels of pollution that frequently exceed recognized standards of safety by truly appalling margins. The Gulf region is engaged in a frenzied building boom anchored literally and figuratively in petroleum. If there is an apt symbol of the global energy binge now underway—and the enduring association of status and waste—it is surely the huge indoor ski-slope in a shopping mall in Dubai, soon to be topped by an even larger version under construction down the road.

The situation of a warming, toxic, degraded, planetary environment—and an exponentially growing population now topping six billion—has fundamental consequences for architecture and for the culture we collaborate in producing that defines both its character and reception. While it is surely the duty of critics to hold the line for architectural quality—to celebrate the artistic achievements of contemporary architects such as Tadao Ando, Zaha Hadid, or Frank Gehry, and to explain expressive nuances and systems of meaning—we are mistaken if we think that the territory of formal analysis can simply be isolated from other concerns, protected by the mantle of "free expression," or by the notion that all artistic works engage the world at comparable distance. A poem written in the nineteenth century by Emily Dickinson on the back of a scrap of paper and relegated to the drawer is a very different affair than a gigantic sealed glass building in the desert or a huge titanium flower in Spain. Not to contravene the First Law of Thermodynamics, but there is no question that, in our sphere, energy can be lost. Virtually no material embodies more energy than titanium. And the BTUs blown cooling Dubai or Vegas might clean all the drinking water of Africa.

It may be that the duty of architectural critics nowadays is less to rise in defense of "architecture" than to defend the planet from too much of it. Our tasks are immediately different from those confronted by Clement Greenberg, Anthony Blunt, and other art critics of less hybrid forms of expression. Because every work of architecture maps a set of social relations, because every work of architecture accounts for a complex of distributive decisions about global resources, and because every work of architecture colludes in the literal creation of the world climate, criticism cannot escape taking these matters into account. However hard it may attempt to retreat behind the veil of "objectivity," criticism is always a form of propaganda, precisely because these inescapable dimensions of architecture ineluctably render its judgments political. The duty of the critic, therefore, is both to consider the larger meanings of his or her preoccupations or circumspections and to empower his or her readers with an analytical tool with which to make the environment more comprehensible and tractable—to make the *public* more critical. To be sure, this can mean—as it did in the debates that originated the era of postmodernity—the fight to defend the aesthetic basis of architecture, to protect it from vulgar theories of reflexive instrumentality: a work of architecture is always also a work of art.

This political aspect of criticism is engaged directly by the dire condition of the environment and architecture's role in creating or curing it. Given architecture's fundamentally conservative position at the end of a chain of decisions, and as the product of the concentration of fiscal and material resources, the task of critics—like that of those social reformers who had such a strong impact on building practices in the nineteenth and twentieth centuries—is to fight for the renewal of the legal and conceptual frameworks of building to make sustainability as uncontroversial an element in architectural culture as sanitary plumbing, fire-safety, or seismic protection. This is a model that demands action before the fact, not simply the canny analysis of the object once standing. But it also means that the nature of connoisseurship—instead of being an arcane, distancing, elitist practice—must be enriched by additional categories of expertise and judgment, that we must empower ourselves to lovingly describe both the lush patina of oxidizing COR-TEN™ and elegant systems for the passive extraction of hot air.

This form-follows-disaster model also becomes widely influential in the wake of quicker-moving natural catastrophes, including the South Asian tsunami of December 2004, and Hurricane Katrina in August 2005. Katrina was both a remarkably terrible and remarkably clarifying event. Like the tsunami, it called into question large-scale patterns of settlement, including the logic of building (and rebuilding) on endangered coastlines, the destruction of natural wetlands, barrier islands, and other forms of natural protection—even the viability of one of the US's most important cities, New Orleans. It also has resulted in dramatic debates about logical building typologies and construction methods, and has, with blistering impact, revealed the deep distributive inequities that underlie all those patterns. If ever architectural criticism were offered a synthetic, focal, moment, this was it: the conjunction of environmental, social, structural, economic, and expressive issues was a "perfect storm." It was also one of those moments at which the task of criticism was widely dispersed, an event that obliged almost every observer to formulate opinions on core questions of architecture and urbanism.

Katrina showed that there is both a very widespread common language for the discussion of architecture and that its deployment is instantaneous in demanding circumstances. Could it be that the complaint by many critics in these pages about their marginalization expresses the pain of a self-inflicted wound? Could there possibly be greater public interest in debating the form of the city, the role of architecture, the laying out of infrastructure, the meaning of community, than there has been in the wake of Katrina? Architects have scarcely been parsimonious with suggestions, and their contending variety has provided a smorgasbord of setups for critical intervention. And these are the times and places where our intervention is important, where lives—not brands—are at stake.

Disasters *are* criticism, because they force reflection on their origins and interrogate the structure of life—both social and physical—that we are accustomed to thinking of as normal. One sometimes uses the phrase "a disaster waiting to happen" to describe a situation that is susceptible to a known form of trouble: an unreinforced building in an active seismic zone, a "fire trap," or a slum of injurious, fomenting injustice and discontent. Clearly, such sites demand the work of criticism and give it purpose: critics can be the canaries in the coal mine. But it is misleading to suggest that architecture has an invariably positivist trajectory, that the cycle of challenge and reform repeats itself uniformly as outcome. Critics must distinguish disasters of our own creation and identify developments, which, in the guise of reform or "safety," are actually regressive, perpetuating rather than ameliorating our jeopardy.

These unnatural disasters form an urgent motive for all of us, and architecture must be discussed both in its role as accessory and as the ledger in which these circumstances are recorded. No more stark instance of this exists than the exponential growth of slums. Half the world population now lives in cities, and of these half live in slums. It is not possible that the architecture of a billion and half people should be outside our purview, that we should reserve our focus for the historic cores of unsustainable megacities, or myopically cheer the fevered growth of their gigantic, perpetually inadequate infrastructures and their generic architectures and environments. We must not confirm these deadly patterns, whether through enthusiasm or indifference, or by confining our practices simply to projects that fall within conventional notions of "quality." Architecture is—and records—a living condition; our choice of focus will either defend or subvert ideas of freedom, equity, and difference.

Writing this as the airwaves are again dominated by images of destruction in the Middle East, another deeply influential set of disasters of our own making leaps to the foreground. There's an old joke about "military music" being a perfect oxymoron. Unfortunately, military architecture is no such thing, and the history of architecture and urbanism is inextricably interwoven with the exigencies of warfare, a connection that seems only to deepen of late. Our "father" Vitruvius devoted a major portion of his treatise to the arts of fortification, and the Roman imperium spread its colonizing tentacles via cities that elaborated the gridded order of military camps. Until very recent times, cities were literally surrounded by walls, and defensive measures certainly might have been part of the Neanderthal schmooze at that primal campfire.

We continue to live with the consequences of our own violence. During the Cold War years, both America and China pursued policies of dramatic de-urbanization as a defense against the atomic war, and even the neutral Swiss—who have the resources to put plenty of cash behind their anxiety—legislated a bomb-shelter in every basement. As ever, civic investment in guns short-changed butter and deformed the idea of public culture, the site where an architecture of life most urgently needs to flourish. Make no mistake: this is a zero sum game. Every base and bunker built means one fewer library, school, sewer, housing block, or clinic. As hundreds die every day in Iraq, as bombs blast Beirut and Gaza, as rockets rain on Haifa, the images of shattered bodies and buildings scream that our addiction to violence must be controlled for architecture itself to live. Isn't it our task to help banish forever this evil branch of the family, the one that builds Security Fences, Pentagons, pillboxes, refugee camps, Kalashnikov-stuffed caves, and the rest of the infrastructure of violent death?

The 9/11 attack galvanized a discussion of architecture and planning that was nearly universal in New York. This was the direst physical disaster the city—which has been spared the direct effects of war since the days of the Revolution—has ever faced. As a result, New York and other American cities are now decking themselves out with a huge defensive apparatus that is transforming both the cityscape and the way in which we inhabit it. Thousands of bollards and anti-bomb flower-planters litter the streets. The building code is undergoing another revision to better prepare structures to withstand attack. Although much of this is sensible from the standpoint of "normal" emergencies—more secure escape stairs are important in a fire, whatever its origins—much of it reflects a manipulated paranoia that only serves the end of a contracted and manipulated public realm. The slow progress of rebuilding at Ground Zero has been an endless object lesson in the relationship of architecture and power, and in the way in which the public meanings of building are established and controlled.

Architecture's highly ambiguous role in all of this has provided endless opportunities for critical reflection, and—in this most media-saturated environment on earth—the discussion has been brisk if ultimately ineffectual in influencing an outcome that has been, for the most part, decided outside the democratic arena. However, the use of 9/11 to produce the vast new apparatus of Homeland Security—and to manufacture consent to it—has also provided a bridge for architectural criticism to enter one of the most challenging realms it currently confronts: the importance of virtual space and its arrangements to any serious contemplation of the built environment. While it is still possible to sustain a degree of enthusiasm for the liberatory possibilities of the electronic "global village," it is also clear that the conjunction of new technology with state and corporate power has had dramatically different consequences.

Those bollards and blast-proof lobbies are the visible tip of a giant iceberg of surveillance and manipulation that has fundamental implications for our relationship to space, affecting the nature of our rights, our privacy, our ease of movement, and our freedom of association and assembly. These are core issues for architecture, and they are being challenged from all sides, whether by suicide bombers, police departments, or multinational hucksters. These forces see architecture militarily, as a phenomenon that either complies with and advances their agendas or as an obstacle to be destroyed, whether literally or by being made transparent to their panoptic gaze. Architectural criticism must find a way to confront both what it can and cannot see, and to recognize that its own situation has been radically changed, and will become even more marginalized if it insists on being no more than the instrument of intellectual and spatial nostalgia.

If the magnitude of the 9/11 tragedy exceeded that of others, the response has been in many ways familiar. New York's great debates about its future often have followed focal events. The Triangle Shirtwaist fire of 1911, in which 146 garment workers—mainly young women—died because they could not escape, led directly to improved regulations for building safety. The construction in 1915 of the Equitable Insurance Company building— an early skyscraper that rose 540 feet straight up from the street—galvanized the rapid passage of New York's pioneering 1916 bulk-zoning laws that invented the "classic" stepping profiles (designed to bring daylight to the public street) that characterized our buildings until the dopey, modernist-inspired revisions of the 1960s. The 1963 demolition of the much-loved Pennsylvania Station (designed by McKim, Meade, and White in 1910 after the model of the third-century Baths of Caracalla in Rome) was a defining moment in the birth of the preservation movement that has been so crucial, in good ways and bad, to ideas about the relationship between stability and change in a city that was suddenly forced to confront its own historic character.

If I seem to return over and over to the confrontational role of criticism, it is because criticism itself can arise only in situations in which there are alternatives. Criticism defines a position within a context in which others are also possible, and uses its tools argumentatively, to demonstrate the logic and consequences of a point of view. Architectural criticism is rhetorical in its obligation to persuade, and political in its obligation to the social, to the distinguishing dimension of architecture. In choosing the location of an argument, the critic selectively distorts, looking for sites of opportunity to persuasively reveal the results of his or her experience and analysis.

In a society governed entirely by "tradition," there can be no criticism because of the presumption that everything has already been consented to (or in which the very idea of consent is foreign), and that the only task of the intellect is transmission or reproduction: the paradigm is fixed. Once, however, the idea of the plural is broached, criticism becomes both necessary and inevitable.

Debates about the importance of traditional architectures (and modernism now takes its place among them)—whether focused on the authenticity of style, on prescriptive social morphology, or on the importance of *l'art pour l'art*—arise only in the context of challenge, of the availability of other ways of seeing and doing. If there has been a general drift in critical theory over the past thirty years or so (however "Western" one might elect to see this phenomenon), it has been to interrogate the idea of the absolute: the notion that the "truth" is stable and universal. While there are many who question the implications of such "relativistic" reasoning and the dangers it poses in particular to the ethical dimension of life, it nonetheless seems clear that the world *is* radically diverse, and that even common objectives can be approached from many directions. The reality of difference also means that the importance of tradition—however this is understood—must be argued in ways that are comprehensible to those who stand outside it. A critic cannot simply assert the timelessness of any given traditional architecture, but must connect it to its role in culture, its ability to fulfill a building's obligation to the environment, its importance as an element in humanity's mosaic of achievement, its ability to conduce the happiness of its inhabitants; or—to address the ethical obligations of the other more directly—must invoke the importance of tolerance for another's free choices.

Such choices about architecture are made a billion times a day, and each of these depends on some mechanism of distinction. Whether it's the bank that "redlines" a poor neighborhood for disinvestment, the suburbanite selecting wallpaper at the Home Depot, the board of trustees at a museum hiring a star architect in hopes of attracting crowds, the bomber pilot "illuminating" a building for destruction, the developer looking for a cheap patch of land, the preservationist defending a historic church, or the favela-dweller sorting through a scrap pile looking for something with which to patch his roof, the built environment is not an unconscious product but a compilation of choices based on an infinite repertoire of criteria. Architectural criticism, as a discipline, can only operate in the context of this blooming of preferences, contingencies, and demands.

To find our own ways through this thicket of determinacies, however, we must formulate criteria that we must then constantly hone and test. There are four ideas that we should all bear in mind. The first is that architecture is always instrumental. Building alters the way people live, the way the planet is configured, the availability of resources, and the way space and its memory are organized. Architecture is not an abstraction, but a concrete proposition about human activity. In analyzing architecture, this means—a second point—that we should never understand our task as standing above the quantitative. The relevance of architectural criticism is founded in its cognizance of the measurable, one of the origin points of architecture itself. Building exists in a social, ecological, and gravitational environment, and can and must be weighed on the scales of survival and equity. We cannot ignore the resources buildings consume, the environmental and social effects of their operation, and their adequacy to people's material needs.

Third, architectural criticism must never lose sight of the artistic dimension of its object, while remembering all the while that architecture's aesthetic expression is uniquely contingent. This does not disqualify any system of meaning, however arcane. It does insist, though, that it account for its compatibilities with the other systems of signification that architecture invariably contains. This relationship can be critical—even antagonistic—but it cannot, by definition, be absent. And finally, architectural criticism is obliged to support the primary duty of architecture itself: making life better. This is the lamp that should illumine every building we make and every sentence we write.

2007

59

Go Down Moses!

Robert Moses is back! In a sentiment that has been brewing for several years, the city's erstwhile master builder has come in for a heavy dose of revisionism. When so many of our big projects seemed vexed by incompetence and stymied by community opposition, the nostalgia for a *man who can get things done* is running rampant. And Moses was that in spades. As Lewis Mumford put it, "In the twentieth century, the influence of Robert Moses on the cities of America was greater than that of any other person."

As the result of a three-part show—at the Museum of the City of New York, the Queens Museum, and Columbia University—curated by architectural historian Hilary Ballon, as well as a fascinating book, *Robert Moses and the Modern City*, co-edited by Ballon and Kenneth Jackson, and swelling media coverage, New York is burning with Moses fever. There is, in fact, much to celebrate in his forty-year career. Moses built on a mighty scale—parks by the hundreds, enormous public swimming pools and magnificent beaches, glistening suspension bridges, elegant parkways, remade waterfronts; a legacy that forms the basis of much of what is great about New York today.

Since the 1960s, however, Moses has been more remembered for his dark side, for the half million poor people displaced by his projects for highways and urban renewal, for the neighborhoods he destroyed, for the psychotic roadways he wanted to keep slamming through the city. Mumford—joined by Jane Jacobs and many others—came to revile Moses, a view fixed by Robert Caro's titanic 1976 biography, *The Power Broker*, which accused Moses of having "used the power of money to undermine the democratic processes of the largest city in the world." In urbanist Robert Fishman's slightly more ambivalent words, Moses—who did not shy from comparing himself to Baron Haussman—"combined the high-minded idealism of a public servant with the insults and innuendoes of a Tammany politician."

While I agree that it is important to celebrate the constructive side of Moses's achievement, I want to devote this column to the brief for the dark side, the cautionary lessons of this history. For all his successes, Moses did very bad things, and there are three indelible charges that continue to have enormous relevance, both for how we remember Moses and for how we plan today. These are, simply put, that Moses pioneered and ruthlessly wielded a set of fundamentally undemocratic instruments for planning; that his priorities were distorted to the detriment of a more "holistic" view of urbanism; and that he was a racist whose project disproportionately harmed the poor and people of color.

Although Moses was not the inventor of the public authority, his refinement of its instrumental power and his use of that apparatus to consolidate sweeping control in his own hands was dramatically innovative. From the headquarters of the Triborough Bridge and Tunnel Authority on Randall's Island, Moses presided over a freestanding empire that was essentially immune from public review, and that wielded powers of condemnation, bonding, and revenue collection that made it virtually autonomous. Moses ruled like a king, dispensing largesse, ignoring opposition, and ruining the careers of those who stood in his way. While the chastening example of his dictatorial methods continues to be a caution, it is striking that the major planning projects in New York today—including Ground Zero and the West Side Yards in Manhattan and the Atlantic Yards in Brooklyn—are all enabled by the special powers of condemnation and immunity wielded by their owners, the Metropolitan Transit Authority and the Port Authority of New York. The baleful specter of Moses also surely hovers over the current national expansion of governmental powers of eminent domain and seizure of private property in order to advance not public but private interests, so dramatically pioneered by Moses in projects like Stuyvesant Town and the raft of urban-renewal developments built under Title One of the 1949 Federal Housing Act.

Although it would be perverse to criticize Moses for not being more sweeping in his ambitions and activities, his life's work was focused on three main areas: parks, roadways, and urban renewal. While Moses's park building was both visionary and refined, his activities on behalf of highways and "slum clearance" were deeply fraught. And this repertoire begs the question of the range of things that these priorities excluded, to the city's detriment, including, most prominently, attention to mass transit as well as other elements of municipal infrastructure—such as schools, hospitals, and sewers. Because Moses was so successful in realizing his agenda—and in attracting funds for it—this triplex both diminished the prospects for other projects and framed for years the core agenda of planning itself.

As Ballon and Jackson write in the introduction to their book, the seeming discrepancy between the marvelous parks and the nightmare neighborhood destruction is often accounted for by a "two Moses" theory: "the good Moses of the 1930s . . . associated with a faith in government's ability to act on the public behalf, and the bad Moses of the 1950s," whom they link to "a loss of faith in the government to act wisely, particularly in urban affairs where governmental programs, however well intended, had destructive consequences." Their semi-redemptive argument seeks to situate Moses's activities in a wider context, in which he appears not as the arch-fiend but as a supernumerary devil, reflecting larger trends in public opinion and the shifting availability of national government programs and financing.

In this reading, Moses's clean-slate urban renewal is simply a particularly successful extension of a more general consensus about the large-scale excision of "diseased" areas of the city and the displacement of the poor—a way both of retaining middle-class vitality and of exploiting the clearance money flowing from the feds under Title One. Similarly, the highways Moses sought to blast through the city in the later part of his career (and which, in their blithe outrageousness, planted the seeds of his undoing) are seen as rational, if reflexive, responses to the 90 percent financing available for the interstates, which proved suicidally irresistible to so many American cities. And there's the implication that, while Moses may have been unashamedly racist (the evidence is disgustingly abundant), so were lots of people in positions of power.

These arguments have a few problems. Moses's road-building career began long before federal legislation financed its acceleration. Indeed, his very success was formative in creating the culture in which the automobile was seen as the irresistible alpha in the traffic hierarchy and in which public transportation was invisible. To the degree that he held a theory of the city, it was thoroughly modernist in its priorities, and—like Corbusier and CIAM—saw cities primarily as a conductive medium for speedy circulation. When the interstate legislation was being drafted, Moses was adamant that, contrary to initial planning, "the interstates must go right through cities and not around them." That this vision of the city defined by its regional circulation sinews and their unobstructed movement through town was in the air for much of the twentieth century in no way exonerates Moses. He was not simply the passive recipient of the good news—he was present at creation.

The same is true of his roughshod tread on neighborhood ecologies. While Moses may have thought he was pursuing a higher calling to advance the public good, he cannot be judged simply in terms of the durability of his projects, their architectural quality, or even their adaptability to changed circumstances—parks built for the middle class that now find themselves in neighborhoods turned poorer. Nor, on the other hand, does it suit to see Moses's work as the product of his own authoritarian personality, to freight his project with psychic biography. His aggrandizement of power, his dreadful effects on the lives of so many people, his distortion of the constructive energies of government, are not incidental to his "real" legacy: they are his legacy. While the comparison may be hyperbolic, a focus on the architectural—even public—quality of his achievements risks the same kind of distortion that a view of Mussolini through the filter of

Terragni or the train schedule does. How do you create a "balanced" view of someone who was "also" a monster?

Clearly, the contribution of Robert Moses cannot be addressed simply as a question of architecture or planning, but must engage issues of culture. The authors of *Robert Moses and the Modern City* have written with balance and insight about a very complicated case, and the catalogue of work the book compiles is invaluable, and in many ways breathtaking. But the risk that Moses poses today is in the conflation of vision and unilateralism. At the level of planning, I am disquieted by the growth of so-called "public-private partnerships" which often represent not simply the abdication of the duty of the public sphere to assure that the common good will contain a full measure of equity in results, but also an end-run around democracy itself, bypassing the hard work of guaranteeing that the voices of all citizens will be heard and acted on with equal weight.

As we daily witness the mayhem in Iraq, the disaster of our attempts to impose our vision of the common good on a body politic that sees the effects of these intentions as both disenfranchising and deadly, it is wise to be wary of any imperious man on a horse who claims to know what's best for us.

2007

60

The Jungle Urban: Welcome to Petropolis

Pink Floyd was playing on the loudspeaker of the ferry that transported our bus over the Rio Napo into the 2,700-square-mile Yasuní National Park in the Amazon basin in Ecuador's Oriente. After hours of slow progress over rutted roads through a largely denuded countryside, we'd missed a ferry and had milled for an hour in a shore-side scene of extreme informality—hot sun, muddy, littered paths along the river, lazing dogs, scattered houses, a little shop, dirt parking lot for waiting vehicles. The scene on the other side, however, was more like Guantánamo. From the dock, we walked along narrow chain-link passages topped with razor-wire, passed though a magnetometer, had hand-luggage x-rayed, passports compared to a list sent in advance, and our watched bus taken into a camouflage-painted metal shed for the once-over. No Coke stands or pleasantries here. Instead there were gun-towers, searchlights, signs forbidding alcohol and drugs, and M-16-toting men in uniform—from the Ecuadorian army and private security firms with Orwellian names (Servisafe, Servipro): an unexpected gateway to paradise.

Yasuní is one of the most biodiverse areas on the planet—a UNESCO "world biosphere reserve"—a river-laced rainforest teeming with life and home to the indigenous Haorani people. And to oil. Crossing the river, we were entering "Block 16," one of the giant concessions that have platted Oriente since 1967, when a consortium of Texaco and Gulf discovered huge oil reserves there. By mid-1972, exploitation was in full swing and a 312-mile pipeline had been constructed from the now booming village of Nueva Loja (universally called Lago Agrio—Bitter Lake—after Texaco's headquarters in Texas), to the coast from which the crude is shipped abroad, primarily to the US. The high security was intended to protect this resource, to secure the jungle against incursions by terrorists, smugglers, narcotics traffickers, poachers, loggers, and settlers. Of course, it did nothing to protect the area from the traumatic impact of petroleum itself.

The effects of oil on the Ecuadorian landscape have been profound. On the one hand, it has fueled a boom economy, which—especially in the go-go seventies and eighties—generated much middle- and upper-class prosperity and government investment in public infrastructure. On the other, oil has been an environmental disaster. Thousands of square miles of rainforest have disappeared. The lives of numerous indigenous peoples have been forever disrupted. And vast areas have become toxic. According to a class-action lawsuit filed in 2003, Texaco—and its successor Chevron—have not simply dumped close to twenty billion gallons of toxic wastewater (much of the oil is extracted by the injection of water under high pressure and, rather than following standard practice of deep re-injection of wastes, the company simply dumped it in ground-level pits, saving itself $3 a barrel), but have spilled thirty times more oil in the jungle than flowed from the Exxon Valdez. Often referred to as the "Rainforest Chernobyl," the devastation has polluted huge areas of land and aquifer, spiked cancer, spontaneous abortion, and other disease rates, spreading these poisonous effects as far as Peru. The class-action lawsuit, which attempts to recover the cost of the estimated $6 billion cleanup, continues to work its way at a snail's pace through the courts, as does an Ecuadorean government suit claiming fraud on Chevron's part.

The oil concessions—covering thousands of square miles—have a very specific spatiality, a format that is, by stages, turning the forest not simply into a degraded, toxic environment but into an urbanism, a city of a new "disarticulated" character that combines webs and nodes, formality and informality, density and dispersion. Its components include grids of seismic trails (three-meter-wide pathways in which a 2–5 meter deep hole is dug each 100 meters to hold 10–20 kilos of dynamite for acoustic exploration), networks of wells and toxic dumps, pumping stations, refineries, tank farms, pipelines, helicopter landing zones, airports, roadways, security checkpoints, military installations, and a proliferation of camps, depots, towns, strips, and villages. In an environmental lawsuit filed against Atlantic Richfield in 1993, the plaintiffs inventoried—in this one concession—339 wells, 18,000 miles of seismic trails, 300 miles of roads, 600 toxic waste pits, and 1,368 helicopter landing sites. Welcome to Petropolis.

The roadways slashing through the rainforest instigate both extraction and attraction, becoming the medium for still larger territorial reorganization. As roads are built, forest is cleared to make way for three rows of agricultural plots, each 250 by 2,000 meters, creating a space twelve kilometers wide and, in aggregate, hundreds of miles long, a vast linear settlement occupied by "colonos" from elsewhere in the country—well over a quarter of million have poured into Oriente since the discovery of oil. Much of this is pasture land: rainforest soils are a poor basis for conventional agriculture, and clearing the jungle dooms the richly symbiotic biodiversity it supports. The pattern brings a new economic organization as well as new styles of agricultural activity, new homesteads, new villages, and new towns. Much like the Jeffersonian gridding of the American West, however, the remorseless geometry of subdivision accomplishes a dramatic literal and conceptual shift: what was once "wilderness" becomes urban, part of a global system. The long miles of farms and villages in the cleared jungle and the checkpoint at Block 16 are part of the same Petropolitan urbanism that produces the freeway morphology of LA and Houston, or the glittering skylines of Dubai or Kuwait City.

Of course, an urban environment requires urban citizens, and the boom has attracted hundreds of thousands. But what of those already there and their sedulously un-urban lifestyles? Two years after Texaco discovered the huge reserves of oil in Oriente, the Ecuadorian government created a protected "reserve" for the Huaorani. Desperate to cash in on the oil but anxious about the potential cauldron of conflict between native peoples, oil workers, and the accelerating influx of settlers and tourists, José María Velasco Ibarra, the president at the time, handed the protectorate's administration to the Sumner Institute of Linguistics, a protestant evangelical group that had been active in Ecuador from the early fifties, specializing in the translation of scripture into native languages.

Like their missionary predecessors from centuries past, their tragic endeavor entailed forcing the "natives" into villages, establishing schools with the Bible at the center of the curriculum, and introducing capitalism. The results included forest-clearing for larger fields, agricultural specialization, a money economy, and the rapid introduction of alien cultural forms, from trousers and radios to beer and zinc roofs: the natives were being urbanized, made into model citizens for a new order. Resistance was not long in developing, and there were numerous instances of speared priests and oil-workers. More importantly, there has been remarkable grassroots political organization and raised consciousness by native peoples, a crucial result of which was the formation in 1986 of CONAIE, the Confederation of Indigenous Nationalities of Ecuador, which has now become a major political power working on behalf of both human and environmental rights.

In 1989 the Ecuadorian government, faced with declining oil prices and eager to keep its revenue stream flowing, prepared—with financing from Conoco Oil—a new "management" plan for the as-yet untapped Yasuní Park, under which half was zoned for oil company use, the other half for the Huaorani. In 1993 a modified plan was put into place in which the Huaorani were nominally incorporated into the administration of the combined entity. For them, this meant jobs as security guards (in their own formerly peaceable homeland), oil workers, and new—and desperately inappropriate—houses for some, generally clustered in what can only be described as concentration camps. This for a people that has, for millennia, lived nomadically. It also meant the ravages of imported diseases and a rapid education in modernity.

This is not the place to settle the question of the rights of indigenous people, or to debate the respective arguments for literacy, technology, and participation in national life versus the logics of protecting the ability of "primitive" peoples to defend and continue historic patterns of settlement and life. The point is simply that the lives of these people have undergone tremendous rupture, and their culture has been sent down the road to extinction on the basis of somebody's idea of the greater good—that of the Ecuadorian economy—which continues to float on oil (as it had earlier done on monocultures of cacao and bananas). Oil sales provide close to 50 percent of government revenue (about half of which goes to the military), and since the final nationalization of oil in 1989 has put the government in the admirable position of actually owning the source of its own income.

The machinations in Yasuní, with the repeated redrafting of the borders of the park, the concessions, and the ethnic reserves (for a people whose imaginary did not house the concept of such borders) are part of a broader system of overlapping territories defined by relations of property that inscribes in the jungle the patterns of modern space and exchange. Northern Oriente shows how all of this rose to a flashpoint of toxic weirdness. Those troops in Yasuní were not simply protecting the oil, but keeping out the cocaine industry (increasingly forced toward and over the Ecuadorian border by the US-sponsored "Plan Colombia") and its own networked system of extraction with its parallel labyrinth of roads, airstrips, laboratories, villages, and flows of capital.

Like any city, this one overlays infrastructures, territories, interests, technologies, densities, communities, histories, and morphologies. Its differences from the "post-urban" edge cities that have become the characteristic mode of urban growth in so many parts of the world are not of kind, but simply of degree. Both patterns are environmentally corrosive and conceptually predicated on the domination of distributed rather than concentrated systems. And both are based on a model of urban development that privileges extraction—of oil, cocaine, or land values—over sociability, permanence, or culture. Although only half the planetary population—by traditional means of measure—lives in the cities, the planet itself is immeasurably more urbanized.

Yasuní, like the Amazon basin, throws this into such sharp relief because the rainforest remains our paradigmatic "state of nature"—the antithesis of urban civilization—and because, as our green sensibility grows (and the jungle disappears), we have come to understand the degree to which our own survival depends on the fate of the forest. In much the same way, respect for indigenous peoples and traditions is an emblem of our understanding of the risks of globalization's obliteration of difference and freedom of economic action. The Huaorani have probably had it, but in their demise it is urgent that we see ourselves.

2007

61

Trumped Again

The form of the city rises from the convergence of legislation, imagination, ambition, and resistance. This complex of forces is getting a workout a few blocks from my office in lower Manhattan, where Donald Trump and partners are building the Trump SoHo, a forty-five-story "condominium hotel" containing 400 apartments—ranging in size from 425 to 10,000 square feet—priced at $3,000 a square foot and said to be selling briskly. The tower, which is going up fast and is scheduled to open in spring 2009, sits adjacent to SoHo and will be, by far, the tallest building in an area characterized by structures of six to fifteen stories. Like most Trump projects, the architecture, by Handel Architects, is merely bland: another glass box. Because of its size, however, it whimsically rescales the entire neighborhood, permanently marring the low roofscape that stretches downtown and culminates in the lower Manhattan skyline. It's a view I take in every morning as I walk to work, and the new tower already constitutes an awful scar on the sky. As urbanism, it's vandalism.

The controversy that surrounds the building, however, focuses on questions beyond size. Use is the real issue: the hotel-condominium bifurcation is Trump's strategy for building a residential structure in a neighborhood zoned for manufacturing—the last such district in lower Manhattan. Although this zoning category does not permit residential structures, it does allow conventional hotels, which the code describes as facilities where units "are rented on a daily basis" and used "primarily for transient occupancy." The condo hotel is a relatively new real-estate product, introduced to New York in recent years and, to date, only in areas with residential zoning. It's clear, though, that the zoning code was written well before any of its framers could possibly have imagined this particular bending of the idea of a "transient hotel."

Because of this lack of specificity and obvious precedent, Trump has needed to finesse the nature of the project's occupancy to create a standard of transience. According to the deal struck between him and the city (through a "restrictive declaration" now described as "voluntary"), although the tower is clearly an apartment building—that is, a building filled with units that in every way resemble apartments, with kitchens, baths, bedrooms, and the rest—individual owners will be permitted to occupy their apartments a maximum of 120 days a year, and no more than twenty-nine out of any consecutive thirty-six days. There appears, however, to be no obligation to rent when vacant, although there will be obvious financial inducements to do so.

Despite gales of criticism from activist groups (who recently staged a demonstration at the construction site) and the discovery during excavation of a cemetery from a pioneering abolitionist church that once occupied the site, the project has moved ahead at breakneck speed. Recently, if tardily, a consortium of community organizations has announced a lawsuit against the city for permitting the project. The city has promised to defend it, arousing further outcry about the use of taxpayer money to pull Trump's chestnuts out of the legal fire.

The suit's claim will undoubtedly focus both on the appropriateness of the building—which will be a tough battle against arguments that it is, thanks to the loophole, technically "as of right"—and, perhaps more promisingly, on Trump's claim that it is actually going to be a hotel. Here the issue devolves on whether what walks, flies, and quacks like a (residential) duck is actually another species. Trump has advertised the units as "residences" (there has been a quick pulling of ads that cross this line), and the legal confrontation will surely fix on the semantic technicalities of the meanings of "transience." To be sure, the jet-set masters of the universe who buy into the property are an extremely transient class, but this certainly can't have been what the framers of the code had in mind when they distinguished "residential" hotels (not permitted) from "transient" ones (allowed).

One obvious question is why Trump and his partners aren't simply building an actual hotel on the site. According to Julius Schwarz, executive vice president of the Bayrock Group (which initially secured the site with the Sapir Organization before bringing in Trump for his inimitable cachet) and the managing partner for the project, "It's a financing mechanism" designed as a hedge against a potential glut of hotels.

> You can model it out ten years. Right now, there's a shortage of hotels. So people are going to be building hotels and the rates will eventually come down. Hotel rooms will always be in high demand, but you can't rely on the $1,200-a-night rates. Even with a very high-end luxury hotel like this, you have to convince a lender. That's the most important thing; otherwise the deal doesn't get done.

What this is likely to mean is that the lawsuit will focus on Trump's intentions and on the enforceability of his "voluntary" agreement to limit the days his high-rollers are actually in the building. Will he really send the concierge to remove the owner of a $10 million unit about to stay for a thirtieth straight night? It likewise seems highly unlikely that the New York City Building Department, which is responsible for enforcement, will have either the resources or the inclination to monitor 400 apartments on a daily basis to see exactly who's behind the closed doors. The scope for scams and greased palms is virtually limitless, and the only real question is whether the city actually believes in the enforceability of the arrangement or is simply acquiescing in a situation it knows to be absurd.

The fate of the lawsuit is not clear, and seems a long shot for this particular project. Part of the intent of litigating, however, is to force the city to close the loophole in the zoning code that has permitted the tower. The lawsuit also seeks to head off similar "Trojan horse" projects that might rise in other manufacturing zones around Manhattan, including chunks of Chelsea, Greenwich Village, Tribeca, SoHo, and the Garment District, among others. Unfortunately, the planning department has not indicated that it sees any urgency in revising the code. Big buildings for big money are at the top of the municipal development agenda, and the site, although it is in an industrial district, adjoins some of the most expensive residential areas in the city.

The building's real affront, though, is broader than the fact that another developer has found another way of manipulating the zoning laws to his advantage: the effect of such projects on the city's mix of uses and its mix of people. Certainly, the outcry would have been less had the site, which was vacant, been developed with a twelve-story building for moderate-income families or an art center. And although I tend to idealize a vision of urban vitality that still includes manufacturing and other industrial uses, unfortunately the inhospitality of both the national economy and the local real-estate market to such activities is powerful. But the category of manufacture also encodes the *idea* of a working class, and the widespread resistance to the city's tide of luxurious residences and class-A offices reflects alarm at the increasingly monochrome, if glossy, character of the city.

Like the nation, New York lacks an adequate industrial policy, and Trump SoHo represents the transformation of an "obsolete" industrial district into something more congenial to the current market. This metamorphosis reproduces, at the scale of the city, something that is going on globally, spatial segregation—or zoning—of continental reach: New York's industrial neighborhoods are now in China or Mexico. What is sacrificed locally, though, is not simply blue-collar employment, but an idea of what constitutes a city that includes self-sufficiency and diversity. One of the things that makes a city great is the spectacle of equity, a palpable right to both its places and possibilities. We rely on public space and public policy to lay out a framework for this freedom.

The motto emblazoning the construction marquee surrounding the new project is succinct: "Possess Your Own SoHo." In the vulgarity of their sumptuary shenanigans, Trump and his hotel are fine symbols of an urbanism of pure extraction that has little interest beyond the bottom line. For those who can afford multimillion-dollar apartments they will occupy only a month at a stretch, possession displaces participation as the reason to be in the city, and their privilege is a growing affront.

2007

62

Asian Alterity: What's the Difference?

The spirited defense of difference that has formed so much of the core of our politics during the past quarter-century is the product of a mingling of liberation and anxiety. Perhaps the most nuanced propositions have flowed from feminism and its efforts to negotiate not simply the crucial idea of sexual difference but its historic and contemporary reduction to essentialist positions: singular and immutable readings that pinion the idea of woman, refusing both cultural and individual fluidities and the complex dialectics of relationship, as well as the liberties of choice that must underlie any democratic account of how we become who we are.

In the cultural territory, similar essentialisms dominate both in the vulgar reaches of the left, with its too expansive, quasi-biologistic formulations, and on the right, with its fundamentalisms of civilizational clash and flat-earth maps of the distribution of virtue. Such distortions notwithstanding, difference is indispensable, both the animator of our subjectivity and a bulwark against the fascist homogeneity and tight control of the neoliberal corporatist politics that have succeeded modernist universalism, extracting useful sameness from any memory of the project of justice.

But the celebration of "authentic" difference runs its own risks, and we are obliged to question the sources and meanings of the differences that confront us. We must fear not simply the tyranny of essentialism—unnuanced ideas of "woman" or "Asian" or "Western"—but also the false distinctions of a culture that thrives on the production of illusory segmentations based on the need to create a blizzard of meaningless choices that will dupe us into the hysteria of consumption that makes the system go: the Teriyaki Burger in Tokyo, the Kimchee Burger in Seoul, the Curry Burger (strictly veg) in Bangalore.

Even more threatening than this is the risk that an under-examined insistence on the abstract value of difference will threaten the vital idea of equality. Ideas of alterity can be used as instruments for manipulating the kinds of inequalities on which political and economic power thrive. And they can be used to dilute notions of justice by exaggerating the claim that human values and rights simply and "naturally" differ from society to society in such fundamental ways that we can evade the real distinctions between democracy and authoritarianism, whether in the guise of cultural choice or some form of political inevitabilism. We stone you for disagreeing with us because that's how we are: how dare you take your patronizing, orientalist attitude to this!

What is the role of architecture here? As both cultural symbol and operational instrument for organizing social activity, architecture speaks powerfully to all of us. But the slow-growing particularity of its forms, their rootedness in history and place, does not relieve us of the obligation to examine the actual points of attachment between form and meaning. Neo-traditionalists around the globe are geniuses of decontextualization, of the insistence that forms fix meanings, rather than channeling them in their perpetual shifts. What more disrespectful attitude to the past than to insist that neo-traditional architecture (in whatever guise) defines its correctness eternally, however far removed from its originating contexts of meaning.

What this means is that Asian alterity must be continuously invented and that its substance must be conducive rather than merely symbolic. That the world's tallest corporate skyscraper should be vaguely reminiscent of a pagoda is indescribably trivial, reducing Asia to a brand, ignoring traditions of stewardship, community, and character for the glibbest form of styling. In fact, when any of us undertakes to design in Asia, we are obliged to invent it anew, to conjure some respectful amalgam of tradition and the individual talent. The meanings that establish the differences in which we collude are in continuous flux, only legible in the compound perspectives of the present, defined by the relativity of observation and participation. We set the boundaries, and the wisdom and generosity of our willingness and power to agree and to share are the markers of non-oppressive alterity. This we must value.

2007

63

The End(s) of Urban Design

Urban design has reached a dead end. Estranged both from substantial theoretical debate and from the living reality of the exponential and transformative growth of the world's cities, it finds itself pinioned between nostalgia and inevitabilism, increasingly unable to inventively confront the morphological, functional, and human needs of cities and citizens. While the task grows in urgency and complexity, the disciplinary mainstreaming of UD has transformed it from a potentially broad and hopeful conceptual category into an increasingly rigid, restrictive, and boring set of orthodoxies.

In many ways, the enterprise was misbegotten from the get-go. The much marked conference at Harvard's Graduate School of Design in April 1956 is both a useful origin point for the discipline and reveals the embedded conflicts and contradictions that have brought UD to its current state of intellectual and imaginative inertia. For José Luis Sert—Dean of the GSD, convener of the gathering, and president of CIAM since 1947—the conference was surely part of a last gasp at recuperating the increasingly schismatic CIAM project, which finally collapsed at the CIAM 10 meeting in Dubrovnik the following year, largely because of the growing dissent of the younger Team 10 group, one of whose mainstays, Aldo Van Eyck, had groused that since CIAM 8 in 1951 the organization had been "virtually 'governed' from Harvard."

Sert's project was both a strategy for including US cities in the ex-pat ambit of the Euro-modernist urban fantasies of the Charter of Athens and a bid to recover the lost influence of architecture—erstwhile mother of the arts—from its dissolution in an urban field dominated by planners. In his introductory remarks, Sert observed, "Our American cities, after a period of rapid growth and suburban sprawl, have come of age and acquired responsibilities that the boom towns of the past never knew." This trope of maturity, suggesting that American cities were reaching a point where their undisciplined native morphologies needed to be brought under the umbrella of some greater idea of order, has proved durable (as has the repeated appropriation of the Harvard imprimatur for the personal ideological projects of imported celebrities from Sert to Gropius to Koolhaas).

Sert identified two hostile forces at which urban design was to be directed. The first was the "superficial" City Beautiful approach, which, he argued, ignored the "roots of the problems and attempted only window-dressing effects," presumably both by failing to observe the "functional city" strictures of the Athens Charter and through its nostalgic forms of expression. The second hemming discourse was that of city planning itself which, Sert suggested, had evolved to a point where the "scientific phase has been more emphasized than the artistic one." Urban design, by contrast, was to be "that part of city planning which deals with the physical part of the city . . . the most creative phase of city planning and that in which imagination and artistic capacities can play a more important part."

The delicacy of this criticism surely reflected the dilemma of modernist urbanism, with its growing conflict between a proclaimed social mission and a dogmatic formalism less and less able to make the connection. Nonetheless, Sert's contention that academic planning had become preoccupied with economic, social, policy, and other "non-architectural" issues was certainly true, and fifty years of subsequent experience—marked by intramural indifference and open hostility—only reinforced the conceptual estrangement. The other pole, the assault on the beaux arts formalism of the City Beautiful movement—a weirdly anachronistic straw man in 1956—was to prove more contradictory, if unexpectedly prescient. Sert, after all, was arguing that it was necessary to create a discipline that would restore an artistic sense to urban architecture, but he clearly had issues of taste with the City Beautiful, whatever his affinities might have been for its scale of operation, its proto-functionalist zoning, and its foregrounded formalism. The charge of superficiality, however, was not simply an orthodox modernist riposte to historicist architecture; it was meant to resonate with the social program embedded in CIAM's discourse—the sputtering effort to globalize European styles of rationality in its putative project of amelioration—and to concretely realize insights shared with planners who lacked the inclination and the means to produce architectural responses.

This constellation of arguments—that cities were important to civilization, that abandoning centers for sprawling suburbs was no answer, that design could reify, for better or worse, social arrangements, and that "correct" and deep architectural projects that commanded all the physical components of city-building could solve their problems—has dominated the field of urbanism from the early nineteenth century to the present. And the critique of this discourse has also had a consistent focus: we must be wary of all totalizing schemes, especially those that propose universal formal solutions to complex social and environmental problems, that obliterate human, cultural, and natural differences, and that usurp individual rights through top-down, command application.

Many of those gathered at the conference clearly felt some disquiet not simply at the 1950s America of conspicuous consumption and sprawl, but also at the America of urban renewal, then in the years of its raging glory. Strikingly, the non-designers in attendance—including Charles Abrams, Jane Jacobs, Lewis Mumford, and Lloyd Rodwin—were those to voice the claims of the intricate social city, to decry the racist agendas of urban renewal, to argue for the importance of small-scale commerce, and to denounce the "tyranny" of large-scale, market-driven solutions. Indeed, the presence of this group—none of whom were members of either the architect-dominated CIAM or Team 10—represented the seeds of doom for the constricted urbanism promoted by CIAM, the inescapably contaminating *other* that continues to haunt the narrow project of urban design.

This critique of the CIAM project was scarcely news. In his indispensable volume on CIAM, Eric Mumford quotes a letter from Lewis Mumford that sets out his reasons for declining Sert's invitation in 1940 to write an introduction to what was eventually published in 1942 as the remarkably flakey *Can Our Cities Survive?* As with the demurral of the non-architect conferees of 1956, Mumford's disagreement was with a reading of the city that seemed to exclude politics and culture, to reduce the urban function to the schema of housing, recreation, transportation, and industry. "The organs of political and cultural association," wrote Mumford about an especially conspicuous lacuna in Sert's polemic, "are the *distinguishing* marks of the city: without them, there is only an urban mass."

In 1961—a year after Harvard formally established its degree program in urban design—Jane Jacobs published *The Death and Life of Great American Cities*, still the definitive critique of functionalist urbanism. As the sixties progressed, this attack on the forms and assumptions that comprised the pedigree of virtually every aspect of contemporary urbanism came hot and heavy from various quarters. The civil rights movement exposed the racist agenda behind much urban renewal and highway construction. The women's movement revealed the sexist assumptions underlying the organization of suburban and other forms of domestic space. The environmental and consumer movements showed the toxic inefficiencies of the automotive system and the selfish, world-dooming wastefulness of US hyper-consumption. The counterculture protested the anemic expressive styles of modernist architecture and the homogeneous spatial pattern of American conformity. Preservationism celebrated the value of historic urban textures, structures, and relationships. Advocacy planning and the close investigation of indigenous "self-help" solutions to building for the poor espoused user empowerment, democratic decision-making, low-tech, and private expressive variety. And the assault on functionalist orthodoxy fomented by both rebellious visionaries and liberated historicists within the architectural profession made CIAM's writ seem both sinister and ridiculous.

All of this called into question the form the new urban design would take, as well as what urban ideology it would defend—its response to the complex of social, political, and environmental crises everywhere exposed and exploding. New York City was to be the most visible battleground, and 1961 opened the decade with a clarifying statement of thesis and antithesis: the simultaneous publication of *Death and Life* and the passage of a revised bulk-zoning law that overturned the pioneering regulations of 1916—with their codification of street walls and set-backs—in favor of the paradigm of the slab in the plaza: the official enshrinement, at last, of the *Ville Radieuse*. This was controversial from the outset—such planning had already dominated public housing construction and urban renewal for years—and the atmosphere in the city was roiling. The tide was turning against Robert Moses, Le Corbusier's most idiomatic legatee, who, thanks to Jacobs among others, was soon to suffer his Waterloo downtown with the defeat of a planned urban renewal massacre for Greenwich Village and of the outrageous Lower Manhattan Expressway, intended to wipe out what is now SoHo to speed traffic across the island.

This triumphant resistance—galvanized too by the contemporaneous loss of Penn Station—helped both to create an enduring culture of opposition and to revalue the fine grain of the city's historic textures and mores, asserting the rights of citizens to remain in their homes and neighborhoods. Jacobs's nuanced conflation of neighborhood form and human ecology was—and continues to be—precisely the right theoretical construct to animate the practice of urban design. Unfortunately, although her example continues to be tonic for neighborhood organization and defense, her legacy has been deracinated by its selective uptake by the far narrower, formally fixated concerns of preservationism, by an ongoing strain of behaviorist crime-fighters (from Oscar Newman to the Giuliani "zero tolerance" crowd) and by the spreading mime field of institutionalized urban design, narrowly attached to its Disney version of urbanity and its fierce suppression of accident and mess: the wellsprings of public participation and the core of Jacobs's argument about urban vitality. And Jacobs's focus on a circumscribed set of US environments and disdain for the idea of new towns unfortunately helped retard the investigation of how her unarguable ideas about the good city might inform other realizations.

Nineteen sixty-one was an urbanistic *annus mirabilis*, bringing publication not only of Jacobs's text but also of Jean Gottman's *Megalopolis* and Lewis Mumford's *The City in History*. This astonishing trifecta—to which I would add Rachel Carson's *Silent Spring* of 1963 and Ian McHarg's *Design With Nature* of 1969—provided the headwaters of a critique that urban design shares with virtually all thoughtful students of the city. Together they reinstated the conceptual centrality of ecology—first systematically introduced by the Chicago School decades earlier—in the production of urban models. But ecology is not a fixed construct, and is comprehensible only in its specific inflections. On the one hand, an ecological understanding of urban dynamics can promote stewardship, community, and responsibility. On the other, it can support a fish-gotta-swim determinism that implies that the urban pattern is as genetic as male-pattern baldness, and that urban design is equivalent to intelligent design, revealing only the inevitable.

In this debate, Mumford retains special importance (although his reputation is often submerged as the result of his boorish and myopic treatment of Jacobs). Mumford was an unparalleled reader of the forms and meanings of the historic city, direct heir of the regionalist ecology descending from Patrick Geddes, and an unabashed fan of the garden city so reviled by Jacobs: the omega point of Mumford's urban teleology was the movement for new towns, incarnate in a history spanning Letchworth, Radburn, and Vallingby. Mumford was utopian in the received modernist sense, a believer both in the therapeutic value of thoughtful order and in the importance of formal principles, qualities he actually shared with Jacobs. But Mumford also understood the depth of his oppositional role, and saw with clarity the way that the "pentagon of power" inscribed itself in the tissue of the city. For Mumford, the city was infused with the political, and he understood its future as a field of struggle for an equitable and just society. Alas, this principled insight only seemed to reinforce his unyielding formal partisanship.

Within the academy, skepticism about urban design's narrowness as a discipline paralleled its consolidation and growth. In 1966, Kevin Lynch published the first of an increasingly critical series of articles in which he sought to distinguish urban design from a more expansive idea of "city design." Lynch's critique was—and is—fundamental. Objecting to urban design's fixation on essentially architectural projects and its reliance on a limited set of formal typologies, Lynch argued throughout his work for an urban discipline more attuned to the city's complex ecologies, its contending interests and actors, its elusive and layered sites, and for complex readings, unavailable within the discipline of architecture, that would allow the city to achieve its primary social objective as the setting for variegated and often unpredictable human activities—behaviors that had to be understood from the mingled perspectives of many individuals, not simply from the enduring modernist search for a universal subjectivity, however "egalitarian."

But Lynch's was clearly a minority view, and urban design as practice rapidly developed along the lines he feared. In 1966—the year of Lynch's initial sally (and of Robert Venturi's *Complexity and Contradiction in Architecture*)—John Lindsay set up his Mayor's Taskforce On Urban Design, which soon morphed into the Urban Design Group (UDG), inserted as a special, semi-autonomous branch within the City Planning Department and intended to make an end-run around its lumbering bureaucracy. The Planning Department was itself then in the throes of producing a new master plan for the city, the last such to be attempted. Despite the inherent dangers of giant, single-sourced plans, this ongoing, willed incapacity to think comprehensively now haunts the city with a counterproductive imaginative boundary—a suspicion of big plans that refuses, however provisionally, to sum up its parts.

The Department's plan—ambitious, out-dated, and strangely reticent about formal specifics—was ignominiously turned down by the City Council in 1969, victim both of its own unpersuasive vision and of a then-boiling suspicion of master planning in general. Urban design represented a clear alternative to the overweening command style of such big, infra-structure-fixated, one-size-fits-all, urban-renewal-tainted plans. Reflecting the reborn interest in neighborhood character and the relevance of historic urban forms, the UDG's main m. o. was to designate special districts, each subject to customized regulatory controls intended to preserve and enhance (and sometimes invent) their singular character. This district-ing—and its zoning and coding strategies—was later extended politically by the devolution of a degree of planning authority to local Community Boards, part of a larger wave of administrative decentralization that, cata-strophically, included the school system. The move to neighborhood plan-ning, however, has proved a generally positive development, if seriously undercut in practice by the restricted budgets and limited statutory author-ity of the boards themselves and by a continuing failure to balance local initiative with more comprehensive vision.

The work of the UDG was very much the product of its time, weighted toward the re-establishment of traditional streetscapes threatened by modernist zoning formulations and visual sensibilities; the Group's recom-mendations were an amalgam of prescribed setbacks, materials, arcades, signage, view corridors, and other formal devices for consolidating visual character. These prescriptions defined, at a stroke, the formal repertoire of American urban design and fixed its more limited social agenda on support-ing the centrality of the street (whose life was the focus of Jacobs's urban-ism), and efforts to reinforce the "character" of local identities in areas like the Theater District, the Financial District, and Lincoln Center, where it sought to create hospitable, reinforcing environments for already concen-trated but weakened economic uses.

The operational conundrum in the approach lay in finding the means for finessing and financing the formal improvements intended to engender the turnaround, and the search for implementation strategies produced two problematic offspring that remain central to the city's planning efforts: the bonus and the business improvement district (BID). The importance of these instruments has only grown as government has become increasingly enthralled by the model of the "public-private partnership," the ongoing re-description of the public interest as the facilitation of private economic activity—government intervention to prime the pump of trickle-down.

The bonus system, which exchanges some specified form of urban good behavior for additional bulk or for direct subsidy in the form of tax relief or low-rate financing, is founded on a fundamental contradiction: one public benefit must be surrendered to obtain another. In the case of increased bulk, access to light and air and limitations of scale are traded for an "amenity"—for a plaza, an arcade, or simply a shift in location to some putatively underdeveloped area. With financial subsidy, the city sacrifices its own income stream, with whatever consequences for the hiring of teachers or police, in favor of the allegedly greater good of business "retention" or a projected rise in property "values" and downstream taxation. Of course, both systems are rife with opportunities for blackmail and corruption, and these continue to be exploited fulsomely.

While BIDs do not involve the same levels of public subsidy, they collude in creating a culture of exception in which the benefits of urban design (and maintenance) are directed to commercially driven players operating outside normal public frameworks, disproportionately benefiting the rich neighborhoods able to pony up for the improvements. This nexus of special districts and overlays, bulk bonuses, tax subsidies, BIDs, preservation, and gentrification has now coalesced to form the primary apparatus for planning in New York and most other cities in the US. This outcome is yet another triumph for neoliberal economics: the now virtually unquestioned idea that the role of government is to assure prosperity at the top, an idea that has produced both the most obscene national income gap in history and the unabated froth of development that is rapidly turning Manhattan—where the average apartment price now exceeds one million dollars—into the world's largest gated community.

Urban design has acted as enabler in this precisely because of its ostensible divorce from the social engineering of planning, nominally expressed in its circumspect scales of intervention and its re-sensitized approach to the physical aspects of urbanism. In New York—where our municipal leadership evaluates all development by the single metric of real estate prices—the Planning Department has largely refashioned itself as the Bureau of Urban Design, executor of policies emanating from the Deputy Mayor for Economic Development, the city's actual director of planning, the man who would be Moses. While attention to the quality and texture of the city's architecture and spaces, both new and historic, is of vital importance, the role of design as the expression of privilege has never been clearer. Whether in the wave of celebrity architects designing condos for the super-rich, the preservation of historic buildings and districts at the ultimate expense of their inhabitants, the sacrifice of industrial space in favor of more remunerative residential developments, or the everyday cruelties of the exodus driven by the exponential rise in real estate prices, the city seems to everywhere sacrifice its rich ecology of social possibilities for simply looking good.

The most important physical legacy of the UDG approach is the 1979 plan for Battery Park City by Alexander Cooper (a former member of the UDG) and Stanton Eckstut, which—because of its successful execution and succinct embodiment of the new traditionalist lexicon of urban design—has achieved a conceptual potency unmatched since the Plan Voisin. This project, created *ex nihilo* on a spectacular landfill site, was controlled by a newly created state authority with a raft of special condemnation, bonding, and other powers, including relief from virtually all local codes and reviews (another Moses legacy and an ever-increasing element in the collusive style of large-scale development in the city), and attempted to channel the spirit and character of the historic city in a completely invented environment. It was surely also heavily influenced by the seminal *Collage City* of Colin Rowe and Fred Koetter, published in 1978, an argument for looking at the city as a series of interacting fragments, a promising strategy dissipated—like so much subsequent urban design—by inattention to the contemporary capacity for assuming meanings derived from the formal arrangements of Imperial or seventeenth-century Rome. Battery Park City, by translating the UDG's historicist ethos of urban design as a contextual operator into an agent for something entirely new and literally disengaged from the existing city, was the crucial bridge to the emerging New Urbanism and its universalizing polemics of "tradition."

Like many subsequent New Urbanist formulations—not to mention the original cities from which its forms were derived—Battery Park City has its virtues. Its scale is reasonable and its look conventionally orderly. Its waterfront promenade is comfortably dimensioned, beautifully maintained, and blessed with one of the most spectacular prospects on the planet. Vehicular traffic is a negligible obstacle to circulation on foot (although there's almost no life on the street to get in its way). The deficit is the unrelieved dullness of its bone-dry architecture, the homogeneity of its population and use, the repression of alternatives under the banner of urban correctness, the weird isolation, the sense of generic simulacrum, and the political failure to leverage its economic success to help citizens whose incomes are inadequate to live there.

By the time of the construction of Battery Park City, the assault on modernist urbanism and the spirited defense of the fabric and culture of the historic city had long been paralleled by a withering interrogation of life in the suburbs. These were not simply the most rapidly growing component of the metropolis, but were—largely under the analytical radar—increasingly taking over center-city roles en route to becoming the dominating edge city of today. The difficult reciprocities of city and suburb were long-standing as both facts and tropes. Indeed, the city itself was first recognized as a "problem" at the moment its boundaries exploded to produce the idea of the suburban during its industrialization-driven expansion in the nineteenth century. At that moment were realized the political, economic, social, technical, and imaginative forces that created the repertoire of forms of the modern city—the factory zone, the slum, and the suburb—as well as the array of formal antidotes that constitute the lineage of urban design. Moreover, the invention of the city as the primal scene of class struggle, of self-invention, of a great efflorescence of new ways of pleasure and deviance, of habit and ritual, and of possibility and foreclosure, had immediate and deep implications for the creation and valuation of fresh form.

The mainstreaming of urban design in the sixties and seventies was, in part, a product of the diminished appeal of the suburbs, contingent on a parallel revaluing of the city as the site of desirable middle-class lifestyles: the happinesses that a previous generation had understood itself obliged to flee the city to achieve. The widespread critical revisiting of suburbia, which was showing strong signs of dysfunction and fatigue, gave urban design's project both relevance and register by establishing it as an instrument of a broader critique of the sprawling spatiality of the postwar city. Like the threat to city life posed by the obliteration of neighborhood character, the attack on suburbanism was both formal and social. Strip development was reviled for its chaotic visuality and its licentious consumption of the natural environment. Highways were defended from obtrusive billboards and honky-tonk businesses through "beautification." Suburban living was criticized for its alienating, "conformist" lifestyles. Racist and sexist underpinnings were assailed. Tract houses were denigrated for being made out of ticky-tacky and looking all just the same. Cars were unsafe at any speed. Even the nuclear family was becoming fissile, chafing at life in its split-level castle.

However, like modernist urbanism, suburbia was not simply the automatic outcome of market forces and its hidden persuaders, but had a strong utopian tinge. Heavily ideological realizations of the American dream of free-standing property, new frontiers, and unlimited consumption, the suburbs felt, to millions, like manifest destiny. However, as they leapfrogged one another farther and farther into the "virgin" landscape, their destruction of the very qualities that had defined them became an increasingly untenable contradiction. The critique of the one-dimensionality of suburban sprawl that arose as a result was both social and environmental, and it reciprocated on both levels with the development of more deeply ecological views of city and region. This was advanced by such observers of the meta-scale as Jean Gottman; by a series of mordant observers of suburban forms, from Peter Blake to Pete Seeger; and by social commentators like Vance Packard, Herbert Gans, and Betty Friedan, who analyzed their patterns of consumption, conformity, and exclusion. And the boomer generation—invigorated by rebellion and fresh from its intensive introduction to the newly accessible cities of Europe—confronted its own oedipal crisis and increasingly drew the conclusion that it could never go home again to the pat certainties of its parents' uptight lifestyles. As it had for centuries, the city represented an alternative.

But comfort and consumption had been too thoroughly embedded, and the vision of the city that emerged as the model for urban design was highly suburbanized—suburban conformities reformatted for urban densities and habits. The incrementalism of urban design, although conceptually indebted to the generation of activists that had risen in defense of the fragile balance of neighborhood ecologies, had none of their rebellious edge: urban design became urban renewal with a human face. While it took a little longer for the "this will kill that" antinomies of suburb and city to become theoretically reconsolidated in the neither-here-nor-there formats of New Urbanism, a consistent disciplinary discourse was quickly consolidated under the rubric of "traditional" urbanism. This formulation provided— at least initially—what seemed a very big tent, capacious enough to shelter neighborhood and preservation activists, modernists looking for a reinvigorated schema for total design, defenders of the natural environment, critics of suburban profligacy, and cultural warriors in pursuit of transformative lifestyles of various stripes.

Collisions were inevitable, and urban design's prejudice for the formulaic, for a reductive "as of right" approach to planning based on the translation of general principles (formal variety, mixed use, and so on) into legal constraints, was necessarily imperfect. And each of the positions that urban design sought to amalgamate into its increasingly homogeneous practice came with its own evolving history and arguments about the bases of correct urban form, replete with potential incompatibilities and often driven—like the city itself—by a refusal to be fixed. Questions of the relationship of city and country, of the rights of citizens to space and access, of the limits on their power to transform their environments, of zoning and mix, of the role of the street, of the meaning of density, of the appropriateness of various architectures, of the nature of neighborhoods, of the relations of cities and health, and of the epistemological and practical limits of the very knowability of the city, have formed the matrix of urban theory from its origins, and its constant evolution is not easily repressed.

This continuous remodeling of paradigms for the form and elements of the modern good city is also—and necessarily—an architectural enterprise. Models of the city—from those of Pierre L'Enfant to those of Joseph Fourier, Ebenezer Howard, Arturo Soria y Mata, Le Corbusier, Victor Gruen, and Paolo Soleri—remain indispensable conceptual drivers for urban progress, for making urban life better by refreshing choice and by holding up one pole of the indispensable dialectic of permanence and provisionality that describes the city. Unfortunately, such concrete visions have become thoroughly suspect—victims of the failed experiences of modernist urbanism—tarred with the brush of authoritarian totalization, by the willful insistence that every utopia is a dystopia, that certain scales of imagining can only come to bad ends. The theoretical underpinnings of urban design seek to deflect—and correct—this problem by claiming to find principles situationally, via the sympathetic understanding and extension of styles and habits already indigenous to the sites of its operations. The imputation is not simply that urban design is respectful in some general sense, but that its formal preferences—because they are "traditional"—embody consent.

In staking this claim, urban design operates as a kind of prospective preservationism. As a result, it becomes radically anti-contextual by assuming that the meaning of space, once produced, is fixed—that an arcade is an arcade is an arcade is an arcade. By extension, it remains an item of faith for urban design that, however far removed from its originating contexts of meaning, an architectural object retains the power to re-create the values and relationships that first gave it form. This is a remarkably utopian position in the very worst way. Urban design's project to reconfigure America's towns and cities along largely imaginary eighteenth- and nineteenth-century lines, enabled and buttressed by rigorously restrictive codes, is chilling not simply for its blinkered and fantasmatic sense of history, but also for its reductive and oppressive universalism and staggering degree of constraint.

But what exactly—beyond its stylistic peccadilloes—does urban design presume to preserve, and how does it know it when it sees it? In the already-existing city, the recognition of living social systems and accumulated compacts about the value of place are necessary points of departure for any intervention. The formal medium for generalizing from such situations is the identification and analysis of pattern, the translation of some specific observation about the experience of people in space into a broader assertion about the desirable. This mode of inquiry—whether practiced by Aristotle, Baudelaire, Walter Benjamin, William H. Whyte, or Christopher Alexander—mediates between the limits and capacities of the body, a rich sense of individual psychology, and a set of assumptions about the social and cultural relations immanent to a specific place and time. Each of these is susceptible to great variation and, as a result, any pattern produced by their conjunction will inevitably shift, however slowly.

Architecture can respond to the dynamism of social patterns by closely accommodating well-observed particulars, by creating spaces of usefully loose fit, or by proposing arrangements that attempt to conduce or facilitate specific behaviors outside the conventions of the present and familiar. The last of these possibilities—which can include both amusement parks and prison camps—always understands architecture as an agent of transformation because, by being inventive, it brings something experientially new to a situation. And, because it changes the situation, it begs the question of the terms of participation, of the means by which a user or inhabitant is persuaded to take part, of the difference between coercion and consent. Here is the central dilemma for utopia, for master planning, for any architecture that proposes to make things better: what exactly is meant by "better"? And better for *whom*?

The language of pattern seeks to deal with this problem either by the quasi-statistical suggestion that the durability, "timelessness," and cross-cultural reproduction of certain forms are markers of agreement, or by more direct psychological or ethnographic observations and measurements of contentment and utility. Urban design borrows the aura of such techniques of corroboration to validate the grafting of a particular system of taste onto a limited set of organizational ideas. This entails a giant—and absurd—conceptual leap. As framed by the Congress for the New Urbanism (CNU)—the Opus Dei of urban design—pattern is not understood in the manner of Levi-Strauss's *Tristes Tropiques*, but rather that of *The American Builder's Companion*. These patterns do not emerge from the patient parsing of the networks of social behavior in some specific community, but from pure millenarianism—from the idea of the utter singularity of the "truth"—that produces tools not for analyzing patterns but for imposing them. The validity of these patterns, promulgated in insane specificity, is established tautologically. Because obedience produces a *distinct* uniformity, one to which particular values have already been imputed, urban design argues that its codes are merely heuristic devices for recovering traditional values and meanings *already* encoded in the heart of every real American: faith-based design.

Urban design has successfully dominated physical planning both because of this resonant fundamentalism and because it has, from its inception, been able to appropriate a number of well-established reconfigurings of "traditional" architecture. Urban design's remarkable timing allowed it both to claim to embody the meanings of the historic city and to fit into a space already replete with a range of tractable and demanding prototypes—or patterns—produced by the market without direct benefit of academic theory and prejudice. The current urban design default is, for the most part, a recombinant form of various developer-driven formats for suburban building that themselves became prominent in the sixties and seventies. The extensive emergence of greenfield "town house" developments (often as a means of realizing the appreciated value of inner-ring suburban land), the transformation of shopping centers to "street"-based malls, the proliferation of "autonomous" gated communities, the rehabilitation of exclusionary zoning to restore traditional styles of segregation, and the uninterrupted semiotic refinement of the appliquéd historicity of virtually all the architecture involved, had, by the sixties, already become ubiquitous. And behind it all loomed the synthesizing figure of America's preeminent twentieth-century utopia: Disneyland. The theme park is the critical and synthetic pivot on which both the ideological and formal character of urban design continues to turn.

Disneyland—fascinating not just to a broad public but also to a gamut of professional observers including Reyner Banham, Charles Moore, Louis Marin (who memorably described it in a 1990 book as a "degenerate" utopia), and even Kevin Lynch—is urban design's archetype, sharing its successes and failures and grounded in a common methodology of paring experience to its outline. Disneyland favors pedestrianism and "public" transport. It is physically delimited. It is designed to the last detail. It is segmented into "neighborhoods" of evocative historical character. It is scrupulously maintained. Its pleasures are all G-rated. It's safe. Grounded in the sanctification of an imaginary idea of the historic American town, each park enrolls its visitors in its animating fantasy with an initiating stroll down a Hollywoodized "Main Street" that acculturates its diversity of guests to a globally uniform architectural inflection of good city form.

But what's most relevant about Disneyland—like all simulacra—is the power of its displacement. Disneyland is a concentration camp for pleasure, the project of an ideologue of great power and imagination, the entertainment industry's version of Robert Moses. Disneyland is not a city, but it selectively extracts many of the media of urbanity to create a city-like construct that radically circumscribes choice, that heavily polices behavior, that commercializes every aspect of participation, that understands subjectivity entirely in terms of consumption and spectatorship, and that sees architecture and space as a territory of fixed and inflexible meanings. Like shopping malls or New Urbanist town centers, Disneyland provides evanescent moments of street-style sociability within a larger system entirely dependent on cars. And, of course, no one lives in Disneyland, and employment there is limited to "cast members" working to produce the scene of someone else's enjoyment. Girded against all accident, Disneyland produces no new experiences, only the opportunity for the compulsive repetition of its rigorously programmed repertoire of magic moments.

America's greatest export is entertainment: hedonism has become our national project. But our cultural mullahs—from Michael Eisner to Pat Robertson—want to tell people exactly how to have fun, to force our product on them, just as we force democracy on Iraq or "Love Boat" reruns on Indonesia. Urban design, with its single, inflexible formula, is also produced for customers—or worshippers—rather than citizens. This fetish for the correct betrays to the core the urbanity evoked by Jane Jacobs, the vital links between sociability, self-determination, and pleasure. The sixties—which Jacobs did so much to help found—were constantly engaged in sorting through the meanings and relationships of pleasure and justice. Crystallizing slogans—like "Tune In, Turn On, Drop Out" and "Beneath the Pavement, the Beach"—were post-Freudian assaults on an enduringly puritan style of repression, and saw free expression and the pursuit of pleasure as instruments of cooperation and equity, ways of making a connection between the personal and the political, insubordinate fun. One of the singularities of postwar American culture was surely the degree to which the terms and proprietorship of enjoyment became both central to the character of the national economy and the object of struggle and critique. The movements for racial, gender, and sexual equality, the spread of environmentalism, the revaluing of urban life, and the assault on colonialism and its wars were all filtered through the perquisites of prosperity, which insistently argued that the fight was never simply for bread but always also for roses.

Urban design, from its origins, was a way into the system, a means for architecture to recover its lost credibility and continue its own traditional role as an instrument of power. The perfect storm of urban design's invention was a miraculous convergence of the overthrow of the old modernist formal and social model, a broad reappreciation of urban life, a freshly legitimated historicism with a new sophistication in the formal reading of the structure and conventions of urban environments, an expanded system of consumption that particularly glamorized European lifestyles (we were suddenly eating yogurt), and the scary emptiness of available late-modern alternatives like the megastructure. Its success was also immeasurably aided by the defection of many architects from the field—a desertion that continues to mark a political split in the profession, reinforced by the inexorable drift to the right of the CNU and its fellow travelers.

Indeed, the social and political priorities of a large cadre of baby boomer architectural graduates led, for quite a few, to a suspicion of architecture itself, which—seen as an inevitable coalescence of power and established regimes of authority—became an impossible instrument. The focus on "alternative" architectures, on small-scale, self-help solutions, and on repair rather than reconstruction, all foregrounded notions of service and consent, disdaining grand visions of any sort as incapable of embodying the shifting, diverse, and plural character of a democratic polity. Such arguments were only reinforced as the decade wore on by the easy connection between DDT and urban renewal at home with Agent Orange and carpet-bombing in Vietnam. The consequences were both inspiring and crippling, discouraging a large cohort of fresh-minted architects and planners from establishing themselves in mainstream practice either permanently or temporarily, turning many to communalism, self-reliance, lifestyle experiment, and various modes of righteous exile. Seeking gentler solutions and warmed by a soft, Thoureavian glow, youth culture created a profusion of alternative communities in the form of urban communes, squatted abandoned tenements, rural settlements under karmic domes, or nomadic enclaves cruising in psychedelic school buses—even if such places were more envied than engaged by the majority who, for their part, pursued altered consciousness through other means.

Because of their anti-authoritarian foundation, these styles of settlement never received—never could receive—a formal manifesto that strategically summed them up, despite a profuse, if diffuse, literature ranging from *The Whole Earth Catalogue* to *Eros and Civilization* to *Ecotopia*. Nevertheless, this collection of forms and actions was clearly a cogent urbanism, one

that continues to inform contemporary debates, if only because the boom-
ers who were their authors are now in their years of peak social authority, dragging their lingering consciences behind them. Without doubt, the
environmental ethos of a light lie on the land and of self-sufficient styles of
consumption, the fascinations of the nomad as an urban subject, the ideal
of a democratic architecture expressively yoked to new and cooperative
lifestyles, the antipathy to big plans, the prejudice for the participatory, and
the fetishization of the natural are the direct progenitors of today's green
architecture and urbanism.

The debilitating paradox of these positions lay in seeing the meaning of
assembly—and citizenship—as increasingly displaced from fixed sites and
patterns. The ideas of the "instant" city and global village were seductive
constructs for a generation for which the authority of permanence seemed
both suspect and dangerous. The ephemeral utopia of the rock festival was,
perhaps, the most coherent expression of an urbanism that sought to operate as a perfect outlaw, and suggested an architecture of pure and invisible
distribution, a stingless infrastructural rhizome that established a planetary
operational parity, a ubiquitous set of potentials accessible anywhere as
a successor to the city. The idea of the oak tree with an electrical outlet
and a world grid of caravan hook-ups was the ultimate fantasy of a post-
consumption nomadology, resistant to the Man's styles of order—a "place"
in which possessions were to be minimal, nature at once wired and undisturbed, and money no longer an issue. The vision was warm, silly, and
prescient: virtuality before the fact. Like the rock festival, this was a clear
proposition for organizing a world in which location has been radically
destabilized, and it anticipated one of the great drivers of urban morphology today with its web-enabled anything-anywhere orders.

One group—Archigram—was particularly successful in formal-
izing all of this, tapping, with insight and wit, into the tensions between
the contesting technological and Arcadian visions of the era. Operating
on the level of pure but architecturally precise polemic, Archigram was
a master of *detournement*, of playing with goaded migrations of meaning,
and at embedding critique in the carnivalesque. From their initial fascinations with the high-tech transformation of nineteenth-century mechanics
into the "degenerate" utopias of the megastructuralists, Metabolists, and
other megalomaniac schemers, they moved quickly to describe a range
of nomadic structures: moving cities, aerial circuses floating from place
to place by balloon, self-sufficient wanderers wearing their collapsible
"Suitaloons." They proposed the infiltration of small towns and suburbs by
a variety of subversive pleasure-parasites and sought, during the productively unsettled post-McLuhan, pre-Internet interregnum, to reconfigure
the landscape as a new kind of commons, a global fun fair. Operating
within the bounds of the physically possible and producing a stream of
intoxicating forms, their project was once hugely influential formally and

almost completely ineffectual politically. Not exactly an unusual fate for countercultural product.

However, the most important attempt to create an alternative style of formal urban practice at the point of emergence of urban design was advocacy planning, which—given the nature of the times—arose as explicitly oppositional, dedicated to stopping community destruction by highways, urban renewal, and gentrification. In its specifically physical operations, the focus was on restoration and self-defense, on the delivery of municipal services to disadvantaged communities, on the repair of the frayed fabric of poor neighborhoods, on tenement renovations, community gardens, and playgrounds in abandoned lots. The redistributive logic of advocacy work looked on architecture and planning with suspicion as an instrument of destruction or privilege. The problem—an analysis descending from Engels—was not a lack of architecture, but the fact that too much of it was in the wrong hands.

While this was both a logical and a consistent position, its morphological modesty was a hard sell for anyone eager to build, and offered no clear proposition for greenfield sites, and certainly no strong insights for transforming the suburbs, which were also viewed with suspicion as enemies of diversity and as economic threats, sucking the inner city dry of resources. Advocacy's visual culture, such as it was, was very much fixed on community expression, on self-built parks, inner-city murals, and the improvisational workings of the favela, its own over-romanced utopia. These preferences were infused by an old dream of a political aesthetic, but advocacy's taste was reductive, looking for the artistic reproduction of social content only when it was presumed direct, when it was authored (not simply authorized) by "the people." This position, which looks to produce design as midwifery, continues to enjoy substantial currency in a range of community-based design practices and has found coherent ideological backing both from the school of "everyday urbanism" and from the progressive wing of planners and geographers—for whom equity and social justice are the gold standard—that is still the most lucid voice on urban issues in the academy.

These multiple strains remain the dialectical substrate of urban design today. A matrix of traditionalism, environmentalism, modernism, and self-help configures the practices—and ideological accountancy—for virtually all contemporary design that purports to build the city. Although every current tendency embodies some degree of conceptual hybridity, the basic terms of the argument about urbanism have remained remarkably consistent from the nineteenth century to the present. What has shifted—and continues to shift—are the political and ideological valences associated with not simply each formation but also their rapid pace of conceptual and ideological reconfiguration, and the promiscuity of meaning and representation that attach to and slip away from each. These migrations of meaning are crucial: the way we make cities marks our politics and possibilities, and the struggle over their form is, as it has ever been, deeply enmeshed with the future of our polity.

Today, US-style urban design—global exemplar from Ho Chi Minh City to Dubai—has arrived at a set of concerns and strategies, as well as a formal repertoire, that is as limited as those of CIAM, though with an ultimately even more chilling social message. The current default is essentially a splicing of modernist universalist dogmatism, City Beautiful taste, and the cultural presumptions of neoliberalism, producing its urbanist double spawn: gentrification and the neo-traditional suburb. Not since the modernism of the 1920s has a visual system so successfully (and spuriously) identified itself with a particular set of social values: the elision of an architecture of stripped traditionalism (a pediment on every Shell station and 7-11) with the imagined happinesses of a bygone golden age has been breathtaking.

It was surely no coincidence that this specificity grew out of a more general turn to the right, with the new Republican majority that took to historicist expression as a means of instant authentication and prestige, all with a redemptive gloss derived from a thin idea of the social authority of convention that culminated in the mendacity, indifference, and sumptuary Hollywood taste of Reaganism. New Urbanism was the perfect theory of settlement for the Age of Reagan, the urbanistic embodiment of "family values," forcefully enshrined at the very moment that American culture was moving in the direction of transformative diversity. The New Urbanists' success is surely the result of making common cause with a right-tinged social theory, the puritan-inspired vision of a "shining city on a hill" that ascendant neocon intellectuals and the burgeoning religious right thought to so embody the values of a "traditional" America, and the New Urbanist idea of a single set of correct urban principles is surely balm to those upset with the dissipation of real Americanism under the assault of an excess of difference, the threatening pluralism of an America no longer dominated by WASP culture, a place of too many languages, too many suspect lifestyles, too much uncontrollable choice. As Paul Weyrich, founding president of the reactionary Heritage Foundation, recently remarked, "New Urbanism needs to be part of the next conservatism."

Of course, this oversimplifies both origins and outcomes. The broad acquiescence to the neo-traditional approach that characterizes American urban design is also the result of its proclaimed embodiment—sometimes tenuous and occlusive, sometimes genuine and persuasive—of many of the elements of more progressive approaches to the environment that provided much of the amniotic fluid for its gestation. Indeed, the powerful attraction of neo-traditional urbanism must be seen not only in its neoliberal, end-of-history arguments, in which historicism stands in for capitalism and "modernism" for the various forms of vanquished collectivism, but also in its claims on the inescapably relevant politics and practices of environmentalism—a genuine universalism with a very broad consensus. Self-proclaimed as the nemeses of sprawl, as friends to the idea of neighborhood, as advocates for public transportation, and as priests of participation, the New Urbanism and much of the current urban design default would seem to be a logical outgrowth of many of the progressive tendencies so lively at their origins. A number of the tendency's nominal proponents—Peter Calthorpe, Doug Kelbaugh, Jonathan Barnett (a UDG stalwart) and others—tilt to these positions as priorities, designing with greater tolerance, modesty, and depth. Moreover, the CNU cannot be faulted for seeking solutions consonant with the scale of the problem: the idea of the creation of new towns and cities is crucial not simply to the control of sprawl, but also to housing the exponential growth of the planet, urbanizing at the rate of a million people a week.

In fact, nothing in the Charter of the Congress for New Urbanism, with its spirited defense of both urban and natural environments and its call for reinvigorating both local and regional perspectives, is likely to be opposed by any sensible urbanist. The controversy, rather, is over the dreary and uniform translation of principles to practice, the weirdly religious insistence on "traditional" architectural form, the dubious bedfellows, and, most especially, the weakness of most New Urbanist product, almost invariably car-focused, class-uniform, exclusively residential, and without environmental innovation. At this point, the clarion principles seem so much cover, much as the CNU's vaunted instrument of community participation—the charrette (one of advocacy planning's more successful tools)—seems most often used not to produce new ideas or to give citizens *entrée* to the process of design, but to manufacture consent for New Urbanist predilections. No matter what the input, the outcome always seems the same.

Such remorseless formal orthodoxy is what killed modernism, and it is not exactly surprising that the New Urbanist Charter and Congress are structural vamps of the Charter of Athens and its organizational vanguard, CIAM, nor that it relies on charismatic, evangelizing leadership, the star power that is such a uniform object of CNU derision. This is the very definition of old-fashioned utopianism. The net effect is a vision that reproduces the self-certain, universalizing mood of CIAM both formally and ideologically, but that offers a new, if equally restricted, lexicon of formal behaviors. The ideological convergence of modernist and "New" Urbanism is striking. Both are invested in an idea of a universal, "correct" architecture. Both are hostile to anomaly and deviance. Both have an extremely constrained relationship to human subjectivity and little patience for the exercise of difference. Both claim to have solutions for the urban crisis, which is identified largely with formal issues. Both purport to have an agenda that embraces an idea of social justice, but neither has a theory adequate to the issues involved. Finally, both are persuaded that architecture can independently leverage social transformation, become the conduit for good behavior—the factory grinding out happy workers/consumers.

It is not surprising that the two most celebrated formal accomplishments of the New Urbanism—Seaside and Celebration—are both figuratively and literally Disneyesque. That is, both are programmed and designed to produce a specific visual character held to channel a fixed set of urban pleasures. Such pleasures are encoded in stylistic expression and heavily protected against deviancy, in a privileged typology in which the single-family house is the invariable alpha form, in highly static and ritualized physical infrastructures of sociability—the porch, the main street, the band-shell—in compaction and the careful disposition of cars, and in an idea of sociability rooted in homogeneity and discipline. These are model environments for a leisured class, and they do produce both a dull seren-ity and a set of spaces for "public" activity with clear advantages over the thoughtlessly cul-de-sacced McMansions whose pattern they interrupt.

Seaside is the Battery Park City of the New Urbanism, its first compre-hensive codification and expression, and a clear expression of its possi-bilities and limits. A small, upper-middle-class holiday community, it is modeled on the indisputable charms of Martha's Vineyard, Fire Island, and Portmeirion—environments whose beautiful settings, consistent architectures, and common programs of relaxation support that special amiable subjectivity of people on holiday. These atmospheres are both delightful and artificial, and their viability as precedents for more general town-making is limited precisely by the inevitability of their exclusions, the things that one takes a vacation to escape: work, mess, encounters with the non-vacationing other, unavoidable inequalities, demanding formal variety, schools, mass-transit, unsightly infrastructure, non-conforming behaviors, and so on.

Celebration, an actual project of the Disney Corporation, is slightly closer to the idea of a town. It's larger, its residents work (if elsewhere), it has a bit more social and economic infrastructure and a slightly wider spread of price-points for the buy-in, but—like most New Urbanist product—is mainly a re-patterning of the suburbs. Celebration's sole economic sector is consumption, and its residents are no less dependent on the automobile to get to work than suburbanites anyplace else. Like Seaside, its orderliness is assured by strict covenants that conspire to produce both hygienic conformity and the vaguely classical architecture that is of such bizarre importance to the New Urbanist leadership. The Homeowner's Associations that provide the necessary instruments of governance and constraint are, as organizations, something between co-op boards and BIDs, with similar agendas to maintain property values, to police levels of otherness, to secure the physical character of the place, and to supplement and evade normal democratic legality.

Although New Urbanists' work has been primarily suburban, their rhetoric derives much of its authority from the example of the city, and there has been much reciprocation between the New Urbanist project and the broader workings of American urban design in the richer and more resistant environment of actual cities. Both tendencies understand their performative tasks as the provision of "urban" amenity, and the good city is primarily associated with the ability of its physical spaces to support a rich and intricate visuality that promotes what are, in practice, the pleasures of the yuppie lifestyle and its program of shopping and dining, of fitness, of stylishness and mobility, and of a certain level of associative urban connoisseurship, based on the recognizability of their programs and architectures. To the degree that they embody a social or political affect, it revolves around old-fashioned forms of bourgeois decorum and the deployment of a limited set of signifiers of sustainability. Over the past twenty-five years many American cities have seen dramatic—if restricted—transformations in form and habit, and virtually no town of any size now seems to lack zones replete with sidewalk cafes, street trees and furnishings, contextually scaled architectures, artistic shop-fronts, loft-living, bike-paths, and other attractive elements from the urban design pattern book. This collusion of pleasant infrastructures has, in fact, emerged as the salient professional measure of urban quality.

I had the opportunity, not long ago, to look over plans for a major extension to the core of Calgary, a succinct encapsulation of the progress of urban design since Battery Park City. The plan had many fine features, including light rail, mixed-use buildings, variegated scale, attention to solar orientation, a well-manicured streetscape with a wealth of prescribed detail, and a strong rhetoric of urbanity. But the net effect was formidably dull, and its gridiron plan and fastidious coding insufficiently responsive to the possibility of exception—a foreclosure visible in the plan's un-nuanced response to the very divergent conditions around it (river, park, rail-yard, and downtown core), in its limited ability to accommodate architectures (such as a proposed university complex) that might be sources of creative disruption, and in its standard-issue pattern book of formal moves, from its little plazas to its proscriptions on non-conforming signage. The image of the plan conveyed in a series of winsome renderings was a perfect rendition of urban design's certifying palette of amenities—the wee shops and artistic signage, the Georgian squares, the bowered streets—all depicted in an apparently perpetual summer.

The Calgary plan was Starbucks urbanism, a suitable home for forms and traditions already translated into generic versions of themselves. With its derivation from the idea of the isolated district in its descent from the *tabula rasa* of urban renewal through the special districting and BIDs that succeeded it, the plan was more inflected by ideology than by place—by urban design's Platonic city form, increasingly identified with the Seattle/

Portland/Vancouver prototype. Of course, these are cities that have achieved many successes and, as a default for urbanism, one could surely choose a lot worse. The issue is not the many good formal ideas embodied in the urban design—or the New Urbanist—paradigm, but rather in their roles in dumbing urbanism down to create a culture of generic urban "niceness" intolerant of disorder or exception, in stifling the continued transformation and elaboration of urban morphologies under the influence of new technical, social, conceptual, and formal developments, and in disallowing the influence of communities of difference. Urban design and the New Urbanism are the house styles of gentrification: urban renewal with a human face.

The problem with this is not with the pursuit of the subtle visualities and comfortable infrastructures of humanely dimensioned neighborhoods, it is rather with gentrification's parasitic economy—feeding on the homes of the poor, on precisely the order of mix central to the arguments of Jane Jacobs. Today's dominant urban design is all lifestyle and no heart, and has nothing to say to the planet's immiserated majority, whether Americans victimized by our obscenely widening income gap or the billion and a half people housed in the part of the world's cities undergoing the most explosive growth: slums. Modernist urbanism, for all its ultimate failings, was the extension of social movements for the reform of the squalid inequalities of the urbanism of the nineteenth century, and the clear subject of its address was slum-dwellers—men and women victimized by oppressive economic arrangements and by the urban environments that grew out of them, the workers' houses of Manchester, the *Mietkasernen* of Berlin, and the tenements of New York. If the sun, space, and greenery of the Radiant City and its identical architectures appear alienating and vapid today, it's crucial to think about what they were meant to replace: the dark, disease-ridden, dangerous, hyper-crowding of the industrial city.

The New Urbanism substitutes sprawl for slum as its polemical target, and its ideal subjects are members of the suburban upper-middle class whose problem is a mismatch between existing economic privilege and inappropriate spatial organization. The difficulty here is of having too much, rather than too little, and if this is a rational observation from the perspective of the environment, it is a radically different issue from the perspective of what is to be done. What's missing is an idea of justice, a theory that addresses not simply the reconfiguration of space, but also the redistribution of wealth. The reduction of urbanism to a battle of styles is a formula for ignoring its most crucial issues. For example, there is no doubt that the neo-traditionalist row houses that have replaced the penitential public housing towers being demolished in so many American cities represent a far more livable alternative. But it is equally clear that the net effect of the Hope VI program behind this transformation is the cruel displacement of 90 percent of the former population, and that arguments about architecture obscure the larger political agendas at work. Likewise the continued, virtually unquestioned, association of modernist architecture with progressive politics has long since been insupportable, given the lie by the real meaning of urban renewal, by its expressive congeniality for multinational corporatism, by the ease with which it becomes the ready emblem of the Chinese ministry of propaganda, by the abandonment of politics by most of the leading lights of the architectural avant-garde.

At a conference in New York last year convened by the Cities Program at the London School of Economics, Rem Koolhaas began his presentation with a slide of Jane Jacobs, whom he snidely denounced as an anachronism and an ideological drag. As a leading advocate of a robust, top-down idea of bigness and as one of globalization's most sophisticated and visible model citizens, Koolhaas was surely consistent in recognizing Jacobs's position as an affront to his own ethical ambivalence and corporatist cultural proclivities. And it was surely an enjoyably naughty performance to stage in front of New Yorkers for whom Jacobs is widely thought a saint. Koolhaas has a fine aptitude for irony, for blurring the line between critique and apology, accepting the market-knows-best inevitability of what he appears to disdain and then, self-inoculated, designing it. For him, critical interrogations of the mega-scale and its received formats are simply doomed, and any attempt to redirect the forms of the generic global city is hopeless naiveté.

"New" Urbanism and Koolhaasian "Post"-Urbanism represent a Hobson's choice, a Manichean dystopianism that leaves us trapped between *The Truman Show* and *Blade Runner*. There is something both infuriating and tragic in the division of the urban imaginary into faux and fab, and the tenacious identification of the project of coming to grips with what is genuinely a crisis with the cookie-cutter conformities of the former and the solipsistic, retro avant-gardism of the latter. Cities are becoming inhuman in both old and new ways—in the prodigious growth of slums, in the endlessness of megalopolitan sprawl, in the homogenizing routines of globalization, and in the alienating effects of disempowerment. But the scale has so shifted that the future of cities is now implicated with an inescapable immediacy in the fate of the earth itself.

Urban design needs to grow beyond its narrowly described fixation on the "quality" of life to include its very possibility. This will require a dramatically broadened discourse of effects that does not establish its authority simply analogically or artistically, but that is inculcated with the project of enhancing equity and diversity and of making a genuine contribution to the survival of the planet. Our cities must undergo continuous retrofit and reconfiguration, their growth rigorously managed, and we must build hundreds of new towns and cities along radically sustainable lines as a matter of utmost urgency. It also means that Sert's call for an urban discipline that narrows the field of its intelligence to formal matters has become a dangerous anachronism, that the aesthetics of the urban must recapture the idea of their inseparability from the social and the environmental: as an academic matter, this will entail more than another repositioning of urban practices within the *trivium* of architecture, planning, and landscape. Finally, urban theory must renounce, once and for all, the teleological fantasy of a convergence on a singular form for the good city.

The thwarting configuration of the traditionally isolated design disciplines must now yield to the broader relational understandings of environmentalism and take up the challenges of finitude and equity. This refreshment of design's epistemology is a necessary and inevitable outcome of our ability to read both global and local ecologies as complex, comprehensive, and contingent, and to see our own instrumental and haphazard roles in their workings and meanings. It is simply no longer possible to understand the city and its morphology as isolated from the life and welfare of the planet as a whole, or to shirk the necessary investigation of dramatically new paradigms at every scale to secure happy and fair futures. Cities— bounded and responsible—must help rebalance a world of growing polarities between overdevelopment and underdevelopment, offer hospitality to styles of difference that globalizing culture does not require, and rigorously account for and provide the means of their own respiration without prejudice to the survival of others'. This calls for the recovery of the "utopian" idea of heroic measures *and* a rigorous defense of the most widely empowered ideas of consent.

Which brings us back to those two model New Yorkers, Jane Jacobs and Lewis Mumford. Both loved cities passionately, and both dedicated their lives to understanding their character and possibilities. Both fought tirelessly to help give shape to the inevitability of urban transformation based on the desire for social justice and a deep connection to an urban history that inhered in intersecting forms, habits, and rights. Neither argued for the stifling imaginary fixities of a golden age, but each saw the good city as an evolving project, informed by the unfolding possibilities of new knowledge and experience. Jacobs celebrated her centuries-old neighborhood but happily rode the subway that ran beneath it. Mumford lived in the suburban fringes but never learned to drive. Each found happiness in a different relationship to the city, and both based their advocacy on preferences they actually lived. A future for urban designing must not dictate the good life, but instead endlessly explore the ethics and expression of consent and diversity.

2007

64

Big Brother Is Charging You

As part of his recently released plan for "New York 2030," Mayor Michael Blooomberg is actively promoting a scheme for congestion pricing in the busiest parts of Manhattan. Modeled on programs in Singapore, London, and Stockholm, the system is intended to curb vehicular traffic (and to raise money for public transportation) by imposing charges ($8 for cars and $21 for trucks) to enter the borough below 96th Street. The proposal has the support of virtually every *bien-pensant* urbanist in town, although it has met some resistance, particularly from the outer boroughs and suburbs where car dependence is highest and public transport thinnest. And there are many who suggest that the burden of the charges will fall disproportionately on the poor.

I certainly support radical measures to reduce traffic in Manhattan, and congestion pricing has a good track record in the cities that have tried it. But there is something disquieting about the system. The arguments that it will be a trivial burden to the man in the Mercedes and a serious one to the busboys in the battered banger have real merit. But what really chills me is the means by which the system will be run. As in London, routes into the city are to be guarded by cameras that will photograph all incoming cars and record their license numbers—information that will be used to generate billing. And the system will presumably be capable of other levels of photographic observation, and is sure to be linked to other networks and databases administered by our anxious state.

Earlier this month, the front page of the *New York Times* carried a story headlined "Police Plan a Web of Surveillance for Downtown—Like London Ring of Steel—A Call for 3,000 Cameras—New York Seeking More Antiterror Aid." These cameras would join close to 5,000 private and public security cameras already in operation in lower Manhattan. Technologically speaking, the plan is identical to the apparatus for congestion pricing, both for its reliance on cameras and license-plate scanners (and its potential to incorporate face-recognition software and other suspicious algorithms) and for the massive, largely unregulated database it will compile. While the police disingenuously offer that a CCTV camera on the street is simply equivalent to an additional cop on the beat, civil libertarians suggest that there is an important difference between simply being observed in a public place and having information about your movement, activities, and whereabouts, recorded, stored, and shared.

The authoritarian risks of such systems are thrown into particular relief by their congeniality to more unabashed authoritarian regimes. The Chinese government is in the process of installing more than 20,000 CCTV cameras in the city of Shenzhen (with face recognition software provided by a US-financed company, China Public Security, incorporated in Florida) that are to work in tandem with new ID cards for all residents. These cards will have embedded chips (again with software from China Public Security) that are to contain staggering amounts of information, including work, credit, and reproductive histories, religious and ethnic data, medical insurance status, transit payments, landlord phone numbers, police records, and room for lots more. And the Shenzhen police already have the capacity to track the location of all cell phones in use in the city. Clearly, such invasive systems threaten any reasonable idea of a right to privacy.

This transformation is fundamental. Cities—and the organization of space in general—are key media by which we sort out the boundaries between public and private, and the public side of the equation is increasingly squeezed. The dramatic acceleration of surveillance post-9/11 is one marker of the contraction, and police agencies, public and private, are enjoying virtual carte blanche to intrude both in the traditional public realm—the streets of the city—and in the private as well. As David Harvey observes, "The 'war on terror' has everywhere been deployed as an excuse to diminish political and civil liberties." The profusion of datamining, phone taps, biometric screening, DNA testing, and other intrusive technologies are political and cultural developments of truly frightening implications, erosions of our most basic freedoms. The supportive incorporation of "terror" as part of the standard repertoire of architectural and planning due diligence—like fire or seismic protection—is astonishingly sinister and far exceeds any simple utilitarian account. As a profession, we are far too compliant in advancing this threatening regime.

The contraction of the public realm, however, extends beyond these Orwellian developments. Public space is produced from the private: in democracy, the commons is always a compact about what is to be shared, what reserved, about where we choose to interact with the other. There's been a lot of criticism from certain academic quarters about traditional notions of public space, about over-identifying the idea with streets, squares, parks and other historic settings for the face-to-face. This critique is predicated both on the idea that these spaces fail to acknowledge the existence of multiple publics and that a purely spatial definition of public space is inadequate in the internet (or any other) age. While the idea of a one-size-fits-all public arena surely risks its own oppressions, spaces of free access are foundational to civil liberty, and winnowing them, whether for nominally progressive or for out-and-out reactionary reasons, is very risky. Public space that excludes the civic—supporting only private forms of exchange—puts our democracy under radical threat.

Consider Starbucks. The problem with Starbucks isn't the instance but the aggregate. I've just returned from several weeks in the suburbs, and Starbucks was a lifeline. Not simply the only source of decent coffee for miles, it was also an oasis of conviviality with its comfortable chairs, free newspapers, and relaxed vibe. The Starbucks we frequented was part of a big shopping center, sandwiched with a couple of other smallish shops between a monster supermarket and a gigantic Lowe's box. Not that we had no choices: another local supermarket had a kind of satellite Starbucks right inside the store, along with a pharmacy, a bank, and various category-stretching elements of the supermarket itself: bakery, liquor store, deli, hardware, florist, and so on. Being there, I felt a little like Nikita Krushchev on tour, visibly staggered by the sheer scale of the operation and of the choices on offer in American capital's most perfectly staged spectacle of consumption.

The problem with the suburbs (and increasingly the city) lies both in the homogeneity of their formats and the frequent elusiveness of a genu-inely public realm—the fact that a coffee always comes from Starbucks or Dunkin' Donuts and that the "street" on which these stores sit is always a parking lot or supermarket aisle. The difficulty is not the lovely houses and gardens, nor the qualities of neighborliness they can produce, but an interstitial tissue that is only negotiable by car. This is a toll even more severe than the downside of congestion pricing—financially, in the alienat-ing effects of hours spent sealed up alone, and for those people it excludes. Over years of visiting elderly parents in the suburbs, I have watched their possibilities contract in a system in which a carton of milk or a visit to a friend require an increasingly perilous drive on the highway.

It's Sunday in New York, and I've just returned from a walk to buy a coffee . . . at Starbucks. There's one a block away and, as I've mentioned, the coffee is tasty, despite the foolishness I feel when forced to order a "grande" instead of a medium. While strolling over, I've counted the security cameras on the single block between here and there. There are fifteen visible to me. Fifteen. This paranoid voyeurism by the authorities surely contracts our relationship to the spaces over which we—whatever "public" we happen to belong to—exercise proprietorship, and in which we feel comfortable and "at home." The line between the friendly cop on the corner and Big Brother is not obscure.

I'd love to get some traffic out of the neighborhood, but those cameras may be too high a price to pay. Such are the ambiguities of unfreedom that the exclusion of cars on the one hand and their indispensability on the other can be servants of the same agendas of monitoring and control, while at the same time their use (or non-use) remains emblematic of the freedom at the core of what makes both cities and suburbs desirable to their denizens. Technology is a human artifact and its role in culture is neither autonomous nor neutral. I have no doubt that we are at a watershed in terms of the way in which we deploy technologies of surveillance, mobility, and control, and that the character of the public realm is under enormous threat from both too much government intervention (by the get-government-off-our-backs creeps in power) and the concession of too much of the public realm to private interest. A shopping mall in not the same as a street, and a security camera on every corner is not a pal.

2008

65

West Side Story

New York's powerful deputy mayor for economic development, Dan Doctoroff, recently resigned, something that had been rumored for a time. Doctoroff, who came to the city from a master-of-the-universe career as a private equity dealer, has left—with scarcely a murmur of disapproval—to become head of Bloomberg LP, the Mayor's very own multibillion-dollar financial reporting company. While there is apparently nothing illegal about this, it does affirm once again the degree of control of the city by an interlocking directorate of government, finance, and real estate–development interests, and the tendency of players to move seamlessly from one sector to another. This cozy relationship finds its parallel at the national level in the kind of reciprocal arrangement that has Cheney going from government to Halliburton and back to government, with the resulting engorgement of Halliburton on no-bid contracts in Bush's war in Iraq.

While in office, Doctoroff accomplished a great deal, much of it constructive. He became the city's de facto head of planning and was frequently compared to Robert Moses for the scope of his activities and energy. This favorable comparison resulted from a long-growing national feeling that government has been incompetent (what politician nowadays doesn't run against the government?), incapable of delivering the goods, too mired in the ethos of welfare, too estranged from the can-do mentality of big business. The electorate has bought into this to a remarkable degree. Our bluest of blue-state towns has now been run for fifteen years by Republican mayors—Giuliani and Bloomberg—who have pursued the sort of tough-on-crime, big-business-friendly policies of the national party. The results have been very successful by certain measures: crime is down dramatically, and real estate prices have never been higher, with the city still seemingly immune to the current national meltdown. And Bloomberg, in particular, has used the city's rising revenues for substantial improvements in many areas of public service.

Of course, there are downsides. Many people seem to have forgotten Giuliani's vicious authoritarianism. And the obscene income gap that has grown so dramatically in both the nation and the city means that New York in general—with Manhattan as an extreme case—is becoming increasingly inhospitable to any but the wealthiest, a culture too skewed to remorseless getting and spending. While, by many measures, the "quality of life" in the city has improved—the subway is better, the streets are cleaner and safer, the fizz of construction is everywhere—the question must be asked: better for whom? Certainly not for kids in public school, where improvements proceed at a glacial pace and a two-tier system has most parents who can afford it sending their children to private schools. Nor for those squeezed from their homes by the cruelties of the market.

Doctoroff made his first big appearance on the city scene as a promoter of New York's unsuccessful bid for the 2012 Olympic Games. The center-piece of that effort was a proposal to build a giant stadium on the last truly vast tract of developable land in Manhattan, the commuter rail yards on the West Side. After the Olympics, the stadium was to be the home for the Jets football team. The massive structure would have joined the even more massive Javits Center nearby in hulking isolation, and conspired to further isolate the area from the riverfront. In a district very poorly served by public transportation, the stadium would have created massive traffic problems and a vast social vacuum. Widely opposed, it proved a non-starter with the public, and both it and the bid for the games went down in flames.

After the Olympics debacle, the city has moved to a more comprehensive approach and produced a zoning and public infrastructure plan for the area to encourage a more "mixed" strategy. The plan includes the extension of a subway line and a clear, if not exactly inspired, formal armature for development. The linchpin for the plan is the rail yards—twenty-eight acres of opportunity for big bucks, with the sky as the limit. (In comparison, Ground Zero offers a mere sixteen acres.) The owner of the yards, the Metropolitan Transportation Authority, has put the site out for bids, and five proposals were recently submitted by a roster of the usual development and architectural suspects. In making its selection, the MTA, in what might be interpreted as no more than the exercise of its fiduciary responsibility, is likely to focus entirely on the bottom line, this being the Republican definition of civic virtue. As at Ground Zero, the choice is protected by the ability of the agency to make its decision with too much independence from public review, and by a program—12 million square feet of buildings, a cultural bauble, and a park in the middle—that fixes the project's scale at a level of sublime unreason.

One of the keys to the magician's art is misdirection: we are fooled, tricked into looking at the wrong thing. Recent presentations of the five schemes have all focused on the architecture, which plays its usual supine role in distracting our gaze from necessity to invention. (The five teams are Steven Holl for Extell Development; SOM, Diller Scofidio + Renfro, Thomas Phifer, SHoP, SANAA, Field Operations, and Handel Architects for Brookfield Properties; Murphy/Jahn, Cooper Robertson, and Peter Walker for Tishman Speyer and Morgan Stanley; Pelli Clarke Pelli, FXFOWLE, and WRT for the Durst Organization and Vornado Realty; and KPF, Arquitectonica, and Robert A. M. Stern for The Related Companies.) As many have remarked in the media, none of these schemes will have any necessary bearing on what is finally built, and all will be subjected to the usual closed-door deal-making between the MTA and the developers, as each seeks to max out its profits and minimize any investment that detracts from the mellifluous *ka-ching, ka-ching* playing in their collective cortex. They will, nonetheless, surely claim, as they stand behind their lovely renderings and models, that the best "design" has won.

In listening to one very well attended public presentation by the designers of the five schemes, I noticed another interesting form of misdirection. We are all greatly attuned to matters green nowadays, and each of the teams pressed that component to the fore, often with the landscape architect most prominently featured in making the case. (By the way, the Bloomberg administration has, under Doctoroff's direction, produced what is, in many ways, a very impressive plan for the city's sustainable growth, which is clearly having at least a rhetorical impact.) The evening was filled with talk of microclimates and runoff capture, of lawns and bosks, as if the schemes were somehow primarily about parks and not about the areola of ninety-story monstrosities that would surround (and, in most instances, cast into darkness) the open space. The environmental ethos—the very least we should expect from all of our building—was meant to lull and to camouflage. Ironically, for all the dulcet claims of up-to-date urbanism, we were served a massive dose of towers in the park. Of course, every scheme was depicted on a glorious summer-of-love day, all blue skies and blooms.

Although many sought to establish pedigree via comparisons to Rockefeller Center, the more apposite analogue is the Albany Mall. (Ah, those Rockefellers: we have them to thank for the original World Trade Center, as well. Not the best batting average.) The genius of Rockefeller Center comes from its architecture, its compactness, and its brilliant elision with its surrounding context. The Albany Mall is dreadful for its architecture, its Brasilia-like spatial extravagance, and its context-of-no-context megalomania. Four of the five schemes simply accepted the client-proposed Albany Mall parti of a rectangular green space with its long axis running east-west, lined by huge buildings with the jumbos generally at the east end, on axis or framing it. By and large, despite the claims of the authors, I was not persuaded that these parks—flanked by giant towers along their southern edges—were likely to be bathed in the photoshopped sunshine depicted in the renderings. Nor was I convinced that the orientation of the skyscraper-walled park toward the river would do much to prevent a massive generation of the Venturi effect on dark and windy winter days. And the literal link of the schemes to the riverfront showed truly massive failures of imagination: virtually every project seized up on its cliff-faced podium beside the riverside highway, then extended a single tragic tendril across the road to the skinny shoreline park.

Two projects had merit (ironically, the two that handicappers already think are most likely out of the running). Although I was ambivalent about the architecture as well as about the solar implication of the decision to put high towers to the south and a low bar building to the north, Holl's scheme took strong cognizance of the mandate to overscale and did something about it. By putting his park on a suspension structure over the tracks instead of on a massive platform, and by building his towers on the flanking terra firma, his plan simply costs less and allows the developer to use the savings to reduce the overall scale of the thing. This is civic thinking. While I was uncertain of how Holl would solve the meeting of his suspension structure with the avenues (likely to produce a walled condition) and how much of the strength of the scheme would be lost if the individual buildings were franchised to other architects, this was still a very serious piece of design. But these cavils are probably moot. Lacking the indispensable anchor tenant brought by several other developers, the proposal is likely to sink.

The other seriously worked out project was that of Brookfield Properties, with an architectural team dominated by SOM but ornamented by a cadre of hipper practices. This was the one scheme that seemed to come to grips with the thornier issues of planning the site in its real particularity, and to do so with intelligence. The biggest difficulty presented in building over the yards lies not so much in the need to span them, but in the very substantial change in grade from east to west, raising a classic problem of too-simple placement of buildings at the artificial grade of a podium. The Brookfield design (presented that evening by its landscape architect, James Corner) has a succinct and elegant modulation from street to podium, creating, on its southern edge, strong spaces at both lower and upper levels, and smartly integrating the High Line (the disused railway viaduct that runs from the site through the neighborhood to the south and is now being converted to a park). This was also the only scheme to subdivide the central park, creating two distinct spaces of differing character—an approach that strikes me as far more rational, both environmentally and programmatically. Much too much architecture, though.

Whether any of this wisdom will wind up in the project selected remains to be seen. Although the whole operation has been the object of uniformly scathing reproach by architectural critics, most of that is itself hemmed by the developers' intended misdirection. Little is written about the larger planning, morphological, and artistic implications of building a clutch of Empire State Building–scaled towers at this edge of the island. Little is mentioned about the distributive ecologies of use. And despite the pieties about sustainability (the acceptable face of social responsibility), few voices can be heard questioning the real social content and effects of a project motivated primarily by the further fattening of the city's most privileged classes. Rupert Murdoch or Si Newhouse or Goldman Sachs will wind up with shiny new headquarters. Others will be obliged to look elsewhere. What a waste of a precious public resource.

2008

66

An Architectural Tourist on Omotesando

The cherry blossoms were at their peak on a Thursday in late March when I went for a stroll in Ueno Park in Tokyo. A nimbus of white glowing pink with dramatic dark branches etched through it floated above the crowds strolling, photographing, and picnicking on blue tarps spread beneath the trees. What could be more Japanese than such civic reverence for this short-lived phenomenon in all its tender aesthetic frailty? Of course, everyone's behavior was exemplary: not a scrap of litter, and no one disrespecting the pedestrian flow.

Tokyo is a shrine to convulsive order, at once chaotic and fastidious. The density of graphic information, of building, of infrastructure, of people, of circumstances, is like nowhere else on earth. It is a city constantly recon-figured by juxtaposition, and remarkable in its tolerance of diversity in scale. (How does the market allow this, I wonder?) All over the city, small structures jostle with midsize and large ones in a counterpoise of energy and repose. It's an enduringly fabulous place, and the mingling of tradi-tion, originality, and money has made it a center for design. This sensibility extends from the postwar generation of Japanese modernists to the current day, and no country has produced a more refined and innovative cohort of practitioners or an environment more hospitable to contributions from abroad—a place at once insular and open.

For the architectural tourist, the epicenter of attraction these days is a street called Omotesando and the neighborhood around it. The street itself is unusual for Tokyo: broad and bowered by elegant zelkova trees, it slopes at a mild but palpable incline, enlivening its section and experience. Sidewalks are wide and conducive to promenading, and offer an opportune arena for a parade of youth-culture fashionability. After the heterogeneous crowd at Ueno, the more homogeneous—if totally fashion-forward!—scene on Omotesando is striking. Surely, Japanese kids are as meticulously put together as any on the planet, and the style of the day is exquisite, at once recombinant and singular. The kids on the street in their raffish, sexy, distressed, vaguely aggressive but ultimately conformist get-up challenge the salary-man uniformity of black suits that sets the adult-world tone, while reproducing its assumptions. In both cases, precision matters, as it always has with Japanese culture and architecture.

Kids have red hair blown big, low-riding jeans, and zooty watch chains, a uniform slouch of nonchalance and languid gait, tiny skirts and short shorts (pockets dangling out below the hem) with knee-high stockings, endless variations on the tarty school-girl look, four and five layers of clothing in a range of overlapping lengths, filmy, gauzy skirts topped by thick leather jackets worn with tough boots, studs galore (if not so many visible tattoos), shades and specs perched on the head—a seething rhapsody of uniform insubordination. Omotesando is a place to preen, to study, to practice style solidarity, and to shop.

The famous-architect-designed buildings that line the street are almost all name-brand, upmarket shops, and the street is both a collection of the architecture of boutiques and a boutique for architecture. The brands gather: Prada, Vuitton, Tod's, Dior, Chanel, Bulgari, Dolce, MoMA, Lauren, Vuitton, Fendi, Celine, Fcuk (not to mention McDonald's, Starbucks, and Sharkey's Pizza). And here, too, the leading brands of contemporary architecture: Ando, Ito, Sejima, Kurokawa, Aoki, Maki, Herzog & de Meuron, Kuma, and Tange. The corroborating symmetries between the goods and their packaging are dense, and speak volumes about the contemporary deployment of style—its utility as advertisement and value enhancer, and its assertive enforcement of the permanent elision of culture and consumption. On Omotesando, the loop between architecture, shopping, and the subjects who buy into it is hermetic and complete.

I found the place at once a cause for celebration and for depression, as well as a good spot to reflect on the way in which architecture accretes its meanings. Here are buildings that reflect the profession at its best, most inventive, and most artistic. The remarkable collection richly addresses so many issues that are native to all architecture: the play of light and shade, opacity and density, the expressive meaning of structure, the logic of geometry, the nature of materiality, the tectonics of gravity, the flow of space, the meaning of scale, the limits of meaningful adjacency, the intertwining of form and function. What fun! What inspiration! What detailing!

But as much as I was dazzled by the assembly of talent, this orgy of superluxe selling soon started some synapse flashing the word Darfur in my brain with increasing and annoying frequency. Ah, the sanctimonious prig in me spoiling my pleasure once again. I grew mildly agitated between sips of cappuccino. What does all this superlativeness owe the rest of the earth, if anything? Nowadays we often dispatch our political responsibilities through the medium of environmental action, and this is surely most important. But these buildings seemed tenacious in taking not the slightest cognizance of green issues. Sealed up in perfectly gasketed glass and slathered in the finest finishes, this gathering—in its own conformity of indifference—certified the amazingly AWOL behavior of our stars to architecture's social side and our own complicity in promoting this narrowed meaning of form. Somewhere, I blundered across a Patagonia store with its advertisement: "1 Percent For The Planet." That about sums it up.

Okay. Enough ranting. What about the architecture? There is some marvelous work. Herzog & de Meuron's Prada is striking in the cityscape, jutting appealingly just above its roofline context. The diamond-gridded structural wall, with its mix of bubbled and flush glass panels, is a lovely thing, and the interior is luminous and dramatic. Circulation is suave, carpet is white, clerks are impeccable in gray. At Tod's down the row, Ito claims inspiration from the angularity of the branches of the zelkovas out front, and creates a facade of big, irregular openings that play against the rectilinear form of the building. The interior is less successful, with too much action and too little resolution in the overbusy details. Part of the problem—which also occurs at Prada—is that exterior walls that depend on the play of non-orthogonal openings must resolve the crisis of intersection with floor slabs that are perforce horizontal. Herzog & de Meuron simply allow the slabs to butt against the building's skin, which doesn't look too bad. Ito fusses away on the interior, using surface details to try to resolve the meeting of the irregular openings with the right-angled floors and walls. This dissipates the greater potential of a more direct approach.

The building that most impressed me was Ando's big Omotesando Hills complex, which combines a shopping mall on its lower floors with two levels of apartments on top. The facades—in a lovely green glass—are expressed rectilinearly but complexly, and embody several rhythms in deft syncopation. The mall is particularly successful. Part of the reason is Ando's usual impeccable detailing. Another part (and this is true of much of the city as a whole) is that the shops themselves are small and establish a continuity of interest and through-the-wall interactivity that enlivens the whole. But the best move—brilliant, really—was creating circulation that's continuous, up a gently inclined ramp that rises along the long sides of the space. The incline derives from the slope of the street outside, so the first long run can be accessed from the sidewalk at both its high and low ends. The rest of the spiral continues, in effect, the rise of the street up through the building. This is both extremely urbane in itself, and also solves one of the big formal problems of shopping malls: the dull stacking of space with point circulation strapped on at key spots. It's a great section, as well as an homage to Maki's well-known Spiral Building down the street.

I was also quite taken by Kengo Kuma's One Omotesando building (which has a truly elegant projecting cantilever on its upper floor), by several other Ando buildings sprinkled throughout the neighborhood, and by Sejima and Nishizawa's straightforward but thoroughly crisp glass box for Dior. And, lurking not far away is what is, for my money, the finest modern building in Tokyo, Kenzo Tange's superb stadium for the 1964 Olympics. Here is architecture with chops! Spotting it down streets from the midst of boutique-land is a good reminder of the power of building when it goes beyond the endless buffing and fuss that comes from thinking of architecture as a species of jewelry.

When I was in school, we were often pompously taught that buildings were to be divided into "foreground" and "background" types, and that the former always depended on the presence of the latter for their meaning. Omotesando—and Tokyo more generally—gives the lie to this particular piece of pat convention. Indeed, the street—which is lined not simply with one modern gem after another, but also more conventional kitsch and everyday mediocrity, from Ralph Lauren's usual dopey ersatz classical drag to the goofy green mansardic item next to Tod's—has no "background" at all. It works both because it is simply dense with interest and because the environment—charged up by both the wonderful street and the forgiving labyrinth of lanes that run off from it—is easy with variety, excess, and density.

So, can an architectural tourist of good conscience have a good time on Omotesando? Of course! I am not trying to argue that Prada must immediately be converted to an AIDS clinic or glassy Dior to permaculture greenhouses. I am simply raising a question: why must fashion be the most fashionable thing we create?

2008

67

Learning from the *Hutong* of Beijing and the *Lilong* of Shanghai

"I do like the grandiose"
Mao Zedong, 1958

I had been to China frequently, but somehow, until a few months ago, never to Beijing. Like many cities in China, it's intimidatingly vast and growing like Topsy. Unlike other cities, though, it is laid out with an orthogonal monumentality, with huge boulevards, widely spaced buildings, and a thick aura of imperium.

The prototype for the city as a whole is the famous Forbidden City, described by Marco Polo as the finest, most complete palace complex on the planet (". . . no man on earth could design anything superior to it . . .")—an astonishing monument to dynastic power. Centralized authority loves recursion, seeing its favored forms deployed at every site and scale; official Beijing is an exemplar of this merger of symbol and control. As Versailles is to Haussmann's Paris, the Forbidden City is to both historic and contemporary Beijing. And the Forbidden City was itself conceived recursively, as the terrestrial expression of celestial geometry.

The astonishing building program the city has undertaken in preparation for the coming-out party of the Olympics is an obvious extension of this attitude. The insistent grandiosity, the incredible extent, the mobilization of labor, the fixation on symbolism, and the centralization of planning—all announce a representational project as well as an urban and architectural one. The city proclaims its importance at every turn, from its humongous airport to its endless ring roads and millions of saplings planted to proclaim its greenness, mitigate the toxic air, and obscure in Potemkin fashion the remnant disorder beyond the highways.

That so many of the striking buildings of this effort are designed by foreign architects is also powerfully symbolic. For millennia, China has been known for shutting out the impact of non-Han barbarism. The country's modern history, in particular, has been defined by the struggle against colonization, invasion, and influence by imperial powers and ideas, including the now-disappearing resistance to capitalist ideology. Indeed, as China heads in breakneck fashion down that particular path, it is laying in an infrastructure that reflects the architectures and attitudes from our own high-water mark of capitalist consumption in the 1950s and 1960s. The car and its implications are embraced enthusiastically, creating prodigious traffic jams, freeways galore, pollution, and sprawl with all its components, from gated suburbs to numbing commutes.

The wanton hybridity of this urbanism is very much of a piece with global developments and, as elsewhere, the splicing produces forms that are alternately freakish, fascinating, forbidding, and familiar. For a culture that is immersed in an internal argument about "opening" to the outside, the conflicts between tradition and globalism are of striking importance. A revelatory incident in this debate was surely the closing last year of the Starbucks that had been operating within the Forbidden City since 2000. Closing the store was the result of a petition drive that collected half a million signatures in protest of this "affront to China's dignity." But where to draw the line?

China has been struggling with issues of indigenousness and influence for many years. If the current model for development is strongly shaped by the multinational metropolis—the format for cities from Los Angeles to Dubai—the Maoist period was in thrall of Soviet models of mass housing, heavy infrastructure, and Stalinoid monumentality, as well as the desire (most radically expressed during the Cultural Revolution) to expunge remnants of the decadent, classist, imperial past. But the confrontation between native and imported formulations also led to the creation in the nineteenth century of a building type that proliferated in huge numbers and continues to offer a valuable solution to questions of life in the city while engaging both the happinesses and the anxieties of influence. It also suggests an important strategy for mediating the compatibility of large and small, surely one of the most vexing issues for the postmodern environment.

Visiting the Forbidden City, I was struck both by its fabulous refinement and enormity and by the way it defines its differences between public and domestic spaces. The emperor's sleeping quarters within the Inner Court, in particular, seemed surprisingly minuscule, scaled to the intimacy of village life, small rooms around a little courtyard in dramatic contrast to the gigantic spaces of official encounter nearby. Here, the intrigues were also personal, and it was easy to imagine the habitual weirdness of the eunuch standing outside the royal bedroom timing the emperor's congress with his concubines with a burning stick of incense. Talk about performance pressure!

The Chinese have a longstanding genius for domestic architecture, and a visit to the *hutong* of Beijing—the fast-disappearing neighborhoods of courtyard houses, laced with small lanes and commerce, sanctuaries of both intimacy and variety in the midst of a city too rapidly doing away with the best of its public character—affirms the singularity and brilliance of their historic accomplishment. Such places offer an alternative vision to the modernist constructs that shape the city today and provide an irreplaceable element in the urban repertoire that demands to be not simply conserved but extended.

If the *hutong* of Beijing represent a kind of pure Chinese urban expression (though one with affinities with other courtyard aggregations in Asia and elsewhere), the *longtang* (or *lilong*) of Shanghai, and the similar *lifen* of Wuhan, which I have recently studied with my students, represent a composite architecture that is the successful outgrowth of a previous encounter with imported models. These neighborhoods developed in the wake of the Opium War, when Shanghai was forcibly opened to foreign settlement as a treaty port (Wuhan, on the Yangtze River, was another). In 1845, the local government promulgated its Settlement Law, defining both the site and the legal character of these foreign enclaves. Among the stipulations of the law was that foreigners could not lease houses to Chinese, who were forbidden to live in the settlement areas.

Fewer than ten years later, a rebellion broke out in the city and large numbers of Chinese began to seek safety within the foreign concessions, leading the occupying powers to unilaterally revise the land law by discarding its no-Chinese stipulation. The result was a massive real estate boom that led many of the corporations (including the legendary Sassoon, Jardine Matheson, and Gibb Livingston) that had previously profited from the trade in opium and other commodities to shift focus to real estate, both by letting existing properties and by building new ones at the periphery of their immediate spheres of influence.

The architecture of these new neighborhoods quickly developed into the *longtang* type, a two-story row house located along a straight and narrow lane. Initially, these houses kept the layout of traditional courtyard compounds, compressed and deformed to accommodate the party-wall condition, regular geometry, and small site constraints of their urban situation. They nevertheless retained a small entry court and a sense of sequence from the public street through a private gate into a sequestered interior realm, as well as utilizing traditional forms of construction, materiality, and style. Hybrids.

As the type developed further, it was incrementally transformed. The little courtyards gave way to parlors or to unenclosed or semi-enclosed gardens. Layouts were adjusted to suit smaller, non-extended families. Rooms were organized according to more "modern" notions of function. Houses grew to three stories or were configured as flats. And the developments began to accrete decorative and morphological aspects of Western architecture. By the time the type had run its course in the 1940s, examples in Spanish, Tudor, Moderne, and other styles had blossomed, and close to three-quarters of the population of the city was housed in some form of *longtang*.

What makes this architecture remarkable, however, is less the character of its individual elements than the way it functions urbanistically. Typically, you enter a *lilong* (a neighborhood of *longtang*) through a gateway off a major street, then turn left or right onto a lane. From the entry axis, smaller cross axes lead to parallel lanes, creating semi-autonomous neighborhood formations on part or all of their blocks, sometimes connected to adjacent developments. The lanes are almost purely pedestrian, and often support an array of retail and other commercial activities, including offices and small-scale manufacture. Each of these places is a little world, housing the necessities of daily life and powerfully conducing a sense of community through the inevitability of encounter with neighbors in the lanes. Although densely packed, the low scale of the buildings—which face lanes both front and back—permits the penetration of light and air.

The quality of the *lilong* varies enormously, and many—built from the get-go for the poor—were surely wretched places, lacking adequate sanitation, shabbily constructed, and without public amenities, especially green space. But the model is brilliant. Although they are enclaved, they are not forbidding "gated" communities. In the insane hurly-burly of the city, they are islands of relative calm. And, in the face of the alienation by numbers of the modern metropolis, they create a tractable scale and an extremely rational increment of development, promoting the kinds of mutual interaction that more contemporary high-rise projects (the default alternative) seldom achieve.

Although the architectural types that make up the *hutong* of Beijing differ from the *lilong* of Shanghai, their organization is similar. Low, tight, and small, they are wonderful: pedestrian, intimate, and diverse. Indeed, so singular, delightful, and increasingly rare are these places, many are fated for gentrification. On my recent visit, I went house-shopping with a Chinese colleague who hoped to find a congenial situation in one of the better *hutong*, but the prices were at Manhattan levels. The market may be cruel, but it's not stupid.

To lament the disappearance of these tight-grained communities has become something of a bromide, and the issue of saving endangered places is hardly foreign to the Chinese. The mistake is to reduce the question to one of preservation, to see these forms as an unrepeatable historic condition. As we all confront the need to create radically more sustainable forms of urbanism and restore the morphological basis of communities worldwide, we have a lot to learn from the *lilong* and *hutong*.

2008

68

Covering the Territory:
Three Films by Amos Gitai

Amos Gitai's remarkable film, *House*, is as artful a piece on the tectonics of memory as I've seen. Although he declares in the film that the house under depiction is a metaphor for the history of Jerusalem, it is actually more direct than that—not an embodiment of history but a piece of it. Watching *House*, and the later *House in Jerusalem* and *News from Home*, their theme emerges clearly, and I was particularly struck by the culture and equanimity of those called on as witnesses, each testifying to the Rodney King appeal: why can't we just get along?

There are reasons. People talk past each other. A key subtext in the films is the language of transmission—the way speakers use Arabic, Hebrew, French, English, or Romanian maps the subjective authorities of occupation. The original owner of the house and his descendants appear almost entirely in English, and much is read in the devolution of accents. Father speaks in courtly, heavily accented English. Son, a doctor like his father, is completely fluent and his language modern, but the accent is distinct. Granddaughter speaks like an American, and one of the most telling moments in the middle film is her explanation that she and her friends speak to each other in English when they visit a shopping mall in Israeli Jerusalem, lest some fanatic finds them out as Arabs and takes his revenge for some imagined crime.

The trilogy constantly focuses on linguistic heritage as a token of authenticity. Israeli immigrants from Belgium and Switzerland conduct their interviews primarily in French, breaking into Hebrew from time to time. In the final episode of the trilogy, the current occupant of the house—who in the previous film spoke mainly in French and admitted discomfort in Hebrew—begins in French but switches to Hebrew when political push comes to shove. Several Israelis express degrees of delight in an alienation from the ancient language and lurch back and forth between it and an "original" tongue. The film's remarkably polyglot soundtrack is effectively an argument for the available discourses of cooperation—the resources available to laborers and professors alike to articulate a territory of linguistic mediation, a way in which the kind of multiple identities available to all of the film's protagonists is a bridge just out of reach. Gitai's emblematic search for meaning in translation and hermeneutics is played out in *A House in Jerusalem* in his incessant questioning of passersby as to the meaning of the name of the street—Dor Dor V'Dorshav—on which the house sits. Of course, the name—which means, more or less, that each generation provides its own interpretation (of the Torah), couldn't be a better ready-made for this evocation of the politics of interpretation, transformation, colonization.

House, with its purer focus and more immediately relevant cast of characters, is the most resonant of the films, an amazing work. The DVD I saw opens under the imprimatur of censorship, declaring its own derivation from a bootleg copy of the original, before it fell under the tender mercies of the Israeli authorities. Its opening shot is remarkable: Palestinian quarrymen—forbidden to use explosives—driving stakes into the raw stone face, cutting blocks for the occupier's villa, a house abandoned by its Arab owner—a member of the Dajani clan, one of the most prominent in Palestine—in 1948. The scene is evocative of other stonework—the Phaoroh's, the rhythmic hammering of chain gangs, name it. I was particularly arrested by a resonance with *The Fountainhead*, another film in which the metaphor of building stands for the project of polity. In the scene I'm thinking of, a glistening, bare-chested Gary Cooper—unable to stand the compromises of the architectural profession—has become a quarryman, hewing the stone for other men's buildings. As for the stonecutter in *House*, this brutally dignified labor establishes the moral authority of the man who wields the hammer. The labor theory of value is made flesh (and stone).

In its reprise in *No Place like Home*, the two-toned cadence of the quarryman's hammer opens the lushly colored film in verité black and white, a lodestone for its moral compass. As the fresh footage begins with Gitai's voice-over, the music turns to Beethoven, indeed to the Emperor Concerto. This cultural marker recurs later in the film, during another voice-over in which Gitai speaks about his Bauhaus-trained father whom he quotes citing Mies van der Rohe's eprigram—"God is in the details"—a view he assimilates to his own discipline. Again, the soundtrack of the Zionist project is sublimely European. The cut here is to the music of a power saw in the hands of a Palestinian at work on the construction of a building next door to the eponymous house at the heart of the three films. Zionism is again represented, in the full flush of irony, as alienated from labor. Indeed, its dependence on exploited labor forms one of the recurring tropes of the trilogy.

Gitai has a remarkable eye for domestic space and for the rituals of home hospitality, and the three films are enacted in a series of interiors—of the Dajani family, of the occupant of their old house, of the next door neighbor, of Palestinian workers and their families. The central players—the

Dajanis, the current occupant, and her neighbor—live in lovely places, big and beautifully furnished as if to abstract the question of justice from the terrain of needs. It is perhaps one of the most striking aspects of these films that the central actors in the dispute are so uniformly educated and cultured, and that all are likewise imbued with strongly secularist views and a compelling sense of reasonableness and liberalism. There are no totalizers and annihilationists in these films, and it is from the seeming intractability of the injustices represented—precisely because they are so radically undeniable—that the films take their almost elegiac tone. In the confusion of proferred cups of coffee and pages turned in family photo albums, in which the gatherings, settings, and costumes are so indistinguishable, Gitai eloquently depicts a situation that feels tragically absurd.

In the last of the films, there is an unusually extended sequence shot at the home of the Dajanis in Amman that focuses, in particular, on Rabija Dajani, a cousin of the house's owner. In the economics of the trilogy's unfolding, her extended screen-time suggests her importance to the films' embedded polemic. She welcomes the filmmaker into a luxurious house—in the "best area of Amman"—furnished in a remarkably baroque style I once heard described in Egypt as "Louis Farouk." The filmmaker is clearly enamored of Rabija Dajani, and understandably so. A vigorous and charming woman in her eighties, she is also a resolute secularist and feminist. "I never cover my head," she asserts, and the flower poised behind her ear recurs in photos of earlier times. She recalls her romantic first marriage (opposed by the family) and describes her progressive social work career in the days of the Mandate. She speaks of working for the emancipation of women—"We started in the forties in Jerusalem"—and beguilingly asserts her credo, "I believe in freedom, don't you?"

There's a musical track to affirm this. A young member of the clan strums an Oud and sings a fervent love song, man to woman. The instrument recalls the score of the middle film, in which its sound pervades the film's atmosphere with a more modern score that nears stridency in its repetition and volume. It's clear that Gitai is in love with this woman—she is irresistible—and her extended appearance closes with an almost coquettish image of parting as she lingers at the gate of her house bidding the filmmaker farewell. Images of modernized women function powerfully in the film, and these figures of liberation are used to narrow the discourse of occupation—and the questions of Israel and Palestine—to a contest of reasonable people, and to make its unreasonable character the more salient through the exclusion of the opinions of fanatics (other than fanatical rigidities of the quotidian).

The current occupant of the house is another impressive woman, who grew up in Turkey, departing for Sweden and Switzerland before settling in Israel. Her photo album contains images of family gatherings in Istanbul. These are indistinguishable from those of the Dajanis, and the men wear tarbooshes and suits and ties. Indeed, the owner, Claire Cesari, speaks glowingly of her childhood experiences, switching from French to Hebrew to underline the importance of her central observation: "I think secularism is the most precious thing Turkey gave us." The spine of the trilogy lies in its foregrounded frustration with the irreconcilability of competing but common secularities defeated by the inescapable presentness of history, as well as in its production of a wealth of examples of Palstininan/Islamic rationality. It falls to the next-door neighbor—the entertainingly named, Belgian-born Misha Kishka—to produce the photo-album with a large number of missing, holocaust-slaughtered, relations.

Perhaps the most striking female figure in the films appears in the middle episode. There's a moment in *A House In Jerusalem* in which the filmmaker interviews an Israeli archaeologist in a cave-like underground site. While dilating on archaeology as the "study of human beings," he directs an Arab laborer carrying a stone, another Sisyphus, to get his burden out of the way. The metaphor/trope of archaeology and excavation is recurrent in the history of Israel as a marker of the state's authenticity and author-ity, and Gitai has himself identified documentary films with archaeology, narratives with architecture. The trilogy seeks to establish the priority of recent history through the same mechanism, and the long scene under-ground is direct and evocative, rich in both fact and metaphor, the cave Platonic in the ambiguous shadows it casts.

If the scene pivots on the figure of the Israeli archaeologist, it is brack-eted by the figures of the Palestinian laborers—again moving stones at someone else's behest—and by a much weirder presence. Throughout the sequence, we catch glimpses of a young woman strangely crouched in a corner of the cave, and she is eventually interviewed. She turns out to be a convert to orthodoxy—and to Zionism—from Pennsylvania, and she is waiting in the cave to immerse herself in a ritual *mikva*, in a bath that seems to spring from the stone to offer its selective purification. We do not know why she is crouching or how this transaction will take place—how she will find privacy, how the feminine boundaries of the water source will be established. At the end of the scene, we do see a young orthodox man showering in the purifying water, but his relationship to the woman and hers to the water remain opaque.

The young woman is articulate, her English native although she speaks mainly in Hebrew, and she functions for the film as another in a series of passionate aliens whose authenticity and rights are among the central ques-tions begged by the trilogy. Although a number of Palestinians ritually invoke religious phrases, none appear in religious contexts and none invoke Islam as a source of rights or grievances. The affective power of religion is almost entirely—and prejudicially—loaded on the Israeli side by way, in effect, of producing a surer secularism on the part of the aggrieved Palestinians. Indeed, it is part of the power and strategy of these works to suggest that rights are vested most prominently in those who can produce the most pitch-perfect Enlightenment versions of laity as a buttress to their claims for justice. Another of the Dajanis goes so far as to admire Israeli democracy—"You can do something to change things"—and to denounce Arab authoritarianism—further evidence of Palestinian reason and assimilation to modernity.

In the end, these films are amazingly eloquent in unpacking the burdens of the past on the present, and the way in which this saturation by historicity deforms all possible futures. The same Dajani who praises Israeli democracy is clear: "You can't get the future unless you manipulate the present." Cesari, the current occupant of the house, is more sanguine about the burden of historical intractability, saying "I didn't do it and I won't undo it. I didn't write history—history is just what it is." In *House*, there's an interview with an Arab worker who speaks Hebrew and declares that he is without hope for Palestine: "Everyone says what they want but the truth exists" is his crystalline view. Perhaps the most eloquent summary—very close to the filmmaker's own position—comes at the conclusion of the final installment of the trilogy, in a conversation with the son of the stonecutter in the first film, who finally expresses anger, eschewing the bittersweet, courteous sentiment of the Dajanis.

He speaks directly, putting the films' underlying questions into words, even as the coffee and hospitality flow. He is living in a house he has built "illegally" because of the criminal obfuscations of the occupation, which has now ordered it demolished. He insists that he is entitled to land that "belonged to his grandfather" and—in Hebrew—wonders why a Russian immigrant has rights that are denied to him. His questions are painfully succinct and his arguments—which close the trilogy—seem irrefutable. And he has a word for the filmmaker about the utility (or futility) of his project: "Your film is about the past, I want to talk about today."

I have edited two books about the question of Israel and Palestine, both critical of the Israeli position, and I imagine that this is one of the reasons I've been invited today, another being the fact that I am an architect. As someone who, although Jewish, has, as an American, stood outside the situation, I have felt some disquiet in my own work as a participant in helping to stage the spectacle of Israeli anxiety for the wider world. This is not exactly foreign to the issue of who is authorized to a certain critical intimacy, not a thousand miles from the question of whether blacks can call each other "nigger" or Jews can tell anti-Semitic jokes. Amos Gitai's remarkable trilogy establishes its political bona fides both in the powerful resistance its argument and evidence offer to Israeli policy and in the way it uses the spectacle of its author's own disquiet and failure as a sign of authenticity. It succeeds because our guide speaks though the lens of failure.

Alberti described houses and cities as larger and smaller versions of each other. I do not agree with this, and think that contemporary architectural theory has been mistaken in its desire to read too much about social relations at the scale of the dwelling, to inscribe or evoke processes that are only legible in larger orders of organization and behavior. Gitai's trilogy, however, discovers a house that is an instance, not a generality, and fashions from its history—not its form—an argument about the site of justice.

2008

69

Bucky and Me

In the early summer of 1967, my mother and I traveled to Montreal to see the Expo. The main attractions were Safdie's Habitat and Buckminster Fuller's great dome. How different they were! Habitat was stolidly gravitational, a weighty pile of boxes dramatically deployed but thoroughly, traditionally compressive. And, like much of modernism, Habitat was bound to a happy image of Mediterraneaity, the prismatic forms of villages sculpted in sun, the same font of tectonic delight that so thrilled Le Corbusier; it aimed to be the ultimate merger of the Mediterranean and the megastructure.

Bucky's dome, by contrast, was tensile and light, a gossamer thing with a synergetic structure that was virtually not there. It was Habitat turned inside out, a global enclosure with its particulars subsumed beneath its organizing whole, rather than aggregated to create the whole itself. If Habitat's surfaces were meant to be awash with greenery, the breathing dome produced its own climate and grew its garden indoors. Into this space of potentiality, things could simply be inserted—factories, "standard of living packages," exhibitions, radars, airplanes.

The two projects were united, however, by one of the sturdiest tropes of modernity: the idea that the conjunction of architecture, technology, and mass production had the potential to re-socialize the project of building, to direct scientific efficiencies to redress the problem of shortage, especially of housing. For Safdie, the idea of those factory-built boxes shipped and stacked promised urban densities on the quick in a form at once radical and familiar. But it was a heavy industrial vision, demanding massive investment and highly centralized organization.

Bucky's lifelong quest for mass-produced housing came from another direction. His most innovative work along these lines—the series of prefab houses beginning with the 4D House (patented in 1928) and culminating in the Dymaxion Dwelling Machine (patented in 1946)—had as its predicate a winnowing of materials and a simplification of erection that had much more to do with kit building than the assembly line. The entire Dymaxion house was to be shipped to its site in a big tube that contained all its elements, none of which weighed more than ten pounds, allowing the whole thing to be put together in a few days by a single person. Indeed, the total weight of the house itself was a svelte 6,000 pounds, in contrast to a traditional house of similar size, tipping the scales at 300,000 pounds. Doing more with less was an abiding credo for Bucky, but one that ramified far beyond the less-is-more aesthetic of modernist minimalism. His genius at such paring down continues to secure his relevance.

In this preoccupation with the weight of things, from cars to planets, Bucky was concerned not simply with economy but with shortage. Although this commitment is sometimes derided as so much mystical palaver, Bucky was an authentic pioneer in the movement for global ecology: his career was dedicated to making global systems both legible and logical, to "reforming the environment, not reforming man." This is clear throughout his copious—if often baroque—writing, as well as in the projects and research he inspired. One of the most important (and lucid) of these—still very much worth reading—is John McHale's *The Ecological Context*, of 1969. Before he met Bucky, McHale was an artist and a leading light of the British Independent Group, described by Reyner Banham (also a member) as the "Father of Pop." McHale's interest in Fuller dated from the fifties, part of his general fascination with the intersection of technology and culture and of his broader penchant for futurism. He joined Fuller at Carbondale in the sixties, participating in the massive World Resources Inventory project and eventually striking out as an extremely rigorous and pioneering analyst of global ecology, a bridge-builder—like Bucky—between spheres of knowledge and action.

I took another trip a little later, in 1967 (this time without mom), to Haight Ashbury. It was, after all, the Summer of Love, and San Francisco was the place to be. One of the most commanding artifacts in the recent retrospective of Fuller's work at the Whitney Museum was a film showing Bucky holding forth to a young crowd in Golden Gate Park at the height of those delirious days. I never did hear one of Bucky's marathon orations, but this tape gives a good hint at his mesmerizing power. There he sits, a gnomic, grandfatherly presence in a black three-piece suit and watch chain, among the flower children, entirely at home. It's a question-and-answer session, and Bucky is remarkably succinct, compassionate, persuasive, and smart. He bounces babies on his knee. His answers are satisfying, whether he dilates on the history of specialization, the pernicious character of the nation-state, the need to turn global resources away from warfare and toward constructive activity, or questions of tetrahedral geometry, the formal quantum of the universe for Bucky. In every sense, this was a man thinking outside the box, gently drawing others along.

Although he was the rage with the counterculture, Bucky has long had an ambiguous relationship to the architectural profession and its canon. It may be his polymathic project that engendered this; the comparison with Leonardo, whom nobody would simply call an architect, is apposite, if slightly generous. But Bucky surely has more in common with an Edison than a Mies: he was an inventor, mathematician, geometer, cartographer, ecologist, manufacturer, industrial designer, moralist, epistemologist, world systems thinker—a collusion of abilities that sometimes produced architecture but found its way there through nonorthodox working methods and winding trains of thought. His architecture did not emerge from the profession's traditions, but produced it in a series of consolidations of other approaches: architecture was a solution, not an objective.

One of the few to appreciate his project consistently was Reyner Banham who, in *The Architecture of the Well-Tempered Environment* got it just right, citing

> Paul Valéry's contrast between Eupalinos, the architect, and Tridon, the shipwright. The former was preoccupied with the right method of doing the allotted tasks, and deploying the accepted methods of his calling, and seemed to find a philosophical problem in every practical decision. Tridon, on the other hand, applied every technology that came conveniently to hand, whether or not it was part of the shipbuilding tradition, and treated the sayings of philosophers as further instruction on the direct solution of practical problems.

Bucky—who early imbibed a nautical tradition and whose late project for a floating Habitat was called "Triton City"—fits this description to a T. This made it tough for the profession to internalize him as one of its own.

The cool reception surely also stemmed from the fact that Bucky authentically delivered modernism's promises, that he pulled its chestnuts from the fire, revealing its product to be far less than it claimed. In *Theory and Design in the First Machine Age* (1960), Banham deploys two telling visual comparisons, the first between Corbusier's villa at Garches (1928–30) and Bucky's Dymaxion House (1927–30). Corb's familiar work embodies its modernity by entirely representational means—through its starkly planar composition, its free plan, its slim pilotis hoisting it above the ground plane. Fuller's house, on the other hand, is authentically radical in its suspended construction, its use of light, non-traditional materials, and its organization around a pre-manufactured mechanical core—form following function to the point of defamiliarization. On the very next page Banham contrasts a design by Gropius for the body of the 1930 Adler Cabriolet with Bucky's Dymaxion car of 1933. The Adler looks thoroughly antique, with a few minor modifications around the margins; Bucky's car looks, and acts, like the future.

Fortunately, Fuller's influence exceeded the architectural profession. The domes were received not simply for their celestial iconography (the first picture of the "whole earth" was not taken until the sixties), but for their astonishing practicality and for their suggestively communal style of enclosure. Bucky pursued the construction of various "geoscopes" meant, like his undistorted Dymaxion Maps, to model the world and display quantitative information about it. (He had hoped his Expo dome would do this but the technology wasn't yet there). He was, in project and proclamation, constantly hectoring us Earthlings to pilot our spaceship by gathering all possible navigational data to control—to take responsibility for—our collective destiny.

The insistence that thought, that the universe, was recursively patterned was at the core of Bucky's investigation and beliefs—his metaphysic. The central artifact of this quest was geometry, and the centrality of his four-vectored organization has received posthumous vindication in the discovery of the family of "fullerenes"—carbon allotropes structured like geodesics that are keys to the world of nanotechnology. Here, too, is a lesson for architecture today, which largely continues to be at a loss for its mission. Modernism foundered theoretically in its unstable oscillations between formal invention and the project of creating new styles of human subjectivity. The one was not really radical and the other was intrinsically beyond its ken (if not its hubris). Bucky asked a more interesting question: "What can I do for my fellow man that doesn't take away his freedom?" Instead of falling into the sterility of modernist politics, Bucky looked beyond architecture to the macro-scale of the global systems and flows that produced the criteria for building, and to the micro-scale of the geometric organization of space that provides the efficient substance of construction. A Platonist in his gut, he knew that ideas produced the meaning of form.

I find Bucky more and more inspirational, especially for the freedom of his research. Two projects done with Shoji Sadao in 1960 make the point. The first of these is the much-ridiculed dome over midtown Manhattan, criticized either as "impractical" (how to buff the glass, how to get the traffic through) or as simply a megalomaniacal expression of an environment overly controlled. Such criticisms miss the project's simple point: the membrane has a surface area approximately 1/64th that of the aggregated exteriors of all the buildings within it, and Bucky argued that the larger the dome, the greater the energy conserved. The Manhattan dome is simply rhetorical, a device to describe the environmental inefficiencies of standard practice. Likewise, the Cloud Nine project for a series of sphere cities floating in the atmosphere is both an acid dream and the embodiment of a very simple set of physical calculations, suggesting that if we could actually build such giant geodesic balloons, they would stably hang, fresh moons lightly elevated by elemental forces. Bucky surely knew that the magic in the universe was there for the figuring out.

2008

70

Three Freedoms

In his 1998 book, *Development as Freedom*, Amartya Sen focuses his analysis on the power of free individuals to be active agents of change, rather than passive recipients of distributed benefits. "Freedom," he writes, "is the primary end as well as the means to development." For Sen, development is powered by the constant effort to remove impediments to individual participation and potential—what he calls "unfreedoms"—and he measures progress in five categories: protective security, economic facilities, political freedom, social opportunity, and transparency guarantees.

Sen's schema is not simply relevant to the developing world: it offers a sensible index of the quality of urban life and character in general, and urban public space in particular. I believe that spatial relations both record and potentially promote the progress of freedom, and that freedom is the project of democracy. This is something most of us believe in, despite the mood of contempt for public institutions and for the project of democratic empowerment expressed by our increasingly reactionary government and manifested by the ongoing privatization of traditional elements of the public sphere, by the domination of the so-called public-private partnerships that seem to define larger and larger components of social life, and by the dramatic contempt for the very idea of civic responsibility that has been thrown into such high relief by the appalling behavior raised to high relief by lack of any post-Katrina planning or reform.

Public space—a shifting and not entirely determinate realm that embodies a range of historical and cultural meanings—emerges, in the reading of Jürgen Habermas and others, somewhere "between civil society and the state . . . the sphere of private people coming together as a public." Although Habermas is not much concerned with the spatialization of the public sphere, it is clear that the activity of "coming together" is often enabled by an appropriate cultural and physical space, by the removal of a number of Sen's unfreedoms that block free and direct encounter. Public space has been body-based for thousands of years, imprinted directly on the fabric of the city, governing its morphology and its styles of distribution of public and private realms, and it seems foolish to abandon the connection, especially now. The emergence of the disembodied means of interaction enabled by the web (with its own imaginary publics), which assail the physical and by the force of the flattening stresses of generic global culture that rip into the idea that the public is multiple, comprising innumerable publics with differing interests, habits and agendas, make the tractability of the physical realm all the more crucial.

In particular, as the conference organizers have noted, the form of the American city increasingly presents profound challenges to the idea of democratic space—something I understand to be not completely isomorphic with the idea of public space, but close enough. The point is simply that such space is produced, and that space only becomes truly public when there exists a citizenry that is equipped to use it. Thus, *democratic* space is—above all—a space that embodies the idea of freedom, and freedom can be measured in access to choices, choices unimpeded by oppressive unfreedoms. As the Orwellian arguments that recently sunk the "Freedom Center" at Ground Zero for the unacceptable risk that it would become the actual site of free expression underline, these issues loom very large and very near.

In the city, freedom of choice manifests itself in a set of physical arrangements that reproduce or enable more general ideas about democratic freedoms in a specifically material context. In particular, there are, it seems to me, three freedoms that figure particularly in the process of urban design and planning, freedoms that form the basis for judging the success of the good city, and that have direct translation into the physical configuration of urban space. I do not propose that the realization of the spaces of freedom should lead to any single morphology, nor do I mean to assess the relative personal degrees of freedom represented by Walden Pond, Times Square, or the Café Sha Sha. I do mean to suggest, however, that it is possible to talk about the quality of freedom in the array of collective physical arrangements densely and dynamically assembled in the city.

The first is freedom of assembly, the main expression of democracy in space, a concept enshrined in the constitution. By definition, physical assembly requires a space that is conducive to it, and the range of such sites—streets, plazas, parks, cafés, meeting halls, ballrooms, front stoops—signal, in their variety and fit, how publics gather and mix. The history of urban public space lies in the particular institutions that house it—the *agora*, the souk, the piazza, the public green; the coffee houses of Georgian London or Imperial Vienna; the cafés and boulevards of the Second Empire; the bars and speakeasies of old New York; the Casa del Popolo and the Maison du Peuple. Like every other aspect of the physical design of cities, however, the spaces of assembly do not invent the right to it. And these spaces—however rich their variety—can be turned from their empowering potential by surveillance, policing, indifference, or simply unfamiliarity with the styles of their use. Nevertheless, a democratic heterotopia can only be that—comprising many different publics and spaces, their mix the product of endless arrangements and deals. While it is important not to fall into the historic trap of thinking that architecture invents social relations, it is equally important to remember that it does not simply describe them: it supports and defends them.

Freedom of assembly itself depends on a second freedom: freedom of access. A democratic city is one in which it is possible to move freely and easily from one place to another. This freedom can be frustrated in numerous ways. Selective access to the means of mobility prevents the unprivileged from transiting the city. Overregulation of the space of movement can relegate styles of assembly to the overly predictable, like the "Public Games" in North Korea or the parking lot at Wal-Mart. And access devolves not simply on the means of motion but on the legibility of the network. We know that this can be frustrated at some outer margin by both the grid and the labyrinth, each of which produces its own special confusions, the one by promoting a universal sameness, obliterating all distinctions, and the other by creating such an endlessness of the irregular that memory becomes incapable of recreating a pathway, no matter how many crumbs are left behind. Here, too, we find an argument for limits and boundaries—both internal and external—which function as media of both difference and clarity.

One of the crucial styles of assembly in the good city is accidental. This possibility depends both on urban morphology and on the mechanism by which people and activities are distributed throughout the city. Accidents refresh private life in the city by assuring that encounters with the public realm are not always predictable. Absent this mechanism, public life becomes like a succession of Soviet Party Congresses in which the outline of democracy can be traced in the raising of hands by the delegates, but in which the outcomes are always predictable. In the urban context, this translates into the nothing-can-go-wrong affect of Seaside/Truman Show planning, the little Pyongyangs of repressed curiosity.

The idea of the stimulating accident is not universal: not every accident is a happy one. We do not wish to bump into our ex-boyfriend every time we step out of the house any more than to be struck by a laundry truck. The city is not simply an aleatory mechanism consecrated—like some surrealist parlor game—to producing unexpected juxtapositions. Good cities are those that find some happy balance between chance and choice, resistance and flow and the mechanisms of clarity and confusion both have their roles to play. The final judgment about the equilibrium between these valences of urbanity must always be suspended: the reciprocation of these qualities cannot, by definition, reach a point of absolute predictability, save the predictability that one is likely to have a reasonable number of surprises negotiating the town.

Which brings us to the third freedom: use and expression. This third freedom is an inflection of the first: free assembly is not simply the right to gather, but to gather for a reason, even if the reason is to do nothing in particular. Freedom of use and expression is complex, and comprises at least two specific components. The first is the general freedom to do as one wishes, and here I am inclined to a fundamentally libertarian view. That is, I think people—and groups of people—should generally be allowed to do as they please as long as no harm comes to others. Inasmuch as the range of such elective activities can be inventoried, the good city will strive to provide the enabling physical infrastructure to support the maximum number of such choices, including those that cannot be predicted.

This requires not simply a non-oppressive and malleable variety, but a set of recording institutions, accumulators of memory, the second element of the third freedom. While free expression is important in and of itself, its meaning in democracy can be thwarted if it is robbed of the possibility of having an effect—repressively tolerated. The exercise of free expression in the city should therefore result in ongoing changes to the city, and the nature of such changes—whether in the form of urban spaces or the deployment of urban uses—is a meaningful, if complicated, register of the success of the urban public.

Given this collection of freedoms, the question for the city—and the American city in particular—is what specifically to include in our conceptual and physical operations that will stimulate the deployment and enjoyment of these possibilities. It is important to be humble here, to keep the cart and horse in their traditional alignment. Once again: although cities can be great incubators of democracy, this is not a product of their design. Nevertheless, the expression—the living—of democracy depends vitally on the media available to it, and here the city is utterly central, a lexicon of association.

Freedom of assembly depends on its spaces, and we are remiss if we ignore the innumerable precedents and instances that guarantee the continuation of established cultures of assembly and that undergird our own efforts to enlarge the repertoire. Sneering at streets and plazas, diverting their functions into malls, vapid labyrinths, excessively programmed spaces of recreational activity, or into hyperspace, simply will not do. On the other hand, the habit of urban designers simply to ornament their projects with the shriveled iconography of assembly—Cinzano umbrellas shading café tables or Disneyesque greens in towns with no governance—must be seen for what it is: a fraud. We have witnessed a spectacular instance of the lack of correspondence between assembly and power in the sorry history of the planning of Ground Zero, in which a public desperate to participate has been repeatedly gathered, put through the paces of free expression, and then completely ignored by the real power. It's important, therefore, not to sentimentalize assembly per se but to understand it and defend it as a mechanism of empowerment, a means of removing unfreedom. Still, as the fracas over the organization of demonstrations against the Republican convention in New York last year so vividly revealed, the right of assembly must not simply be defended as a right in and of itself, but the production of the spaces for such assembly is a vital precondition for assembly's very possibility.

Freedom of access demands a double investigation, one that embraces both forms and means. To restate a basic conviction: the embodiment of this freedom demands that the body be placed in the alpha position. The free body represents a paradigm of independent motion and, as such, should live at the point of maximum privilege. In this sense, all else is prosthetic, a means of extension. Thus, there is a fundamental economy that balances the embodied right of movement against varying degrees of mediation. If machinery is required for every encounter, if we cannot meet our friends and neighbors without recourse to technology, something vital is lost. This is an extreme, and the all too familiar nightmare of mediated access has at one end a world of constant, meaningless motion, and at the other a condition of total immobility, a life shared only through the ether.

Urban accessibility can be measured more practically in the relative weight given to different means of motion. In Houston, three-quarters of the surface area at grade is given over to automobiles, to their movement, storage, and service. The largest component of the physical public realm in New York City is the network of streets, of which something like a third is devoted to the storage of private motor vehicles. Imagine the transformation were a single lane on every street to be switched from the automotive system to the pedestrian realm. Immediately, we could redesign our idiotic style of waste disposal, provide storage for everyone's bicycles, increase street trees by 50 percent, offer myriad small-scaled social spaces, and the list goes on.

I have long been intrigued by traffic in India. There's something that feels democratic about it. From building front to building front, the space of circulation is shared by all modes. Instead of our style of segregating means of motion by energy level to avoid "conflict," the Indian system offers free access to cars, pedestrians, trucks, buses, motor-rickshaws, bullock-carts, elephants and, of course, those ubiquitous cows. Indeed, it is the licensed dissent of the bovine hordes, the sacred right of cows to simply plop and snooze wherever they choose, that guarantees the viability of the system. It works because it is slow, and it relies on an intricate web of negotiations between all elements of the system, all of which are parties to the deal. While I do not advocate this precise mix for our own cities, its fundamentals—minimal segregation enabled by a slow pace that dilutes the kinetic advantage of large and energetic vehicles—seem very sound.

Which leads me, in conclusion, to a few words about freedom of expression. In Indian traffic, expression is a key component of the viability of the system, a byproduct of its intense diversity. The same cycle of diversity and harmonization should also govern larger patterns of urban organization in democratically conceived cities. This does not simply mean the endeavor to anticipate multiplicity: it requires that the dogmatic organization that structures our cities—the ongoing regimes of zoning and segregation—be critiqued and thwarted. The decision about what may be where within the city might be said to be the city's own measure of free expression, and here too our prejudice should be for latitude rather than constraint. Especially in post-industrial, massively linked, service-oriented economies like our own, this style of expression should flourish, should offer one of the key engines of urban transformative logic.

Again, we are confronted with democracy's project to nourish both difference and accommodation, a process with no end. Indeed, the end of the process can only be the death of the activity of democracy itself, which thrives on its own renewal. The city structures its expressive freedoms around a cycle of invention and integration, the deepening of consent and the thickening of agreement. Great cities are formed in the interplay of genius and compact and—as they grow historic—the compass of their morphological elaboration both shrinks and deepens as agreed conventions and rituals—as history—takes ever stronger hold on the public imagination, and as the body of laws and habits that define its spaces becomes more elaborate. The imposition of new formal or behavioral paradigms on the body politic can therefore be expected to be greeted with increasing resistance when they assail urban characteristics that publics within the city have come to love and expect. We observe this every day in events like the current outcry over the Bruce Ratner/Frank Gehry scheme to massively rebuild a piece of downtown Brooklyn, irretrievably altering its character, for better or worse.

Free expression in the city is therefore a combination of private preferences and public conduits. Its legibility is to be found in the range of useful places in the city for speaking and gathering, for being heard by urban publics in all their diversity, and for living life as one wishes to live it. This will necessarily register in the architecture and organization of the city, in its variety, flexibility, hospitality, difference, dimension, and neighborliness. While every city must find its own road to singularity, we must hold firm about these principles and ask of our work as urbanists if what we do enlarges or contracts the space of possibility for the enjoyment of freedom. Only the vigor and justice of the public realm can assure full access to our private desires.

2008

71

The Plot against Architecture

With Apologies to Philip Roth

After the election of Lindbergh to the presidency in 1940, the anxiety in the business community about doing business with Germany, which had reached such a pitch in Roosevelt's second term, relaxed considerably. Of course there remained a certain sense of reserve in some quarters, but the profit to be made supplying the military needs of the Reich were so substantial that any political restraint was swept away. In particular, Henry Ford—who became Lindbergh's Secretary of the Interior—was quick to supply the Reich with trucks and other vehicles.

Indeed, Ford's advertising came to heavily feature pictures of its two-ton trucks doing service on the eastern front, and the slogan "Keeping the Red Tide at Bay" appeared over lurid images of Ford convoys rolling east, filled with chiseled storm troopers ready to do battle with the Soviet enemy. In a number of these ads, a tide of prisoners could be seen marching west to captivity. Although there were sporadic protests, many of these prisoners were marked by what were clearly meant to be "Jewish" features, and Ford himself continued to be forthcoming about the dangers of "World Jewry" and the importance of the war in curbing its invidious influence. This continued the jeremiad he had begun in the 1920s with his "investigation of the Jewish question" in his newspaper, *The Dearborn Independent*, subsequently published as *The International Jew*. Here Ford urged that in the cleansing of America from the various scourges that afflicted it, "the International Jew and his satellites, as the conscious enemies of all that Anglo Saxons mean by civilization, are not spared."

In the early years of the war, Germany also became a considerable tourist attraction, despite the sporadic and largely ineffective British bombing of its cities. Indeed, for the groups being shepherded by their energetic *Hitler Jugend* guides, a trip to a well-appointed shelter became an almost obligatory part of the tour. Many returned home in disappointment that no raid had interrupted their journeys through the New Germany and travel agents were eventually obliged to include a simulated air-raid on their itineraries if the real thing proved unavailable.

The groups that made these visits included many branches of the German-American Bund, worker groups from the factories that were supplying armaments and materials, a constant stream of contractors bidding for orders big and small, as well as interested citizens from many walks of life. Visits also became *de riguer* for many architects and planners. As the war provided more and more resources to the Reich, and as its sense of its own destiny grew more and more firm, Hitler's massive program for Germany's reconstruction became an ever higher priority, and the highways, housing projects, civic buildings, and urban development proliferated.

Under the indefatigable direction of Albert Speer, this reached a truly enormous level, and there was much derisive comparison with the efforts of Roosevelt's Works Progress Administration, most of which was abandoned following his defeat in 1940. *The New German Architecture*—the title of a glossy publication issued by Goebbels with an introduction by Philip Johnson entitled "A New International Style" in which he renounced the austere modernism he had previously advocated—found a wide audience in the United States. Enthusiasm for the "German model" reached such a level that Lindbergh responded with his own program of superhighways, and with the short-lived New American Village project. America's emergence from the Great Depression via these public projects was materially assisted by the rapid and profitable growth of an arms industry that was able to sell to Germany, Britain, and the Soviet Union. Lindbergh and his economic advisors—among whom Ford was the most prominent—pursued their "guns and butter" policy with some success.

The New American Villages were both a public works program and a critical component of Lindbergh's efforts at ethnic and population redistribution, part of his *Life with Your Neighbors, Life with Your Kind* initiative—the so-called Coughlin Plan—that had begun in 1941, shortly after Lindbergh took office. Eager to court the celebrated radio priest Father Coughlin, Lindbergh appointed him special advisor for community affairs and quickly agreed to the massive effort that hoped to refigure much of the American landscape under the banner of "One Nation, Divided," a slogan with special resonance in many southern states. This project was administered by Lindbergh's Office of American Absorption, which quickly began its work "encouraging America's religious and national minorities to become further incorporated into the larger society."

Philip Johnson's involvement with the project was partly serendipitous. Because of his long involvement with fascist and proto-fascist causes, including his frequent trips to Germany as a reporter for Coughlin's newspaper *Social Justice* (for which he had written enthusiastically about Nazi policies and about the war, deriding in equal measure the French, British, and Jews), and because of his spirited public embrace of Nazi architecture, he was invited to the controversial dinner at the White House that President Lindbergh gave to celebrate the first state visit of Foreign Minister Von Ribbentrop to Washington. Thanks to his close relationship with Coughlin, Johnson was seated at the president's table. His place fell opposite the first lady Anne Morrow Lindbergh, herself seated to the right of Von Ribbentrop. Coughlin was on Johnson's immediate left, next to Henry Ford.

Coughlin found the opportunity to discuss his redistributive project irresistible, and launched into what was by then a well-rehearsed argument—drawing variously on biblical and eugenic sources—about the necessity for the "harmonious sequestration" of incompatible components of the population, particularly Negroes and Jews. That particular evening, he dilated on the ideal of small-town America, suggesting that the corruptions of "big city cosmopolitanism" might be addressed through both the concentration and "protection" of racial groups and the benign influences of "traditional villages with traditional houses and traditional ways." This formulation found enthusiastic support from Von Ribbentrop, who not simply urged Coughlin on but turned to Ford and said (as Johnson later reported), "*Lieber Heinrich*, just imagine: one thousand Greenfield Villages for America!"

Ford—with whom Coughlin had long discussed the matter—agreed to press Lindbergh on the initiative and proposed, on the spot, to prime the pump for the project by financing the design and construction of ten model villages on the assembly-line model. "Works for cars and tanks, don't see why it shouldn't work for houses," Ford offered. Johnson sensed an opportunity in the making and joined the conversation with enthusiasm. Recognizing that something well beyond style was at stake, he spun out the argument he had begun to make in *The New International Style* in a way that he thought would have special appeal for Henry Ford. Turning to the automaker, Johnson made his point with vigor.

> Modern architecture is about *process*, about a way of doing things, about harnessing the logic and might of industrial production for the masses, the people, the *volk*. The way a building—or a town or a city—looks should be an expression of a nation's will to form, a will that must grow from it rootedness in history. You cannot not know history, of course.

Warming to the subject, Johnson proposed the homology between the *klein Dorf* and the small town, arguing the alignment of the purity of their architectures—half-timbered Gothic and white painted "classical"—with the purity of the inhabitants. "The danger is not from the wisdom of tradition, it is rather from its corruption, from the mingling of disparate streams, which is as sure a formula for degeneracy in building as it is for degeneracy in the population." Johnson, who now had the ear of the table, including Lindbergh, went on to extol the virtues of having a Führer devoted to architecture as a means of channeling and vitalizing "the people's sacred blood and soil," and compared him to Thomas Jefferson, another leader who understood the national project as the conjunction of philosophy, building, and the organization of "the space of the nation." He ended his impassioned oration with a seething dismissal of "Franklin Delano Rosenfeld" and his "bad dealers," and a highly unfavorable comparison of "puny new towns laid out by and for socialists" with "the bright order and social power" of Theresienstadt, to which he had recently paid a visit. In the glowing article he had published about it in *Social Justice*, he'd written that this "handsomely gilded ghetto represents a fine and final solution to the Jewish problem that so taxes the nations of the civilized world."

By the time dinner was over, Ford had engaged Johnson to direct a project for the creation of ten New American Villages, and Johnson soon established offices in Dearborn and Washington to undertake the work. His first initiatives were to establish the Congress for the New American Town to propagandize for the initiative and offer a neutral harbor and conduit for architects and planners eager to participate in what was envisioned as a huge gravy train, and to hire Walt Disney as the primary design consultant. This latter move was variously regarded as scandalous (mainly by architects) and brilliant (by almost everyone else). Johnson—who was, at this point, untrained as an architect—had a deep appreciation for Disney's artistry, his mass appeal, and his politics (Disney had been generous in his support of the Lindbergh campaign, and his racial views were in constellation with those of Coughlin, Ford, and Johnson). In addition, Hitler's own enthusiasm for Disney was well known: not simply were Disney cartoons a regular feature of evening entertainment in the Chancellery, "When You Wish Upon a Star" was—along with the "Horst Wessel Lied" and the overture to *Tannhäuser*—a favorite tune. Speer reported that Hitler had begun whistling it as they stood at the Palais de Chaillot, overlooking conquered Paris.

Johnson was also inspired by the great popularity of the Rockefeller-financed reconstruction of colonial Williamsburg and, of course, Ford's Greenfield Village, an imaginative re-creation of his boyhood home, understanding them as "architectural distillates of the nation." As Johnson put it in his Charter of the Congress for the New American Town,

Architecture must have a *theme*, a cultural portrait that at once gives it meaning and simplifies its expressive component in such a way that the people can easily identify it. As with any other product of mass manufacture, the underlying armature will be usefully and efficiently repetitive. However, by precisely locating those suggestive inflections that will right away evoke the Rabbi or the Minstrel, those people they represent can be, as it were, put in their place.

The construction of New Plantation, Alabama and New Warsaw, Arizona (privately referred to by Johnson as Coontown and Kikeville) began within three months of the launch of the New American Village initiative. Sensitive to the fact that the earlier program to disperse minority populations to "unprepared" areas of the country had resulted in numerous "disturbances," including dozens of murders and lynchings, New Plantation and New Warsaw were sited in what were held to be more hospitable climes. New Plantation, in fact, returned blacks from cities in the north-east and mid-west to an area of the country from which many had fled just a generation or two before. The Arizona site was tucked in a corner of a Navajo reservation, established during a prior concentration regime. In fact, after Roosevelt returned to office in 1942, New Warsaw became an internment camp for Japanese Americans—a hat trick of ethnic separation.

Formally, the towns were virtually identical. Each had an axial main street, lined with two-story row houses and culminating, in the case of New Plantation, at the portico of the Uncle Remus Baptist Church, and in that of New Warsaw at the very similar portico of Temple Jolson. Behind this main street lay a neat grid of roads along which small wooden houses were carefully aligned. The architecture, however, was carefully inflected by the Disney scenographers, right down to what appeared to be long-faded (but actually freshly produced) signage and advertising in Yiddish in New Warsaw and an ancient-looking locomotive at the siding of the New Plantation Station, periodically fired up to take residents in a similarly old-fashioned-looking coach on a short loop around the town, its public address system blaring the specially composed "Zip-A-Dee-Doo-Dah" (a tune which, after the war, became a hit number in Disney's 1946 *Song of the South*). In fact, traffic to and from both towns was highly restricted, largely confined to new arrivals periodically dropped off by bus and the sporadic supply of goods.

This latter was one of the initial difficulties the Office of American Absorption had with the towns. Although the planners had kitted them out with shops, schools, civic and religious buildings, and extensive landscape buffering, they had neglected to provide for any economic basis for their survival. In the case of New Plantation, the assumption had been that the sharecropping economy would provide appropriate subsistence. In fact, this was the only employment locally available, but given the size of the town it obliged residents to seek work many miles away. As a result, the town was largely and rapidly hollowed out and—despite the meting out of sometimes draconian punishments—the houses were covertly dismantled to provide timber for shacks built on the distant fields its population tilled. Johnson's own direct architectural contribution to New Plantation seems to have been limited to the much publicized "Tar Baby Caryatids" which held up the front porch of "De Gen'ral Sto" on Main Street.

At New Warsaw, Johnson and his planners assumed that the relocated Jews would be able to survive on, as he put it, "those ducats they've all squirreled away," or on the largesse of their wealthy coreligionists. In fact, there was much disagreement within the Jewish community about how to respond to the situation. At one extreme were collaborationists like Rabbi Lionel Bengelsdorf of Newark, who made common cause with the program—actually serving as titular head of the OAA—in the hopes that appeasement would spare the Jews further trouble. At another were the "New Zionists" who saw the Arizona town as a possible bridgehead to a Jewish state, and a group of them attempted unsuccessfully to start agricultural enterprises on the unyielding sands of the Arizona desert. Most of the community was simply divided between outrage and fear, especially as the scope of the Nazi atrocities in Europe came to be known. In the end, the economy of New Warsaw depended on covert gifts from the free Jewish community—still the major portion of American Jewry—and from piecework for the garment industry, goods driven back and forth from Los Angeles in dilapidated cars by the so-called "cloakies." Indeed, many of the neat clapboard houses grew to resemble the sweatshops of New York, whose workers had been the parents of so many of those resettled in New Warsaw.

On October 7, 1942, following the assassination of Walter Winchell, the Lone Eagle took off on a solo flight in the *Spirit of St. Louis* to rally his constituency for his social programs and his ongoing insistence that the United States stay out of "Europe's war." His disappearance—many alleged he had ditched his plane in the Atlantic to be picked up by a German U-Boat—resulted in the return of Roosevelt to office, and with it the unraveling of the New American Village project and the return home of its internees. New Plantation and New Warsaw were the only towns completed before the end of the Lindbergh presidency, and there are no physical remains today, although they survive in numerous publications from the time, including issues of Johnson's glossy—if short-lived— monthly, *America Builds*. His editorial in the first issue might serve as an epitaph for his career:

> Architecture serves power and every architect must do its bidding. In this he has no choice. Lucky the architect with the opportunity to work for power that wields the truth. In this, today's America—and today's

Germany—have a near monopoly. I glory in the opportunity to bend to this hurricane of national will and to direct its power to blowing out the reeking miasma of impurity that holds America back by my unquestioning obedience to my masters.

2009

72

A Letter to President Obama

Dear President Obama,

I am extremely heartened that you are planning to address our miserable economic situation with a massive investment in infrastructure. This is not simply a logical and efficient way of translating dollars into jobs (although it's always important to ask for whom), it is an investment in the long-term future of the country. Although I am writing this in December and don't know precisely what the shape of your program will be, I appreciate that it will be of a magnitude commensurate with the problems at hand. You've already suggested that it will be the largest investment in public works since the building of the interstate highway system in the Eisenhower days, and that in the interest of speed you will be seeking "shovel-ready" projects. While I understand that the Eisenhower analogy is meant to suggest magnitude and "shovel-ready" efficiency, I urge you to be cautious about additional implications. The last thing we need is more highways, and those "shovel-ready" projects will tend to reflect old priorities, not the change we need and can believe in.

Here are ten suggestions for a stimulus program that will help remake our cities and take them into the new century.

1. Prepare for the post-automotive urban environment. After taking care of the most pressing repairs to bridges and roadways, initiate a massive aid program for the creation of a post-automotive urbanism. This will mean enormous investment in urban mass transit, intercity rail, as well as a planning and design regime that puts human locomotion— on foot, on bicycles—at the very top of the transit hierarchy. Both our cities and suburbs need radical redesign to incorporate systems that are in fundamental sympathy with urbanity. Instead of offering subsidies to convenience cars (look at the damage done to cities by the availability of irresistible financing in which the feds picked up 90 percent of the tab for the construction of interstates), the government should encourage compact cities that consume less energy and offer a good mix of uses. Subsidies should go for removing traffic lanes, not adding them. The

effects of such "greenfill" would be to increase urban greenery (mitigating the heat-island effect and refreshing the air), offer space for pedestrians and public transit, and rebalance the use of what is far and away the largest component of our public built space.

2. Reconceive the automobile industry. Do not simply bail out the car companies, but force them to rebuild based on a new paradigm. This should include both their involvement in sustainable forms of mass transportation and a dramatic reconsideration of what an automobile should be in our era. Although moving rapidly away from fossil power is crucial, so is the production of cars that are specifically designed for cities. Instead of large, dangerous vehicles optimized for the highway, we need a new class of small, slow, nonaggressive, clean cars for the urban environment—cars that fit comfortably with reduced roadways and the expansion of the pedestrian realm.

3. Rebuild the sewers. We need a massive program to reconstruct our water and sewage systems. Money should flow to eliminate sewers that mix storm and waste water in order to reduce pollution and conserve and appropriately reuse scarce water resources. We must also introduce graywater systems and bioremediation facilities everywhere possible to further manage this life-giving asset.

4. Green America's buildings. Raising standards for insulation and weatherization and greening the roofs of our buildings is perhaps the single most efficient expenditure we can quickly make to reduce energy consumption. Because such work does not require large organizations, it is most likely to benefit smaller businesses. Moreover, what could be a more suitable activity than a WPA-like intervention in both training and implementation? America has an obscenely large prison population. Instead of allowing it to languish, why not institute a large-scale program to train inmates in the skills necessary to green the country, creating a CCC work-relief program for the new century and a new cadre of small entrepreneurs. Imagine this huge cohort insulating, green-roofing, planting urban forests, repairing and expanding parks, managing urban agriculture, organizing recycling and reuse programs, and then returning to their neighborhoods to act in the vanguard of their sustainable transformation.

5. Convert rapidly to renewable energy. Undertake a Manhattan Project–scaled effort to convert our energy systems to renewable sources. After decades of palaver, it's time to put up or shut up about this. We have come to understand that there is no silver bullet—no single system—that will move us beyond petroleum. And it has likewise become clear that much of the technology for rapid conversion already exists: wind-, hydro-, tidal-, gradient-, and solar-energy systems are ready to go and ready to be applied at all scales, not simply concentrated in the hands of giant utilities. Let us subsidize a vast conversion (and vastly discourage the use of

such disproportionately dangerous, expensive, and dirty technologies as oil, coal, and nuclear energy). Let us also dramatically increase investment in research on the next generation of possibilities. Such expenditure is one of the most efficient ways of leveraging investment.

6. **Build schools.** Speaking of research, let's spend billions on building and repairing academic facilities. I may be prejudiced, but years of teaching have convinced me that good schools are the most important key to both prosperity and equity. Our underfunded and unequal school systems are both an embarrassment and an obstacle to real progress. While I will not offer my opinions on testing, vouchers, school choice, or any of the other educational policy controversies of the moment, I am certain of one thing: beautiful, spacious, and well-equipped school and university buildings can make an enormous difference in the self-esteem of students and the effectiveness of teachers and researchers.

7. **Build public housing.** The bursting of the housing bubble has not simply helped plunge the economy into recession, it has been an object lesson in the distortions of the market. The profligacies of credit extended to those who could not afford it—often on incredibly deceptive terms— and the widely bruited fantasy that prices would simply rise forever, have helped to demonstrate once again that anyone who believes uncritically in either the wisdom or justice of the market is foolish. Despite the fall in prices, the nation still faces a crisis of both housing affordability and quality. As the national income gap continues its obscene growth, both the poor and the middle class are being squeezed out. It's time to get over the old politics of indirection and get back to the direct provision of vital services. We massively subsidize home ownership via mortgage-interest deductions but can no longer bring ourselves to support the idea of public housing as something government can build directly. Yet a third of Americans live in substandard or unaffordable housing, and the market has shown neither the inclination nor the ability to solve this problem. Government can. But subsidy strategies—whether offered to homeowners or developers—are not enough. It's time to step in both to repair and renew existing public stocks and to construct millions of new units. To be sure, we've learned the lesson of public housing built meanly, housing that simply concentrates the poor in new ghettos. So let's get on with something better, housing that will allow our cities to be fairly shared by all their citizens.

8. **Build new cities.** When the Cold War came to its close, there was much talk of what might be done with the "peace dividend," the funds freed up by the disappearance of the Soviet threat. It's time to pay that dividend. While I'm as Keynesian as the next born-again New Dealer, it's clear that the trillions in giveaways and bailouts to the fat cats in the financial sector under Bush and the huge sums you propose to spend

on stimulus will have a disastrous effect on our out-of-control national indebtedness; the Chinese are unlikely to buy our paper forever. Huge savings are also needed, and the one truly soft spot in the budget is defense, which currently consumes a trillion dollars a year. (According to an article in the *Washington Post* by Linda Bilmes and Joseph Stiglitz, the war in Iraq alone will eventually cost $3 trillion in direct and indirect expenses.)

You have pledged to withdraw our forces, but why stop there? How about cutting defense spending in half and using the money for something constructive? Of course, it doesn't make sense to simply fire our military personnel, discard their resources, or sever the intricate cultural connections of the military-industrial complex. Let us, instead, give the military and its contractors a new task commensurate in grandeur and importance with warfare: building cities. As towns from Fort Wayne to Fort Worth attest, the military has long played a crucial role in setting our urban pattern and providing necessary infrastructure. At a time when the automobile-induced pattern of edge cities and sprawl has spun completely out of control, what better antidote is there than the systematic construction of hundreds of new towns on a radically sustainable pattern? And what better use is there for a military that has been growing for two centuries than to put it to work converting its thousands of bases into new cities and towns?

9. Reconstruct New Orleans. I was surprised at how little New Orleans was discussed during the campaign. Although the levees have been repaired to a point and prime tourist areas restored, the city remains massively depopulated and little has been done to rebuild most of the neighborhoods destroyed. Why not step up to the plate? We take it for granted that federal money—via the Army Corps of Engineers!—will be spent on flood-mitigation measures. But why not spend on the rest of what needs to be done? I find it beyond ironical that we have poured tens of billions of dollars (huge portions of which have been squandered due to inefficiency, corruption, and greed) into "rebuilding" the Iraq we destroyed, but have yet to make an even remotely similar commitment to our own devastated city. Instead, we do not simply countenance racist inertia but even sanction the destruction of the city's public housing stock. Make this city great again. Send in the Urban Forces! Then, on to Newark and Detroit!

10. Clean up the place. There are around 1,300 "Superfund" sites in the US, and the rate of cleanup has slowed to a snail's pace. Part of the reason is political: there are no funds in the Superfund. Another is the difficulty in compelling polluters to do the remediation themselves. The economic crisis will only increase the number of companies in bankruptcy or otherwise able to plead poverty. And the Superfund sites are only the tip of the toxic iceberg. Our cities continue to be plagued by air and water pollution,

by dangerous materials, and by overwhelming amounts of solid waste. Taken together, this is a public health emergency. As you move to reform our medical delivery system, it would make a lot of sense to look to the causes of our ill-health; to make the country beautiful; and to restore our land, air, water, and woods to something a lot closer to pristine. We'll all breathe easier.

2009

73

A Cut through the City

Not long ago, a small mid-block building was demolished not far from my office downtown. The excision was a revelation. Because of a sequence of low buildings in succeeding blocks, it was suddenly possible to look through a huge cut in the city that reconfigured the backs of the big buildings—with their ornamented, public facades on the avenues—into a long series of fronts. The space is like none other in New York in its proportions and architectonic character, the elegant austerity of these previously unseen elevations making a place both lyrical and tough. Looking at it, it's easy to imagine further transformations, an accessible swath of public space stretching five blocks through the heart of town.

The uneven development of the city—its cycles of boom and bust—drives the production of innumerable morphological accidents, yielding spaces of unexpected character. Behind the building where I had my office several years ago was a parking lot, flanked by an old cobbled street. My building, fourteen stories high, was on the eastern side of the space. The other sides were flanked by much lower structures—two to six stories—and the accidental piazza that resulted was of a rare proportion. It would have made a superb public space, easily captured and configured.

Unfortunately, nature and real estate abhor a vacuum: this space was eventually occupied by another fourteen-story building designed to look like the twin of the first and the piazza was lost forever. It will also be the fate of the demolished site that launched the view of the blocks-long cut up here in SoHo to be refilled by a rising tower. These evanescent states are both part of the genius of the development system—poignant, short-lived urban phenomena—and tragic exemplars of its limits. Caught in a situation that both produces and destroys its own greatness, we are too often unable to value this kind of revelatory anomaly until it is too late. Who can save it?

Part of the problem is that our planning is done with instruments too blunt and sluggish to properly accommodate unexpected or serendipitous circumstances, events we simply do not see. Landmarking can't preserve these spaces because, even though they may occur in historic districts, they are new, not part of an already legible pattern. Nor can zoning, which is a system for managing the upper limits of use and density. In economically robust times, everything presses this envelope.

The conundrum was made especially clear to me at a recent conference at Cornell organized to discuss the "NoMa" (North of Massachusetts Avenue) development in Washington, DC. This is a concerted effort to build out a series of largely derelict blocks just north of Union Station and a stone's throw from the US Capitol. The project has been in various stages of deal-making and development for seventeen years, and was propelled forward by an eminently sensible move: the creation of a new station in its midst along the existing Metro line. This, coupled with a bike route of suburban reach and a location next to the city's expanding downtown, has created the nexus for a classic transit-oriented development.

Unfortunately, because of a lack of resources and municipal planning chops—part of the disenfranchising legacy of the District's lack of home rule—the opportunity to plan creatively has largely been lost. The morphological possibilities of the site remain hemmed by the demands of the block pattern of the L'Enfant plan, the early twentieth-century imposition of a city-wide 130-foot height limit, a uniform FAR 10, and the giant infrastructure of the railway as it fans out to approach the station. The result is a plan that treats the literal blank slate of the site as an infill problem, each developer taking its parcel to the physical limits while letting function be dictated by the invisible hand. Thus, what was heading toward a reasonably harmonized mix of housing and offices was first skewed dramatically to offices and will now fall into a state of arrested development as the result of the national economic collapse.

The end-state of this project will be seriously constrained by its failure to "capitalize" on the spatial possibilities opened up by its strong relationship to transportation and its rare anything-possible beginning-state. And although all the actors involved diligently tithe the idea of a mixed-use, authentically neighborhoody, green, and design-intensive place, they all claim to be powerless to achieve anything beyond the alleged market and planning defaults. Nevertheless, the DC planning department—which now has unusually enlightened leadership—continues to struggle to retrofit the unbuilt project with decent streetscapes and a set of secondary uses beyond mere retail. Stay tuned.

The irony of the accidental plaza suppressed in New York and the impossibility of producing any plaza, legible center, or sense of hierarchy and variety in Washington lies in the fact that while the founding physical conditions are opposites, the conceptual cage in which both are locked is identical. Most of us can recognize decent urbanity when we see it, but we are constrained by the inefficiencies and limits of paradigms that are too narrow, too limited, too unimaginative. Whether it's the treacly reproduction of historic forms devolved from any meaningful context, the brutalizing celebration of capital's "creative" destruction as unassailable spirit guide, the slavish futures of current fashion, or the devil-made-me-do-it obedience to the "as-of-right" city, the results too consistently fail to satisfy the basic tenets of good city life.

Like many others, I am both wonderfully impressed by the energy of the new Obama administration and increasingly skeptical of the flow of stimulus funds to the big banks and corporations whose ineptitude and greed got us into this mess. After years of seething at the Republican and "new" Democrat mantra of government incompetence and irrelevance, it is stunning to see how quickly the fat cats and indifferent libertarians have turned to the collectivity to pull the singed chestnuts of flaming capital out of the fire. And yet, the application of stimulus structurally repeats the old Republican fantasy of wealth's distribution: by making life agreeable for the rich, benefit will trickle down to those less empowered.

Our cities need a stimulus package that works from the bottom up and—from us architects—a mighty stimulus package for the imagination. At NoMa, it is only the disenfranchised government, left without powerful enough administrative tools, without funds, and with influence too diminished, that can and should act to secure the genuinely highest and best use of the site. While build-out (when it eventually occurs) will certainly result in a greatly enhanced revenue stream, and while many argue that this money should return to the site in the form of improvements, this is both too late and contravenes the larger fiduciary obligations of the public sector, which must always balance the competing claims of the citizenry as a whole. The tax-increment financing model and the Business Improvement District overlay masquerade as community empowerment, but actually function to sustain the disproportionate enabling of the already empowered.

While I have deep skepticism about top-down approaches to planning and the too-frequent privileging of the formal over the social in dealing with questions of the city, there are many occasions on which government must decisively step in and set the agenda, the standard, and the solution. To invariably associate such intervention with the dystopian stylings of Robert Moses, Albert Speer, or Walt Disney is to be stupid about the real obligations and possibilities of the collectivity. How tired I am of hearing endlessly about the so-called "public-private" model (as if there were any other in a democracy), when all it amounts to is a cover for the public's giving away the store, acting on the same grasping profit model as those corporations whose only idea of public interest is sucker rates on adjustable mortgages and credit cards.

Now that the government has moved so swiftly and insistently to plan the economy, has embraced its role in providing medical care for all, is ponying up untold billions to save Afghanistan, perhaps the same kind of bold responsibility might be taken for the mess at home. Bailing out General Motors is not exactly transit-oriented development.

2009

74

Trouble in Paradise

Earlier this year, I was in the Emirates to give a lecture and was invited to visit the school of architecture where one of my hosts taught. Segregated by gender, the place was a Foucault fantasy made concrete. On one side of the building lay the studios and classrooms for women students, and on the other—in mirror image—the rooms for the men. Between them were faculty offices, all of which had two doors, one to each side. The dean— natty in Armani—explained to me (as if the whole thing made sense) that the office doors were locked on the women's side on Mondays and those on the men's opened so male students could enter for meetings. On Tuesdays, the configuration was reversed. When my colleague proposed an academic exchange, I demurred, unwilling to contemplate the discriminatory logistics.

In June—the fortieth anniversary of my college graduation—I thought back to those halcyon days and remembered that one of the reasons I chose the college I did was for its "co-education." As a progressive-minded teen, I thought it was absurd that places like Yale and Princeton were simply for boys: I couldn't imagine living in such a weird environment for four years, marinating in a pool of upper-crust testosterone. This recollection arrested my smug liberal bile at the Gulf school's setup, reminding me that it wasn't long ago that our most prestigious universities were predicated on an even more extreme form of gender separation. A little of my self-righteousness ebbed, not at the thing itself but at the idea that such an arrangement was cast in stone and intractable. Indeed, we use such notions to demonize the Muslim other, as unsusceptible to change, forever fixed in its ways.

The Gulf states offer profligate lessons in uneven rates of modernization and change and serve as a museum of the weird cultural forms that come from their extreme hybridity: the Guggenheim and the mosque; the megamall and the burka. You know the drill. Dubai is, of course, the locus classicus of this over-the-top style, and my recent visit was both jaw-dropping and depressing. The bubble has burst in a big way and craning towers—including a fairly fabulous-looking rendition of the world's tallest—stand incomplete and empty, blowing zillions of BTUs to keep the square miles of carpet cool to off-gas undisturbed. And yet, down the road in Abu Dhabi, Masdar city rises, as lavish an experiment in urban sustainability as any on earth.

While the planetary implications of the region's potlatch of (mostly) antisustainable practices are clear, the fallout from the crash has far sadder implications. The economies of the Gulf are enabled by imported labor, and most of these states have populations that are at least 80 percent foreign. And when jobs disappear, so must their holders. We've all read the tales about the laid-off ex-pats abandoning their leveraged Mercedes in the airport parking lot as they split for home. The story making the rounds during my visit was about the Bangladeshis and other South Asians who form the backbone of the construction industry and who work in conditions of near servitude. Made redundant in massive numbers, many are too humiliated and desperate to let their home villages—dependent on their regular remittances to survive—know that they are unemployed, and are too fearful to reappear empty-handed. While it may be an urban legend, the tale being told was about workers standing by the highway, waiting for the approach of a fast and expensive car, and throwing themselves under the wheels in the hope that some of the insurance might find its way back to their families.

I repeat this story not to belabor the cruelties of the Gulf's capito-feudal system but to evoke its ragingly complex dynamism, the intimate links so visible between culture, environment, development, and human success. The segregated architecture school in the midst of the most fabulous display on the planet of what currently passes for architectural "invention," and the downside miseries this volatility engenders, suggest more fundamental issues for the condition of architecture, how we conceive of it, and how we convey its values. This is not a random collection of observations raised to clarity by the designated weirdness of this particular place, but a summary of the expanded site of architecture's production: education, finance, construction, culture, place, sustainability, history, politics.

We have not moved swiftly enough to embody such consciousness and knowledge in architectural education, and Dubai stands as a particularly clear object lesson in our own confusion: this is an environment designed by the world's best and brightest, and, for many, a paradigm of global inevitableness. The fetish for form that has characterized the profession and the schools for the past few decades has slighted much more urgent matters, and it will come as no surprise to regular readers of this column that issues of the environment and social justice (linked inextricably) are those I feel must foreground both the ideology and the pedagogy of contemporary architecture. Just as gender-segregated education must be interrogated, so the received organizational formats of architectural education need to be questioned and revised. Having taught in dozens of schools and visited hundreds, I remain struck by the antique model of the design disciplines that still informs education: variations on the *trivium* of architecture, planning, and landscape. These ossified rigidities seem increasingly incapable of coming to grips with the real state of the planet.

There are some small signs of movement, especially in the stirrings of fungibility on the part of planning and landscape. Although I run a program in urban design, I have a fundamental disbelief in any unitary discourse of the city and try to offer access to many. Originally conceived as a way of recuperating physical design from a planning profession that had fallen in thrall to the social sciences, urban design is often taught simply as big building, and fixates excessively on historic patterns. But urbanism's most desperate needs devolve on the new morphologies of sustainability and equity that an exponentially urbanizing world so urgently needs. The urban population increases at the rate of a million people a week and, to me at least, that means that we need to create numerous new cities on an urgent basis, cities that are able to provide for themselves and provide rich lives to diverse populations.

The emergence of "landscape urbanism" as a position, if not a discipline, is a hopeful sign. Not simply does the conceit represent the rejection of a hard boundary between the practices of landscape architecture and urban design and planning; it stands, in theory, for a more holistic view of the environment and the indispensability of an integrated perspective in thinking about projects that exceed the architectural scale. And it suggests a strategy of inclusion, rather than an endless consideration of what the disciplines are not. Still, from the perspective of education, it feels a little like rearranging the deck chairs while preserving distinctions that have outlived their usefulness. As environmentalism becomes more and more the central authority for all design, why retain any boundaries at all?

I've been dreaming about a school of design that takes the unity, not the autonomy, of disciplines as its predicate, a way of opening the field to the real possibility of its diversity. Our boldest experiments haven't gotten us too far. The Bauhaus focused, in varying degrees, on social production, but retained disciplinary compartments and continued to see architecture as the eternal mother. It had indifferent ideas about the city and virtually nothing to say about the environment. More idiosyncratic, home-grown experiments like Taliesin or Arcosanti also fixated too much on the leading role of architecture (and the infallibility of their particular popes), and were passionately unscientific, though they did have deep commitments to craft and the earth. Alas, architecture's historic and dangerous conflation of megalomania with the big scale led them to social and organizational dead ends.

Our divided professions tenaciously guard their turf and look disdainfully at neighboring disciplines. How tiresome this is! While I am not suggesting that each designer be an impossibly learned polymath, I am arguing that the common ethical and environmental basis for design is becoming more and more apparent and more and more urgently part of the necessary equipment of anyone who aspires to take an active role in shaping the planet. One solution is to give each student entering a school of design a common grounding on which to build later specialization. This would include rigorous introductions to the environment and natural systems, deep immersion in the social and economic modes of production of the built world, and a vivid grounding in the global histories of physical responses to the question of habitation at every scale.

Providing this foundation will take time. Just as so many undergraduate architecture programs are formulae for fundamental illiteracy (too much time spent learning structures and CAD, none on Shakespeare, Oceanic art, or *The Tale of Genji*), so this reform of the design curriculum carries risks. If the years devoted to education aren't expanded, then something crucial must be eliminated. Or we can begin to think that design education might be dedicated to producing activists who are prepared either to step into the design environment in a literate and engaged way or to continue to deepen a particular specialization. I don't argue that the professions must die as autonomous pursuits, rather that we recognize—with new kinds of degrees and new kinds of schools—their deep common basis and the need for new and refreshed syntheses.

Received writ prescribes isolating the men from the women at that school in the Gulf without any particularly satisfying arguments—beyond obedience or human frailty—and so does it keep our own practices and people apart. Witness the appalling state of the planet; we clearly need to educate designers differently. This will mean focusing on what brings us together rather than what keeps us apart. Designers should be equipped with the knowledge of what makes a building sustainable, what drives construction workers to despair, what makes the city humane, what deepens our connection to the landscape, what gives us a sense of real connection to each other.

2009

75

Discipline and Punish

Not long ago, I agreed to serve on a jury organized by the New York City Department of Design and Construction to choose the architect for a new jail in the Bronx. I did this with considerable trepidation. America is a society that has far too many prisons, and our rates of incarceration exceed the numbers in every other country on the planet that keeps records: close to 2.3 million of our citizens are incarcerated and over 7 million are in the system, including those on parole or probation. And it isn't simply the numbers. The system is racist at its core, and we convict people of color with a disproportion that can only be attributed to prejudice. Fact: African-American men have a 32 percent chance of serving time at some point in their lives (the rate is 69 percent for high school drop-outs), Hispanic men 17 percent, white men 6 percent. Forty-five percent of inmates nationwide are African-Amercan although they are only 13 percent of the population. Moreover, the uneven sentencing practices (including the ludicrous "three strikes" and mandatory term regimes, as well as rampant judicial whimsicality), the degraded, violent, and overcrowded conditions of facilities, and the lack of meaningful job-training and rehabilitation for inmates, all mean that the system has spun out of control. Our prisons are not simply brutal, they are breeding grounds for criminality.

Prisons, however, are a vigorous growth industry, and billions of dollars can be made building, staffing, and running them. According to Architects, Designers, and Planners for Social Responsibility (ADPSR), the number of prisoners has increased 700 percent in the past 20 years (bringing it to about 700 percent of the rate in Britain, the highest in Europe) while the total US population has grown only 20 percent and crime rates have actually dropped. The Pew Center reports similar statistics and observes that our inmate numbers exceed the *aggregate* of all thirty-six countries in Europe. Moreover, the rapid privatization of our prisons has engorged a growing "prison-industrial complex" that, Halliburton-like, has turned incarceration into big business. As ADPSR and others point out, every time someone is sent to jail, the Corrections Corporation of American or Wackenhut (a brand now owned by the CEO Group) hears a sparkly *ka-ching* as the cell door slams shut. Such market-based incarceration incentivizes cramming the slammer and throwing away the key: during the prison boom of the 1990s, a new prison was opened every fifteen days.

ADPSR has been in the vanguard of those arguing for prison reform and, some years ago, started an initiative to persuade architects and others in allied disciplines to refuse to undertake any prison-related work. Their petition drive has now attracted over a thousand signers, many of them distinguished practitioners. But such a pledge of non-cooperation is not the same as disengagement from the issue. After all, throughout architectural practice we know that problems must be solved not simply on the supply but on the demand side of the equation. It is fundamental to sustainable practice, for example, that we reduce energy consumption, not simply build new power plants. Likewise, with the incarceration crisis, our work must first reduce the flood of prisoners by struggling for equal justice, rebuilding broken lives through education and rehabilitation, attenuating our draconian attitudes toward such nonviolent "crimes" as drug-use, and fighting against the punitive attitude that increasingly pervades American public opinion and media.

But the humanization of our prisons also requires active engagement, and this means that architects of conscience must challenge the system from within. Such opposition encompasses many dimensions, but all must focus first on keeping people out of jail—through a social and economic culture that eliminates crime in the first place and through sentencing practices that are not simply retributive—and on establishing some sense of rational and humane proportionality in the expenditure of public funds. This has a clear spatial component. The Spatial Information Design Lab and the Justice Mapping Center in New York have produced a series of revelatory studies of what they call "million dollar blocks." What they've discovered is that the prison population comes disproportionately from a relatively small number of urban neighborhoods, and that, in the flow of people from city to prison and back,

> the criminal justice system has become the predominant government institution in these communities and that public investment in this system has resulted in significant costs to other elements of our civic infrastructure—education, housing, health, and family. Prisons and jails form the distant exostructure of many American cities today.

This is a remarkable observation, and cuts to the core of the relationship between architecture and justice. With its binary approach to crime and punishment, our system overlooks the issue of environment. We encourage crime by the way we spatially segregate people and disproportionately spend resources: because these million-dollar blocks receive their (relatively enormous) portion of public funds in the form of prison "services," they are disenfranchised in all of the areas of investment—from schools to sports fields—that might make a difference in halting the cycle of abuse and retribution that forms the substance of far too many lives.

Still, such problems do not mean that prisons themselves should not be attended to, that they should not change from sites of discipline and abuse to spaces of hope and repair. During the architect interviews for the Bronx jail, I brandished a story that had appeared in the *New York Times Magazine* in June, depicting a prison in Loeben, Austria, characterized by its architect as offering "maximum security outside; maximum freedom inside." Though surrounded by a moat-like space and walls topped with concertina wire, the building had "cells" that were more like apartments, with all the furnishings and fittings to lead a life of some dignity and with at least as much comfort as my freshman dorm room. This idea that prison should not *ipso facto* dehumanize and psychically cripple people who will eventually return to society is breathtaking in the simple dignity it offers.

I had hesitated for quite a while before agreeing to join the jury. I decided to participate because David Burney, the head of the agency, is a huge friend of architecture and a genuine *mensch*, because I made a number of "working-within-the-system" arguments to myself, and because I wanted to influence the results by helping to direct the contract to a firm capable of excellent architecture and, perhaps, to people genuinely committed to the idea of reform. I was also persuaded by the fact that New York City has been strong in advancing a vision of community-based corrections, not just placing jails in proximity to courts but making them accessible to the families and neighbors of prisoners. This approach represents a clear step toward reintegrating justice and communal life, helping to reverse our contemporary desire to get the miscreants out of sight. The most appalling manifestation of this tendency is the rise of "prison towns," a gulag of prisons (often clustered together) in remote areas that become the grim sustenance for entire rural regions. America now has more prisoners than it does farmers.

I arrived at the jury with a combination of skepticism and hope. Talented people were up for the job and I was curious about how they'd thread this architectural and ethical needle. The project was not for a prison but a detention center—a place for people awaiting trial, many of whom would presumably be found innocent. Moreover, it was a replacement for a nightmarish floating prison that travelers from LaGuardia Airport may have seen lashed to the Bronx shore opposite the prison complex on Riker's Island. As an object, the barge represents degradation made form, and replacing it is imperative. The site for the new building is just ashore of the penal ship's location, on an environmentally sensitive and potentially wonderful shoreline.

The architects' presentations were remarkably similar. Like anyone eager for a job, all the firms tailored their Powerpoints to expectations about what the panel wanted to hear and to current defaults of professional responsibility. Each team touted its adept deployment of computerized "Buidling Information Management" systems, and the way in which this would allow seamless communication and management. BIM represents not simply a general promise of up-to-date computational competence, it suggests a kind of panoptic understanding of the building process not unrelated to the theories of surveillance that have been so influential in theorizing prison design since the days of Jeremy Bentham.

Not unexpectedly, each team also stressed its green credentials, promising high environmental ratings on the LEED scale and sensitivity to the delicate site. As in so many other situations, the whiff of green-ness was surely meant as a surrogate for a raft of other social concerns and a signifier of responsiveness to issues of community. While not slighting questions of sustainability—which must be at the heart of everything we designers do—I saw such eco-speak as a weird displacement. I'd recently received a letter from Raphael Sperry, a leader of ADPSR's prison initiative, describing the dilemma faced by architects trying to get LEED credit for daylighting while wrestling with security regulations that prohibit windows within reach of prisoners.

And so it went, to a certain extent, with the architects who presented to us. Inviting gardens out of reach. Beautiful shoreline paths never to be strolled by the "users" of the project. I kept having flashes from the scene from *All Quiet on the Western Front* where the German soldier, having survived almost to war's end, reaches from his trench toward a fluttering butterfly only to be nailed by a sniper. While I greatly appreciated the larger civic impetus behind the rich landscape strategies, I was perplexed at how little the teams actually talked about incarceration, which is—short of the flat-out barbarism of execution—the worst thing we empower the state to do to us. Especially vexing was the fact that this was a pre-trial detention center which, by definition, prioritized "public safety" over due process and the right to liberty. As the outsider on the jury, it fell to me to ask each team the same question: what is your position on imprisonment? I certainly didn't expect anyone to take the ADPSR line (all of us in the room had clearly made our peace with the legitimacy of the project), but I desperately wanted someone to make a case for innovation in what was the central architectural and programmatic issue for the building.

Each of the teams, of course, had a "corrections" specialist on board, and one of these answered me with some eloquence and compassion. While none of the presentations suggested any architectural responses that much exceeded the idea of a clean, well-lighted, orderly, and relatively calm environment, it was clear that everyone wanted to work up to the current default for these places—but there wasn't much to suggest any were prepared to go beyond it. I don't know if it was the play-it-safe nature of an interview for a giant job in front of a public agency, but the only architectural passions on display were for sustainability, efficiency, and form. We picked the team that we felt was led by the most creative designers.

I do hope that, as this project evolves, their powers of imagination will extend into the dark recesses of the most problematic building type our "civilized" society requires. As the economist Glenn Loury has put it, America has constructed "the largest infrastructure for mass incarceration in history." This is a mark of enormous and sinister failure. Architects must fight not simply to "humanize" this awful archipelago, but to challenge its causes at the root. We are citizens first.

2009

76

Eutopia Now!

"Our most important task at the present moment is to build castles in
the sky."

Lewis Mumford, *The Story of Utopias*, 1922

Utopia gets a bad rap. For a generation of scarred scholars, including
Hannah Arendt, Karl Popper, Isaiah Berlin, and others, Auschwitz was
utopia's inevitable omega point. For them, utopia was the implacable enemy
of pluralism, freedom, and individualism—values at the very core of liberalism. After Hitler and Stalin, the utopian virtues of harmony, leisure,
peace, prosperity, pleasure, health, cooperation, freedom, and love seemed
simply part of a rhetoric of deception and delusion, values that could not
be produced by—were, indeed, antithetical to—utopian styles of desire.
This anti-utopianism was an attack not simply on a mode of thought, but
on the horrifying political project to realize "utopia," which they had all
witnessed.

The fear of the totalitarian results of universalizing ideologies is both
historic and legitimate. The Nazis and the Khmer Rouge were both utopian
in the sense that they were the enforcers of reductive blueprints that sought
a radical transformation of society through the reconfiguration of its
human subjects on the basis of some higher good. But to retrospectively
trash every utopian writer—from Bellamy to Plato—every utopian experiment—from Drop City to Brook Farm—and every utopian urbanist—
from Ebenezer Howard to Filarete—is to slight a discourse that is vital
and useful, and to pile skepticism on sunniness as a style of argument:
something that architects and planners simply cannot abandon.

Such bright, Emerald City imaginings are tough to sustain nowadays
(in *Blade Runner*, it's always raining), and we muzzy advocates risk being
tarred as fascists or—worse—as superannuated, hopelessly naive fossils
of the "sixties," that utopian decade. Nor does it help that so much of our
contemporary critical discourse is rooted in a broad pessimism, in the kind
of over-aestheticized styles of negation that have gripped so much architectural theory. "If" writes Rey Chow, "the terms for grasping the classical

order of things are resemblance, analogy, continuity, and propinquity, those for grasping the modern world have to do with estrangement, difference, discontinuity, and distance." This is the *heimat* of dystopia, the sum of our fears, attuned to the threat of cruelty rather than the possibilities for joy. Foes all of totalizing master narratives, we are too fearful of the flipside nightmare to see the upside of the imaginary, and so surrender the useful, constructive, example of the all-at-once.

But to evoke dystopia is also to make clear that utopia always embodies the means of its own critique. While it's hard to trace the origin point of utopia, its form always conflates paradise and politics: a portrait of both the forms and the means of ethical social organization rolled out as a fiction. Like the binarism that structures so many views of the afterlife—every heaven needs its hell—utopian argument oscillates between portrayals of better possibilities than the present and the idea that things could be a lot worse. In utopia's discourse, the static is dangerous: inaction either perpetuates a drear present or brings on the maelstrom. Just as paradise and the inferno represent the perfection and degeneration of the societies to which they are meant to appeal, so utopia deploys the same metaphor of construction to ideas of perfection and degeneration both. The dystopian tradition—with its reserves of both terror and irony—runs from Plato (whose vision of the ideal city was produced dialogically in relationship to alternatives less ideal, and for whom the very unrealizability of that city was its predicate) to More to Swift to Malthus to Yevgeny Zamyatin to Orwell to Philip K. Dick to half the movies at the multiplex. Utopia, properly imagined, is always obliged to explain why it isn't a nightmare, whether in its outcomes or its methods.

Theorists of utopia recognize not simply a distinction between utopian and dystopian styles of argument, but also distinctions within the category of utopia. These differences are not precise but are invariably organized around the poles of prescription and critique. Russell Jacoby—one of several sympathetic left utopian revivalists writing today—distinguishes "iconoclastic" and "blueprint" utopias, paralleling Fredric Jameson's split between the utopian wish and the utopian form. Françoise Choay writes of "progressivist" and "culturalist" utopias. There are golden ages and far horizons. While one appreciates the need to distinguish, let us say, Ernst Bloch from Yona Friedman, there may be less to these distinctions than meets the eye. It bears repeating that it is the nature of the utopian project to speak its wish through the medium of form, however inversely or obscurely. This is the source of both its power and its problem.

A utopian argument always includes the idea of construction—some series of human measures to bring about the "ideal" thing itself, however vaguely, provisionally, or fictitiously described. The condition of utopia is that it *proposes* its own realization, a deliberation with an outcome: without its *topos*—the idea of place—utopian thought would simply lapse into some other style of ethical, metaphysical, or political speculation. And this is why it is so important—as precisely the only way of speculating concretely about a projective connection between architecture and politics. To design utopias is to enter the laboratory of politics and space, to conduct experiments in their reciprocity. This laboratory—unlike the city itself—is a place in which variables can be selectively and freely controlled. At the point of application, of the concrete, utopia ceases to exist.

The *topoi* of utopian urbanism have remained remarkably consistent for centuries and originate in the homology between city and society, begging questions of boundedness and growth, of the relationship of publics and their spaces, of the right dimensions and organization of communities, of the character of the beautiful in just societies, of the connectedness of built and natural, and of the interaction of subjectivity and space. Within the territory of architectural utopias, these issues can be invoked in various ways, and the idea of the blueprint—of the model—is always rhetorical. While utopia and dystopia may simply be different figures used to produce the same argument, the special power of dystopia is both that it clarifies the risks in the present and that it is mute about specific alternatives to *its* alternative.

For those fearful of the inescapable immanence of the totalitarian in utopia, dystopian representations have the advantage of insulating the critic against the risk of excess prescription. But it's an irony of criticism that will only countenance utopian thinking in dystopian form that it requires a literal-minded, fundamentalist hermeneutics—that it takes its utopia straight: not so different from the kind of biblical exegesis that fixes the birth of time exactly six thousand years and twenty-three minutes ago. Envisioning the new in anything approaching its all-at-once is seen as an incitement to the bloody obliteration of the now unless it is figured as a warning. Chilled by the risks of idealism, such critiques of utopia are simply too fixed on the Platonic lie to see the value of dreaming.

Utopia is a *telos*, not a floor plan. But it uses such plans as its metaphor, and the design of the city as medium for political argument. Any blueprint, however metaphorical, begs the questions of how real, how accurate, how practical, how close, how specific—as well as how provisional and how contingent—the representation is. Because utopia is always a fiction, a fabricated reality, it must work by opening up a useful difference between the current now and a hypothetical one. As suggested by Jameson and Jacoby's classifications, these questions are always of degree. No reasonable person would take Thomas More's utopia as a literal proposition—its very distance from its present locates its space in critical, not practical, territory. It is, nevertheless, a code of behavior, and its prescriptions no less "real" than those of the garden city.

Karl Mannheim—a writer friendly to utopian practice—described planning as the "rational mastery of the irrational," a description that also nicely fits psychoanalysis. Like a dream, a city is constructed from the concrete, but it constantly reconfigures the familiar in new—and sometimes startling—ways. We create the city by interacting with it, by changing its capacities of connection, appearance, behavior, imagination, and exchange through the dialectic of template and accident, knitting its fabric out of zillions of feedback loops to create a present—not an eternal—particular. Henri Lefebvre is right to call the city an "oeuvre"—a work rather than a thing. This is at once fundamental and vague. Both things and processes can go wrong, and the history of planning—like utopia's—is the ongoing perception that things are not completely right with the city as we know it, that outcomes are unsatisfactory. Utopias argue outcomes by inversion, dystopias by extrapolation.

Every politics—from Plato's to Marx's—deploys some format for the prospective and some theory of the good. Utopia is the rationalist's paradise, and its great modern complication is science. With its instrumentality and aura of positivism, science—and its parallel systems of economic, social, and logistical organization—has materialized a new realizability for massive social undertakings and supplied an ethical (if controversial) cover. There is a reason those Red States are afraid of Darwin: biology resituates creation. Technology has, in both its representation and its reach, contributed to the myth of its own autonomy, a god-like set of truths working themselves out beyond human agency.

It is no coincidence that the most extensive contemporary work of utopian—and dystopian—imagination has taken place in science fiction, which has assumed a central social role in the popular understanding and critique of space. Our imaginative world is richly populated with Cyborgs and Hobbits, with their kingdoms and planets, their cities and architectures, monsters and saints, which map contemporary forms of paranoia just as our utopias—from Club Med to Vegas—limn our own possibilities for hope. I think it can also be argued that these representations—because they are founded on ideas of social values and relationships—have contributed to a larger vision of the city as a social arrangement, rather than an artifact. From Solaris to Gaia to the Superorganism, consciousness, too, is being defined upwards.

The bleakness of most postwar "science fiction" is understandable, and a generally pejorative descriptor that has had the effect of largely shutting down formal utopianism (depicted as impractical at best and deeply sinister at worst) by reinforcing the dominant negative reading, by making the forms of our anxiety too mesmerizing, and by repetitively fixing imaginative territory within familiar limits. Most of this falls along the Huxley/Orwell polarity of soft (*The Truman Show*) or hard (*1984*) styles of total control, reflecting the same fears as those of the more theoretical anti-utopians about modern universalisms and the risk of subjectivity reduced to Agambenian bare (or unthinking) life, or any other form of existence without a capacity to transform itself—the kind of centralized authority required to realize utopian organizational schemes in literal precision. And it doesn't hurt that the fears themselves—of slavery, concentration camps, faceless multinationals, mind control, genetic engineering, the duping simulacrum, and all the rest—are both authentic and ubiquitous.

In a more specifically architectural way, it surely doesn't help that the trope of "the city of the future" serially infuses our actual building construction. It's hard not to be a Platonic idealist—and an anti-utopian skeptic—when the world is so littered with realizations of models that first saw life as speculations about what the city might best be. I've recently returned from Korea, much of which is an astonishingly precise reproduction of the Ville Radieuse, right down to its oversized roadways and dysfunctional separations of uses. A few weeks before, I'd been to Almaty, which is rapidly acquiring a crust of gated golf communities—the end of the line of the garden city, yeoman to duffer—Ruskin hands Morris his niblick and drives. The main drag in Dubai is lifted intact from the 1939 General Motors pavilion. Vegas is the apotheosis of postmodern semiotic recombination, a world of signs. Crystal City, Virginia, is a megastructure at Metabolist scale. The afterlife of these "utopian" morphologies is both fertile and foul.

Although I want to argue that the critical reinvigoration of the formal repertoire of the urban is crucial to both the practice of architecture and the fate of the earth, this can only happen in an intimate and searching relationship to politics. Given the city's necessary relationship to global resources and their distribution, as well as its role in the fateful, breakneck, alteration of the planetary environment, it's clear that much of the field of a specifically urban politics forms around these urgent questions. It's also evident that the nature of the autonomy of individual cities within tightly laced systems of global economic and political organization is becoming a more and more crucial issue for both individual and federated forms of freedom. As ever, today's utopias must strike new balances between liberty and limit.

In contemporary political articulation, what worries us most about utopia is that it is hostile to diversity, that it obliterates accident and difference. This is an understandable anxiety. The discredited modernist utopia is dominated by a single political figure: equality, which it simply understands arithmetically. While struggles to realize myriad forms of human equality must always drive any progressive politics—in fact, must always form its predicate—the idea can take on a very nasty inflection when pushed to its mathematical limits. The camp is a dystopia of sameness, the equality of bare life, of life outside the political. The postmodernist dystopia runs a special variation on this mode of dread, evoking styles of manufactured difference, at once winnowed and infinite. Today's urban nightmare is the city in which the differences are simply architectural: the contemporary articulation of utopia's historic preoccupation with the formats of idealized geometry.

In the critique of modernist planning exemplified by Jane Jacobs, utopia and the master plan become strictly analogous. This elision between *any* visionary physical thinking and a particular style of operations with a known history of negative consequences led to a suspicion of big plans in general, especially if they make claims for a strict isomorphism between form and values. This anxiety applies both to contemporary utopias of formal order—like those of the New Urbanists with their unwaveringly modernist sense of the correct—and utopias of devolved restraint like those of "everyday" urbanists and preservationists, or of Jacobs herself. Although all of these deploy the rhetoric of a golden age, including the idea of the golden age in some especially valued present, their shared claims to a more democratic style of planning, their political underpinnings, unite them with the longer history of utopian urbanism, including its modernist branch.

I do not wish to dismiss any of these arguments, but to argue that the consistency of their political claims suggests the actual (if camouflaged) vigor of utopian urbanism and a widespread (if rhetorical) agreement about the notional qualities of a good, democratic life, predicated on the defense and cultivation of difference, opportunity, and enjoyment. There is, however, a deep contradiction in the idea of an exclusionary diversity that invalidates the special authority of any particular formal utopia: the idea that a contemporary utopia cannot be expressed as a formal singularity with universal aspirations. If, as I am arguing, to be a utopian is to embrace a strong principle of tolerance, open-endedness, and continuous disputation over the reasons for it, this means that there will be many translations of principles into practice, that there must be many utopias, that the fantasy of a single point of formal convergence must be trashed in favor of an inexhaustible multitude of non-homogeneous outcomes. Utopia is important precisely because it is *not* a city, but a representation of one. The necessary singularity of *any* utopian image will be alleviated by multiplicity—every utopia adds to the repertoire of urban possibilities—and by a general recasting of urban utopianism as the study of points of departure rather than end-states. For utopians, history cannot end.

If the task of utopia is to expand the repertoire of urban formal differences, it must be on behalf of a politics that values difference in some particular way, not as one more consumer choice—Coke or Pepsi, Frank or Rem. What utopia *represents* is always also an idea about social relations, which are constrained or made legible through the medium of architectural, urban, or territorial organization. At a minimum, this means that the set of utopias should be heterotopic and multiple, providing an armature for thinking about mutability, and some proposition about limits, however extreme. The counter-argument is that any *projective* representation that exceeds a certain scale must be a representation of thwarted difference precisely because it is not the product of actual clash and collaboration, of differences voiced by different actors. But this argument denies the usefulness of the imaginary and of fantasy in fueling interpretive diversity, the role of artists and thinkers operating in their special spheres, and the fact that utopias add to rather than subtract from the global store of ideas.

Resistance to scaling—one of utopia's liberties—ignores the true dimensions of our crisis. Need I dwell on it? Six and a half billion people. Half in cities. Half of these in slums. The urban population is growing by a million people a week, and most are poor. By 2015, according to the UN, there will be 358 cities of a million or more; by mid-century, 1,000. Of these, at least twenty-seven will be megacities—cities of more than 10 million—of which eighteen will be in Asia. Our wildly imbalanced distribution of resources produces the twin crises of overdevelopment and inequity. There are limits to growth, and the engine of continuous economic expansion is already running up against the hard edge of the earth's finite bearing capacity: for everyone in the world to live as we do would require the surface of two additional planets. Consider China, where rates of automobile ownership are at the level of the US in 1912, and policy is to catch up with the Jones's ASAP. Already, Beijing has the most toxic air of any city on earth. What will happen if this great leap forward is successful? To their credit, the Chinese government is beginning to accelerate green moves, but the ice cap is melting fast. The canary in the mineshaft has croaked.

The only rational solution to these interlaced crises is to construct many radically sustainable new cities. These must be a new kind of city—one that builds on thousands of years of thinking about and making good cities, one that recognizes a radically reconfigured urban situation as its inescapable site, one that that takes the survival and happiness of the species as its predicates, one that finds and defends numerous routes to meaningful difference, and one that advances the project of freedom. There is intense need for research and speculation into what the forms and agencies of these cities might be. There is, in short, a desperate need for utopia.

The force of utopian thinking lies in its disinterested projection of places that are nowhere yet but already all around. We may all agree on the utopian bromides I've just uttered, but their bridge to form is rightly fraught and radical, a shift in categories, from should-be to could-be. This is the moment when utopia ceases to be utopian and can no longer claim the defense of abstraction. But how do theory and critique morph into worldly practice? How do the vivacity of hope and the particularity of formal expression characteristic of utopia take the next step into becoming? Since this is at the center of my own architectural project, I would—rather than surrendering its operational potential—like to finesse it orthographically and discuss not utopia but "eutopia," following the usage and meaning of that prescient eccentric, Patrick Geddes. The switch makes explicit the ameliorative agenda of the project, eliding its fiction with real opportunity.

I adopt the prefix "eu"—*better* place—advisedly, despite its risky resonance with another project of improvement—eugenics—which, in its arc from medicine to murder, offers a much more resonant image of the utopian fallacy than any utopia that simply operates on the body of the city. Geddes's biologism also seems useful at a time when biology is increasingly displacing physics as our emblematic scientific endeavor. This is reflected in the current crisis of architecture in which the frantic search for formal complexity—for angularities in seeming defiance of gravity, for explosiveness, for knotting up the loose ends of quantum mechanics, for the coy inevitabilism of hands-off scripting—has become an increasingly uninteresting and narrowly aesthetic preoccupation. The discursive shift to questions of urbanism reflects both this shift in paradigm and a certain repoliticization of the urban. It is no coincidence that our renewed interest in the city parallels the rise of environmentalism and the greening of historically red concerns.

Geddes himself was greatly interested in eugenics and its translation into urbanism, but his take was unusual, even twisted. Geddes pioneered a respiratory model of urbanism, and his work on the interaction of cities and regions helped to build the ecological understanding of cities as elements in the larger planetary environment. Eugenics was enabled by the rise of modern theories of evolution, the discovery of the biological basis for the mutability of species, and the attempt to control it for some purported good. Its practical implementation depended on specific mechanisms, on mutations at the genetic level and the nature of the generational transmission of human characteristics. Geddes's biology, however, was that of the losing party to the debate about inheritance—which was still lively at the turn of the last century—casting its lot with Darwin's predecessor, Jean-Baptiste Lamarck, and his belief in the heritability of non-genetically acquired characteristics.

Geddes's urbanization of Lamarck, however, turned its defective biology on its head, effectively redeeming it. By analogizing the city with an organism, Geddes formulated the idea of a *social* heritage that resided in the forms and behaviors of the city and which, by being both fixed and endlessly transmissible, could indeed be passed down the generations. The concept—never mind the science—is crucial because it offers utopian speculation as both a site and a regulator, the idea of the city as an accumulation of the social, the complexifying result of a history of compacts and arrangements that are the encoded source of the evolutionary character of the city itself: urban memory. However, memory—like evolution—is produced conflictually, and the future of the city is always forged from a shifting set of uncertainties and perspectives.

The city is a historical phenomenon, and the act of envisioning its future cannot be undertaken without accounting for its past-in-present. Which gets us back to Jane Jacobs and her own particular and powerful style of utopianism. To be reductive, this includes two components. The first is the idea of the good city as a self-organizing system, the outcome of maximized participation by its inhabitants through the medium of a free, but disciplined and caring market. In Jacobs's utopia, participation is not necessarily political in a direct sense but constitutes a particular way of being-in-the-city that, because it is demandingly (and pleasingly) interactive, amounts to a kind of political suffusion, analogous to the *agora* and the *polis*, to cite the physical and political components of that most resilient of retrospective utopias, Athens.

The other element of Jacobs's utopia-in-the-present is morphological, and her work is an intensely prescriptive utopia of form. That the particular forms she celebrates are derived from the contemporary condition of certain parts of certain American cities of eighteenth- and nineteenth-century origin does not make her project any less utopian: it shares the same idea of a fixed and reciprocally determining relationship between good form and good life that also underlies the speculations of le Corbusier, Sitte, Howard, Fourier, and, for that matter, Plato. Nostalgia can also be utopian. Like that of all of these predecessors, Jacobs's work is the product of a particular idea of the good, and, like all utopias, it begs the difficult question of dissent, and therefore requires a perpetual questioning of what the question actually is.

Presumably Jacobs would argue that a self-organized system constructs itself through an internalized dialectic of demurral, and that its outcomes always embody an integrated force of critique; or that the model she foregrounds is specifically—even uniquely—capable of nurturing diversity, of accommodating the needs of difference. Jacobs thought that this condition of critical mass, critical mix, and critical thinking could be achieved and conserved by a combination of direct action, a fairly heavily modulated market, and intelligent design—in short, by the forces already at work to produce the neighborhoods she idealized. But, as is often—and relevantly—asked about Jacobs's work, how can this set of prescriptions work on the *tabula rasa*? Is it possible to make a new city based on her ideas?

I think the answer is yes, but that her morphological arguments cannot stand outside her politics, and that their nexus is very particular to a special time and place—Greenwich Village in the 1950s and '60s. Here's the nub of the historic morphological fallacy: the idea of the reversibility of the relationship of form and politics, of creation and representation. The dispute between "everyday" urbanists and "new" urbanists, for example, might be said to represent the divorce of the co-dependent components of the Jacobs schema, and this leads to the characteristic incapacities of both "practices" and the fruitless argument over the more authentic matrimony. The set of politics is always larger than the set of architecture, which means that although architecture can be political, there is no such thing as a political architecture.

But let's get back to the question of diversity as a widely held value that tests the idea of the good city. The question is one not of difference per se but of the match between differences and desires, and the question of how these are produced and valued. Consumer culture provides one model, with its inculcated narcissism of the small difference and its apparatus for making meaningful the choice between a thousand breakfast cereals. The urban equivalent often focuses not simply on the diversity of a single class of goods but—as Susan Fainstein and others have pointed out—on the diversity of the opportunities for a single class of people. While the Time Warner Center in New York has an extensive mix of restaurants, residences, hotel rooms, and offices, and is therefore at some level a paragon of "mixed use," it is a mix directed at a very particular group of people— the extremely rich. And, upmarket and down, the mix is not exactly self-organized. One Hundred and Twenty-Fifth Street in Harlem has moved from a blend of small, individually owned retail and commercial establishments to a standardized array of multinational outlets—from the Gap to Starbucks—that remake the local on the model of the shopping mall. Fainstein sharply traces the migration of the value of diversity from critics on the left to proponents of growth like Richard Florida, who explicitly separates the ideas of diversity and equity, frankly describing his famous "Creative Class" growth machine as a "diversity of elites."

If freedom is opportunity, then diversity is the predicate of choice, and the enlargement of choices theoretically is a good thing. But the idea of enlargement must deal with which choices in particular are fertile areas of growth and how choices—as well as their construction—are distributed throughout society. The city is a distributor and modulator of choice and opportunity, as well as a medium for invention of new possibilities. Its success can be judged by the harmonization of choices and desires; by the accessibility and convenience of choice-making; by its creativity in the invention of those choices; and by the consequences of what is chosen by its citizens. If we are to continue to speak about the idea of good cities, it will continue to be necessary to distinguish Athens from Gomorrah. More important, though, is that choice be shifted from choosing between existing *things* to an idea of choice as an *act* that creates things, the ability to invent a life (or a thing) of your own.

While the logic of a broadly constructed politics of diversity grounded in fulfilling and "authentic" choice-making seems a slam dunk, questions still remain for the idea of diversity, and here again I will channel the muse of Geddes and return to a biological model or analogy. Biodiversity is a core issue for biological and ecological communities, and its value is assessed in a number of ways. Much of the debate today centers on the question of extinction, and there is hot discussion about its rate—with Norman Myers's famous 1979 estimate of 40,000 species lost every year setting the outer limit of alarm—and about the impact of human alteration of the environment (cutting down the rainforest, emission of greenhouse gases and other contaminants, and so forth) on this effect.

In arguing *why* extinction is a bad thing, a number of positions are offered, and most have some resonance with questions of human social diversity and with the role of cities as habitats for this process. Just as the rainforest is the planet's most biodiverse environment, so the city is its most socially diverse, and the two are complementary sites for making this argument by analogy. Both are very large systems and both can be imputed with "intelligence." Interestingly, one of the most frequently made arguments in favor of species preservation—perhaps because it is a compelling one for the communication of scientific concerns—is a general appeal to our immediate self-interest in the unknown, to the possible cures we will miss, sources of nutrition we will lose, exotic materials we will be denied, energy answers we will never know, beauty spots never to be visited, and questions we don't yet know to ask.

The issues for diversity raised by the question of extinction (including the extinction or discontinuous transformation of the historic city) include the loss of social or genetic memory and the attendant loss of opportunity, as well as the quasi-economic issue of the productivity which ecologists (suggestively) always study in terms of communities. There are three key diversity effects on the ecological productivity of such ecological communities. The first is "complementarity," the idea that species coexistence—diversity expressed in spatial terms—is made possible by "niche partitioning," by the different resource requirements of different species. This suggests that a more diverse community will use available resources more completely and efficiently. In the social territory, complementarity offers a self-interested argument for cooperation, another value we prize politically.

"Facilitation" is another, more explicitly synergistic, effect wherein one species modifies the environment in such a way as to facilitate the well-being of another. This includes the enrichment of the soil by nitrogen-fixing plants, the distribution of seeds by fruit-eating birds, or the benefit of "nurse plants" that alleviate water and temperature stress in their young neighbors. Finally, the "sampling effect" suggests simply that there is a greater likelihood of finding a species of great inherent productivity in a patch that is more diverse. The sampling effect includes both elements of variety and scale, and is an enabler of greater facilitation and complementarity through diversity.

The word *sampling* is a particularly suggestive one for the city, and its various usages cut a number of ways. Sampling is key to the genetics of rap music, crucial to its meaning-in-mutation. Lyrics, beats, tunes, riffs, and licks from existing music are lifted and spliced into the frankly recombinant new organism. This is an operation that is intrinsic to the elaboration of cities as well as being a potentially risky one. Cities, after all, are clearly recombinant mechanisms, but not completely aleatory ones. Like "natural" selection, the city is defined by the way in which accidental inter-actions collude with more calculated events to produce new species, conditions, events, insights, and possibilities. Rules of attraction and repulsion are received, invented, evolved, and discarded.

As a directional, historical phenomenon, such development begs the question of progress. In a simplified Darwinian sense, progress is associated with survival, and the value most conducive to survival is "fitness." In the social realm, other values, many of them less assured and more transitory, stand in this position. The city—as a container, crucible, and selection of values, many of which are translated into space—deploys more subjective and contradictory tests for determining fitness, including tolerance, economic benefit, power, delight, and so on. While the old law tenement may have been a remarkable fit for the mercantile environment of nineteenth-century immigrant New York, it was not fit for habitation, and its mutation through legislation (the law selected certain characteristics—ventilation, insolation, sanitation—and transformed the old organism into a new one that embodied these qualities) was clearly eugenic.

However, as the example of the tenement should suggest, the genetic, evolutionary model is a tricky one, and Geddes's theory of the heritability of acquired social characteristics through their inscription in the forms and habits of cities will take us only so far. The fault-line divides the two ways in which I've used the idea of sampling. In many ways, our contemporary urbanism is a giant Sample City, a recombinant, eugenic organism that—like the television system—produces an endless number of juxtapositions, splicings, and constructs. While there is an obvious creativity in this, as well as a certain recherché artistry of de-familiarization, the problem is that these recombinations often depend on a narrowing stock of possibilities rather than an expanding one, like the illusory mixed use of the Time Warner Center. Here, diversity is a cover, and the "real" global city is the outcome of actions by a small number of producers of possibility who themselves "sample" opinion and demographics and construct environments in which the identities produced by those samplings are reconciled with their (the producers') desires in order to smooth the efficiencies of large-scale consumption from increasingly concentrated sources through the calculated construction of a series of useful publics. Such triangulation is a profoundly political exercise.

If there's an overarching condition for judging an ecosystem, it is the idea of "health," and our interventions—whether active or passive—in assuring a healthy environment are rich with politics and the social. How do we measure the health of an environment? We measure our own in terms of longevity (the antithesis of extinction), of the presence or absence of disease, and of quality of life—all phenomena as easily analogized with the rainforest as with the city. A healthy ecosystem is one that is productive (in the senses described above) and stable, and diversity is crucial to both. For planners, the idea of community stability, while complex, is, like diversity, a widely shared value. Ecologists correlate diversity and stability in a number of ways. These include the idea of "averaging"—the greater ability of diverse systems to account for differential responses to change by members over time; and "negative covariance"—the idea that if some species do better when others are not doing well, a greater number of species in the system will lower the overall variance, a mark of greater stability. Competition is a great source of negative covariance, of insurance. The presence of a "redundancy" of species buffers the system by offering a greater number of possible responses to disturbance: resistance to invasion because of a fuller use of resources and the likely pre-existence of the invading property or process, and resistance to disease through diversity's ability to limit the epidemic effect in any particular species.

As the history of utopia abundantly proves, the construction of analogies can be a dangerous thing. Some, however, are more resonant than others at any given moment and—it seems to me—biology has special meaning just now. We are facing a crisis as a species, and the need for the transformation of architecture and urbanism into a genuinely "organic" practice is urgent. Not simply has the modernist vision of machines for living become hopelessly limiting—architecture's media are increasingly ecological, and the elision of built and natural form has long since ceased to be a purely visual matter. The emergence of such disciplinary hybrids as "landscape urbanism" is both an acknowledgement of this communion and a demand for the necessity to model at scales from patch to planet. We cannot exist without the embodiment within us of all of such voluntary evolution.

But what about justice? What about freedom? What about community? The neo-Lamarckian model that Patrick Geddes develops finds its aptness in its embodiment of the vector of choice, in opening up the field of values that can be actively contested by our own agency, and by the infinite and unfolding mystery of the noosphere—a space only accessible through human comprehension. The risk, to repeat, is that our participation will be hemmed by a system of "post-democracy"—described by Jacques Rancière, Chantal Mouffe, and others—in which power and choice are so radically disarticulated and distributed to non-state actors (from corporations to NGOs) that politics becomes a sham, and we are all trapped in an automatic individualism, without the possibility of collective action or real participation—which is to say, robbed of the possibility of dissent.

Biodiversity—with its aleatory, evolutionary component—presents a pregnant model for urbanism, for the continuous renewal and interrogation of its forms and habits. The continuous mutation at the core of the production of biodiversity suggests an urbanism that seeks to increase the number of collisions of both people and forms, maximizing the recombinant and frictional energy of their interaction. Politics is the means by which the results are vetted and found fit, and a tractable density is the medium of its survival and articulation. Diversity is not simply a value in and of itself: it is evidence—of the exercise of the Lefebvrian "right to the city," that is, of the right to imagine its future; of tolerance, the waning of "unfreedoms"; of invention; of the health of the planet; of the rightful dissimilarity of individual ideas; of the fraught character of any fixed "consensus"—that which, according to Rancière, annuls the more fundamental democratic value of "dissensus."

At the end of the day, though, the question is whether—and if so, how—the work of physically producing the city can channel these values. Sometimes, the connection is direct: certain "freedoms" have necessary spatial implications. Freedom of assembly and freedom of movement depend on conducing spaces, and both virtual and representative alternatives—by piling on shadowy mediations—cannot be allowed to annihilate the encounter of bodies, the right to the street. Other equities—the right to affordable housing, the right to the city, the right of neighborhood choice—are not so susceptible to physical solutions, whatever role they may play in the contour of good outcomes. And accidents—the genesis of unfolding diversity—cannot, by definition, be planned.

Urbanism's problem is to create a sticky—but non-imprisoning—surface for inhabitation and meaning. The utopian project has always been about expanding the repertoire of possibilities, about fertilizing the present with arguable alternatives. As a representation, the modernist utopia may have depicted the annihilation of variety, but as an artifact in context, it was also an addition to the reservoir of possibilities for the form of the city. And a responsive one—the embodiment of new modes of production and social organization, new technologies, new ideologies and political arrangements, new styles of representation, new feelings for form and space. It demands to be read *differently*, and so continues as a useful instrument for the investigation and description of diversity.

Since I am asserting a Eutopian basis for these ideas, I conclude this overview by offering a constellation of desires for a better city. These criteria are meant to be actionable, a basis for bringing good city form closer to "reality."

Let's call it a manifesto!

Manifesto: Twelve Qualities for Eutopian Cities

1. Strictly Neutral. How do you measure sustainability? By keeping strict accounts of inputs and outputs. And against what standard? I begin with a utopian impossibility, an end-state never to be achieved but still to be constantly measured. The economic model that most closely describes the mechanism of urban self-sufficiency is that of import replacement. In her classic *The Economy of Cities*, Jane Jacobs argues that this process has been

the historic driver of rapid urban growth and differentiation from the earliest days of cities. Although generally used to describe a strictly economic dynamic, the idea also contains a teleological component. It begs the question of why cities grow and, implicitly, contains a notion about the limits of growth.

This balance between political autonomy and environmental self-sufficiency has a clear vector of scale and, once again, the only reasonable solution to unchecked growth is to create new cities, lots of them. Of course, this process is taking place all the time and answers to no designer but the invisible hand, which can only draw the bottom line. The default is simply the undisciplined growth of existing towns, coalescing in the global spread of the interstitial ooze of edge city sprawl. We lead the way. The American economy directs the majority of urban investment and development not to traditional urban centers, but to the endless periphery of the multinational globopolis, producing a new kind of distributed space that owes its fealty only to capital.

Eutopian urbanism seeks the neutrality of going it alone. The goal of self-sufficiency—of urban neutrality—is to provide a primary measure of a city's responsiveness to the biosphere and an inventory of global economic and environmental justice. A city striving to support itself will—through this predicate of economy—find a more meaningful and defensible place in a world community increasingly characterized by weak states and powerful corporations. Equally crucial, the self-sufficient metropolis will limit its growth by harmonizing its production with the bearing capacity of its site and the desires of its population. Economies of scale are not based on an ever-increasing gyre of size. True economy is a proportioning system, a means of balancing needs, wants, and resources. The self-sufficient city will find the medium of its own singularity by evolving an economy that does not simply reproduce a universal pattern of supply and demand based on the corporate invention of want, but which engenders forms that incorporate historic habits, desires, and uses. It will specialize for both competitive advantage and self-identity, and—because of the depth of its internal economy—promote welfare and exchange among its citizens; and it will ever be open to question.

2. Limited. The debate over compact, bounded cities needs to be continued. But bounding is still crucial: a primary agenda for any urban growth is the retention of the difference between what is urban and what is not: a proposition about both character and edges. While we may prefer to think of nature as an artifact—a pet-like remnant of rationalist ideology—the continued existence of the "natural" environment is crucial for both our psychical and our physical survival. The only cure for sprawl is to call a halt to it, to build cities in which boundaries are clear and cities that are able to continuously inventory the means of their own survival,

differentiation, hospitality, and assets. This will produce a double cycle of growth. The first phase—that of enlargement—will limn the expanded territorial requirements of the city. The second—characteristic of "historic" cities—will be an ongoing differentiation in place. As cities mature and become successful, this differentiation will devolve on a set of shrinking physical sites, resulting in the continuous growth of complexity rather than extent. In the democratic city, this will be provided both by an accumulation and interrogation of dissent, the opposition that will serve to limit the ease of involuntary transformation, favoring the most widespread—and differing—styles of compact, rather than the autocracy of the top-down or the emptiness of predigested choice.

3. Open. Free access is the precondition of free assembly, the most important manifestation of democracy in space. Open cities imply that the structure of their internal differences will not prohibit free movement within them or the exercise of free choice by their citizens about where to live or how to be. The open city, whatever its physical limits, will be founded on hospitality, on a willingness to accommodate difference and to welcome outsiders. Of course, such cities cannot survive without a reciprocal willingness by other cities to incorporate similar freedoms and without a global effort to insure that all cities find their fair shares of the world's wealth. The vast army of refugees and migrants that mark the modern world are produced by a globalization in which the greatest mobility belongs to capital, which enjoys a circuit of choice born of unfettered opportunism sustained by radical inequality. Open cities will offer people their own free choices, based on desire, not coercion or desperation.

The open city will also be a place in which the bounding membrane is permeable to nature. The hard boundary of growth will extend only to the spread of the inorganic outwards, not to the penetration of the natural environment inwards or to the accessibility of the not-city to those who live in the city itself. For them, the horizon will always be dual, offering both the opportunity to plunge deeper into the urban labyrinth and to find an easy track out. No particular form, whether the grid, the cluster, the corridor, or the gradient, holds any special authority here. All must ultimately be judged not by their intentions but by their effects.

Finally, the Eutopian city will move beyond the historic strictures of zoning to a far more open planning format. Zoning arose as an instrument for segregating obnoxious uses and dangerous people, and a means for making the functional organization of the city more legible (a project that fascinated the framers of the Athens Charter). However, as the world moves, however unevenly, to more benign forms of manufacture, as the digital revolution offers individuals greater freedom of choice about where to be, and as we cease hating our neighbor for her culture, color, or class, the city can become more like a loft, ready to adaptably accommodate a legion of differences, choices, refusals, and eccentricities anywhere. The open city will be one of endlessly refreshed juxtapositions. Of course, this happy picture takes as its unassailable predicate a reversion of control to the people, the end of involuntary mobility, the defeat of manufactured consent, the purity of tolerance, and the eternal power of dissent.

4. Body-Based. Green urbanism—Eutopia—sees cities as *habitats*. Placing and maintaining ourselves in healthy environments is central to its task. There is some holy writ here: whatever the augmenting mix, self-propulsion has priority. Setting aside the current utopian horizon—eternal life and perfect health—the Eutopian city will strive to accommodate and comfort all sorts of bodies, and will privilege human locomotion as the source of their mobility and bodily comfort as the source of their dimensions. City air makes you free, but only if you can get a breath.

The walking city ramifies in its architecture. Easy accessibility mainly generates an architecture that is low. I've lived on the fifth floor of a walk-up building for over twenty years, the natural limit for stair-climbing on a regular basis. The modernist would say that the exercise of mobility in both horizontal and vertical axes is crucial to the health of the organism, but only achieves this mobility by an alienating sequence of encapsulations, elevator to car to elevator to . . . Messages that urge us to buy a vehicle and start driving, patterns that offer no alternative but the automobile, the growing predominance of the elevator high-rise, even the fantasy of the infinite reparability of our bodies through drugs, surgery, or other centrally administered forms of "self-help"—all contribute to the marginalization of the body as a driver of form. Unless it is restored to the center, architecture is dead.

5. Diverse. In the US, most households already live in non-nuclear family arrangements. As our affinities become increasingly elective and our lifestyles more diverse, our urban architecture must accommodate a broadening range of choices. We rely on our environments not simply to reflect the reality of our desires, but to authenticate our differences. This implies a city of numerous good, expanding, and tractable choices—a city that extends tolerance to the point of celebration. The goal of architecture is happiness, but our pleasure must not be purchased at someone else's expense; the Eutopian city has no tolerance for the ghetto. The post-zoning loft city will be especially adept at the push-pull of local transformations that will allow diversity to flourish without exclusion. Its boundaries will be both flexible and creative, ecotones not walls, places where the mingling of desires and expressions will constantly produce new ones. This is not some fantasy of an impossible future, but the reflection of a reality that already exceeds our ability to house it.

6. **Neighborly.** Neighborhood bridges the Athenian and the medieval ideas of the commune to that of the metropolis. The neighborhood is the fundamental increment of urban social and formal organization and the medium of urban propinquity. If walking is the alpha means of urban circulation, then the basic construct of urban organization—the neighborhood—will be both sized and differenced to accommodate people on foot. This suggests that neighborhoods should be highly mixed in use, supporting the range of daily necessities—employment, education, commerce, conviviality—that are crucial to full and active life. The legibility and tractability of the neighborhood is also central to the spread of a democratic polity. Urban politics is not simply about a site but also a condition, and neighborhoods are essential to the creation of human autonomy as well as being the birthplaces of urban sociability.

If we are to participate fully in the life of the planet, we must have the right to control our bodies and our homes and the right to participate in the management of our immediate environments. Good neighborhoods make this immediacy clear and, by investing them with rich possibilities, we help offer the rich choices that give meaning to collective decisions. Neighborhoods—whether in Greenwich Village, Vallingby, or Djakarta—are the foundation for neighborliness, the greatest virtue in the repertoire of urban citizenship, the core of global civility. That these bonds are produced even under the worst physical adversities is a testament to their abiding importance. The real struggle for neighborhoods, though, is in finding the means to be non-exclusionary.

7. **Many-centered.** Public assembly is foundational for both democracy and sociability. Facilitating such gatherings is perhaps our most critical task as designers, and the measure of such interactions our most useful index of urban success. We have increasing difficulty speaking of public space, both because of the surge of privatization—the global flood of gated communities, shopping malls, and theme parks—and because of a suspicion of its traditional physical forms, the streets and squares, the parks and cafés, of historic urbanism as anathema to our multiplicity. Such places, however, are bulwarks for the expression of our rights, and still strong symbols of the meaning of collectivity. The bodily right of access is fundamental, and is guaranteed by the spaces that we set aside as public. Indeed, the humanity of the city can be measured, in part, by the character and the care reflected in such spaces. The good city reflects an accumulation of social compacts about how to use it, about how to be urban. Strolling the plaza at sunset, sipping tea as the world passes by, picking up a team for soccer in the park, skateboarding under the highway—all of these are the treasures of urbanity, and displacing them in the name of innovation or "security" is both stupid and pernicious.

Although "netizenship" and other forms of virtual adjacency are marvelous means for augmenting our relations around the planet—for organizing affinities that transcend our immediate environments—we abandon the face-to-face at our peril. Being green means recognizing the patterns of our own sociability. It is not simply a distraction from what might seem more pressing principles, but a crucial rearticulation of the terms of political argument for managing a globalizing culture. To the degree that the ownership of the urban and natural environment—and America and its ideological allies are pressing for the rapid devolution of the global commons into private hands—marks the world distribution of wealth, its stewardship becomes the marker of what once was called class struggle. However, equally crucial to the character of the green city—which I understand as conceptually fully interchangeable with the idea of the just city—is the way in which it fulfills the primal role of democratic space, providing the setting for both the deliberate and the accidental meeting of bodies.

8. **Complex.** The city is a propinquity engine, a means of organizing the meeting of bodies in space. Creativity and democracy both thrive on the accidental, on the unexpected and continuous enlargement of possibilities. The city must be filled with useful margins and edges, with human ecotones, rich sites of interaction between neighboring ecologies that permit the growth of differentiation and complexity. The good city is marked not simply by the wealth of its choices, but by both the efficient and the unexpected means of discovering them. The production of such accidents depends, to a degree, on our ability to get lost in the city. This is not an absolute value: cities should not be places of fear, nor is every accident a happy one. There's a clear distinction between what might be called "traditional" forms of urban confusion—the result of complexity, irregularity and unpredictable changes—and more "modern" forms based on the alienations of indifference, on the confusion that springs from too much sameness. Indeed, this modern style of "equality" in which our rights are identified with the surrender of all those features that make us and our environments unique, is the greatest enemy to true freedom, freedom based on the enrichment of choice through our own power to question it. Expanding and critiquing the field of good choices is at the core of our duty not simply as architects and urbanists, but as democratic citizens and good neighbors.

9. **Local.** Given the rapid evisceration of the idea of locality by the onslaught of multinational culture, new strategies must emerge for authenticating the individuality of place. A green, minimum-energy, self-sufficient city will be closely attuned to the particulars of its bio-climate, shifting culture, and local resource base. By understanding itself as habitat, the green city will aim for a style of homeostasis that keeps place both dynamic and particular.

Rejecting the paradigm of the continuous sealed environment of the multi-national corridor and the endless city of sprawl, the green city will engage both the politics and the forms of its own particularity. There are three potential sources for such differentiations of form. First, the weight of culture and history—the fabric of memory and of consent—must be served. This does not mean the limp conservation of forms that have been totally wrested from their originating contexts of meaning. Rather, it means that forms and habits that remain vital are reproduced and that living textures are re-used.

The second source is responsiveness to the bio-climatic particulars of place. These are the emergent morphologies of "green" urbanism, and their unfolding will be the most dramatic and important source of the physical transformation of the city. Here, though, best practices will emerge regionally, and there will be strong logic for repetition; many of both the technical and formal defaults for these newly imagined cities will become widespread. Urban singularity—the unique identity of Venice or Fez, Paris or New York, Istanbul or Dakar—is not automatic or "natural." Finally, in the Eutopian city, to preserve and legitimize difference we must increasingly rely on artistic invention to set the terms of urban singularity. And why not? We have arrived at a moment in which the design of cities can be dramatically re-engaged as a discourse of the harmonization of the received with the freshly imagined. It is possible to speculate about forms that are both logical and never before seen. This is a core task for Eutopia.

10. Appropriately Technologized. We can keep loving technology—a Kindle can save a copse. But it is time to move on from the giant energy model. Technology is refreshing itself at an astonishing rate, but we're coming up short with applications and cost-benefits, and too often cannot answer the question of why we bother. Appropriate technologies of sustainability will be foundational in the disposition of the elements of the city and in their particular configurations. The repertoire of shading, insulating, managing wind, using indigenous materials, carefully considering life-cycle from "cradle to cradle," reducing embodied energy in construction, incorporating renewable means of creating electrical energy—all will contribute to the formulation of an architecture of particularity and suitability within the larger context of local wishes and memories, demands, and perplexities.

11. Green. This is literal. The Eutopian city will be green and act it. We will surely be thrilled by the marriage of new and historical knowledge about sustainability in the gestation of the forms of Eutopian cities. Buildings will be shaped for sun and air, wastes remediated at every scale, toxins removed, propinquities engendered and shifted, conventions refined, fresh climaxes achieved, compacts agreed or denied. And precedents and models will be attended to, including earlier runs at Eutopia. Among these will surely

be the garden city, which, to its endless credit, sought self-sufficiency, compact dimension, human scale, and a kind of proto-environmentalism that reflected the rapid rise of the natural sciences and the first stirrings of the concept of a global ecology.

The salient characteristic of the garden city was that it was green. Garden cities were an early effort to redress what was perceived as a dramatic imbalance in human relations with the natural world. Just as contemporary Darwinism resituated the species within the family of worldly creatures and dealt a mortal blow to received ideas of human exceptionalism, so the protagonists of the garden city—and successors like Patrick Geddes—redescribed urbanism as a sheltering activity with a prominently biological basis. The opening up of the city to an idea of necessary cohabitation with the plant and animal kingdoms produced a new morphology of inclusion, derived from a fantasy of the balance represented by the village life of a previous age. This restoration of the putatively superior social principles of small town and village life was to be advanced not simply by a turning back, but by new technologies of movement and communication that allowed the garden city not simply to be scaled up from a village model but also networked with a hoped-for galaxy of new towns of similar character, with abundant green space in between.

We still have much to learn, not simply from the example of these propositions but also from the way in which the ideas of the garden city have been twisted and degenerated as they've morphed into vapid suburbanism and one-dimensional visions of new towns too simple, too monochrome, too unquestioning, as if the life of a fictitious past could be revived through the reproduction of its forms. The lesson of these places and this movement, however, must be redirected. The creation of new towns is not opposed to the idea of the big city in general. Big cities remain central to the human project and unique in their ability to deliver lives of richness, confusion, and diversity. Rather, the idea of the garden city must be applied to its own bastard, suburban sprawl—the real nemesis of urban and planetary sustainability.

Our new and newly green cities will owe a great deal to this earlier project, and not just in the terms suggested above. If one can make a blanketing statement about the character of these cities, it is that they will literally teem with green. This proposition might seem both too obvious and too simple. But an abundance of plant life in cities will mark their efficiency and progress in the future and color our new global environmental consciousness. For virtually every issue cities confront, nature has an answer. Our new urban gardens—ubiquitous on every horizon—will supply us with oxygen, absorb pollution, control temperatures, provide habitat for our fellow creatures, offer us food, grow construction materials, calm our gaze, and instrumentalize our autonomy. This condition must become the default. Our lives depend on it, on remembering something we've always known but must learn again.

12. Equitable. The *sine qua non*. If urbanism has a teleology, an intelligence behind its design, it must entail the facilitation of justice.

"Politics . . . turns on equality as its principle," writes Jacques Rancière, and this is where, again, we begin. Mapping human relations at every scale, the city stands as both an incredibly succinct representation and a monumentally complex and efficient facilitator of contact, a distribution and collation engine. As the instrument of our manifold community, cities—unlike rainforests or rocket ships—are saturated with the political. Any claim to the contrary is disingenuous. Fairness and joy, in forms both known and not yet known, is the end of politics, the condition that gives meaning to the abstraction of an empty equity and insistently presses the demand of the beautiful on the town.

2009

Acknowledgments

Details of the original publication of the chapters collected here are given below. Note that only chapter numbers are used since many titles have been changed for republication.

1. *Harvard Design Magazine* 12 (Fall 2000).
2. *Architecture Magazine* (June 2001).
3. *Architectural Record* (July 2001).
4. *Metropolis Magazine* (September 2001).
5. *Architectural Record* (September 2001).
6. Michael Sorkin, *Starting from Zero: Reconstructing Downtown New York* (New York: Routledge, 2003).
7. Michael Sorkin and Sharon Zukin, eds, *After The World Trade Center: Rethinking New York City* (Routledge, 2002).
8. *Architectural Record* (May 2002).
9. *Architectural Record* (July 2002).
10. *Architectural Record* (August 2002).
11. Sorkin, *Starting from Zero*.
12. Sorkin, *Starting from Zero*.
13. *Architectural Record* (December 2002).
14. Sorkin, *Starting from Zero*.
15. *Architectural Record* (January 2002).
16. *Architectural Record* (November 2002).
17. *Architectural Record* (March 2002).
18. *Achitectural Record* (July 2002).
19. *James Wines & Site: Architecture in Context* (Orléans, France: Éditions Hmx, 2002).
20. *Slate* (January 2003).
21. *Architectural Record* (September/August 2003).
22. *Architectural Record* (July 2002).
23. *Architectural Record* (September 2003).
24. *Architectural Record* (May 2003).
25. Sorkin, *Starting from Zero*.
26. *The State of Architecture at the Beginning of the 21st Century*, Bernard Tschumi and Irene Cheng, eds. (New York: Monacelli Press, 2003).
27. *Architectural Record* (November 2003).
28. Not previously published.

29. *Perspecta: The Yale Architectural Journal* 35 (2004).
30. Steven Graham, *Cities, War and Terrorism: Towards an Urban Geopolitics* (Oxford: Blackwell, 2004).
31. Constance M. Lewallen and Steve Seid, eds, *Ant Farm 1968–1978* (Berkeley: University of California Press, 2004).
32. *Architectural Record* (January 2004).
33. *Architectural Record* (April 2004).
34. *Architectural Record* (June 2004).
35. *Architectural Record* (August 2004).
36. *Arcade* (Autumn 2004).
37. *Architectural Record* (October 2004).
38. *Domus* 875 (November 2004).
39. *Architectural Record* (December 2004).
40. *Perspecta* 37 (2004).
41. Fiamma Montezemolo, Yepez, *Here is Tijuana!* (London: Black Dog Publishing, 2004).
43. *Architectural Record* (2004).
44. *Domus* 877 (January 2005).
45. *Architectural Record* (February 2005).
46. *Architectural Record* (May 2005).
47. *Architectural Record* (October 2005).
48. *Architectural Record* (December 2005).
49. *Architect's Newpaper* (July 2005).
50. *Architectural Record* (August 2005).
51. Jerilou Hammett and Kingsley Hammett, *The Suburbanization of New York* (New York: Princeton Architectural Press, 2007).
52. Thom Mayne, *Fresh Morphosis: 1998–2004* (New York: Rizzoli, 2006).
53. *Architectural Record* (February 2006).
54. *Architectural Record* (June 2006).
55. *Architectural Record* (July 2006).
56. *Architectural Record* (November 2006).
57. Unpublished talk given to the International Association for the study of Transnational Environment (2007).
58. Mohammad al-Asad with Majd Musa, eds., *Architectural Criticism and Journalism: Global Perspectives: Proceedings of an International Seminar Organised by the Aga Khan Award for Architecture in Association with the Kuwait Society of Engineers, 6–7 December 2007, Kuwait* (Turin, Italy: Umberto Allemandi & C. for Aga Khan Award for Architecture, 2007).
59. *Architectural Record* (March 2007).
60. *Architectural Record* (June 2007)
61. *Architectural Record* (December 2007).
62. William S. W. Lim, *Asian Alterity* (Singapore: World Scientific Publishing Company, 2007).
63. *Harvard Design Magazine* (Fall/Winter 2006/2007).

64. Douglas Kelbaugh and Kit Krankel McCullough, eds, *Writing Urbanism: A Design Reader* (London and New York: Routledge, 2008).
65. *Architectural Record* (February 2008).
66. *Architectural Record* (May 2008).
67. *Architectural Record* (July 2008).
68. Unpublished at the Museum of Modern Art's "Amos Gitai: A Roundtable Discussion," New York, NY, (October 5, 2008).
69. *Architectural Record* (November 2008).
70. Unpublished talk given at Princeton University (2008).
71. Emmanuel Petit, ed., *Philip Johnson: The Constancy of Change* (New Haven and London: Yale University Press, 2009).
72. *Architectural Record* (February 2009)
73. *Architectural Record* (May 2009).
74. *Architectural Record* (August 2009).
75. Unpublished.
76. *Harvard Design Magazine* 31 (Fall/Winter 2009/2010).